Design: Ben Cracknell Studios

© 2008 Thames & Hudson Ltd, London

First published in 2008 in hardcover in the United States of America by
Thames & Hudson Inc., 500 Fifth Avenue, New York, New York 10110

thamesandhudsonusa.com

Library of Congress Catalog Card Number 2006940559

ISBN 978-0-500-25138-6

Printed and bound in China by Everbest Printing Co. Ltd.

Contents

Introduction: The Terrible Tide of War

War and history are inextricably linked. The writing of history was first developed in ancient Greece to go beyond a mere account of the events of great wars and try to explain their origins. Even before that the recording of battles and campaigns had become a regular practice among most ancient civilizations.

While the technology of warfare has changed beyond recognition from the ancient mode of hand-to-hand combat with spears, swords and shields, supplemented by javelins, slings and archery, it is widely believed that insights into many of the political, social and psychological aspects of warfare can be gained as readily from studying the ancient world as the modern.

Ancient warfare continues to be studied by modern military specialists for the lessons that can still be drawn from events like the battle of Cannae in 216 BC, where the Carthaginian army led by Hannibal destroyed a much larger Roman army through superior strategy and tactics. The Peloponnesian War fought between Athens and Sparta from 431 to 404 BC remains an essential feature of the curriculum for military academies. The 4th-century BC Chinese treatise on *The Art of War* attributed to Sunzi has become a classic text, read and applied by strategists of all kinds from military commanders to corporate directors.

Although there are other books on ancient warfare, none of them look at it truly globally and few offer much more than a simple narration of the major battles and campaigns, interspersed with descriptions of the personnel and equipment of ancient armies. This volume is unique and innovative because it combines discussion of the course of political events and the evolution of military structures worldwide with expert analysis and explanation of the underlying social, economic and cultural factors that shaped the nature of warfare in the ancient world.

THE ORIGINS OF WAR

If we define war in a broad sense as *any form of collective violence waged between two opposing groups that have been armed and organized for that purpose*, then it might be thought that war has always been with us. In the opening chapter of this book, however, Brian Ferguson challenges this commonly held view, arguing that much of the evidence for early human social development is consistent with the notion that there was 'a time before war'. He demonstrates that 'the terrible stream of war that comes down unbroken into the present' makes its earliest appearance around 8000 BC in northern Iraq and is present in central Europe by 5000 BC. There is no uniform pattern across the globe, however, and war seems to be a relatively late arrival in some cultures. Neolithic fortifications in northern China start from around 3000 BC, but the emergence of war in Japan may be as late as 300 BC. Similarly, some parts of the Americas provide evidence of warfare from the 3rd millennium BC, but in others it

An intricately carved ivory wrist ornament showing the Egyptian pharaoh Thutmose IV (1400–1390 BC) slaying a prisoner of war. It may symbolize the punishment of rebellious Egyptian vassals in Syria or Palestine. Thutmose wears a Nubian-style wig and is crowned with a solar disc; he is watched by the war-god Montu.

does not seem to be present until 500 BC, or even later. Thus the chronological starting point of the chapters in this volume varies considerably, as does the end-point, reflecting the uneven pace of historical change from the ancient to the modern era.

WARFARE IN ANCIENT EGYPT AND THE NEAR EAST

Ancient Egyptian warfare is analyzed by Ian Shaw and Daniel Boatright. They argue that even in the Protodynastic era around 3000 BC the Egyptians were already developing a ritualized religious framework to justify acts of war aimed at increasing territory and seizing valuable resources. By the 6th dynasty of the pharaohs (2345–2181 BC) Egyptian forces were attacking and laying siege to fortified cities in the Levant, which was to be an almost constant theatre of warfare for the next 2,000 years. During the high point of Egyptian culture, the pharaohs of the New Kingdom (1550–1069 BC) had a semi-professional army of conscripts supplemented by mercenaries drawn from foreign lands, such as the Nubians and Canaanites who fought for Ramesses II in 1285 BC at Qadesh, one of the first major battles in history.

The development of Egyptian warfare took place in the context of rivalry with and defence against the peoples of the ancient Near East, considered next by Nigel Tallis. He examines warfare in several famous civilizations, with a special focus on the Assyrians whose reputation as fierce soldiers was well known to the writers of the Old Testament. The Assyrians were one of the earliest people to develop specialized techniques for siege warfare. Relief sculptures from the palaces of some of the Assyrian kings depict the use of battering rams, siege towers and assault ramps against walled cities of the Levantine region.

Nicholas Sekunda reviews the military might that was wielded by the Achaemenid kings of ancient Persia (558–323 BC), whose empire at its height extended from northern Greece in the west to the Indus River in the east, gaining huge wealth in the form of tribute. As Cyrus the Great and his successors conquered Media, Assyria, Babylon, Lydia and Egypt they amassed enormous, multinational armies of spearmen, archers, cavalry and chariots that represented the mightiest war machine ever created up to that time.

THE GREEKS AT WAR FROM THE BRONZE AGE TO THE ROMAN CONQUEST

Ancient Greek warfare is the subject of three chapters which reflect the richness and variety of our sources. Alan Peatfield combines his specialist knowledge of Bronze Age archaeology with his own martial arts expertise to present an innovative and challenging analysis of warfare and combat in the Aegean world during the Minoan and Mycenaean eras. His explanations of the images and artifacts from the Minoan civilization on the island of Crete (3000–1400 BC) suggest that there existed a warrior elite who took great pride in their skills as swordsmen. His interpretation challenges the long-held view of the Minoans as peace-loving, but it accords well with the archaeological evidence and provides a context for the arrival of Mycenaean mercenaries from mainland Greece around 1450–1375 BC. The celebrated Mycenaean cities, with their cyclopean walls and rich warrior tombs, furnish abundant evidence for a sophisticated warlike culture whose military elite, sporting bronze weapons and riding in horse-drawn chariots, lay behind the legends of the Trojan War.

Stories about the warriors who fought at Troy were incorporated into the Homeric poems. These epic tales, composed around 700 BC, provided inspiration for the succeeding generations of Greeks whose military ideals and practices are explored by Hans van Wees. This is one of the great periods of ancient history, when the Classical Greeks developed what many think of as the definitive form of warfare in the western world – the pitched battle between two armies of heavy infantry fighting hand-to-hand. At the heart of such battles stood the Classical 'hoplite' warrior, with characteristic large round shield, crested bronze helmet and thrusting spear.

David Potter picks up the next major stage in Greek warfare – the rapid creation of a new military system by King Philip II of Macedon (357–336 BC). He explains how the Macedonians formed a much more effective army than those of the Classical Greek city-states by combining well-trained and coordinated cavalry and infantry, both lightly and heavily armed. This flexible fighting force enabled Philip to become master of Greece and his son Alexander the Great (336–323 BC) to invade and conquer the Persian empire, laying the foundations for what scholars call the Hellenistic world.

ROME AND HER ENEMIES

The tactical and strategic skills of the Roman generals that brought about the demise of the Hellenistic states were honed in a long series of wars, including a struggle to the death with the Phoenician city of Carthage which included the famous war with Hannibal (218–201 BC). In his chapter on the Roman Republic, Nathan Rosenstein traces the evolution of Rome's armed forces from those of a chieftain and his band of loyal warriors to the legions of citizen-soldiers with which the Romans went on to conquer the Mediterranean. The ambitions of generals like Pompey and Julius Caesar who were not content to pass on their position and power to others, and instead were prepared to exploit the loyalty of their soldiers, led to a series of civil wars. The ultimate victor was Julius Caesar's adopted son, Octavian, later to become the first Roman emperor Augustus.

The new Roman military system that Augustus devised is described in a chapter by Jon Coulston. Drawing on the rich and varied sources for the army of the imperial period (30 BC – AD 284), he shows that it was a highly professional one, organized into legions supported by auxiliary cohorts, which preserved the integrity of a vast empire. Yet, this *pax romana* (Roman peace) came at a high price. Military mutinies and civil wars plagued the empire in the 3rd century AD, leading eventually to the creation of a more regionally based political structure in the Later Roman empire (AD 284–500).

The warfare of that period is discussed by Hugh Elton. While heavy infantry continued to provide the core element of Roman armies, it was their strength in cavalry, backed up by archers and light infantry, that was often the key to any military

A Black Figure amphora, found at Vulci in Etruria, painted in Athens about 540 BC. It depicts two Homeric heroes engaged in single combat: their bronze armour, large round shields and thrusting spears are typical of hoplite warriors.

The pair of warriors on this ornate gold clasp from Bactria (modern northern Afghanistan) wear Greco-Roman-style armour and helmets of local design, and are armed with long, Persian-style swords. Their trousers and heavy boots are characteristic of the nomadic horsemen from the Central Asian steppes.

success. Ultimately, Professor Elton argues, it was not military decline but failures of leadership and political misjudgments, exacerbated by the loss of wealthy territory, that led to the demise of the western empire. The eastern empire was to endure for another 1,000 years.

The enemies that Greek and Roman armies faced from the 5th to 1st centuries BC included Celtic and Iberian warriors. Louis Rawlings shows how individual prowess in combat was central to these warriors' political and social status. Despite their apparently frenzied method of fighting, they could be highly effective. Iberian and Gallic mercenaries, both infantry and cavalry, played a pivotal role in Hannibal's victories over the Romans, including the famous battle of Cannae (216 BC). It is small wonder, then, that Rome's conquest of the Iberian peninsula took 200 years, or that the Gallic campaigns of Julius Caesar were so important in the development of the Roman army.

The chief 'barbarian' power that menaced Rome's eastern provinces was the revived Persian empire, examined by Nigel Tallis. He analyzes the armed forces of the Parthian kingdom that arose in the 3rd century BC. Although their highly effective horse-archers achieved a notable success against the Roman general Crassus at the battle of Carrhae in 53 BC, the frequent conflicts between kings and nobles generally allowed the Romans to maintain the upper hand. The succeeding Sasanian dynasty, however, created a strong monarchy and even captured the Roman emperor Valerian in 260 BC. Thereafter the two empires maintained hostile, but relatively stable relations until the Arabs conquered Mesopotamia and Iran in the mid-7th century.

At various times in their history the Greeks, Romans and Persians all encountered formidable horse warriors from the plains of Central Asia. Jonathan Coulston considers these nomadic tribesmen, usually referred to as Scythians, who were famous for their riding skills and ferocity. For the most part they remained beyond the frontiers of the great empires of antiquity. In the 5th century AD, however, an exceptionally large and powerful confederation of tribes, known to history as the Huns, penetrated deep into Europe, bringing chaos to the northern provinces of the Roman empire under the leadership of Attila, known as 'the Scourge of God'.

INDIA, CHINA, KOREA AND JAPAN

We now turn to the very different cultural and military traditions of South and East Asia. In India, discussed by Robin Coningham and Mark Manuel, where Alexander the Great's conquering army first encountered war elephants, the numerous Indian cultures developed attitudes to warfare and imperialism which differed markedly from those of the Near East and the Mediterranean. This is exemplified by the influence of Buddhist philosophy on the Mauryan ruler Asoka (272–235 BC) who, after a successful but bloody campaign of conquest in Central India, rejected warfare and imperialism in favour of non-violence.

In a wide-ranging chapter on ancient Chinese warfare, Charles Peterson highlights the creation of huge armies, often led by highly skilled professional fighters. After several centuries of warfare, most of the early states were united by the military power of the Qin in the 3rd century BC. The famous terracotta army, guarding the tomb of the first Qin emperor (250–210 BC), provides valuable and detailed information about the types of armour and weapons of Chinese soldiers.

Actual armaments found by archaeologists can be remarkably informative, as Gina Barnes shows in her fascinating account of warfare in ancient Korea and Japan,

These clay models of cavalrymen from Xianyang in northwestern China date from the time of the Former (or Western) Han dynasty (206 BC – AD 9). Its founder Liu Bang was a military commander who fought his way to supreme power. Cavalry forces were an essential element of the Han military system for defence against the Central Asian nomads.

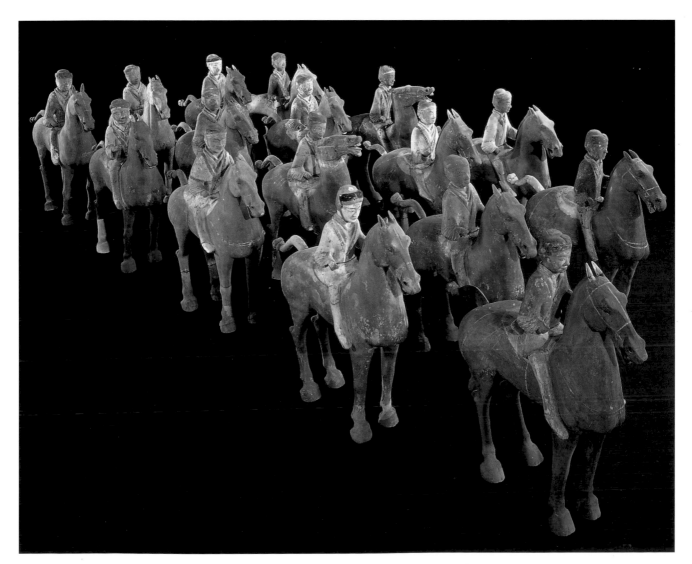

where there are no indigenous written accounts. She traces the influence of military and technological innovations on political and social developments from the 1st millennium BC to the establishment of strong, centralized states with professional armies modelled on those of China.

MILITARISM IN THE AMERICAS

The last two chapters examine the nature of warfare in the ancient civilizations of Central and South America. Here, the term 'ancient' can be applied to a vast historical period from the 2nd millennium BC to the arrival of Europeans in the 16th century AD. Anthropologist and historian Ross Hassig uses a wide range of archaeological, textual and iconographic evidence to discuss the rise and decline of a series of Mesoamerican military powers, starting with the Olmecs. They dominated an extensive trading network with the aid of small but well-organized military forces. The improved military technology and tactical organization of the great city of Teotihuacan allowed it to control a substantial region in the early 1st millennium AD, while Chichen Itzá was a highly militarized city-state on the Yucatan peninsula that lasted from the 10th to the 13th centuries AD. Professor Hassig concludes with the Aztecs, whose ambitious rulers fielded much larger armies than any of their predecessors, led by highly trained, elite soldiers.

The Aztec empire lasted only about 100 years until it was conquered by the Spanish in 1521. A decade later Spanish forces penetrated into South America and brought the great Inca empire to an end. Evidence for the emergence of warfare in this region is patchy, but through careful interpretation of surviving fortifications, excavated human remains, weapons and artistic depictions Elizabeth Arkush demonstrates the centrality of warfare in the Moche and Nasca cultures (c. AD 1–700), and the importance of sacrifice and dismemberment of captives, which continued into the Wari and Tiwanaku periods (c. AD 700–1000). Drawing on both archaeological evidence and the written accounts of the Spanish invaders, Brian Bauer and Joe Szymczak show that the Incas had developed the capacity to deploy large armies in battles on open plains, as well as defending and attacking mountain fortresses. They also had a network of military roads and bridges that rivalled that of the Roman empire at its height.

THE BIG PICTURE

An important theme of this book is the gradual but inexorable trend towards the creation of larger, more diverse and more professional armies among the civilizations of the ancient world. As the scale and complexity of warfare increased, so did the need to recruit more and more subjects and allies who could swell the ranks of armies that numbered in the tens of thousands. The swift rise of the Roman Republic could not have been achieved without the deployment of forces drawn from Rome's extensive network of allies. In the Later Roman empire the incorporation of whole tribes of allies became commonplace as the emperors sought the necessary manpower to protect their frontiers and maintain internal control. Such strategies were perilous, however, as the case of Attila and the Huns shows all too clearly. Looking beyond Europe a similar situation is encountered in the case of Korea and Japan. The introduction of Korean allies into the newly formed Yamato state in the 5th century AD had long-lasting economic and political effects. On the other side of the world,

The figures carved into the sides of this Aztec stone altar are elaborately costumed and armed with weapons suitable for high-status warriors. As with many other ancient military cultures, images of the dominant warrior elite featured prominently on Aztec monumental religious structures.

the mighty Aztec empire was brought down by an alliance between the Tlaxcaltecs, longstanding enemies of the Aztecs, and the small Spanish force led by Hernan Cortés.

We can also see how the practices and technology of war in one part of the ancient world could be transferred to another. The armies of New Kingdom Egypt provide excellent examples of the adoption of military technology from enemies. Powerful composite bows and war chariots were adopted by the Egyptians from the Hyksos and the Canaanites respectively. Nor did the transfer of military technology always occur in what might be the expected directions. It is a little-known fact that the Romans copied their chain mail armour and iron helmets from the Gauls, and their short, wide-bladed swords from the Iberians.

An important cultural legacy of ancient warfare is the prominence of military subjects in the arts. Great cities and temples of the ancient Egyptians, Assyrians, Persians, Greeks, Romans, Chinese and Maya were adorned with impressive stone monuments which gave pride of place to the sculpted figures of rulers leading their armies into battle and winning victories with the assistance of a patron deity. Such monuments also feature images of the successful soldiers leading away bound prisoners or gathering their weapons and other spoils of war.

There can be no doubt that military demands stimulated the organization of ancient societies. The need to maintain and equip the Egyptian New Kingdom's troops in turn led to the rise of a substantial arms industry, which soon came under the control of the pharaonic officials. Both the Romans and the Warring States of ancient China evolved sophisticated bureaucratic systems to register, count and tax their peasant populations as well as to conscript and equip them for war.

Although warfare is clearly a harmful and destructive activity, it nevertheless appeals to our imaginations and stimulates our creative impulses. It was an important driving force in the social, economic and cultural development of the ancient world. Through their examination of the records and remains of ancient civilizations, the following chapters provide fascinating insights into one of the most fundamental aspects of human society.

1 War Before History

Opposite Neolithic cave painting of archers in battle from Tassili n'Ajjer, southeastern Algeria. The Sahara was much wetter then; other portrayals suggest that conflict was stimulated by cattle theft.

Right A skull from a Danish bog body with an embedded bone point, dated to 2500 BC, when war had become endemic across Europe. Death was probably caused by another point found in the breast.

When did war begin? Or has it always been with us? We do not know. Part of the problem is in the definition of 'war', but most anthropologists could settle on simply 'organized, lethal violence by members of one group against members of another'. This is just enough to make the essential point that war is different from murder. It is a group process, it is social. Many believe that socially sanctioned war is as old and commonplace as humanity itself, or maybe older. In this view, war is in our blood, or at least our genes. Many people, without claiming any expertise, simply assume, they *know*, that war has always been our way, from our most distant discernible past. But what are the facts? We will start with 'what?' – what sorts of evidence reveal the presence of war. Then we will move on to 'where and when?' – scanning the globe for the earliest signs of war. With that in hand, we can ask 'why?' – what factors seem responsible for the origin or early intensification of war?

EVIDENCE

The archaeological record varies tremendously around the world – what sort of material past inhabitants left behind, the degree of preservation, and how much archaeological investigation has been done. In addition, the point in time from which good evidence can be recovered varies by millennia across different world regions. But when an archaeological record does develop, war leaves recoverable traces of four types of evidence: bones, settlements, weapons and art.

Skeletal evidence can be definitive, but quite often is not. When a good number of embedded arrow points, unhealed depression fractures on the left fore-skull, 'parry fractures' of the forearm, missing or extra body parts, mutilations, unusual mass burials or unburied bodies are found in a collection of skeletal remains, the presence of war is beyond doubt. But often what is found is one individual. An embedded arrow point could be from a murder, an execution, or a hunting accident, and many forms of non-lethal violence cause skeletal trauma, from domestic violence to culturally structured head-bashing duels. In the past, post-mortem bone damage was often misidentified as proof of violence, an error that gave rise to very bloody scenarios of human prehistory.

Settlement data can also be conclusive – or not. Nucleated settlements, walls with defensive features, defensible locations on hilltops or cliffs, redoubts and lookouts, and settlement destruction are found where war was common. But enclosing walls may also be used to keep cattle in, predators out, or to indicate the status of a settlement; clustered buildings can burn to the ground accidentally; and settlements deep within the lands of a people warring against external enemies may not need to be fortified.

A stone mace or a bronze sword might show the presence of war, but the line between tool and weapon is often not so clear cut. The spear or arrow used to kill a beast can kill a man. Stockpiles of larger arrow points or slingstones are suggestive of battle preparation, but, until a specialized weaponry has developed, such artifacts alone usually cannot confirm the presence of war.

Rock art or carvings in rock depicting interpersonal violence can seem to be compelling evidence of war. But dating of such images is often maddeningly imprecise, within a range of a few thousand years. And what do they portray? One scene from eastern Spain – probably Neolithic – suggests a flanking manoeuvre, but some see the enactment of a ritual. Another suggests an execution, but of whom?

In the past decade, a major controversy has developed over how to interpret the archaeological record described above. Some conclude that war goes forever backwards in time. But others – including the present author – argue that evidence of war emerges out of a warless background. Most archaeologists are in between, clear that any evidence of war amongst many early prehistoric peoples is lacking, yet not going so far as to claim there was a time before war. The next section surveys the global archaeological record for signs of collective violence, so you the reader can form your own opinion. But be forewarned – each area is different.

AROUND THE WORLD WITH A TROWEL

What is the earliest war? That depends on what you count. Cannibalism of enemies, for example, sometimes occurs in war. There are indications of cannibalism among Spanish *Homo antecessor* as early as 780,000 BC, and possible (but debated) cannibalism among later *Homo erectus* in China, Neanderthals in Europe, and among the earliest modern *Homo sapiens* in southern Africa. But cannibalism can be a last resort of the starving, or part of mortuary rituals for one's own dead, so these cases do not establish feasting on killed enemies. In the American Southwest, strong evidence of cannibalism includes a period when there seems to have been little if any war (AD 900–1140), though cannibalism accompanied war later.

For decades, the earliest generally accepted evidence of war has been a burial site excavated during the Aswan Dam construction at Jebel Sahaba, possibly dating to before 10,000 BC. Some 5,000 years later, further south along the Nile, the Khartoum Mesolithic people had stone discs which appear to be maces. Despite these intriguing early finds, African archaeology has produced only a few scattered skeletal indicators of violence from these early periods. Thus, collections of several hundred skeletons from Nubia exhibit high levels of different sorts of trauma, variously and tentatively

Above Rock art from Morella la Villa, Spain. Dating has been disputed, but most believe it is Neolithic. Interpretation of ancient art is always debatable, but this panel appears to show a basic tactical manoeuvre. Two lines of archers clash, while another comes from the side and shoots an enemy in the back.

Below Palaeolithic rock art from Cougnac, France. Such images could be taken as evidence of interpersonal violence, even war, but the wavy lines emanating from the human figure, and going around human figures in other images, contrast with the straight, v-tipped lines sticking into animals in roughly contemporary cave paintings.

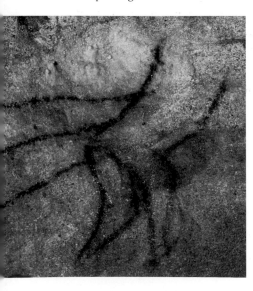

identified with war, non-lethal club or wrestling fights, domestic violence, accident, and even political repression – but all of these come after long interaction with Egyptian civilization. The earlier record in Africa remains a major gap in our knowledge, and could be seen as the future of the archaeology of war.

A more recent entry in the 'very earliest' category comes from Arnhem Land in northern Australia (see box on p. 25). In Australia, or at least parts of it, it seems the fighting never went away. Parry fractures and cranial depressions are common in many skeletal collections. The vast majority of these are healed, suggesting the usually non-lethal club fights observed ethnographically. Females generally had more skull fractures, suggesting much of the trauma may be from domestic contexts, or even a known mourning ritual of bashing the head with rocks. But the earliest accounts of European contact leave little doubt that aboriginal Australians were prepared for deadly encounters with wooden spears.

The first widely accepted evidence of war, the beginning of a terrible stream of violence that comes down unbroken into the present, is found in northern Iraq. The site of Qermez Dere, dating to around 8000 BC (all dates in this section are simplified and should be taken as approximations), has maces and enlarged projectile points, and two other sites about a thousand years younger have between them a major defensive wall, maces and skeletons associated with arrow points. Slowly, irregularly, over the next 3,000 years, war spread throughout the Middle East. Around 4300 BC, on the southern coast of Turkey at Icel, there was a true fort, rather than a walled village, which was destroyed after a century and reoccupied by others of a different culture. But some places where there are signs that war was present – the occasional mace, for example – do not appear to have had much actual fighting. Not until the rise of city-states early in the 3rd millennium BC does intense war become commonplace.

Within the vast, interconnected cultural sphere all around the ancient Middle East, war also developed, due to some combination of military interaction or converging underlying conditions. Mesopotamian-style maces are already present in northern Egypt when the record picks up around 4300 BC. In Central Asia east of the Caspian Sea, and in the high country of Pakistan, settlement defences begin to appear during the 4th millennium BC. The great Harappan civilization of the Indus valley is a long-standing puzzle, with surprisingly few signs of war before and during its peak years, 2500–1800 BC. But after Harappa declined, intensive and spreading warfare is unmistakable.

In China the first defensive pattern appears in the 5th millennium BC among the Neolithic Yangshao in the central Yellow River valley. After 3000 BC, rammed earth fortifications show up across the extensive Longshan interaction sphere of local Neolithic traditions, and in other regions. One location has several bodies thrown down a well. Yet like the Middle East, war signs are clear in some areas, while absent or rare in others. In the Bronze Age, however, war became a way of life.

Reconstruction of the fort at Icel on the Anatolian coast, dating from around 4300 BC. War had been present for millennia, but this represents a new phase. Not a walled village, it appears to be a true fort, with projecting towers, reinforced entrance, and barrack-like rooms with slit windows.

Above A 7,000-year-old bone deposit at Talheim, Germany. At least 34 individuals, 16 children and 18 adults, appear to have been slaughtered and thrown in a pit. More than half have blows to the skull, seemingly caused by farmers' tools.

Below The enigmatic skull nests from Ofnet in Bavaria, dating to around 5500 BC. Some 33 individuals, mostly women and children, are represented in these two roughly contemporaneous deposits. Separate interment of skulls is not rare in burial practices, but peri-mortem bludgeon wounds strongly suggest war killing.

The record for the Korean peninsula begins with specialized metal weapons already present, but in Japan there was a dramatic transition from hunter-gatherers exhibiting little skeletal trauma when war-making cultivators from Korea arrived around 300 BC; then war with high casualties quickly spread.

In Europe the story is more complicated, partly because we have so much information. The very early record is suggestive, but difficult to interpret. Signs of cannibalism have already been noted. In the Upper Palaeolithic after 40,000 years ago there are more skeletons, but only rare suggestions of violence, including a few embedded points. These could be accidental, individual quarrels, or executions. In the 9th millennium BC, warming climate led to the spread of forests and loss of big-game herds. Settled Mesolithic lifestyles developed, a shift from mobile hunting to reliance on smaller, more concentrated wild foods. More human remains have signs of violence, such as the depression fractures on several of the skulls from Ofnet in Bavaria.

In the 6th millennium BC, agriculture began to spread slowly across Europe, reaching the far corners some 2,500 years later. Early agricultural sites generally lack any defensive features, and this status can last for centuries. The earliest pattern of fortification may begin before 5000 BC on Italy's Tavoliere plain, where substantial ditches ringed Neolithic villages. More conclusive evidence of war appears abruptly around 5000 BC at German Talheim and Austrian Schletz, in what appear to be slaughters of settled farmers, slain with woodworking adzes and axes. Signs of violence are scarce or non-existent in most other areas at this point, but by 3500 BC or so, war seems firmly in place across Europe. Forts dominated hilltops, and men were buried with battle-axes. The Bronze Age, beginning around 2300 BC in the Aegean (later elsewhere), is associated with an elaborate weaponry, often ceremonial, linking together warrior elites across the continent (see box opposite).

Bronze Age Weaponry

A warrior aristocracy flourished in the European Bronze Age. In the Late Neolithic, some warrior specialization was already apparent in grave goods, but bronze was a critical addition. Circulating in ingots and finished products, at first almost all of it went into weapons. Bronze spearheads, daggers, and battle axes testify to personal combat by small numbers of elite warriors, probably joined by larger numbers of subservient farmers with cruder killing tools. After 1500 BC, the sword became the paramount weapon. With more bronze in circulation, it appeared in drinking goblets, body ornaments and implements (combs, razors, tweezers and mirrors) for men and women.

The concentrated value of bronze gave more to monopolize, more to fight over, and trade routes were especially militarized. But if elites fought each other, they also traded and built alliances. These interlocking chains connected long distances, spanning peoples who were culturally very different. The whole system supported a network of chiefs, elaborately buried with artistically detailed ceremonial swords, supported by warriors whose swords show ample signs of use. Pictures carved in stone celebrate a martial existence, ideologically reinforcing warriors' political dominance. Even chariots appear, however impractical in northern Europe. At its peak, this shared elite military ethos and exchange joined together most of Europe, from Spain to

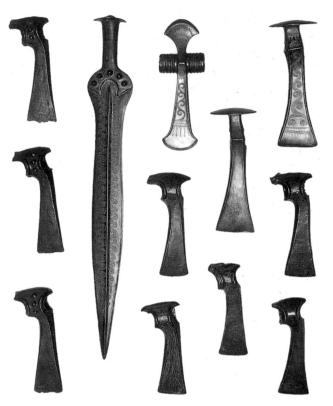

Scandinavia, from the Eastern Mediterranean to England. After 1200 BC, with new ways of fighting – in some areas based on iron weapons – this universe came apart, ending an epoch of a common pan-European culture of the heroic warrior.

Above A horde of Middle Bronze Age (16th–15th centuries BC) weapons from northeast Hungary, including a short sword and both decorated and undecorated battle axes. They were deposited in water, a common ritual practice. The Carpathian Basin was a crossroads of Bronze Age cultures, and these show stylistic affinities with the Aegean and northern regions as far away as Scandinavia.

Left A Bronze Age carving in granite bedrock at Fossum in northern Bohuslan, Sweden. It could represent an actual fight, but given the symbolic significance of both axes and boats in this culture, it might also represent a ritual performance, or even a clan insignia.

Keet Seel ruin, northeastern Arizona, USA. Local Anasazi moved from scattered exposed settlements to begin construction of this defendable location around AD 1250. At that moment, a century-long dry period turned even drier, and all the local people moved to inaccessible sites, with up to 150 people living at Keet Seel. Early in the 14th century, the entire area was abandoned.

Crossing the Atlantic, the early inhabitants of North America did not have it easy. Two of the 39 or so individuals known from 13,000 to 9,000 years ago – some just bone fragments – have signs of projectile wounds, others have cranial fractures. Later archaeology is a patchwork of very different stories for different regions. Since they give such a compelling picture of the variability of war records, and since North America is not otherwise considered in this volume, a region by region overview is in order.

In the eastern forests, one of the earliest large skeletal collections, of hunter-gatherers from about 5400 BC in Titusville, Florida, has 9 of 168 individuals with signs of violence. Elsewhere signs of violence remain unusual, and from scattered, single individuals. By the Late Archaic, 4100–2500 BC, there are a few clear cases of collective killings, such as at Indian Knoll, Kentucky, and the Finger Lakes area of central New York. The subsequent Woodland period seems comparatively peaceful. The rise of the maize-based, urban Mississippian tradition beginning around AD 900 is accompanied by unmistakable signs of intensive warfare – fortifications, empty buffer zones, specialized war weapons and icons. In the Southeast, this intense violence appears to be associated with the rivalries between regional chiefs, which were observed, and utilized, by the explorer de Soto in his meandering, bloody quest for gold in the mid-16th century.

The southern Great Plains region begins with scarcely any signs of violence, just one woman with two blows to the head among some 173 individuals. Much of the area later fell into the militaristic Mississippian orbit. Out of southwestern Minnesota after AD 1250, the Oneota people warred against and ultimately replaced earlier residents. At Norris Farms #36, an Illinois Oneota cemetery, 43 of 264 fairly complete skeletons indicate violence. But it was in the Dakotas that the worst violence recorded for prehistoric North America occurred: one location, Crow Creek, had a mass burial of 486, often mutilated, skeletons, conventionally dated to 1325, but perhaps later.

In the Southwest, there is no clear evidence of war for centuries after the start of maize and squash agriculture (1500–1000 BC). In the Anasazi area (a modern name for an ancient cultural group), during the Basketmaker II period of 500 BC–AD 500, collective violence is clear, including an apparent slaughter of 90 individuals at Weatherill's Cave 7 in southwestern Utah. But the Mogollon and Hohokam cultural areas to the west and south remain without any war indicators that early. Over the next 750 years, the record is variable, but the big shift to war throughout the Southwest came in the 1200s, with defensive settlements – including the famous cliff dwellings– settlement destructions, area abandonments and other compelling signs of war. After 1400, with huge areas already abandoned and populations concentrated in larger pueblos, signs of actual fighting decrease, yet war was still waged when the Spanish arrived.

Native peoples of California had a reputation for non-violence in early historical accounts, but the archaeological record shows something different. A few individuals are found with projectile wounds from as early as the 5th millennium BC. On the Channel Islands near Santa Barbara, a 7,000-year series of skeletons indicates a pattern of club fights begun by 3000 BC, but with few if any fatalities. Around AD 500, the bow and arrow appears on the scene, and so do more skeletons with points. A big increase in war is seen from several California locations from about AD 1150–1350.

The Pacific Northwest Coast has by far the longest documented history of war in the Americas. In the earliest set of human remains, from 3500 to 1500 BC, 9 of 42

Above The central plaza of Monte Albán in the Oaxaca Valley of Mexico was home to more than 300 bas-relief carvings of mutilated war captives, once thought to represent dancers and hence called 'danzantes'.

Below Nasca spirit-being holding a club and trophy skull. Although a number of ancient South American peoples took enemy heads, among the Nasca of the southern Peruvian coast this became a cultural obsession. Heads were interred in other burials, painted on ceramics, and woven into textile designs.

individuals show signs of violence. Fortifications, embedded points and daggers continue in later times. Generally, war appears to be earlier and more intense to the north, in southern Alaska, and only gradually spreads to and intensifies in the south, around Vancouver and Washington state. Throughout the coast, a marked intensification of war is visible in the period from AD 900 to 1400.

Jumping south, Mexico and Guatemala are well known as an area of state formation. Persuasive evidence of war is lacking until some of these states began to develop. The Olmecs, perhaps the first Mesoamerican state dating to around 1150 BC, clearly made war (see Chapter 17). However, the best continuous Mesoamerican sequence comes from Oaxaca. Maize domestication appears in the area around 3400 BC, but the first village palisades and at least one settlement destruction, at San José Mogote, date to around 1500 BC. Signs of war fluctuate thereafter, but generally indicate that raiding is more frequent after 800 BC. The real surge came with the rise of chiefly polities around 500 BC. War increased in scale to the rise of the Monte Albán state two centuries later. It never went away. Incessant conquest struggles still characterized the region at the time of Spanish conquest.

The continent of South America contains enormous variation in ecologies, settlement, political development and archaeological recovery. The historically interconnected Pacific coast and Andean highlands, both divided into multiple distinct valley systems, illustrate how variable localized records can be. In the Norte Chico region of Peru's coastal desert, major settlements with monumental architecture date from 3000 to 1800 BC. But countering expectations, there is an astonishing lack of evidence of organized violence. Other early coastal sites such as San Pedro de Atacama include skulls which indicate a pattern of non-lethal bashings – perhaps individual duels, but not war. However, severed heads have been found from pre-ceramic peoples on the coast, as early as 2000 BC at the Asia site. In the Casma valley, a theocratic state with little if any war appears to have fallen to a militaristic state from the highlands around 1000 BC. Other coastal valley systems do not show a comparable level of disruption. In what would eventually be the Moche area of the northern Peruvian coast, agriculture was practised by 2700 BC, and localized political centralization developed around 1800–900 BC, but there are no hints of war in skeletal or settlement material until roughly 400 BC. Then war signs increase over 800 years, culminating in the Moche state, with internal peace and external war. In other locales regular war does not become apparent until some point from 200 BC to AD 700. The coastal Nasca culture, from AD 200 to 600, exhibits a seeming obsession with trophy heads, in contrast to the highland state of Tiwanaku, peaking around AD 800, which had war but seems relatively un-militaristic. Other highland systems offer their own pattern variations.

The archaeology of other South American areas, particularly the wet lowlands, is much less developed than for the Andes or Pacific coast. Some good information is available, however, for the Orinoco Basin of central Venezuela. One detailed reconstruction from the middle Orinoco finds manioc agriculture in the first small settlements identified in the region by 2100 BC. Maize cultivation begins, slowly, around 800 BC, and then population growth rises for centuries before stabilizing. Signs of war, along with chiefdoms, show up on a tributary of the Apure, itself a tributary of the Orinoco, around AD 550. That was a contact zone between lowland and highland peoples. It took 500 years for this combination to appear throughout the middle Orinoco. But by the time the Spanish arrived in 1530, powerful chiefs in fortified villages could muster armies in the thousands. Once war gets going, it can really go.

The last stop for our global tour is the far-flung Pacific. In New Guinea, so many different groups waged war in front of anthropological eyes that it became a focus for scholarly theorizing. Yet it is one of the least understood areas archaeologically. Evidence of any violence, collective or otherwise, is extremely scarce. One synthetic overview, however, argues that the introduction of sweet potatoes in the Eastern Highland area was followed by a major development of warfare, only a couple of centuries before European observers arrived. The Melanesian islands of Fiji, Tonga and Samoa, colonized some time after 1200 BC, all see the creation of fortified settlements 2,000 years later. On Fiji and some other locations, this was associated with a social emphasis on cannibalism of war captives.

Polynesian colonization of other islands in the Pacific is also fraught with controversy and uncertainty. The expansion appears under way by AD 1, but accelerated later. In this far-flung diaspora, an initial date of war cannot be fixed. Yet over time it became an integral part of Polynesian culture. When New Zealand was reached – around AD 800–1200 – the word for warrior and its cultural elaboration had been brought along. Some of the earliest skeletal remains have signs of inter-personal violence. Hawaii saw separate, hierarchical polities arise after AD 1100, and turn to conquest warfare after 1400. The Marquesas also saw fortifications develop between 1100 and 1400. New Zealand hilltops were covered with fortifications after 1300, and all indications of war increase after 1500, setting the stage for genocidal campaigns once Europeans introduced guns.

Maori hillfort (or Pa) at One Tree Hill, a volcanic peak in Auckland, New Zealand. Located on an isthmus between two bays, it was strategically situated to extract tribute on trade. This may have been the largest Maori settlement in pre-European times, and is one of the largest known earth forts in the world.

WHY DID WAR START? WHY DID IT GET WORSE?

This tremendously varied global record, with all its uncertainties, warns against any simple theory on the origins of war. Contrary to some popular opinions, we know that war did exist before agriculture or civilization. In Europe, North America, Australia and elsewhere, there is unmistakable evidence for war before agriculture, and it is early agricultural societies, often with abundant archaeological remains, which provide some of the most compelling evidence for the absence of war. Nevertheless, over time, war regularly appeared in agricultural societies, and many civilizations became chronic war machines.

It may be that both agriculture and civilization are accompanied by more basic circumstances that greatly increase the likelihood of war. Comparing situations around the world, several sets of circumstances appear again and again in the record before, or as, war developed. Rather than the cause of war, they may be thought of as preconditions that make its inception or intensification more likely. These preconditions are not independent, and many causal linkages connect one or another. But with several of them put together, the stage is set for whatever spark that finally starts the fire.

Sedentism is very important. Fully mobile groups have the option of moving away from conflict. Initial signs of war usually appear among a people who have recently become more anchored in space. Once people have invested in one location, there is something to be both lost and gained through combat. Moreover, the settled points often are unusual locations of relative plenty in broader regions of resource scarcity or unpredictability, coveted, and if necessary, defended.

A shift to more intensive and sedentary resource exploitation typically is associated with another precondition, increasing population density. This may be revealed by larger settlements, but more commonly by a substantially increased number of contemporaneous settlements within the same area. Although population density is not correlated with more intensive warfare among tribal peoples of recent centuries, that may be due to a host of historical circumstances. In the archaeological past, a rough connection is apparent in many cases. The obvious inference is that more people in one area can mean more competition over finite resources, as well as a more fertile medium for political struggle and efforts at domination.

Some scholars have stressed the presence of stored food as a lure for raiders, whether that is foraged (e.g. preserved fish stores) or cultivated (e.g. cleaned wheat). Those are bounties, especially when others experience want, although the ability to haul away food without supplemental transport can limit its significance. Others note that livestock may be even more tempting. Not only is this capital in the original sense, they can transport themselves, and historical herding peoples are often notably warlike.

Other preconditions involve social organization, both horizontal and vertical. One line of thinking is that the development of segmental social structures, such as lineages or clans, is a necessary precondition for war. These preformed groups not only provide a basis of military mobilization, but by establishing collective identities, they encourage a shift from homicide targeted at specific individuals, to the more warlike 'any of them will do'. Although cultural divides can also provide such group identities, it should be stressed that most early cases of warfare appear – when we can tell – to be among people of the same or similar cultures.

The Earliest War?

Two widely separated locations credited as very early cases of war demonstrate the problems of establishing such claims. Jebel Sahaba, a burial site near the Nile in Sudan, contained 58 skeletons, 24 associated with stone artifacts interpreted as parts of projectiles. That convoluted phrasing is necessary because most of these items are simple chips indistinguishable from ordinary stone-working debris. They are interpreted as barbs or points on spears because a few are embedded in bones, and the position of others suggests they were in the bodies. Some multiple burials and cut marks on bones reinforce a military interpretation. However, post-mortem defleshing or repositioning seem worthy of greater consideration as explanations. Dating of the site is very problematic, and is based on comparisons of the stone tools to another regional stone working tradition that is very roughly dated to between 12,000 and 10,000 BC, but could be considerably younger.

In Northern Australia, rock art of human figures, flying boomerangs and embedded spears seems to reveal a very long-term progression from mostly individual confrontations, to group clashes, and to elaborate battles, beginning roughly around 8000, 4000 and 1000 BC respectively. Do they represent a transition from duels, to feuds or contests, to tribal war? Do they represent physical humans at all, or happenings on a spirit plane? Here too dates are very rough, cobbled together from evaluations of material culture, indications of fauna and human adaptations, and the amount of silica crust formation over images. Future revisions of claims for the earliest evidence of war are to be expected.

Above Two adult males from Jebel Sahaba. The individual on the left had six stone flakes, the one on the left 19, two of them embedded in bone, two within the skull (pencil points show the location of some of them). Were these crude tools composite points of projectiles, or perhaps the remains of a defleshing process prior to burial?

Left This rock painting from Ngarradj-Warde-Djobkeng rock shelter, Kakadu National Park, northern Australia, appears to represent one group of men throwing spears at another group. Earlier images portray individual duels. Assigning dates to such rock art is difficult and tentative.

Above Maori trophy head. Traditional Maori warfare involved a mix of conflict over resources, chiefly competition, and cosmological ideas of social power. With the introduction of guns, it shifted to attacks of extermination. The Musket Wars from 1818 to 1840 claimed 20,000–50,000 lives.

Vertical social development means political hierarchy. In ethnography, even the most minimal leaders, such as Amazonian headmen, are known to manipulate potential conflict issues in pursuit of their own private interests. In archaeology, it is not the case that all chiefly systems are warlike, but the vast majority of them are. Chiefly status-striving and competition is a regularly cited explanation of intensive warfare, although 'status-striving' should be read as a gloss for a lot of different interests, involving wealth, wives and power. Not always but often, leaders favour war because war favours leaders – if they win.

Beyond the organization of particular communities, long-distance trade, especially of prestige items, creates a concentration of value that can be plundered or monopolized. High-value trade offers perhaps the tightest linkage between the use of force and its potential benefits. Those who sit atop trade routes, or who can tax or plunder trade, may become wealthy.

One last pre-condition or cause of the inception or intensification of war is a major ecological reversal. This may be purely natural, such as a decrease in rainfall, a river that digs a gorge and thus loses a floodplain, or rising sea levels that push more people together in remaining lands. A particularly striking example is the surge of warfare in many areas of North America from around AD 1100 to 1400. This followed a climatic period which had been favourable for many subsistence activities – notably maize agriculture – followed by a time of cooling and more erratic precipitation which made getting enough food for expanded populations much more difficult. Other ecological reversals can be anthropogenic, such as degradation caused by over-farming or over-grazing. Intense warfare associated with negative ecological change seems to be widespread throughout broad regions, which should raise red flags concerning our current global environment.

26

Opposite On his second visit to Tahiti, Captain Cook was surprised by the sudden appearance of over 200 war vessels, manned by some 6,000 men, with raised platforms for fighting with slingstones, clubs and spears. They were preparing for a punitive attack on a neighbouring island, but the Tahitians did not want Cook to see the battle, and set it for five days after he left. With European contact, Tahitian warfare shifted from limited engagements to territorial conquest.

But if there was a time before war, how did it get to be so common – not just among civilizations, but among tribal peoples around the world? Here four different trends can be identified. First, war began in more places as all the preconditions identified above became more common. Always there are questions of independent invention vs diffusion, but certainly the Middle East, China, Central and South America, and the Pacific represent *sui generis* war traditions. In North America alone, the Northwest Coast, the Southwest, the Eastern Woodlands and perhaps other areas seem to have turned to war all by themselves.

Second, war spread. In Japan, war arrived with people from Korea. In North America, warlike Mississippian chiefdoms spread throughout the midwest and east. Polynesian seafarers carried a war complex to new domains.

Third, the rise of states pushed the development of war beyond their frontiers. Tribal peoples around states probably developed warlike cultures simultaneously with state centres, but expansionist states pushed the process. The rise and fall of states can set off chain reactions of violence, as happened throughout northwest Mexico after the fall of the great city of Teotihuacan in the 7th century AD, or in southeastern Africa with the rise of the Zulu. Long-distance trade routes between states were often highly militarized.

Fourth, contrary to the standard idea that European contact 'brought peace to the savages', the initial effect was usually the reverse. In contrast to the gradual, localized expansion of ancient states, Europeans crossed huge distances and entered entirely new areas of interaction. They brought new plants, animals and diseases that tumultuously transformed local societies. They brought trade goods of iron, glass and cloth, which often became scarce items of great demand, and thus booty or payment for war. Their military techniques and technology, over time, radically transformed indigenous war patterns. The scope of European demand for captive labour or land denuded of prior inhabitants was far greater than the most exploitative ancient empires. All these factors created a bow wave of warfare that spread far in front of actual colonization, and which too often has been mistaken for the 'pre-contact' pattern.

Taking these four trends together explains how the world turned to war in the 10,000 years since its documented origin in northern Iraq. Yes war is ancient, and war has been quite pervasive among the non-state peoples whom we know most about. But it was not always like that. If to claim that there was a time before war – as I do – may seem too extreme for many archaeologists, few with expertise in the subject would disagree that the ethnographic universe of the past 500 years is far, far more filled with war than the early archaeological records of nearly everywhere on earth. Times of written history can be misleading guides to humanity's prehistoric past.

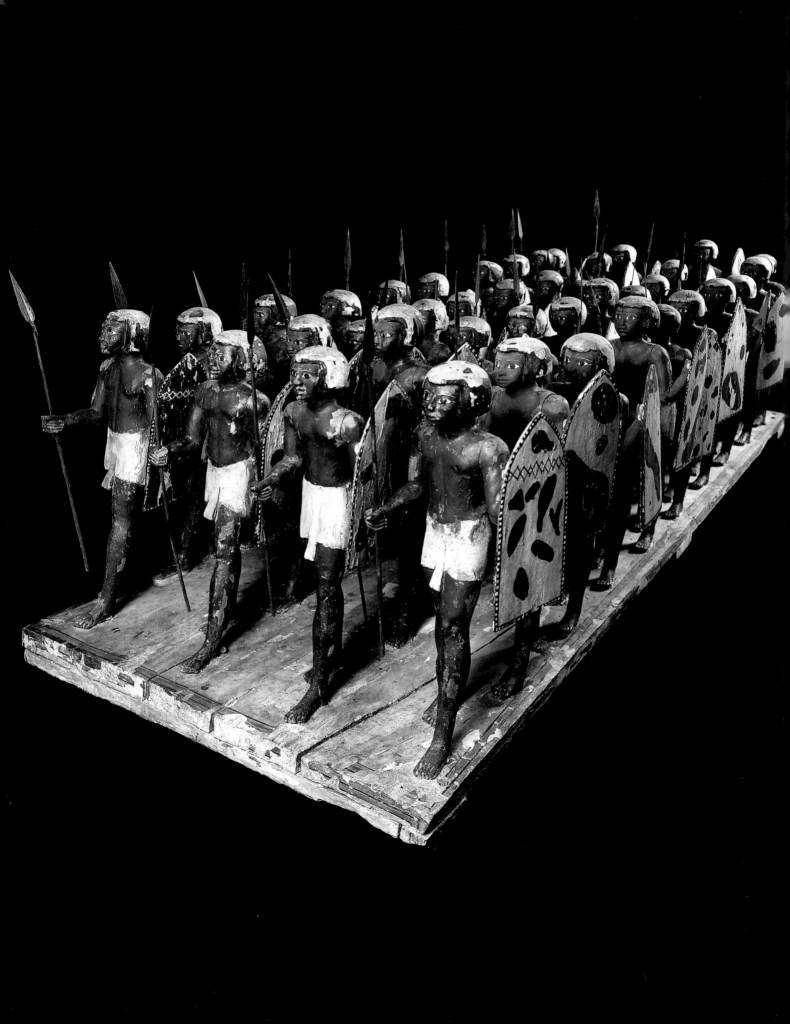

2 Ancient Egyptian Warfare

A wooden model from the 11th-dynasty tomb of Mesehti portrays 40 Egyptian spearmen each carrying a spear comprising a bronze blade on a long shaft. This may simply reflect the difference between the ideal (bronze depicted in a tomb model) and the reality (use of flint).

The evidence for battle in ancient Egypt stretches back possibly as far as the 12th millennium BC when struggles between bands of Palaeolithic hunter-gatherers led to flint arrowheads becoming embedded in the bones of almost half of the individuals buried at Jebel Sahaba, near Wadi Halfa (see box on p. 25).

The most fundamental themes of Egyptian battle were encapsulated at a surprisingly early stage in its history. Carved reliefs on ceremonial palettes, mace-heads and knife-handles of the Protodynastic period (c. 3100–2900 BC) are characterized by a number of constantly repeated motifs: the king smiting foreigners, the siege and capture of fortified settlements, the binding and execution of prisoners, and the offering of the spoils of war to the gods. It is likely that, even at this time, the real political and economic motivations for warfare – the defence of borders and the acquisition of valuable land, livestock, natural resources and slaves – were being masked, to some extent, by layers of religion and ritual, providing both moral justification and a 'universal' framework for the nasty business of war. Egyptian warfare, as in most other cultures, was a mixture of internal conflict (particularly in the three so-called 'intermediate periods', when political control was less centralized) and campaigns against enemies beyond the traditional borders. The regions and peoples with which Egypt came into conflict can be grouped into three basic areas: Africa (primarily the Nubians and Libyans), western Asia (the inhabitants of Syria-Palestine, Mesopotamia and Anatolia) and the northern and eastern Mediterranean (the Sea Peoples).

The earliest battle scene of the Old Kingdom (2686–2125 BC, Egypt's pyramid age, after the first unification of the country), showing archers drawing their bows, has survived on a fragmentary relief from the 4th-dynasty mortuary complex of King Khafra at Giza. The only other known royal depiction of battle in the Old Kingdom is from the funerary causeway of the 5th-dynasty pharaoh Unas at Saqqara, where reliefs show a confrontation between an Asiatic soldier and Egyptians armed with daggers, bows and arrows. This theme of Egyptians attacking Asiatics is repeated in two slightly later private tombs: that of Inti at Deshasha, where there is definite evidence for the use of sophisticated siege technology, and the roughly contemporary tomb of Kaemheset at Saqqara, which shows a scaling ladder on wheels being used in a siege. Both of these scenes suggest that Egypt was already launching military campaigns into Syria-Palestine during the Old Kingdom.

Some surviving First Intermediate Period (2125–2055 BC) funerary reliefs and texts, such as those in the tomb of Ankhtifi at el-Moalla and the tomb of Setka at Aswan, make it clear that this era was characterized by greater conflict between the individual regions within Egypt. Provincial governors continued to play a more military role in the subsequent Middle Kingdom (2055–1650 BC). This is clear from the fact that four important 12th-dynasty officials' tombs at Beni Hasan contain

Right The main sites mentioned in this chapter.

Below This very early example of the classic image of the Egyptian king smiting a foreign captive decorates one face of the so-called 'Narmer Palette' – in this instance however, the facial features of the prisoner seem Egyptian rather than Libyan or Asiatic.

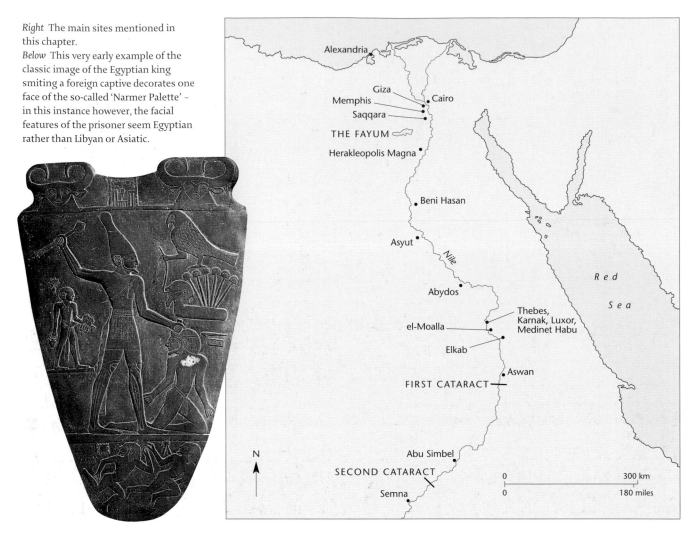

Below A group of archers raising their bows in action formed part of the decoration of the 4th-dynasty mortuary complex of King Khafra at Giza, probably a fragment of one of the earliest Egyptian military narratives.

battle paintings. These battles might have been a combination of smaller skirmishes or might never have taken place at all; indeed it has been pointed out that the scenes of siege warfare at Beni Hasan resemble one another so closely that they may all be fictional. Alternatively, the earliest of them might depict an actual unique historical event (perhaps the Theban assault on Herakleopolis Magna which brought an end to the First Intermediate Period).

The most important surviving military documents from the Middle Kingdom are the so-called Semna Dispatches, which are administrative reports from a lector-priest's tomb in western Thebes. These documents, dated to the reign of Amenemhat III, mostly comprise copies of reports sent to the commander at Thebes from the Egyptian garrison at Semna in Nubia, conveying something of the tedium of military life in between campaigns or battles. One, for instance, describes the routine task of desert surveillance: 'The patrol that went out to patrol the desert-edge near the fortress of Khesef-Medjau ['Repeller of the Medjay'] on the last day of the third month of spring in the third year has returned to report to me, saying "We have found the track of 32 men and 3 donkeys...".'

Right The painted scenes in the 6th-dynasty tomb of Inti at Deshasha provide definite evidence for the use of sophisticated siege technology. In this instance the appearance of the defenders suggest that it is an Asiatic fortified town that is being besieged by Egyptians, rare pictorial evidence of early Egyptian incursions into the Levant.

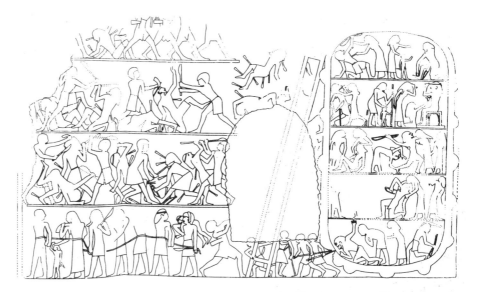

Below Part of a wall-painting from Tomb 15, belonging to Baqt III, at Beni Hasan. The upper row shows wrestlers, whilst the lower three depict a battle scene, including the siege of a fortress.

THE FIRST RECORDED BATTLE IN HISTORY

In the New Kingdom (1550–1069 BC), the Egyptians' principal motivations for attacking foreigners were the maintenance and extension of their own borders, the protection of trade routes and quarrying and mining expeditions, and the acquisition of foreign goods, raw materials and extra manpower. It is a matter of some debate as to whether their pursuit of these aims led to the establishment of an 'empire' in Syria-Palestine, as opposed to a series of economic and political spheres of influence. By the time of the 18th-dynasty ruler Thutmose III, the kingdom of Mitanni (located between the growing powers of Assyria and the Hittites) had established itself as the dominant influence on the city-states of Syria. In about 1457 BC, less than a year after he assumed sole rule, Thutmose III embarked on his first, and perhaps most significant, expedition in order to thwart a 'revolt' of city-states led by the prince of Qadesh and doubtless backed by Mitanni. This campaign culminated in his surprise attack on the city of Megiddo, described in his 'annals' inscribed on the temple walls at Karnak, which is the earliest surviving detailed account of an ancient battle. According to this account, the king chose the most dangerous of three possible routes for his army, forcing them to march slowly and at great risk through a narrow pass, thus allowing them to descend unexpectedly onto the plain of Megiddo, within a few hundred yards of the confederation of Asiatic troops, encamped for the night in front of the city. The following morning Thutmose's troops were then able to launch a frontal attack that routed the enemy. After this success at Megiddo, which was eventually captured after a seven-month siege, Thutmose backed up his military achievements in Syria-Palestine with the creation of a network of garrisons and numerous vassal treaties. In his sixth campaign he adopted a more long-term strategy, taking back 36 chiefs' sons to the Egyptian court so that they could be held as hostages, indoctrinated with Egyptian ideas and eventually restored to their thrones as puppet-rulers.

The next significant battle for which we have even more detailed description was the battle of Qadesh (see box overleaf), which took place in the fifth year of the reign of the famous pharaoh Ramesses II (c. 1274 BC). Tremendous publicity was given to this single military event, which was depicted on no fewer than five of Ramesses II's most important temples (Luxor, Karnak, Abu Simbel, Abydos and the Ramesseum), while the literary account has also been preserved on three papyri.

The sophistication of the system of mud-brick defences, slopes and ditches of the Egyptian Middle Kingdom fortresses in Lower Nubia fore-shadowed certain aspects of medieval castles, with the use of loopholes, berms, counterscarps, glacis and bastions, as shown here in the outer part of the defences at the fortress of Buhen (now covered by Lake Nasser).

The athleticism and discipline of early 5th-dynasty royal soldiers are emphasized here in a fragment of a scene depicting the royal ship of state of King Sahura, from his valley temple at Abusir. The soldiers are possibly carrying rolled-up military standards.

THE CHARACTER AND MAKE UP OF THE ARMY

In the earliest periods of Egyptian history (c. 3000–2100 BC), the army was probably little more than conscripted labour forming a specialized element of the wider conscription of corvée labour, used for major building works such as the pyramids. Because of the amorphous and devolved nature of the Egyptian army in the Old and Middle Kingdoms, it is difficult to estimate its actual size, composition and organization in these early times. The numbers of soldiers given in Egyptian accounts of battles, such as 'many tens of thousands', often seem to be unreliable, and in this instance are probably just intended to give the impression of huge numbers.

In the early Middle Kingdom the army probably functioned in a similar manner, with men conscripted from around the country to participate in seasonal campaigns and on royal building projects. However, by the 13th dynasty there is evidence that Egyptian fortresses in Nubia were defended by full-time soldiers who were based there permanently, as opposed to the earlier rota system of the 12th dynasty.

The Battle of Qadesh

	NEW KINGDOM OF EGYPT	HITTITE EMPIRE
COMMANDERS	Ramesses II	Muwatalli
STRENGTH	c. 2,000 chariots c. 16,000 infantry	c. 3,500 chariots c. 20,000 infantry (not engaged)
CASUALTIES	Unknown (considerably higher)	Unknown (considerably lower)

By the reign of Ramesses II Egypt's main rivals in Syria-Palestine were the Hittites. In Ramesses' second campaign in the Levant, in 1274 BC, the main Egyptian army was passing through the Wood of Labni, just a few miles to the south of the city of Qadesh, and preparing to ford the River Orontes. When two captured Bedouin convinced them that the Hittites were many miles to the north in the region of Aleppo, Ramesses marched on ahead with one division of his army, and began to set up camp near Qadesh, planning to lay siege to it the following day. It was then that the Hittite chariots attacked the second Egyptian division as it was

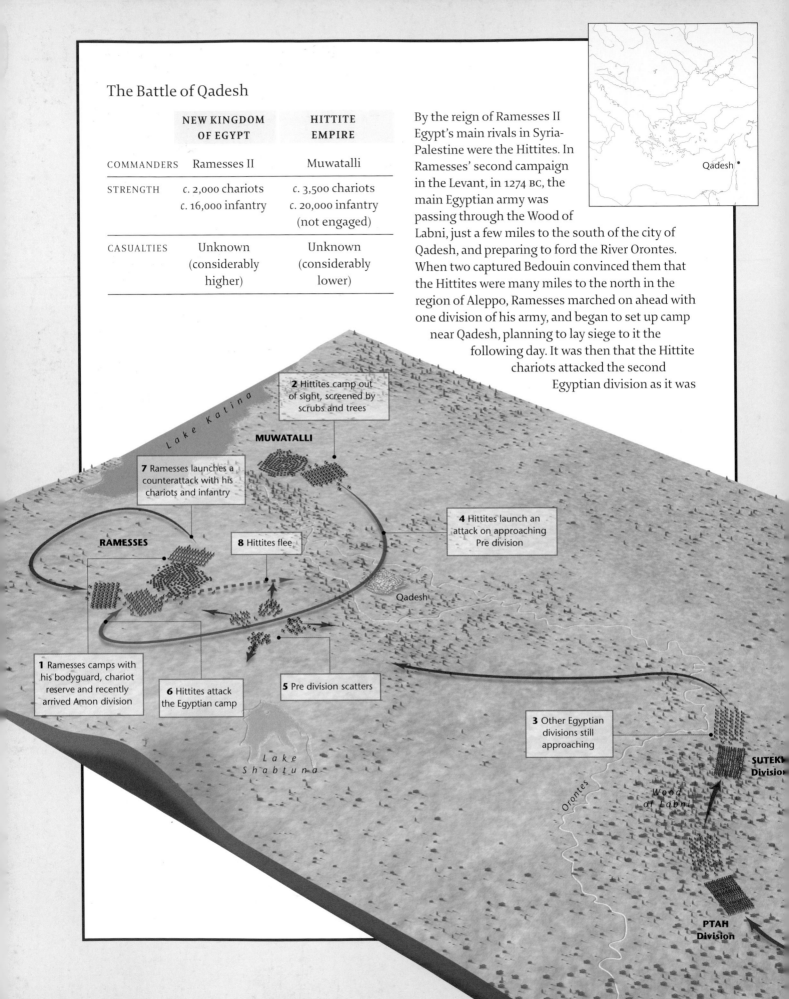

Qadesh

Lake Katina

2 Hittites camp out of sight, screened by scrubs and trees

MUWATALLI

7 Ramesses launches a counterattack with his chariots and infantry

4 Hittites launch an attack on approaching Pre division

RAMESSES

8 Hittites flee

Qadesh

1 Ramesses camps with his bodyguard, chariot reserve and recently arrived Amon division

6 Hittites attack the Egyptian camp

5 Pre division scatters

3 Other Egyptian divisions still approaching

Lake Shabtuna

Orontes

Wood of Labni

ŞUTEKH Division

PTAH Division

on its way from the River Orontes to Ramesses' camp, and while two other divisions were still in the Wood of Labni. Ramesses is supposed to have rallied the combined troops of Amun and Pre in an attempt to rescue the situation, apparently calling out 'Hold your ground and steady yourself my shield bearer! I will attack them like the swoop of the falcon, killing, slaughtering and casting them to the ground.'

Possibly the Egyptians and their king might have been totally defeated at this stage if it had not been for the timely arrival of another group of Egyptian troops who had come north by the coastal route and marched eastwards to Qadesh. The following morning the two armies faced each other on either side of the Orontes. The Hittites still had the numerical advantage, but they had probably suffered heavy losses in their chariotry. Ramesses kept the initiative by launching an attack across the river – this was at first victorious but eventually, through sheer weight of numbers, a situation of stalemate set in. In the subsequent exchange of envoys an uneasy peace was made, allowing each party to claim some degree of success. Although the scale of the commemoration of the battle of Qadesh implies that it was intended to be regarded as a high point in Ramesses' reign, it seems likely that it was at best a case of stalemate, and at worst a severe setback to Ramesses' empire-building.

Above From the Ramesseum, this relief shows a group of fallen Hittite chariotry soldiers and their horses. Many of the casualties have been slain by arrows fired by the king himself as they flee from his chariot.

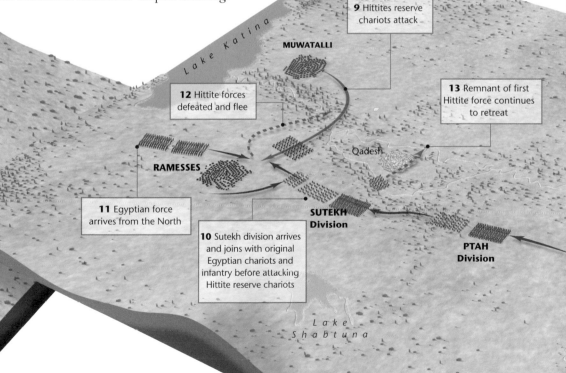

Lake Katina

MUWATALLI

9 Hittites reserve chariots attack

12 Hittite forces defeated and flee

13 Remnant of first Hittite force continues to retreat

Qadesh

RAMESSES

11 Egyptian force arrives from the North

SUTEKH Division

10 Sutekh division arrives and joins with original Egyptian chariots and infantry before attacking Hittite reserve chariots

PTAH Division

Lake Shabtuna

In the New Kingdom there seems to have been a more ready supply of volunteers, whether through individuals inheriting the role of a family member, or through the enrolment of so-called 'mercenary' ethnic groups such as the Canaanites, Nubians and Mycenaeans. It is likely, however, that some form of conscription remained, since, although a small number of troops were based in garrisons abroad, fighting was still strictly seasonal. New Kingdom texts provide us with more reliable figures on the numbers of soldiers, although this is still a much-debated area. In the battle of Qadesh, Ramesses II seems to have commanded an army consisting of five divisions. Opinions concerning the size of an individual division, however, range from 1,000 to 5,000, suggesting anything from 5,000 to 25,000 as the total number of troops in Ramesses' army. A papyrus from the time of Ramesses' father, Seti I, lists military rations that would have fed an army considerably larger than 5,000. It is also worth noting that the Egyptian population in the New Kingdom is estimated at around 3 million, therefore an army of 25,000 Egyptians would have represented just under 1 per cent of the population. Regardless of the overall size of the army or its divisions, for tactical purposes the basic military unit seems to have been a platoon of 50 infantrymen, each under the command of a 'chief of 50'. There were usually five platoons in a 'company' (sa) and about 20 companies in a division (if we assume the higher figure of 5000 per division). The units of infantrymen were reinforced by separate companies of 'elite troops' (neferu) and 'chariot warriors' (seneniu). The numbers of chariots in the Egyptian army would not have been large, with probably a maximum of around 200 operational vehicles and an additional 50 in reserve. As well as the hierarchy of purely military officials there was also a separate, superimposed chain of command made up of officials drawn from the civil administration (such as scribes, quartermasters, adjutants and stablemasters).

A MILITARY CAREER

It is not until the Middle Kingdom that the first evidence of military training appears. In the tomb of Khnumhotep there are a series of scenes depicting men wrestling, as well as what appears to be an actual battle. Similar scenes are found in the New Kingdom battle of Qadesh reliefs, in which Egyptian soldiers are shown practising military tactics and fighting. There is strong evidence that this training could be very tough. A school exercise from Papyrus Anastasi III, also dating to the New Kingdom, describes a boy being inducted into the infantry, sent to a barracks for training, and experiencing harsh discipline, including beatings. A similar text, from Papyrus Anastasi I, shows that life after training was still difficult, describing the aftermath of a long march: 'you stop in the evening; with all of your body crushed and battered; your [limbs] are bruised'. Although these writings are a form of satire written from a scribal perspective, with the deliberate aim of castigating military life and instead promoting the lifestyle of a bureaucrat, the description may well have had some basis in real life.

Despite the harsh realities of military life, the Egyptian army would have been a potentially lucrative career, particularly in the New Kingdom. An inscription in the tomb of Ahmose-pen-nekhbet at Elkab states that he was rewarded with the 'gold of valour', and given slaves and land as a result of his actions on the battlefield. Another text, in the tomb of Amenemheb at Thebes, states: 'I took thirteen Asiatics

Above The tomb of the early 18th-dynasty Queen Ahhotep at Thebes contained a necklace consisting of large golden 'flies', traditionally awarded for prowess in battle. They may have belonged to her son King Ahmose I.

as prisoner of war... then my lord gave me the gold of valour.' Although these texts are from a funerary context and are often thought to resemble personal 'shopping lists' of rewards, they also show the distribution of war booty as well as the issue of medal-style awards ('flies of valour'), actual surviving examples of which are known from contemporary tombs.

Many soldiers also owned land. The Wilbour Papyrus, of the mid-20th dynasty, shows the system of land tenure in several regions of Egypt. A large number of small landholders bear military titles varying from infantryman (*w'w*) to charioteer (*ket*), and this and other texts indicate that any rank of the Egyptian military could be rewarded for their services.

Status and rank are also considered to have been important aspects of a military career in Egypt. Ahmose son of Ebana, for example, describes himself as initially an infantryman, the lowest rank of the military, but his funerary texts suggest that he worked his way up to achieve the rank of crew commander. Such promotion and career development was thus certainly possible; nevertheless, economic status at birth probably determined the potential progression of an individual. Chariotry was a separate wing to the infantry, but it is not clear whether members of the infantry could be promoted to a position where a career with the chariotry was attainable. It is also difficult to know whether regular soldiers (i.e. those without elite connections) were able to attain high-ranking positions.

WEAPONRY: SPEARS, MACES, AXES AND DAGGERS

Egyptian weapons were similar, if not identical, to those of neighbouring lands, especially in western Asia. This was a consequence of the Egyptians adopting technology from neighbouring civilizations, a culmination of several factors. Once a professional army had developed, it is believed that the Egyptian weapons 'industry' became the business of the government, with military workshops initially attached to the temples, but transferring to the royal treasury and military headquarters later in the New Kingdom.

The weapons used by the Egyptians were standardized throughout the Dynastic period, with the main types being the spear, javelin, bow and arrow, and, later in the New Kingdom, swords and chariots. The specific group of key materials used to produce these weapons were wood, leather, stone, copper and – especially in the New Kingdom – bronze. The use of bronze was restricted in earlier times due to the lack of tin in the region, but the Egyptians utilized copper extensively. An analysis of Egyptian axes has shown that arsenical copper was employed as a deliberate alloy from an early period, with tin-based bronzes being used only on a limited scale. Although this reliance on arsenic alloys would not have produced such strong weapons, it would at least have allowed the Egyptians to utilize copper more productively.

The elaborately decorated and primarily ceremonial golden axe and sheathed dagger of King Ahmose I were also found in the tomb of Queen Ahhotep.

Chariots

The Egyptian chariot emerged as part of a process of military modernization at the beginning of the New Kingdom. The Egyptians gained their knowledge of this technology from Canaan, and early 18th-dynasty Egyptian chariots were exactly the same as contemporary Canaanite vehicles.

The Egyptian chariot's light structure restricted its use. Its speed enabled it to be used as a mobile platform for an archer delivering harassing fire against the enemy infantry. But it was almost certainly not employed directly against opposing chariots as it was vulnerable in close combat. It could also not be used on mountainous terrain, and might be easily disabled with a simple spear attack. Although infantry probably played a more important role in actual campaigns, the chariot was closely associated with elite presentation, therefore chariotry-based warfare has survived better in the visual record.

The six chariots found in the tomb of Tutankhamun are particularly helpful in determining the manufacturing process. The lower part of the vehicle was typically composed of two four-spoke wheels with the axle set towards the rear. All the components would be produced from wood and held together using leather, rawhide and glue. Leather straps were added to the wheel to help hold it together and protect it, and rawhide was used to strengthen joints, wheel hubs, and as a bearing for the axle. Such regular use of glue and rawhide was only possible in a dry climate such as that of Egypt. Even so, frequent protection of joints with waterproof coverings, such as birch bark, indicates that the loosening of joints due to moisture may still have posed a problem.

The New Kingdom Egyptian chariot is thought to stand technologically somewhere between the experimental Levantine examples of the 18th–17th centuries BC and the heavier type of the 1st millennium BC, shown in Assyrian reliefs. Designed for speed, lightness and stability, it was arguably the most technically effective chariot ever made.

Above This chariot, part of a scene on a painted box from the tomb of Tutankhamun, is far more elaborate and ornate in design than the physical examples from the same tomb.

Below Tutankhamun's chariots were buried in pieces by the Egyptians. In their reconstructed form, they are by far our best evidence of how these vehicles were constructed, not only in Egypt, but in the whole of the Bronze Age Mediterranean.

Above The 'Hunter's Palette' dates to a period of Egyptian history when internal conflict and state formation were central to military activity rather than foreign invasion. Soldiers are shown holding spears and bows.

Right The iron-bladed dagger of Tutankhamun – a rare example of this material being used in the Late Bronze Age – is likely to have been a gift from the Hittite empire to the Egyptian king, since Anatolia is believed to have been one of the earliest locations for iron production.

The spear was the main short-range weapon. The early examples depicted on a Protodynastic 'Hunter's Palette' consist of a long staff and a leaf-shaped blade with protuberant spine. Old and Middle Kingdom examples of spearheads are usually made of flint or copper and were attached to wooden staffs by a tang at the end of the blade. In the New Kingdom it would appear that bronze was more readily available to produce spearheads; this, along with an increase in contact with western Asia, is believed to be a factor in a design change whereby spears began to be produced with a socket attachment rather than a tang.

The mace was a basic hand-held offensive weapon, which comprised little more than a stick with a pear-, apple- or saucer-shaped stone mounted on one end. This weapon appears to have been used for more ceremonial purposes after the Old Kingdom, though it is possible that the soldiers themselves may have carried the mace as an extra weapon to complement the standard-issue weaponry, especially due to its simple construction.

Axes and daggers were important throughout the pharaonic period. Not only are they depicted frequently on tomb and temple walls, but many examples have been found in archaeological contexts. The dagger was commonly produced from copper alloys and had a regular design for much of the Bronze Age. The introduction of more sophisticated production techniques in the New Kingdom, however, allowed the Egyptians to produce a narrower, sharper blade. Often shown attached to the kilt of the king, the dagger was probably

The sickle sword (or *khepesh*), like this one from the tomb of Tutankhamun, would have been very effective as a slashing weapon used against lightly armoured infantry. The name 'sickle sword', however, is something of a misnomer: on a standard sickle the cutting edge is on the outer side of the blade, rather than on the inside as it is here.

considered to be a weapon of last resort, in a similar manner to the modern bayonet.

A variety of swords have been found in 19th- and 20th-dynasty funerary contexts, though the extent of their use is difficult to determine. The main Egyptian type was the sickle sword (or *khepesh*). It is thought that the manufacturing techniques to produce this weapon were probably acquired from Canaan (now part of modern Israel), however direct imports, through trade or tribute, may also have occurred, as an example found in the tomb of Tutankhamun demonstrates.

The Egyptians more commonly utilized the tang-type cutting axe rather than the socketed axe favoured in western Asia. A particularly common axe in Egypt during the Middle Kingdom was the three-tanged epsilon axe. This weapon possessed three holes, allowing the head to be fastened to the haft with cord or small nails. 'Duck-bill' axes were also common in Middle Kingdom Egypt and remained in use during the succeeding Second Intermediate Period when more rounded forms were developed, before being replaced by a splayed-type weapon with straight or incurved sides that became predominant in the New Kingdom. This change is believed to be the result of the latter type's penetration capability, and the design is widely believed to be a response to the development of body armour. The axe remained an important weapon up to the end of the 18th dynasty until it was gradually supplanted by the sickle sword.

THE BOW AND ARROW

The bow and arrow was the basic long-range weapon in Egypt from the outset of the pharaonic period. The simple (or self) bow was the first known bow in Egypt and was produced from a stave of nearly straight wood, trimmed at each end to produce a tapered effect. Production techniques are believed to have undergone little change throughout the pharaonic period. The wood was required to be long enough to bend but not break, and this may have been accomplished by steaming the wood to increase pliability during the manufacturing process. Simple bows have survived from the New Kingdom, such as the examples found in the tomb of Tutankhamun, which are especially important as several have the remains of animal-gut string still attached. Various depictions have survived from earlier periods, including scenes in the tomb of Khnumhotep at Beni Hasan, and the model of 40 Nubian archers from the tomb of Mesehti at Asyut.

Life in an Egyptian Military Camp

The reliefs depicting the battle of Qadesh incorporate scenes of the interior of Ramesses II's main encampment. Among the details are ox-carts carrying supplies into the camp, a chariot in the course of being repaired, an archer re-stringing his bow, the interrogation and beating of Hittite spies, and a seated soldier whose leg-wound is in the process of being tended. Ramesses' magnificent tent is shown surrounded by the smaller tents of his officers, and elsewhere the seated king discusses strategy with his generals.

Apart from the individuals involved in producing food and weapons for the army, there were also many other workers making a wide range of non-military contributions to the cause. The Theban tomb of Userhet, an army officer in the time of Amenhotep II, contains scenes of barbers cutting soldiers' hair and quartermasters handing out the rations. Another tomb at Thebes, of an army scribe in the reign of Thutmose IV, contains a depiction of cattle being herded into the army camp as food for the troops. Several reliefs from the tomb of the general and pharaoh Horemheb at Memphis depict a military encampment in the reign of Tutankhamun. One recently excavated fragment shows a tent already pitched and another perhaps in the process of being erected, surrounded by soldiers preparing and eating food. Three better-preserved fragments from the same tomb show boys carrying water-skins and food around the camp while the soldiers tend

The military encampment scene from the Qadesh reliefs. A multitude of activities are shown, including soldiers training, men being treated for foot injuries, animals being fed, and weapons being prepared for the upcoming battle.

horses and donkeys, maintain the chariotry equipment and set up tents. Views of the tents of the officers (including perhaps that of Horemheb himself) show that they contain stocks of food and a folding stool and are being fastidiously cleaned and dusted inside by servants. In one of these scenes a squatting scribe is shown writing instructions or perhaps a list of provisions.

The 18th-dynasty tomb of Userhet shows soldiers having their hair cut. A distinctive military hairstyle is common in armies throughout the ancient and modern worlds, generally to instil discipline and *esprit de corps*. In Egypt it is also possible that the form of the haircut was designed to protect the head.

The detailed model of 40 Nubian archers from the Middle Kingdom tomb of Mesheti perhaps shows what the Egyptians considered an ideal rank of soldiery. Each soldier carries a bow in his left hand and several arrows in his right, while they march in unison.

Opposite The head of one of 60 mummified soldiers buried in a mass grave close to the mortuary complex of Nebhepetre Mentuhotep II. The trauma evident on the bodies and the arrowheads found within a number of chest cavities suggest they were killed in battle. These soldiers are thought to have died during the conflict of the 11th dynasty when local Egyptian rulers were attempting to reunify the country.

The arrow had to be made of a light, straight material such as reed (although wooden shafts have also been found) and metal, flint or wooden arrowheads would be attached. Arrows have been found with or without feathers at the end of the reed, although the addition of feathers afforded greater stability and accuracy and thus was probably widely employed. From the study of Egyptian ballistics it is clear that the feathered arrow had considerable force.

The introduction of the composite bow, stronger and more effective than the simple bow, was part of a striking change in military equipment that occurred at the beginning of the New Kingdom. This modernization of the Egyptian army is attributed to the need to keep pace with the military innovations of neighbouring countries and prevent any recurrence of a foreign incursion like that of the Hyksos in the Second Intermediate Period (1650–1550 BC). The composite bow was made from a wooden core with a layer of sinew applied to the back. A layer of horn was applied to the face and the whole bow was then covered with a protective sheath made of ash- or birch-bark. All the composite bows found in Egypt are from tombs, though they appear to have been neither especially rare nor costly, since many derive from non-royal tombs.

BATTLE INJURIES AND DEATH

At the end of the 3rd millennium BC, at least 60 11th-dynasty soldiers were buried together in a rock cut grave near the tomb of Nebhepetre Mentuhotep II in western Thebes; many of these had suffered severe head-wounds probably sustained in the course of siege warfare, and in one case an ebony-tipped arrowhead was discovered embedded in an eye socket. The un-mummified linen-wrapped bodies of the soldiers were preserved by dehydration – despite the absence of any embalming, these corpses are the best-preserved of all Middle Kingdom bodies. Because they were buried as a group and within sight of the royal cemetery, it has been surmised that they died in some particularly heroic conflict, perhaps connected with the Theban rulers' war against the northern dynasty based at Herakleopolis.

Gonzalo Sanchez of the School of Medicine at the University of Dakota has pointed out that the artists' depictions of wounded and dead soldiers in Ramessid battle scenes seem to be medically accurate. In the two scenes depicting the battle of Qadesh, Sanchez identified specific injuries on about 70 per cent of the 63 Hittite charioteers shown breaking into the Egyptian military camp. He found that most of these injuries were inflicted from a frontal direction onto the upper body, suggesting that they derived from close combat rather than long-range weaponry.

EGYPTIAN WARFARE AFTER QADESH: SEA PEOPLES TO PERSIANS

For most of the pharaonic period Egyptian involvement in the Mediterranean seems to have been commercial rather than overtly military, but in the late New Kingdom a number of sea-borne foreign armies began to menace the Delta coastline, posing a new kind of threat. In the second year of the reign of Ramesses II (c. 1278 BC) there was a raid by Sherden pirates, who were defeated and incorporated into the Egyptian army as an elite force of mercenaries. This was the first real indication of the challenge

posed by a loose confederation of sea-going Indo-European migrants (including the Ekwesh, Shekelesh, Tjeker, Weshesh, Teresh, Sherden, Lukka and Denyen) whom the Egyptians described as the Sea Peoples or simply 'northerners'.

In the fifth year of Merneptah's reign (c. 1207 BC) an invasion from the northwest by an alliance of Tjehenu (Libyans), Meshwesh and Sea Peoples was repelled, but by the eighth year of the reign of Ramesses III (c. 1174 BC), a second wave of Sea Peoples had arrived on the Delta border. This time they were allied with the Peleset (Philistines) and their attack came from the northeast by both land and sea. A contemporary text describes the Sea Peoples' advance: 'Suddenly these peoples were on the move, scattered in war. No country could withstand their arms.' The land attack seems to have been checked by a single battle near one of the Egyptian frontier garrisons on the northern edge of the Sinai desert. When they attempted an audacious attack by sea, Ramesses III defeated them again in a great naval battle, which was depicted in a complex relief sculpture on the northern outer wall of his mortuary temple at Medinet Habu. In the long term, however, this solitary sea victory seems to have simply postponed the inevitable, and by the end of the 20th dynasty much of Syria-Palestine had effectively passed into the hands of the Sea Peoples. The surviving account of the ill-fated royal trading mission of Wenamun shows that, in the time of the chief-priest Herihor (c. 1075 BC), at the very end of the New Kingdom, the Egyptian navy could not even maintain their traditional supplies of cedarwood from the Levantine port of Byblos.

The last battles of the native Egyptian pharaohs were desperate defensive struggles, far removed from the empire building of the Middle and New Kingdoms.

Opposite In the marine battle of Ramesses III against the Sea Peoples, Egyptian soldiers are depicted on boats fighting the invasion forces hand-to-hand, while further Egyptian bowmen and slingers fire missiles into the throng.

Right This group of captive Sea Peoples depicted at Medinet Habu, were captured after their battle with the forces of Ramesses III. They are described in the associated caption as 'the fallen ones of Peleset' and are believed to be a cultural group who subsequently settled in the Levant after their unsuccessful invasion of Egypt.

Significantly, many of the military actions of the Third Intermediate Period and Late Period (1069–332 BC) took place on Egyptian soil, as successive waves of foreigners capitalized on the political and economic weakness of their old enemy. In 671 BC the armies of the Assyrian ruler Esarhaddon captured Memphis. In an inscription at Senjirli Esarhaddon described the event with great relish: 'I laid siege to Memphis... and conquered it in half a day by means of mines, breaches and assault ladders; I destroyed it, tore down its walls and burnt it down. His 'queen'..., his heir apparent, his other children, his possessions, horses, large and small cattle beyond counting, I carried away as booty to Assyria.'

During the Late Period the Egyptians found that they themselves were not exempt from the recurrent cycle of conquest, pillage, vassaldom and rebellion that they had for so long inflicted on the peoples of Nubia and Syria-Palestine. Humiliated by the technologically and tactically superior armies of the Assyrians, Persians and Macedonians, the Egyptians could no longer be regarded as major military players in the game of east Mediterranean domination.

3   Ancient Near Eastern Warfare

A detail from the 'Stela of the Vultures' (*c.* 2500 BC) showing the elite infantry of Eannatum of Lagash equipped with armour of crossed belts and helmet, with shouldered long spears in their right hand, and with the typical type of Early Dynastic bronze axe in their left.

The time-span covered by this chapter is, at some 2,500 years (3200–539 BC), effectively half of all recorded history. Moreover, we are dealing with not one but many cultures or civilizations over this immensely long period, spread over a vast and diverse geographical area – encompassing at its heart Anatolia, Syria, the Levant, Mesopotamia (largely modern-day Iraq), Arabia and Iran. Our sources include many images of military scenes on commemorative stelae, figurative stone relief decoration and wall-paintings in palaces, as well as plaques, tiles, inlays, seals and sealings, but their interpretation is not straightforward. In addition, from the late 4th millennium BC surviving texts, written largely on almost imperishable clay tablets, include considerable quantities of official inscriptions and letters, administrative and business records and private correspondence. These give an unrivalled insight into the functioning of the military systems of the ancient Near East, but again, these documents have to be used with care since their message has sometimes passed through the filter of official ideology and propaganda. Finally, some areas appear of a lesser historical significance merely through having had far less archaeological attention than others. For all these reasons, the wider Near East can receive only a summary treatment here, and the main focus will be on Mesopotamia and its hinterland where the combination of pictorial and textual sources is richest.

ORIGINS

Civilization as we now understand it was born in the Near East during the 4th millennium BC, most likely as the result of widespread climatic change, on the alluvial plains flanking the great rivers of the Euphrates and Tigris in southern Mesopotamia, and the Karun and Kerkha rivers of southwestern Iran. The increase in the availability of highly fertile, cultivatable land saw a rapid intensification of settlement and population in southern Mesopotamia. As the climate continued to dry, and more of the potentially productive alluvial plain became available to the burgeoning populations, substantial artificial irrigation became essential – as, unlike other areas, there was too little rainfall for dry agriculture. The need to raise and direct the labour required for economic activity, irrigation, and other major public works demanded more complex forms of social organization, communication and record-keeping in the densely populated south than in surrounding regions. Given that these are also the basic tools for effective military organization, it is not surprising that the structure of the earliest armies was clearly based on those employed for work-crews on civil projects. In the ancient world, even more than today, the nature and structure of army, society, economy and state were directly related and interdependent.

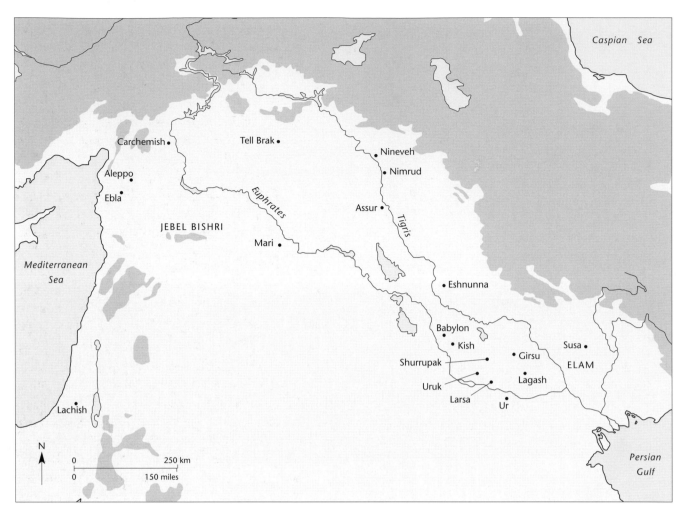

Above The main sites mentioned in this chapter. The courses of the Tigris and Euphrates differed in antiquity.

By the beginning of the historical period it seems that the population of southern Mesopotamia, or Sumer, was composed of two main ethnic groups: those who lived in the south and spoke Sumerian, and those, predominantly in the north, who spoke a Semitic language known as Akkadian. Both groups appear to have shared a common, though diverse, 'Sumerian' culture. The earliest historical records show that southern Mesopotamia was divided politically into a number of small but densely populated city-states and may indicate that the northern state of Kish was larger and once predominant. Urban centres were generally large and came to be heavily defended with fortifications of mud- or baked-brick. Some indeed were vast: the walls of the city of Uruk (traditionally constructed by the semi-legendary Gilgamesh) were 11 km (7 miles) in circumference.

Despite Sumer's considerable human resources there were no local sources of stone, good-quality timber or metal ore, and the city-states of the so-called Early Dynastic period (*c.* 2900–2334 BC) evidently vied with each other to gain control of either the trade routes or sources of supply of these essential raw materials – a situation compounded by endemic inter-state conflict over waterways and productive land. Indeed, the drive for natural resources seems earlier to have resulted in a remarkable, but very short-lived, expansion of 'Sumerian' civilization into Iran, northern Mesopotamia, Syria and southern Anatolia in the prehistoric late Uruk period. Seals from this period in Mesopotamia and southern Iran depict scenes of warfare, and there is now archaeological evidence for armed conflict and the violent destruction of local urban centres in these 'colonized' areas, as at Tell Hamoukar in Syria. Artistic representations show that the bow and stout thrusting spears were used both in hunting and in warfare. Although the depictions are not entirely clear, the type of bow portrayed is characteristically double-curved with reflexed tips which would indicate an advanced composite construction of several layers of wood, horn and sinew. Early Mesopotamian archery is also found in Archaic tablets from Uruk and Elam, with quantities of 'arrows', or 'bows and arrows', issued to officials. Other weapons known archaeologically include clay slingshot, javelin points, stone maces and simple copper axes. Even earlier, one storage room at the small Late Neolithic site of Umm Dabaghiyah contained over 1,000 clay slingshot and many large clay balls for throwing. Arrows were made of reed with either leaf-shaped or transverse arrowheads of flint. Even from this fairly limited evidence, it is clear that we are dealing with a mature military tradition whose origins ought to predate the available pictorial and textual evidence.

The history of the 3rd millennium BC in Mesopotamia shows several key features that will be seen time and again in the Near East. One is the complex, yet sometimes violent, interaction between semi-nomadic and sedentary populations and ways of life; another is the constant struggle to create larger political units both within Mesopotamia, and then, through expansion by military means, into surrounding areas. The counterpart of this state-building is the eventual collapse of these polities during periods later conceptualized by their successors as unnatural anarchy. In the historical period, there is evidence that the Early Dynastic rulers Eannatum of Lagash (c. 2450 BC) and later Lugalzagesi of Uruk established short-lived empires in southern Mesopotamia with limited influence upon territories in Syria and

Right A clay sealing (c. 3000 BC) from Susa in southwestern Iran with an impression made by a cylinder seal. The complete scene has been reconstructed and depicts a ruler shooting an arrow from a composite bow at three naked adversaries, one of whom is fleeing, each already pierced by a single arrow. To the right is a temple on a platform decorated with horns (a symbol of divinity).

Opposite below This stone stela from the site of the city of Uruk (modern Warka, Iraq) shows a ruler hunting lions in two scenes: in the upper with a thrusting spear and in the lower with a composite bow and arrows tipped with transverse arrowheads, probably of flint or obsidian (c. 3000 BC). The lions are shown shot with several arrows, which may indicate use of a fast shooting technique.

Above Fragment of a stone stela from the period of the dynasty of Akkad, showing a soldier with a crescentic axe escorting naked and bound prisoners. It was found on the Acropolis at Susa where it had been taken in antiquity (probably as loot).

Below A limestone inlay (*c.* 2500–2400 BC) from the city of Ebla, showing an unarmoured archer. Although rarely depicted in Sumer itself at this date, military archery is, however, known from textual sources.

Elam. However, around 2330 BC, Lugalzagesi was defeated and swept away by Sargon (*Sharru-kin*, 'legitimate king', 2334–2279 BC) of Akkad in a momentous turning-point in the history of Mesopotamia and the world. For the first time Akkadian became the language for official inscriptions, and the Semitic-speaking northerners achieved general political dominance. Sargon and his dynasty created the world's first true empire and introduced a new concept of kingship and state. They set a standard for conspicuous real and imagined achievement that succeeding generations of rulers could only attempt to emulate. The most significant difference from previous states was in the scope and range of military operations. The kings of Akkad campaigned far beyond Mesopotamia, most spectacularly by ship to the land of Makkan (which is likely to have been either Oman or possibly southern Iran) and these campaigns appear to have had essentially economic objectives in securing trade routes or booty.

ARMIES IN THE 3RD MILLENNIUM BC

The world's earliest coherent historical narrative is an account of a series of wars fought over land and water rights in Sumer. It was waged in the name of its patron god Ningirsu by the city-state of Lagash against the neighbouring state of Umma (Tell Jokha) over a period of about 150 years from *c.* 2500 BC. The most famous of these documents, found at the site of Telloh (ancient Girsu) in 1881, is a fragmentary inscribed stone stela illustrated in relief with scenes depicting one episode in this extended conflict, and now known as the 'Stela of the Vultures' (from the details of birds feasting upon the slain). The main protagonists depicted are, however, the god with his divine standard-bearers and chariot on one face, and on the other the victorious ruler of Lagash, Eannatum, riding in his chariot before a phalanx of his soldiers. The latter are shown marching over the despoiled enemy dead in well-ordered array armed with axe and spear, protected with armour of crossed-belts on the chest and pointed helmets, and behind a wall of large rectangular body-shields. Other artworks, for example the famous 'Standard of Ur' of *c.* 2600 BC, show very similar troops, though in this case long capes are worn for protection instead of crossed-belts and shields. The deadly importance of these highly developed personal and unit defences is revealed in part of the extensive inscription on the 'Vulture' stela: 'A person shot an arrow at Eannatum. He was shot through by the arrow and had difficulty moving. He cried out in the face of it.'

Similar elaborate Early Dynastic victory scenes are known from other sites in southern Iraq, though typically rendered in the form of shell and other inlays – as in the 'Standard of Ur'. Fragmentary examples are also known, for example from Kish, and from Syria, at Mari (Tell Hariri) on the Euphrates and most dramatically from Ebla (Tell Mardikh), which illustrates large numbers of lightly equipped archers armed with self longbows, in addition to the more commonly depicted elite troops.

Right The head of a soldier from the 'King's Grave' at Ur (Tell al-Muqayyar) as preserved, still wearing a copper/bronze helmet. Crushed and distorted after burial, the X-ray shows its original appearance was actually identical to contemporary representations (see below) and reveals the details of construction. Note the holes around the edge of the helmet to secure a soft inner lining and edging.

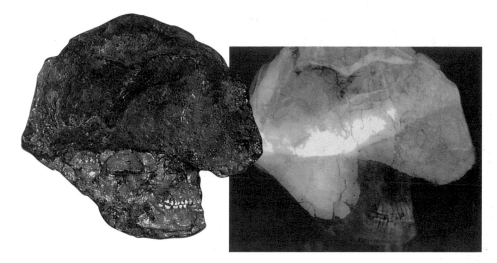

Below This enigmatic object (dating to c. 2600 BC), conventionally called the 'Standard of Ur' (although its purpose is unknown – it was possibly the sound box of a harp), was found in the 'Royal Cemetery' at Ur. Inlays of shell, red limestone and lapis lazuli are set in bitumen on a (long-decayed) wooden foundation. This scene depicts the immediate aftermath of a victorious battle, the routed enemy pursued by charging four-wheeled chariots, while naked prisoners are escorted before a ruler by soldiers wearing helmets and protective cloaks.

The most striking aspect of these representations – the technical sophistication of the military equipment, both defensive and offensive, and their homogeneity over a large area – can be readily confirmed through archaeology. Leonard Woolley excavated copper helmets, still worn by their owners, in the 'Royal Cemetery' at Ur in the 1920s, of exactly the same type shown in contemporary Early Dynastic art. The type of bronze axe head shown has also been recovered from the 'Royal Cemetery' at Ur, and from Kish and elsewhere. The commonest type is a narrow-bladed weapon with a cutting edge on the tip and inner blade, a highly specialized form clearly intended to punch through targets from above – presumably padded copper/bronze helmets – though wide, crescent-shaped slashing blades were also part of the military arsenal.

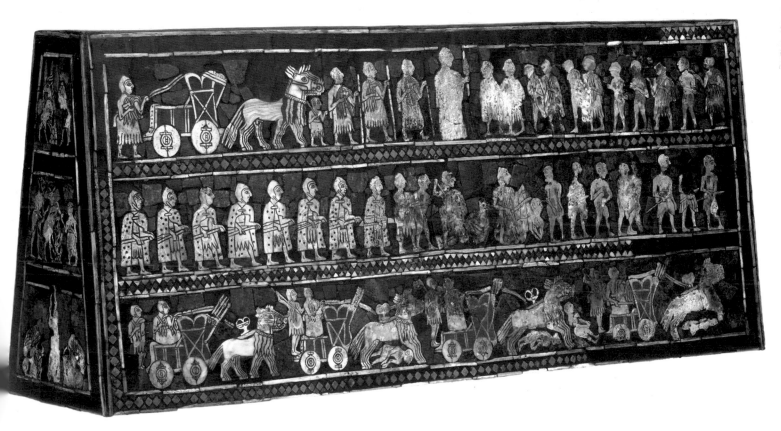

A scene from the 'Stela of the Vultures' (c. 2500 BC) showing the close-ordered phalanx of Lagash advancing into battle behind its ruler, Eannatum. Only the heads of the first rank are shown above the large body-shields. In the wider scene, there appear to be four men armed with long spears, six carrying shields and one, perhaps an officer armed with an axe, at the extreme left. Six rows of spears are shown, so the formation was at least six deep, and possibly represents a company of 60–100 men. Such mixed formations of spearmen and axemen fronted by shieldbearers are also indicated by contemporary muster-lists.

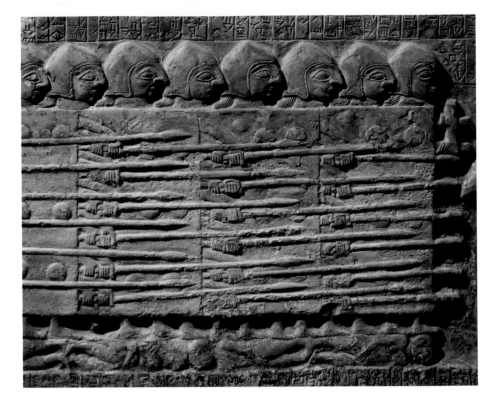

The spearheads excavated are either large bronze pike-heads or smaller javelins, the latter found in graves at the Royal Cemetery in sets of four. These match the representations of javelins in the quivers of chariots and possibly indicate that these graves are those of, presumably, high-status charioteers. Weaponry of this basic type remains in widespread use, with minor variations in design, throughout the Near East until the early 2nd millennium BC. Missile weapons were bows, slings and javelins, while close-combat weapons comprised pikes, spears and javelins, axes, maces, daggers and sickle swords. The sickle-sword was a sophisticated slashing weapon of bronze with a curved blade on a straight shaft and with the cutting edge on the outer edge of the blade.

Shields, known from pictorial sources, have not been recovered through excavation. On the 'Vulture' stela, the infantry of the phalanx are shown in six close ordered ranks (indicated by six rows of protruding levelled spears) behind a front of six rectangular shields reaching from the neck to the ankle, each decorated with nine large, circular bosses. Such body-shields are usually said to be reaching down to, or resting upon, the ground and seem to have functioned more to shield a unit, and as 'a screen for the army' in both field combat and during sieges, rather than as shields for individuals.

MILITARY ORGANIZATION IN THE 3RD MILLENNIUM BC

In Early Dynastic Sumer, the state's palaces and temples functioned as major administrative and economic units, organizing trade and employing thousands of tenants in workshops and on the land. These men and women were organized into specialized crews according to their profession, under the supervision of 'commanders' (**ugula***), 'captains' (**nu-banda**) and, on temple estates, by 'superintendents'

* Bold and italic text in this chapter represent the Sumerian and Akkadian languages respectively.

and 'stewards'. In time of war a city's ruler could mobilize these tenants for military service, the duration and conditions of which are not entirely clear. Payment was in rations and clothing, and later in the Akkadian period seemingly also by land grant for professional soldiers.

In Sumerian, both labourers and soldiers were called **erin**, whereas professional soldiers, guards and retainers were known as **Shub-lugal**, or **aga.ush** and probably formed part of the palace establishment. Texts of *c.* 2600 BC from Shurrupak (Tell Fara), at that time subject to the powerful state of Kish, describe a large royal household. But in many cases the titles held by these men were probably honourary, and reflected the status of their holders as retainers in the royal household. Sargon of Akkad is said to have once been the 'cupbearer' of the king of Kish, for example. One text states that a craftsman from Kish was having his chariot repaired in Shurrupak's palace workshop, which suggests that some of the royal household fought from chariots. Certainly one ruler of the state of Umma had an elite unit of 60 vehicles, and very large numbers of equids were part of the responsibility of one of the administrative departments at contemporary Ebla in Syria.

Military units seem to have had fixed sizes, although the size of similarly organized work-crews varied according to the nature of the work. The largest units are some 670–680 men strong, and described as 'going into battle'. They occur in texts from Shurrupak, and in bodies 800–300 strong in a large muster list from Ebla.

In the reign of Sargon of Akkad we have the first real indication of sizeable professional military forces, when it is said that Sargon's household consisted of 5,400 men (called *gurush* in Akkadian). They were stationed in Sargon's palace at his capital of Agade, where they 'ate bread daily before the king', and might represent nine units of 600 men. The military use of early chariots was thought to have declined rapidly following the Early Dynastic period, but sealings excavated from the site of Tell Brak in Syria showing chariots and equid riders in battle now suggest otherwise. Chariots seem still to have been used as fast mounts for messengers and special 'chariot roads' are mentioned in some texts. There is evidence in the Early Dynastic period for the use of foreign mercenaries from outside Mesopotamia, and this continued under Sargon with evidence of mercenaries from Elam, the Zagros mountains and from the west.

To subdue the strongly independent traditions of the conquered city-states, Sargon replaced their rulers with his own governors who were probably also responsible for the military establishments in their districts. Akkad's brilliance was only brief and would later be remembered as a dynasty that perhaps attempted too much. Following widespread revolts, power in Mesopotamia again devolved to the city-state and to external forces, characterized as barbarous Gutian tribesmen from the Zagros area.

The Victory stela of Naram-Sin of Akkad (*c.* 2254–2218 BC). The deified Naram-Sin, wearing a horned-helmet that proclaims his divinity, strides before his standards and the ranks of his axe-, bow- and spear-carrying men, up wooded slopes on a campaign against the highlanders to the east of his kingdom. Naram-Sin was famed for winning nine battles in a single year.

Chariots and Mounted Warfare

The earliest fighting vehicles appear around 2800 BC as the prestige mounts of divinities, rulers and military charioteers. They were essentially light carts with a high protective front, low sides, and either four or two solid composite wheels (made from three sections of wood) and a single draught-pole with a team of four asses or other equids. Directional control of the team was via a goad (spiked stick), and braking was by reins attached to a nose ring; so although these early vehicles were probably fairly speedy (as confirmed by modern reconstructions), they were difficult to turn and control. These early ass-chariots were actually single-seat vehicles and any second crewman shown was hitching a ride (although this crewman probably threw javelins while, for example, the vehicle threatened to break-up enemy formations or was in pursuit of retreating troops).

combined with the invention of new forms of complete armour for man and horse, result in the 'chariot-system' which came to dominate Near Eastern warfare for nearly 1,000 years. Chariot design only changed significantly in the 1st millennium BC with the increasing use of ridden horses in mounted warfare (at first still acting together as pairs as if a chariot crew without a vehicle). Different harnessing systems and yokes were developed and vehicles became multi-crewed, with up to four men, and with larger teams of three or four horses.

Above Copper model from Tell Agrab, Iraq, of a four-ass, two-wheel chariot, a so-called straddle-car.
Left King Assurnasirpal II of Assyria (883–859 BC) riding in a new design of chariot with a strong 'Y' shaped draught-pole.
Below A clay plaque from Mesopotamia with an early depiction of horse-riding in the 3rd millennium BC.

Asses ridden in battle also appear early in the artistic record, and their use by messengers, or ridden on the march to battle, is attested textually. Horses seem to be in frequent use by the 3rd dynasty of Ur (around 2100 BC). Four-wheeled chariots cease to be depicted as real-life vehicles at around the same time, with two-wheelers becoming increasingly lighter, horse-drawn, and eventually acquiring spoked wheels during the early 2nd millennium BC. From about 1700 BC, developments of these improved vehicles,

This drawing of a design from a Syrian cylinder seal shows the appearance of the early fast chariot in the 18th to 17th centuries BC, as evolved from the cumbersome ass-drawn vehicles of the previous millennium: a light, multi-purpose, two-crew vehicle, with two-spoked wheels, drawn by a pair of horses. Typically depicted as a mount for an elite archer, in its final form (by the late 8th century BC) it had become an armoured, four-crew, four-horse vehicle. This form probably reflected an increasing specialization in roles unsuitable for the more flexible cavalry.

The next successful, but equally brief, attempt to establish a single political entity in Mesopotamia was by the 3rd dynasty rulers of Ur (*c.* 2112–2004 BC). Unlike the imperialistic kings of Akkad, they did not unduly stress their military achievements. Instead their surviving inscriptions concentrate on pious and civil projects: the digging of canals, the rebuilding of temples and the restoration of order. Campaigns were waged to the north and east, the latter securing Elam for the empire, and massive fortification projects attempted to protect the western frontier 'like a bird net' from the predations of semi-nomadic peoples known as **martu** (the 'westerners' or Amorites).

Governors (**ensi**) administered individual cities and their surrounding districts via an astonishingly rigorous and controlling bureaucracy. They were frequently moved from city to city, either to prevent strong local ties developing as a threat to the king, or perhaps to use the talents of an able man in troublesome areas. The duties of a governor were to maintain order in his city, to collect taxes, keep the local infrastructure in repair and to keep the king informed of events in the area. Communications were maintained by the use of numerous royal messengers travelling well-kept roads, as runners or on horse or ass-back. The military responsibilities of the governor were concentrated in the post of 'general'. The two types of official existed side by side in some provinces, although they were sometimes combined in one person (often in outlying areas) whose security depended on the military. The men employed on civilian and military tasks under these governors appear to have been conscripted as before. Royal troops were called **erin-lugal** or **lu-tukul**, 'king's men' or 'men-at-arms'. In border provinces there was special provision of rented land grants (**gun mada**) for the maintenance of substantial numbers of frontier troops.

A NEW MILLENNIUM

In the period following the collapse of the 3rd dynasty of Ur, in the early years of the 2nd millennium BC, there was extensive settlement by Amorites in the old urban centres throughout Mesopotamia and Syria. They were quickly assimilated culturally, and this process of gradual urbanization created numerous small Amorite kingdoms, of which the most important were Aleppo (Yamhad), Qatna, Mari, Larsa and eventually Babylon. The most powerful state in northern Mesopotamia was ruled by Samsi-Addu I (1813–1781 BC), while most of the area to the south of Babylon was controlled by Rimsin (1822–1763 BC) of Eshnunna. But by the end of his reign, from these unpromising beginnings, Hammurabi of Babylon (1792–1750 BC) emerged supreme – defeating all his neighbours through a patient strategy of warfare, alliance and guile.

Military organization in the Amorite states appears to have been very similar and we can see that Amorite tribal organization was combined with aspects of Mesopotamian tradition. The Amorite element in the community seems to have been favoured militarily, as demonstrated by the senior military rank of 'Chief Amorite' (*rab amurrum*).

Soldiers were conscripted through the institution of *ilkum*: a duty to serve the king in return for the provision of land. Holders of *ilkum* were required to serve either on war-service on royal campaigns, police-duties or labouring (such as digging canals and building fortifications). According to the famous Law Code of Hammurabi, if a

The famous Law Code of Hammurabi (dating to c. 1792–1750 BC), inscribed on this black granite stela includes several edicts relating to military law, showing how intimately the military system of recruitment was bound up with civil life. This, like many iconic pieces of Mesopotamian art, was discovered at Susa, where it had been taken as loot following later successful Elamite campaigns.

soldier did not attend a muster or send a substitute, the penalty was death. If a soldier was taken prisoner and his land was granted to another, it would be restored to its original owner, together with the *ilkum* obligation, if he returned, and the temple or the state would pay any ransom required to recover a captive. Officers who appropriated a soldier's land grant or otherwise abused the system were liable to the death penalty.

The greater part of the army still consisted of infantry, organized in companies as before, of which there were two main types: 'fully equipped' and 'light' troops. The latter were used especially for mounting ambushes or skirmishing, and could include guides and scouts. Troops were equipped from palace arsenals and work-shops, and were often moved and supplied by boats, making full use of the river systems; otherwise supply relied on pack animals and carts. Sophisticated systems of fire-signals were used to give warning of impending attack and to mobilize the armed forces in defence. Chariots now consisted of fast horse-drawn two-wheeled vehicles, but do not feature prominently in the warfare of the time and the numbers used appear to be small.

Armies of 20,000, 30,000 or even 60,000 men are known for this period, but smaller forces of 100, 1,000, 2,000 and 10,000 are more frequently mentioned. Great reliance was placed on contingents supplied by semi-nomadic tribes allied or subject to the Amorite kingdoms and on foreign allies: one contingent sent to Mari from Yamhad numbered 10,000 men, another, from Hammurabi, numbered 10,500 and a well-known letter states that 15 allied kings followed Hammurabi of Babylon. A letter from Samsi-Addu I, who at one point held most of northern Mesopotamia and administered Mari (situated on the middle stretch of the Euphrates, at the junction of key trade routes) through his dissolute son Yasmah-Addu, gives instructions for the construction of a 'strong' field army: 3,000 men are already mustered for their military service; 2,000 men are to be levied by Yasmah-Addu from among the tribal encampments. Only 1,000 guard troops will be required, giving a total of 6,000. To these will be added 10,000 men sent by Samsi-Addu. A further 6,000 allied troops are expected to come from Eshnunna.

THE CHARIOT AGE: 1600 BC TO 745 BC

Between the 16th and 15th centuries BC there was to be a sweeping change in the nature of warfare in the Near East. In this period the fast chariot, which had been known for some 200 years, finally reached its full military potential when paired with defensive armour for horse, vehicle and crew and a complete offensive armament for mounted and foot combat (composite bow, a large number of arrows, javelins, hand weapons and thrusting spears). Provided and maintained under royal patronage by a military aristocracy, the concept of the 'chariot-system' was to reign supreme throughout the Near East for nearly 1,000 years and in modified form was to spread into the Bronze Age Aegean states, India and China.

A clue to the origins of this development can be found in the commonest names for metal armour in the Near East: all are derived from the Hurrian word, *sharyani*. During the 3rd millennium BC, the highland Hurrians began to form a growing element in the populations of Syria and northern Mesopotamia. By the 17th century BC several Hurrian states had formed in these regions and within the following

Campaign, Siege and Battle

The ancient Near East was a world of cities, each sited on important routes and highways and controlling the territory and resources of its hinterland. For this reason, the arts of fortification and the techniques of siege warfare became highly developed at an early period. In contrast with the western tradition, the winning of individual field battles mattered less in terms of prestige and written accounts focus instead on campaigns as a whole and the capture of key urban centres.

Neo-Assyrian strategy required that cities be captured quickly before the campaigning season ended, and siege-craft was developed to a peak of efficiency. Battering rams are mentioned as early as the 3rd millennium BC in texts from Ebla, and there are rare scenes on Early Dynastic cylinder seals which appear to depict siege towers (in the form of four-wheeled carts with a ladder behind a high protective front) or battering rams. Siege engines could be prefabricated in city workshops and then transported to the scene of action, sometimes by boat. Such siege trains were of course unwieldy, and we find engines being burnt to prevent them falling into enemy hands.

Mathematical texts deal with the construction of earthen ramps to capture cities (see box on the storming of Lachish). These are set problems for scribes to solve, suggesting that the process of besieging and capturing an enemy fortification was as timetabled and quantifiable as in early-modern Europe.

Battles in the field are treated in stylized terms in art and literature, with representations of conflict often limited to the ruler and his immediate entourage pursuing an already defeated enemy and with texts focusing on the advance to combat and the enumeration of the enemy slain and captured. By contrast, the actual mechanics of battle – what actually happened on the battlefield – are very little known. There is however one description of combat in an Old Babylonian literary text in the form of a seemingly simple, yet sophisticated and multi-layered simile (evoking Ishtar, goddess of war and sexual love):
'The writhing (ranks) will writhe back and forth,
Two women giving birth, bathed in their own blood!'

A limestone relief panel from the central palace of King Tiglath-Pileser III (745–727 BC), showing an Assyrian assault on the city of U[pa] in southern Turkey. Allied or subject spearmen with crested helmets (recruited heavily at this time) climb up ladders while a siege engine attacks under the cover of archery. The archers are protected by large wicker pavises (shields). Neo-Assyrian siege engines seem to have been made to look like powerful beasts, with battering rams fashioned into boars' heads, or, as here, with engines built to look like elephants.

century a confederation of these states between the Euphrates and Tigris, known as the kingdom of Mitanni, had established control over most of Syria and northern Mesopotamia. The skills of horsemanship and chariot warfare were particularly associated with the Hurrians, and a generally high-status class of citizen called *mariannu*. *Mariannu* status was connected with land holdings and could be hereditary, but not all charioteers were *mariannu*, and not all *mariannu* possessed chariots. In the Hurrian state of Arrapha, in northern Mesopotamia, we find *mariannu* charioteers and conscript infantry militia serving as *alik ilki*, 'one who performs the *ilku* duty' as in contemporary Assyria. Pressured by both Egypt, the Hittites and then by Assyria, the kingdom of Mitanni finally collapsed in the 13th century BC, but Hurri-Mitannian influence in army organization and equipment was all-pervasive and can be seen in all the Near Eastern states for which we have evidence, from New Kingdom Egypt to the Hittites (and even Bronze Age Greece), to the Middle Assyrian kingdom and Kassite Babylonia.

Assyria appears to have weathered the calamities at the end of the 12th and 11th centuries BC better than most other Near Eastern states. The later kings of the Middle

The great Assyrian victory over the Elamites at the battle of the river Ulai (*c.* 653 BC), which ultimately led to the destruction of the ancient Elamite kingdom, was depicted in at least two palaces of King Ashurbanipal (668– *c.* 628 BC). This scene shows the collapse of the Elamite army under attack from Assyrian chariots, cavalry and infantry, and the death of the Elamite king (whose head was carried in triumph to Assyria).

Assyrian period waged numerous campaigns against marauding Aramaean tribesmen, sometimes crossing over the Euphrates and raiding in their heartland around Jebel Bishri, but despite these efforts the kingdom fell into a sharp decline after the reign of Ashur-bel-kala (1073–1056 BC). Significant revival in Assyrian fortunes is clear from the time of Tukulti-Ninurta II onwards, which peaks in the reigns of the Neo-Assyrian kings Assurnasirpal II (883–859 BC) and his son Shalmaneser III (858–824 BC).

NEO-ASSYRIAN ARMY ORGANIZATION AND RECRUITMENT

Mitannian practice and a few hints from the limited number of earlier texts suggest that the concept of *dullu* or *ilku*, best known from somewhat later sources, formed the basis of the recruitment of earlier Middle and Neo-Assyrian armies. In its basic form this seems to have involved the obligation of all subjects to serve the king, not necessarily in a military capacity, for a limited period each year, although there were major exceptions to this rule. The citizens of the city of Assur, for example, claimed privileged exemption throughout most of this period, and in other circumstances, service in person could be commuted to a payment in cash or kind, or the equipping of a substitute instead of those subject to *ilku* actually serving in person. This system had major disadvantages: it demanded a high degree of bureaucratic control (though in this the Assyrians excelled), it did not easily accommodate the need for specialists, and it might cause economic and agricultural disruption with the service of key workers far from home as the empire grew. Most importantly, it could, and clearly did, provide military resources for ambitious local magnates in periods of weak central rule, as it seems that the magnates mustered and possibly led their own forces for the royal army.

Shalmaneser III died in 824 BC amidst rebellion and civil war. The major revolt in Assyria against Shalmaneser at the end of his long reign seems to have resulted, at least in part, from the increasing pressures of *ilku* on native Assyrians from his relentless campaigning. Shalmaneser was followed by a succession of weak kings who were unable to prevent a loss of royal authority to powerful magnates or to hold Assyria's conquests in the face of the growing power of the Anatolian state of Urartu. Adad-Nirari III, who did achieve some limited military success, ascended the throne as a minor with his mother Sammuramat acting as regent. Assyrian sources do actually record her on a victorious campaign with her son against the Medes, giving rise to the later Greek tales of Semiramis.

In 745 BC, Tiglath-Pileser III usurped the throne and proceeded radically to reform the government of Assyria. Royal authority was re-established and strengthened and Tiglath-Pileser changed the entire basis of the state by accelerating and formalizing the creation of a professional, regular army. This was through the selective inclusion of conquered territories as Assyrian provinces governed by royal officials as part of a greater Assyria, which were subject to *ilku*, rather than merely levying tribute. Mass deportations of peoples throughout the empire to punish the rebellious were probably also intended to break local loyalties and establish pools of royal manpower throughout the empire. Assyria itself was re-organized into smaller provinces and territories judged not suitable for annexation, but more useful as buffer states, closely supervised by a *qepu* or royal overseer. An efficient postal

Below Assyrian reliefs were originally brightly coloured, but this rarely survives. This polychrome glazed tile of Assurnasirpal II gives some indication of what these colours might have been like. The king drinks from a bowl under a canopy, armed with an angular composite bow. Note the dismounted cavalryman with a bronze helmet, shield on his back, brightly coloured plaited quiver strap, and iron-tipped javelin.

and courier system was established and the king maintained close control over the provinces and received detailed intelligence reports on other states from spies and merchants, some of which survive.

Following these reforms the later Neo-Assyrian army appears to have been composed of three main categories of soldier: elite royal guardsmen; long-term professionals of the *kisir sharruti*, or 'king's corps'; and shorter-term conscripts, the 'king's men', drawn from all the provinces of the empire serving in the army on a regular basis in fulfilment of their state obligations and who formed the basis of the pre-reform army as discussed above. In addition there was the important and large *shaglute*, or 'foreign legion' created from the deported guard troops of conquered kingdoms. Each category comprised chariotry, cavalry and infantry, though native Assyrians may have served only as mounted troops. In addition to the standing army, the soldiers and naval forces of client states could be called upon, and irregular levies made of warriors from subject areas.

Conscription was in the hands of professional *rab kisri*, or 'company commanders', appointed by and responsible to the king, who were allocated a number of settlements from which to make up, train and maintain their companies. Each company would consist of men who probably knew one another and had family ties that would help build unit cohesion and morale. The very name for a company, *kisru*, known since the 3rd dynasty of Ur, means 'knot', and the term neatly implies both cohesion and strength.

Analysis of muster records suggests that each year the best of those eligible for conscription would be picked at muster points (*pirru*) to serve

Above One of the bronze bands which formed part of the decorative facing of a wooden gate from a palace of Shalmaneser III at Imgur-Enlil (modern Balawat, Iraq). It shows in two registers almost the entire repertoire of the artistic depiction of 9th-century BC Neo-Assyrian warfare: assault of cities; walled towns acting as army supply depots; chariots supported by cavalry overturning the enemy; the reception of prisoners; and tribute by the king.

as front-line soldiers or as reserves to make up any losses, while the remainder would be employed as workmen on state projects. Men with particular crafts or skills could use these to fulfil their state service, possibly but not necessarily manufacturing material directly for the army, such as uniforms, armour, or weapons, rather than serving as a soldier or labourer. This service was in theory limited to a set period, probably originally a few months in each year after the harvest, but in reality military necessity could often result in prolonged service.

REFORMS OF SENNACHERIB AND ESARHADDON

Army reform did not end with Tiglath-Pileser III. Other major changes were initiated by Sargon II and Sennacherib (where we find more than one *rab sha reshi* or chief eunuch, one of the highest military commanders in the Assyrian hierarchy) and by Esarhaddon. In particular the latter two kings increased the size of the guard and officer corps: Esarhaddon 'added Egyptian troops to the *kisir sharruti* and greatly expanded the guard chariotry, guard cavalry, *shaknute ma'assi* officers, *shaknu* officers, specialists, and *kallapani*'.

The regular army was composed of two main elements: elite household and guard troops, and permanently maintained units of professional soldiers. There were evidently a large number of high-quality guard troops, in part promoted from the best of the regulars.

THE HOUSEHOLD TROOPS

The king's personal bodyguard, which was almost certainly of Middle Assyrian origin, was called the *sha shepe*, 'at the feet (of the king)'. By the 8th century BC the *sha shepe* consisted of at least two bodies: one of chariotry, probably at least a squadron of 50 vehicles, and a large cavalry formation, perhaps founded before the early 9th century BC. In the detailed report of Sargon II's eighth campaign made to the god Assur it is stated that this cavalry unit was 1,000 strong, and was always stationed by the side of the king. Here it is also described by the name of its commanding officer, in this case the king's brother. A separate but little-known unit of 'Palace Chariotry' (*ekal mugirri*) also existed.

The other guards of the household, the *qurubtu*, or *sha qurbute*, were composed of charioteers, cavalry (*pethal qurubtu*), and probably infantry. The major reform of the

The Assyrian army made extensive use of allied and subject troops. This relief from the Southwest palace of Sennacherib (704–681 BC) at Nineveh shows two Assyrian guardsmen in court dress. The spearman on the right wears almost identical dress to the defenders of the city of Lachish in Judah (see box opposite). He is probably a member of the Samarian regiment, known to be a part of the Assyrian regular army from the time of Sargon II of Assyria.

guards during the reign of Sennacherib created additional units 'of the left' and 'of the right' (known already from Sargon II's reign). The king also seems to have assigned separate household units to senior members of the royal family: the crown prince, the queen and the queenmother. Membership of the guard was a position of high status and great responsibility: *qurbuti* could be attached to other units, or even appointed to command them. A particular role was in collecting fresh drafts of king's men, and acting as the king's representative in settling disputes over recruitment.

There is very little textual information concerning the foot guards, although they are invariably shown arrayed in ordered ranks before the king's chariot on palace reliefs.

The Storming of Lachish

The detailed reliefs of the siege of Lachish show the methods used against a major fortress, the most powerful stronghold of King Hezekiah of Judah, during the Assyrian king Sennacherib's campaign in the Levant in 701 BC. A timber-laced and revetted earth ramp is shown thrown up against the wall, and the remains of the ramp have been identified by the most recent excavator of the site. The wood used in construction was a weak point, and sometimes the defenders could seek to set it alight, itself a risky process as one Assyrian account records this being attempted but, with a change of wind, the flames blowing back and weakening the enemies' wall.

Upon the ramp a wooden trackway is shown, laid down to provide a good surface for the advance of the four-wheeled elephant-like siege engines. These use sharp-pointed 'rams' to lever bricks and stones from the walls. Behind them heavily armoured slingers and archers, stationed behind large reed pavises (shields), are shown shooting at the defenders on the walls while the Assyrian infantry, with lightly equipped archers shooting in support, assaulting the wall with scaling ladders. The defenders try to stop the engines by dropping flaming torches and even burning carts on them, but each engine has a crewman with a long-handled ladle dowsing its housing with water (attempts to overturn siege-engines and towers by catching the ram in a chain, hung down from the battlements, are also known). It seems likely that the elite and well-armoured cavalry and chariot crews operated dismounted during sieges, and groups of three or four men shooting behind pavises (representing such crews) are a usual feature of Assyrian siege reliefs.

These reliefs from the Southwest Palace of Sennacherib at Nineveh show the climax of the Assyrian assault. The desperate defenders hurl flaming torches and even carts loaded with stones in an attempt to destroy the Assyrian siege engines.

The Assyrians appear to have adopted their later military uniform, with practical leggings and boots, from eastern highland peoples (possibly Iranians). This section of a wall painting from the Assyrian provincial centre at Til-Barsip shows guards in court dress standing behind the king who sits in a wheeled throne (only his feet are preserved). It shows that the Assyrian short leggings (or long socks) and boots were brightly patterned in alternate rows of colour.

Interestingly, Herodotus states that the Achaemenid Persian kings always marched accompanied by 1,000 elite cavalry and an elite 1,000-man unit of the 10,000-strong foot guards supposedly nicknamed the 'Immortals'. The cavalry unit is remarkably similar to the 1,000-strong *sha shepe* cavalry of the Neo-Assyrian period and it seems highly likely that the size, structure and organization of Assyrian foot guards, was similar. A corps of 10,000 Neo-Assyrian infantry guardsmen does not seem unreasonable as the backbone of the army.

THE HOME ARMY

Apart from the guards, the core of the later Neo-Assyrian standing army was administered by the chief eunuch in a number of large, seemingly permanent administrative units, or regiments. These regiments were named after the geographical areas or ethnic groups of their original recruitment or the cities maintaining them and seem to have included chariots, cavalry and infantry. The Nimrud texts, dating to *c.* 716–710 BC, record five units raised from the home provinces of greater-Assyria – listed in what appears to be a strict order of precedence – and their associated *rab urâte/rab kisri*, or 'leaders of teams/captains'. The most senior, the largest, and probably the longest established of these units, was the 'Assyrian' regiment, followed by the 'city of Arrapha' regiment, then the 'Aramaeans', the 'city of Arzuhina', and finally the 'city of Erbil' regiment.

The number of these home units evidently increased as each area came under Assyrian influence. For example, the 'Chaldean' regiment was raised and added to the five home regiments around 709 BC. A separate and evidently elite 'ethnic' regiment of the *kisir sharruti* was created by either Shalmaneser V or Sargon II from the guard troops of conquered Samaria in *c.* 726/5 BC. This large unit, with 50 chariots, was maintained as a distinct body like the 'home' regiments.

Finally, in addition to the regiments of the home army and other regular 'ethnic' regiments the Nimrud texts also list the equestrian elite and long-established Assyrian foreign legion, or 'regiment of deportees', under their own commanding officer. This unit, or units, was frequently expanded by the addition of the guards, mounted and foot, of conquered kingdoms. It probably incorporated troops from the powerful Neo-Hittite and Aramaean states of northern Syria, such as Carchemish and Hamath, and later forces from Elam and Egypt. Similar bodies of deportees (usually archers and their families) are known from earlier Middle Assyrian administrative texts assigned to the king and the households of Assyrian magnates.

According to the limited figures provided by annalistic sources therefore, it seems that a regiment of the *kisir sharruti* could have a strength of between 50–300 chariots, 200–600 cavalry and 500–3,000 infantry.

CONSCRIPTS

The 'King's men', who formed the basis of the pre-reform army as discussed above, performed military service as their *dullu* or obligation to the king, They provided charioteers, cavalry and infantry and could be levied from the provinces under the command of their local governors. There are examples under the later Assyrian kings of 'King's men' serving for three years or more, and it might be supposed that the efficiency and enthusiasm of these units varied quite widely. Letters speak of desertions and minor mutinies among provincials as well as attesting to the reliability and competence of Assyrians and other groups, especially the Aramaean Itu'aya : 'I sent their *shaknu* to them with the words: "Come, let me review you and give you your battle-equipment", but they refused to come and (instead) maltreated him....'

With its superbly equipped and organized army, and under a dynasty of exceptional ability, the tiny Neo-Assyrian state dominated and utterly transformed the Near East over a period of some 200 years. However, rivalries for the throne were a great weakness, and in the later 7th century BC debilitating civil wars sapped Assyria's strength. Even by the 8th century BC the demands for manpower by the army had resulted in complaints from officers that their soldiers were only boys, and the powerful guards regiments (recruited throughout the empire and beyond) may even have been, by the end, a fifth-column – following the suggestion that a significant proportion of their men were provided by the Medes. Between 614 BC and 612 BC a festering war with a resurgent Babylonia turned to disaster when the Medes also attacked. The Babylonians and Medes forged an alliance, and by 605 BC Assyria had ceased to exist. However, its military and administrative legacy endured, partially in the Neo-Babylonian state, partly in the Assyrian provinces of the west, possibly partly in Media itself, and ultimately and most strikingly in the army of the mighty Achaemenid empire (see next chapter).

4 The Might of the Persian Empire

The Persian empire was the first of the Near Eastern imperial systems to run as more than a mere extension of national power. As a small nation, they simply did not have the manpower to impose their culture on the mass of peoples they conquered, and were forced to adopt new military and administrative techniques. Mechanisms of family engineering were introduced to increase the Persian population, provincial administration was devolved to the satraps, who commanded local forces, and much reliance had to be made on mercenary forces. In the end, however, these policies undermined the efficiency of the central rule of the state, and contributed much to its military decline and conquest.

THE RISE OF THE PERSIANS

In the late 2nd millennium BC, the Iranians moved into Iran and dispersed west and south. One of the Iranian peoples, the Persians, moved into what later became their homeland, Persis, and became subservient to the Elamites, who had dominated the area from ancient times. In 646 BC the Assyrians invaded Elam and devastated the capital Susa. Henceforward the king in Susa was a *primus inter pares* of a group of Elamite rulers, one of whom ruled over Persis from the eastern city of Anshan. Meanwhile the northern Iranian kingdom of Media under Phraortes (647–625) and Cyaxares (625–585) rose sufficiently in power to overthrow the Assyrians. By the reign of the next Median king Astyages (585–550) the kingdom of Anshan had become a vassal state of Media.

The circumstances under which Cyrus the Great (559–530 BC), king in Anshan, overthrew Median rule in 550–549 are obscure. According to a Mesopotamian source, the 'Cyrus Cylinder', Astyages invaded Anshan, his army mutinied, and he was defeated and taken prisoner. Cyrus marched on and took Ecbatana, the Median capital. Within the span of a single generation, the modest Kingdom of Anshan

Opposite Two 'Immortals' from the polychrome burnt brick wall of Darius' palace at Susa. Their gold earrings and bracelets indicate their status.

Right Composite drawing of a seal impression found on a number of tablets at Persepolis, dating to the reign of Darius. The Elamite inscription informs us that the seal belonged to 'Cyrus the Anshanite, son of Teispes'. It has been suggested that the seal is an heirloom, and once belonged to Cyrus I, the grandfather of Cyrus the Great, though this is disputed.

Few representations remain showing Lydian cavalry, once one of the most powerful military forces in Asia. This watercolour records a painted sherd from Sardis bearing an isolated example. Lydian cavalry seem to have relied most on the use of a long fighting spear.

would be transformed into a world superpower. However, the campaigns of Cyrus were not universally successful, and the early expansion of Persia was full of reverses.

The western border of the Median empire with the kingdom of Lydia lay on the Halys River. Cyrus was soon drawn into conflict with the Lydian king Croesus, and summoned all the subject peoples of the Lydians to secede from their rule. The kings of Cyprus willingly submitted to the Persian conqueror, but with the exception of Miletus the Greek cities remained loyal to Croesus.

Although the Medes were famed as horsemen, the Persians themselves had not yet formed a significant corps of cavalry. The Lydians were also famous as horsemen and were confident of success. But according to one legend, Cyrus achieved victory in 547 by sending camels into battle. The Lydian horses panicked and fled before these strange creatures. Perhaps at this point the Persians decided to form an efficient force of cavalry. Cyrus governed the Lydians with a light hand until a national revolt was led by Paktyes. According to Herodotus, the Lydians were afterwards ordered 'to wear tunics under their cloaks, and boots on their feet, and to teach their sons to play the harp and the lute, and to engage in commerce'. No longer taught the art of war, the Lydians ceased to be of military significance.

Herodotus tells us that the Sakai and the Bactrians were not included in the Median Empire, so Cyrus must have conquered these peoples. Bactria was incorporated into the Empire after the fall of the Lydian capital Sardis. In a further campaign Cyrus' army ran out of food and was reduced to cannibalism, until the Arimaspians arrived with 30,000 wagons with provisions. This incident probably took place in Helmand province in southern Afghanistan. Henceforward the Arimaspians were awarded with the title 'Benefactors' of the king. Cyrus is also reputed to have campaigned in India. On his return to Persia his army met with disaster crossing the Gedrosian desert: only Cyrus escaped with seven men.

Cyrus invaded Babylon in 539. How the conquest was subsequently achieved is shrouded in mystery, but Cyrus won a great victory at Opis on the Tigris, and Babylon fell. Cyrus adopted the title 'Cyrus, king of the world, great king, mighty king, king of Babylon, king of Sumer and Akkad, king of the four quarters'. His empire was the first to rule over practically the entire known world.

Above This cylinder seal (*right*, with impression alongside) shows Persians, protected by composite cuirasses and fighting with spears, in combat with Sakai, who use thin-bladed battle-axes (such as this one from the Ashmolean Museum in Oxford, *above*) which were designed to pierce armour. It is not known if the seal was meant to commemorate some specific historical event, or is a generic image.

Right Achaemenid cylinder seal impression showing two crowned Achaemenid rulers standing facing each other. The image probably symbolizes the geographical division of rule between the reigning monarch and his son, perhaps a reference to Darius and Xerxes. The precise significance of the fire-altar between the two figures is uncertain.

Cyrus' last campaign, in 530, was in Central Asia. The aim seems to have been to stabilize the empire's northern border by subduing her troublesome nomadic neighbours. The city of Cyropolis (*Kuruš-kaθa*) was probably founded at this time. Cyrus crossed the river Araxes but fell in battle against the Massagetae, a Saka tribe, commanded by their queen Tomyris. Other Saka tribes living in the area took the opportunity to throw off Persian rule.

Persian monarchs tended to divide the territory of their empires into more easily governed zones, each one being ruled by a different son. One zone was Central Asia, governed from the Bactrian capital Baktra, which Cyrus entrusted to his junior son Tanaoxares before his death. The king himself usually ruled from the palaces at Persepolis, Susa and Echatana. There is some evidence for a second, western zone governed from Babylon. These subordinate rulers were called *karanos* in Greek, perhaps reflecting an Old Persian *kara-naya*, 'leader of hosts'.

Cyrus' son and successor Cambyses (530–522) annexed Egypt in 525. The pharaoh Amasis relied on command of the sea, for an army could only approach Egypt from the east across the narrow area between the desert and the sea, so Cambyses built the first Persian fleet. It was organized in a sexagesimal system, perhaps borrowed

69

from the Phoenicians. Five recruitment areas each supplied 60 ships: two naval squadrons numbering 30 ships. The defences of Egypt were turned. The Persians then used their naval strength in the west. In 520/19 Otanes, the Persian governor at Sardis, captured the island of Samos.

THE REIGN OF DARIUS (522–486 BC)

Cambyses' death threw the empire into confusion. Eventually Darius, who claimed kinship to Cambyses through a distant common ancestor, took the throne and brought stability to the empire. Modern scholars believe this joint lineage is a fiction, and some have suggested Cyrus and Cambyses were ethnically more Elamite than Persian. Darius may have been the first truly Persian king.

Darius' reign saw campaigns on many fronts, and according to his own version of events he fought 19 battles and seized nine rebel kings in the first year of his reign. One of the first was in 519 BC against the Sakai, some of whom were incorporated within the empire. Most historians believe that Darius also extended the empire to the Indus valley and established a new satrapal capital at Taxila. This campaign may have taken place in 515 (see p. 233).

Darius now turned to the west. Thrace and Macedonia were annexed. Although Persian dominance in Macedonia was short, its influence was profound. The Macedonian army, for example, retained the Persian title *dekas* or 'decury' for the file of infantry, even though it numbered 16 men. Darius then attempted the conquest of the European Scythians, ethnic cousins of the Sakai, perhaps in 513 (see p. 219). The Scythians withdrew and laid the country waste, and Darius was forced to turn back. This was the furthest Persian forces ever marched away from their homeland.

A complex series of events led to an uprising of the Ionian Greeks in 500 BC. The Ionians asked for the help of the mainland Greeks, and the Eretrians and Athenians responded. Initially the rebels were successful, and Sardis was burned, but fortune

A mercenary cavalryman, shown on an Athenian vase of 470–460 BC, armed with a battle-axe and a lasso, a weapon Herodotus (7.85) says was used by the Sagartians. Note the way the spare rope of the lasso is coiled on his right shoulder. This image was probably inspired by the presence in Lower Asia of mercenaries recruited from among the Iranian nomadic tribes of Central Asia.

Dipylon Shields

One common type of shield used by the Achaemenids is of a type known to Classical archaeologists as the 'Dipylon' shield. Shields of this type have a very distinctive shape, with cut-outs at either side of the central portion of the shield. The Dipylon shield was so named when Geometric pottery decorated with pictures of warriors holding shields of this type was discovered during excavations near the Dipylon Gate in Athens.

Above Coins of Mazaios, struck when satrap of Cilicia, show Dipylon shields with a thunderbolt. When the Macedonian Balacrus took over as satrap, his coins continue to show Dipylon shields, but now decorated with his personal sign, the letter *beta*. It is possible that the Dipylon shield continued in use among Balacrus' personal guards.

The shape is probably ultimately derived from the figure-of-eight shields used in the Greek Bronze Age, frequently being shown slung from the neck. Many representations of these shields make it clear that they were made of bull's hide. These large shields were put under tension at the sides to keep the large hide surfaces under tension.

In the Iron Age another generation of shields took their place, which may have been made of other materials as well as bull's hide, but which in general retained the shape of the old figure-of-eight shields. Rather than the sides being sloped back, they are cut out, although the overall shape is similar. In Iron Age Greece the Dipylon shield was frequently slung over the back, allowing the warrior to fight with both arms free. Shields of this type were also used by the Achaemenid Persians. They are clearly shown in the Persepolis relief, but are also attested by other archaeological finds. Persian Dipylon shields were furnished with metal rims and bosses. Greek representational evidence continues to show Dipylon shields in use in Persian contexts down to the end of the Achaemenid period, and perhaps even beyond.

Above The Dipylon shield continued to be shown on Greek pottery down to the end of the 6th century, although archaeologists dispute whether this reflects contemporary military practice, or is rather a 'badge' denoting a hero. On this vase Ajax recovers the body of Achilles.

Left Comparative evidence for the construction and shape of hide shields comes from modern Africa. This photograph from the Cameroon shows a dignitary accompanied by his guards. They carry large hide shields drawn in at the sides to give a figure-of-eight look.

The Persian siege-ramp at Old Paphos, Cyprus, both in a photo-montage of the archaeological section cut through it, and in a more recent aerial photograph. Some idea of the massive scale of this construction is given by the human figures of two archaeologists standing next to the section. Some 422 round projectile stones were found in the ramp, weighing from 2.7 to 21.8 kg (6 to 48 lb). The heaviest of these can only have served as ammunition for stone-throwing catapults. An identically shaped stone weighing 22 kg (48.5 lb) has been found at Phocaea, which was also besieged by the Persian general Harpagos in c. 540. Greek sources would leave us to believe that stone-throwing artillery was a Greek invention of the 4th century, but it has been suggested that the Persians already knew of the technology in the 6th century BC on the basis of this and other evidence.

soon turned against them. In 494 the revolt was suppressed, and the leading population of Miletus was deported. In Cyprus, also involved in the uprising, Herodotus mentions a siege-ramp constructed at Paphos; this has also been identified by archaeological excavation.

The burning of Sardis provoked the wrath of Darius against Athens and Eretria. Furthermore the Athenians had entered into negotiations of friendship in 507. In 490 an expeditionary force was sent out to punish Eretria and Athens. The city of Eretria was razed, and a detachment of 10,000 Medes commanded by Datis, plus some Persian and Saka infantry regiments and attached cavalry, landed at the plain of Marathon. The opposing Athenian army numbered 9,000, assisted by 1,000 Plataeans. The Athenians were afraid to attack with no cavalry, and stalemate ensued. The Persians began to re-embark for Athens where, it was hoped, the city would be betrayed. But when the cavalry had re-embarked, the Athenians attacked. In order not to leave any flank of the opposing line uncovered, the tribal regiments in the centre were drawn up in shallow files, but those on the two flanks were deeper. This made the Athenian line longer than the Persian.

The Athenians charged, driving back their opponents on both flanks. In the centre they were slowed down by scrub, and were driven back. Some of the regiments on the flanks managed to halt their advance, re-form, and attack the Persian centre, putting them to flight. For the Greeks it was of tremendous psychological importance to discover, for the first time, that they could confront a Persian army and win.

Wicker Shields

The war between the Greeks and Persians is characterized as a war between spearmen and archers, or spears and bows. But walls of wicker shields are mentioned by Herodotus, and it seems that the decurions in the first rank of a Persian infantry line carried wicker shields and spears, and, like medieval pavise-bearers, protected the archers who made up the rest of the unit.

The wicker shield, *gerrhon* in Greek, was called a *spara* in Old Persian. This is made clear by the gloss *sparabarai* in Hesychios, where he tells us that the word is equivalent to the Greek *gerrhophoroi* 'bearers of wicker shields'. It is supported by the word *ispar* meaning 'shield' which has survived into Middle and New Persian. Different versions of the wicker shield were carried by the infantry and the cavalry. Infantry shields are large and rectangular, while cavalry shields are smaller, and could be of more varied shape.

The shield was constructed by weaving osiers in and out through a piece of rawhide of the desired ultimate shape of the shield. When the rawhide dried out and contracted it put the osiers under tension. The osiers were thus flexed and the whole construction was strengthened. This combination of materials put under tension resulted in a shield of great lightness yet of great resilience.

Above An interesting depiction of a Persian wicker shield through Greek eyes comes on the famous Oxford Brygos Cup. The Achaemenid warrior shown clearly holds the shield out in front of his body by a single central handle.

The osiers and the rawhide could be dyed different colours, and the osiers were woven through the rawhide in such a way as to give a V- or W-shaped pattern. This is most clearly shown in the case of a shield from the Pazyryk tomb, which could be Achaemenid in date, and in a number of later Sasanian shields found in excavations of a siege tunnel at Dura Europos.

Right The size of the Dura shields, as well as the shape, suggests that these, too, were designed to be used by cavalry. This is suggestively demonstrated in this archive photograph of the Dura excavations. This particular shield has survived well in the dry conditions.

Above The Pazyryk shield came from the *c.* 4th-century BC grave of a Siberian tribal chief, preserved by the cold. It could have been an Achaemenid import, and was probably used by a cavalrymen to judge from its size.

Above Bronze helmet recovered by German archaeological excavations at Olympia. The inscription around the rim informs us that it was dedicated as booty taken from the Achaemenid army, perhaps at the battle of Plataea.

Above Two faces of an Attic vase painted about 440 BC depict a scene from Aeschylus' play *The Persians*. When news of Salamis reaches Susa Darius is summoned from his tomb by a libation, poured by his widow Atossa. He condemns Xerxes for his folly. The play contributed much to the demonization of Xerxes' character.

Below Clay ration document excavated at Persepolis. The names given to the sub-units of the Persian army and their commanders can be reconstructed from documents such as these. This particular tablet, written in Elamite, records the issue of rations to the *daɪabām* of Uštanna in the *satabām* of Mannanda.

PERSIAN MILITARY IMPERIALISM

The death of Darius in 486 is an appropriate point to pause for reflection. The empire, with an estimated population of 50 million, stretched from the Aegean to the Indus, from Central Asia to Egypt. The Greek soldier and historian Xenophon tells us the Persians numbered 120,000: presumably the number of adult males. Over 64 years this small Iranian tribe had subdued most of the known world, a process of military imperial expansion with few parallels in history.

The limited number of ethnic Persians entailed looser methods of government. Cyrus left local administration largely intact. Persians were present at only the highest level of provincial government. The provinces were governed by satraps, perhaps a rendering of the Old Persian *xšaçapāvan*, 'protector of the kingdom'. Herodotus mentions that Darius created 20 districts, called satrapies, as though for the first time, but it seems likely that the system was older.

A number of policies were introduced to expand the Persian population. Multiple marriages were encouraged. Darius himself had five wives and at least 12 legitimate sons. We have much evidence for polygamy and concubines at satrapal courts. Illegitimate sons could hold significant military commands. Strabo reports that 'The men marry many women, and at the same time maintain many concubines for the sake of having many children. The kings set forth prizes annually for those who have the most children.' In his Behistun inscription Darius wishes for his loyal subjects 'may Ahura Mazda be friendly to you, and may offspring be to you in great number, and may you live long!' At Persepolis female labourers who had given birth were given a special ration of flour and wine for a month, while mothers of sons received double. Persis, at least during the reign of Darius, was freed from tribute, which the conquered nations paid. The aim was probably to give Persians sufficient wealth to support large families.

Above A gold model of a chariot, part of the so-called 'Oxus Treasure' found in Central Asia. Though it is not a scythed war-chariot, it probably represents a late 4th-century military leader in his chariot. The head of the Egyptian deity Bes, shown on the front of the chariot, was a symbol which became very popular among Achaemenid mercenaries. In this case it might be the badge of the military unit this individual commanded.

Right Detail of one of the Persepolis relief sculptures showing Achaemenid warriors. Some of these soldiers are infantrymen, presumably from one of the regiments of Persian 'Immortals', perhaps the elite regiment of a thousand 'Spearbearers'. They all wear 'crowns', which was perhaps a distinction restricted to this regiment, and they carry Dipylon shields, more useful for spearmen than wicker shields.

PERSIAN MILITARY FORCES

From their 5th to their 20th year, Persian males were taught horsemanship, archery, and telling the truth. Following this period of military training they remained liable for military service from their 20th to their 50th year.

Persian forces were organized decimally, the base being a regiment of 1,000 (*hazārabām*) commanded by a *hazārapatiš*, 'commander of 1,000', divided into 10 *sataba* of 100 men. Each *satabām* was commanded by a *satapatiš* and was divided into 10 *daθaba* commanded by a *daθapatiš*. Xenophon mentions commanders of 50 and of 5, and Mesopotamian cuneiform tablets mention '50s', while Persepolis ration documents mention a *pasçadaθapatiš*; an 'after' or 'rear' *daθapatiš*. Above the regiment the decimal system was maintained. A division of 10,000 men, formed by 10 regiments, was called a *baivarabām*, or 'myriad' in Greek, commanded by a *baivarapatiš*.

The most famous *baivarabām* in the army were the infantry 'Immortals' (*amŕtaka*), named, according to Herodotus, 'because it was invariably kept up to strength; if a man was killed or fell sick, the vacancy he left was filled at once, so that the total strength of the corps was never less, and never more than 10,000.' It seems that the 'Immortals' were the only permanently embodied force of ethnically Persian infantry maintained by the empire. The main strength of the Persian national army lay in its cavalry, and our sources imply that it was maintained at a strength of 30,000. The commander of the cavalry was termed the *asapatiš*, or 'master of horse' in Old Persian.

The elite regiment of the 'Immortals' were the 'Spearbearers' (*arštibara*), composed of Persian noblemen, forming the king's personal bodyguard. The king's *hazārapatiš* commanded this regiment, guarded the king and controlled access to him. He became the leading figure at court, and his favour had to be won to obtain a royal audience.

MERCENARY FORCES

Persian forces were inadequate either to extend the empire, or to defend it. Mercenaries, both Iranian and non-Iranian, were extensively used. The Iranian peoples of Central Asia – Bactrians, Cadusians and Saka – were an important source. Such forces could be contracted temporarily, but more often they were maintained on a semi-permanent basis. The armies sent on offensive operations, such as the invasions of Greece, were overwhelmingly composed of mercenaries, as were the garrisons installed throughout the empire.

An attempt was made to form a reserve by granting mercenaries, after an initial period of military service, fiefdoms in return for liability for mobilization. We have most evidence for this system from Babylon, though one presumes that reserves were created in all provinces. Greek texts suggest that each satrapy of the empire was expected to furnish a *baivarabām* of troops when a general mobilization was declared. Military fiefdoms could not be alienated, and could be inherited along with the obligation for military service. Over time the system fell into disuse. Plots were farmed out, and military service was replaced by taxation and an obligation to provide manual labour.

THE ROYAL ROADS

The Persians inherited existing road-systems in many parts of the empire, and further developed these resources themselves. The most important Mesopotamian

'Greco-Persian' gem from Asia Minor. Is this a Greek mercenary hoplite as seen through non-Greek eyes? The *pilos* helmet, spear and shield are realistic enough, but did Greek mercenaries really fight naked at this time? This is possible, but it is perhaps more probable that the Anatolian gem-cutter has copied a standard Greek model.

roads were either paved with stone or brick, or had bitumen surfaces. Herodotus first mentions the Royal Road which ran from Sardis to Susa in the reign of Darius, but the system may have existed previously. The road system had an offensive strategic function, enabling armies and supply trains to deploy from one border of the empire to another quickly, increasing the tempo of military operations during a time of imperial expansion on many fronts.

Herodotus describes the staging posts along the road, approximately a day's journey apart: 'At intervals all along the road are royal stages (*stathmoi*) with excellent inns, and the road itself is safe to travel by, as it never leaves inhabited country.' A day's journey was calculated at 150 furlongs, or three parasangs (a parasang measured about 5.25 km (3¼ miles) for a man on foot. It seems that the passage of each parasang was marked with a column: the ancient equivalent of a 'milestone'. A marker of this type, dating to the early Hellenistic period, has been found at Pasargadae. The stages were about 25 to 30 km (15 to 18 miles) apart. When the road passed through a natural obstacle, such as the defile at the Halys River, or the Cilician Gates, the passage was defended by a fortress.

Herodotus talks as if there was only one Royal Road, but there was a whole network. Supplies of water in jars were deposited along the section of the road from Gaza to Egypt: an army could march back into Egypt should it ever become necessary. An actual section of a northern road cut out of the rocks near Pasargadae has been identified. Susa lay at the hub of the system, and clay tablets from Persepolis make

The Achaemenid empire, showing the principal military roads and regions, and the sites mentioned in this chapter.

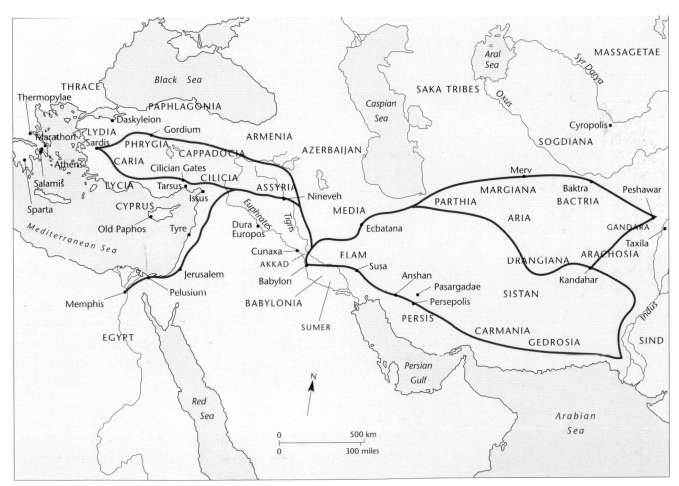

it clear that a 600-km (370-mile) link existed between the two cities, mentioning 22 staging posts along its length. Modern scholars have claimed a plausible route for the road, and have even attempted to locate the staging posts.

As well as overnight accommodation for travellers, the stages supplied changes of horses for the royal couriers, called *pirradazzish,* or 'fast messengers'. Herodotus states 'There is nothing in the world which travels faster than these Persian couriers…. It is said that men and horses are stationed along the road, equal in number to the number of days the journey takes – a man and a horse for each day. Nothing stops these couriers from covering their allotted stage in the quickest possible time, neither snow, nor rain, nor heat, nor darkness.' The Persians also seemed to have developed a system of fire signals to ensure the even more rapid transfer of information from the borders to the heart of the Empire, although little is known of the details.

THE ACCESSION OF XERXES (486–465 BC)

The eldest son of Darius was Artabazanes, born before Darius had taken the throne through a daughter of the nobleman Gobryas. Nevertheless, it was Xerxes, the first son of Atossa daughter of Cyrus, who succeeded to the throne. His mother had used the argument that it should be the first son of Darius 'born in the purple' who should be made king. Darius appointed Xerxes 'the greatest after himself' – perhaps an official title. The consequences of royal polygamy were resolved bloodlessly this time.

In 487 the Egyptians rose. Xerxes marched against Egypt and left his brother Achaemenes there as governor. Some time later, possibly around 484, Achaemenes was killed, but Xerxes was unable to return for the Babylonians revolted, twice it seems, in 484 and 482. Babylon was severely treated and many temples were destroyed. The Babylonians were forbidden to bear arms, like the Lydians previously, and this eventually destroyed Babylon as a military power.

Despite these troubles, in 480 BC Xerxes moved to take revenge for the defeat at Marathon with a massive army. Herodotus, having no other information available, made use of a list of the peoples of the empire compiled by the geographer Hecataeus, and assumed that each of these nations sent a 10,000 strong division against Greece. He calculated that the army numbered 1,700,000. Ctesias, who perhaps used Persian sources, tells us that the army numbered 800,000. In fact most of the army would have been composed of regiments of mercenaries, and was probably much smaller than either of these figures.

The army marched to Thermopylae which led into Central Greece. It was briefly held up by a force of Spartans and others, which was outflanked. The fleet suffered considerable loss at Artemision. The Phoenician squadron was sent south to block off the Greek fleet in the straits between the mainland and the island of Euboea. It was completely scattered, with heavy loss, by a freak storm. This lost the whole campaign, for the Greek fleet was able to escape south.

The Persian army marched on to Athens, and razed the city. The Greek fleet now stationed itself between the mainland and the island of Salamis. The Persians once again attempted to trap the Greeks in the straits, but no longer had the strength to divide their forces. The ensuing battle was lost, as was all chance of outflanking the Greek forces defending the Peloponnese (see box on p. 103).

Right Impression from an Achaemenid cylinder seal. The winged device at the top represents the fortune of the Iranian people. An Achaemenid warrior on the left is shown attacking a Greek hoplite with his spear. He wears a composite cuirass with flaps at the bottom to protect the groin, and at the back a nape-protector. The precise iconographic significance of the scene is difficult to interpret, but it may predict the victory of the Iranians over the Greeks.

Right Persian dress had a great influence on the dress of the subject populations of the empire, and on the Greek concept of what looked oriental. This 4th-century Greek vase shows a mounted Amazon attacking a Greek hoplite. Amazons had previously worn Scythian dress. They now retain the trousers common to both Scythians and Persians, but the tunic shown here is of a type popular with Persians, Greeks and the native populations living in Lower Asia.

Opposite This black-figure aryballos (spherical flask) records one of the conflicts of the Persian Wars. A Greek hoplite (*above*) strikes down at an Achaemenid soldier already brought to his knees (*below*), perhaps a Saka mercenary archer from Central Asia. The Achaemenid soldier carries a wood-framed shield faced in leather, perhaps termed *taka* in Old Persian. Both shields have an apron of thick material attached to the bottom, designed to protect the lower legs from arrows.

Xerxes withdrew, leaving 300,000 troops in Boeotia under the command of Mardonius. The next year, by a skilful manoeuvre involving a second thrust at Athens, the Greek army was coaxed out of its impregnable position on the Isthmus. It advanced to Boeotia, and took up a position in the Plataean Plain. Greek forces were harried by incessant cavalry attack. If the Greeks attempted to move, Persian cavalry inflicted heavy losses with javelins. The cavalry were supported by archers, who loosed their arrows on any section of the Greek line which retreated before the cavalry.

The Greeks suffered these attacks until they were cut off from their water supply, following which they decided to retreat by night into the hills at the back of the plain. The whole retreat was held up, and dawn found the Greeks strung out between plain and mountains. The Persians deployed out of camp and advanced, in some disorder, after the Greeks, who fell under an intense arrow barrage. The Tegean commander recommended attack to which the Spartans agreed, their fighting spirit severely shaken by their military impotence over the last few days. The Greeks reached the Persian line and tore down the wall of *spara* shields. Persian spears were shorter than the hoplite spears and the Persians suffered for it. The Persian archers rushed courageously on the Greeks both singly, or where the *daθapatiš* took a local initiative, in groups of ten. They attempted to lay hold of the Greek spears with their bare hands and break them. This desperate struggle could only postpone defeat. Few escaped: Mardonius himself was killed. The courage of the Persians had not been found lacking, but their equipment and tactics had. More important than any other factor, however, was the Persian inability to deploy sufficient forces to achieve victory.

DEFENCE OF EMPIRE

Greek sources portray Xerxes as a coward: the first Persian monarch who failed to expand the empire. How much this reflected ancient opinion is unknown, but Xerxes simply faced facts. The Persians no longer had the military might, and principally the manpower, to continue to expand the empire. Now the military effort of the Persians would be devoted to its defence.

Persians had been settled in Western Anatolia at least from the reign of Darius onwards. The aim was to provide a pool of Persian manpower which, together with their feudal retainers, could be mobilized in time of crisis. Persian aristocratic families were also given lands in Lydia, Caria and Phrygia. Exactly when this happened is difficult to establish. These land-grant gifts should also be regarded as rewards to the Persian aristocracy for loyal service during the period of imperial expansion. Perhaps there were no longer sufficient lands left in Persis to reward the younger sons of the Persian aristocracy. Mercenary soldiers were also settled in the west upon completion of their service. We also

A number of Achaemenid seal impressions, in this case oval stamp-seals, show Achaemenid cavalrymen in combat with Greek hoplites. These two images repeat a common variant of the motif, showing the cavalryman victorious, his horse striding over the body of one fallen hoplite, while he rides down a second.

Below Wall-painting from Karaburun Tumulus II, near modern Elmalı in Turkey, dated to around 470 BC. The deceased may have been a local noble granted the privilege to wear Persian dress, rather than a Persian noble settled in the area. This fresco is one of the earliest depictions of a thigh-protector fitted to a saddle.

hear of Bactrians and others, presumably ex-mercenaries, settled in Lydia. Loyal Greeks were also given fiefdoms along the Aegean coast. Themistocles, for example, was rewarded with a fiefdom after leaving Athens in around 470 BC. After learning Persian for a year he obtained an audience with the king, and was given the usufruct of a number of cities, a Persian noblewoman as a wife, and the privilege of wearing Persian dress. He called his youngest daughter Asia. She was probably the fruit of this last marriage with a Persian woman.

The settlement of Persian aristocrats, retired mercenaries and loyal Greeks in the west was surely intended to stabilize the Aegean border against Greek attack. The Greeks would have been especially useful, given their local knowledge and contacts. Nevertheless, conflict with Greece dragged on for many years until the so-called 'Peace of Callias' was agreed. The king agreed that his forces would not cross west of the Halys, and the defence of Lower Asia was left to the local forces available to the satraps.

Similar policies seem to have been adopted by Xerxes to settle the Central Asian frontier. Three major Persian families settled there: the dynasties of Ariamazes, Sisimithres and Oxyartes, along with a whole host of dependants. When Alexander the Great invaded Central Asia, Ariamazes commanded a contingent of 30,000 men. Urbanization was boosted by the forcible resettlement of Carians and Greeks from Barke and from Didyma. Xerxes's eldest brother Ariaramnes is said to have 'reigned' in Bactria. This seems to imply a command higher than that of satrap. Perhaps Ariaramnes held the appointment of *karanos* responsible for the whole of the Central Asian border.

Throughout the empire, strategically important forts were placed under commanders (*didapatiš*) directly responsible to the king, and were garrisoned by guards paid directly by the king. This division of powers within the satrapies made rebellion more difficult.

THE DECAY OF EMPIRE

It seems an inevitable fact in the cycle of history that imperial might can either grow or wane. It cannot remain constant. From the reign of Xerxes onwards Persian imperial might waned. Key factors in this decline seems to be the negative effects of the very policies once put in place to create the empire.

From the reign of Xerxes onwards palace intrigue played an increasingly malign role in Persian history. The Court ladies played the key roles in these royal 'soaps': a consequence of the family engineering policies introduced to expand the demographic base. Mothers schemed so their son was chosen for succession. In 465 Xerxes was murdered by his *hazārapatiš* Artabanus, together with his eldest son and heir. Another palace struggle followed the death of the next king Artaxerxes I, who was at first succeeded by Xerxes II (424), then by Sekundianus (424–3) and then by Darius II Ochus 'The Good' (423–405/4), the son of Artaxerxes I by a Babylonian woman. As well as complicating the succession, palace intrigue crippled consistent policy making, as one element at Court schemed for supremacy over another, either through the *hazārapatiš* or the royal wives.

Another increasingly evident feature of the later years of Achaemenid rule is satrapal revolt. The early Achaemenid rulers had been forced to give a lot of independent power to their local governors, yet another consequence of the lack of manpower. As imperial power at the centre became evidently weaker, provincial governors increasing sought to assert their local independence. The problem was most serious in the west.

In 401 the satrap of Sardis, Cyrus 'the Younger', favoured by his mother over his reigning elder brother, Artaxerxes II Mnemon ('the Remembrer') rebelled and

Although only the arm and side of a Persian are shown on this fragment of a Greek mixing-bowl for wine, the partially preserved label ARTOBA suggests that the individual shown is the *hazārapatiš* Artabanus, and that the vase originally showed the murder of Xerxes in 465.

Right An Anatolian warrior, possibly a Lycian, carrying a war-sickle is shown on this stele now in Konya. The stele still exists, but the colours are only recorded in this early reproduction.

Below An oriental archer is represented on this 'Greco-Persian' gem found at the sanctuary of Zeus Messapeus near Sparta. Presumably the archer is not a free Persian, as he does not wear the hood typical for an individual of that status. Note the asymmetrical ears of the bow and the long arrows.

marched east with a huge force of 10,000 Greek mercenaries. Artaxerxes retreated but turned to face Cyrus at the battle of Cunaxa (see box on p.84). The Greek hoplites were successful against the army of Artaxerxes, but Cyrus himself was killed. The Greeks then marched back home. Although the revolt had been unsuccessful, the campaign clearly demonstrated the superiority of the Greek hoplite. The revolt precipitated a Spartan invasion of Asia, which was repelled with difficulty, and the conflict only ended in 386 with the 'Peace of Antalkidas'. In 362 the 'Satraps Revolt' broke out in the western provinces and paralyzed any Persian action there.

Local revolt in the Iranian provinces of the empire also steadily increased, particularly among the Cadusians, Medes and Bactrians. The problem of satrapal revolt was most acute in Bactria, where the satrap had a large number of Persian noble settlers to call on for support. Rather than being due to any local nationalistic feeling, these Iranian revolts were once again caused by the high level of independent power held by the satraps. In two other areas of the empire, however, local revolt had a nationalist dimension.

In 405 Egypt once again seceded, and by 401 all Achaemenid presence in Egypt had disappeared. Persian military effort against Egypt was delayed by further trouble in Cyprus. In 390 Evagoras of Salamis rebelled and, in alliance with Akoris of Egypt, spread his rule from Cyprus to Cilicia, Tyre and Phoenicia. According to Diodorus Artaxerxes 'appreciated the strategic position of Cyprus, and its great naval strength with which it would be able to protect Asia in front'. The king launched a number of expeditions against Cyprus, but at first was unsuccessful.

The Persian first expedition against Egypt took place from 385 to 383. The Athenian general Chabrias successfully defended Egypt against invasion with a palisade built at Pelusium. These field defences may have originally been a Persian concept borrowed by Chabrias. The idea was exported to Greece, and field defences played a major role during the Boeotian War of 378–371. Cyprus was finally brought back under Achaemenid rule in 381, and the Persians were able to start collecting forces for a second Egyptian expedition in 379. An amphibious invasion was launched in 373, but after initial successes the Persians were forced to withdraw.

THE ACHAEMENID REVIVAL

The empire must have seemed at its lowest ebb, but when Artaxerxes II died in 359/8 and was succeeded by his son Artaxerxes III Ochus, the fortunes of the empire dramatically revived. He immediately campaigned against the Cadusians. In the decisive battle Codomannus, a great-grandson of Darius II, won the battle in single combat against a general of the enemy. He was appointed satrap of Armenia. The 'Satraps Revolt' in the west was subdued, and satrapal armies were disbanded in 356. Egypt, which had been in revolt since 404, was finally re-conquered around 342.

83

The Battle of Cunaxa

At the battle of Cunaxa in 401 BC, fought on the flat plain of the Euphrates, Cyrus 'the Younger' placed most trust in his personal regiment of 600 heavy cavalry, which he had recruited from among the Iranian and local nobility in Lower Asia. Both riders and their horses were armoured, and the regiment wore crimson surcoats over their armour. The heavy cavalry fighting on the opposing side, that of Cyrus' elder brother King Artaxerxes II, had white surcoats. The king worshipped the goddess Anahita, and white was the colour of ritual purity. At the head of this regiment Cyrus went in search of Artaxerxes. He realized that a victory of his Greek mercenary infantry over the enemy infantry would achieve nothing if the king was allowed to withdraw from the battlefield alive. Cyrus wanted to seek him out and kill him: personally if necessary. After Cyrus' charge the fighting became confused. Cyrus was wounded and then killed in circumstances which are unclear: three persons seem to have had a hand in his death. Later on the queen mother Parysatis took her revenge on the three, who all died enduring the most excruciating tortures human imagination could devise. Such were the rewards of loyal service to the king. Artaxerxes meanwhile propagated a false story that he had killed Cyrus himself in single combat.

Above The re-conquest of Egypt is celebrated on this cylinder seal from the reign of Artaxerxes III. The king, visible here, spears the last native pharaoh Nektanebo II, while behind him he drags along a row of prisoners by the neck.

Ochus died in 338 and was briefly succeeded by his son Arses, who adopted the throne-name Artaxerxes IV. He in turn was succeeded by Codomannus, who took the throne-name Darius III, in 336. According to our Greek sources the kingmaker behind all these successions was one Bagoas, a court eunuch, who poisoned the first two monarchs before being forced to drink the fatal cup himself by Darius III. This is contradicted by Babylonian sources, who imply that the monarchs died of natural causes, and who give Bagoas the title *ša rēš šarri* 'he who stands at the head of the king'. The precise significance of this title is unknown, but perhaps Bagoas was the *hazārapatiš*.

Paradoxically it was precisely now, once Persian power had been restored by two effective rulers, that the Empire was to fall. At first the danger Macedon posed to the west was underestimated. The disbandment of satrapal forces had weakened border defences, and Alexander was able to achieve a surprise victory at the Granicus. It was only now that Darius began to mobilize his forces in sufficient strength. A general mobilization of both Persian and satrapal forces was started. But, once again, lack of reliable Persian troops was a fatal flaw in the army's strength, and too much reliance had to be placed on non-Persian troops. The two forces met on a restricted field of battle between the sea and mountains at Issus in 333 BC, but Darius was unable to take advantage of his numerical superiority and the battle was lost (see pp. 122–123).

Darius set about assembling a new army while Alexander was engaged in the conquest of Phoenicia and Egypt. His main recruiting ground was the eastern satrapies – too much Persian manpower had been lost at Issus. He also tried to form a body of infantry equipped in the Macedonian fashion with long pikes. The two armies met at Gaugamela in 331 BC. Although the Persian forces were superior in number, they were inferior in quality, and Alexander once again won the day. Darius retreated to Media, and Alexander entered the Persian heartland. Defeat was inevitable as Darius further retreated to Central Asia, hoping to recruit another army from the Persian settlers there. He was killed by his generals, but this was not the end to opposition to Alexander. It took many more years of costly campaigning before he was finally able to conquer the Central Asian provinces of Bactria and Sogdia.

Right The fresco, now destroyed, on the principal wall of the 'Kinch Tomb' in Macedonia is recorded in this watercolour of Simoès de Fonséca. It depicts a victorious Macedonian cavalryman riding down a Persian infantryman. The Persian carries a large round leather shield. These 'targeteers' were probably called *takabara* in Old Persian.

5 Minoan and Mycenaean Warfare

Opposite A 13th-century BC ivory plaque
from Mycenae Chamber tomb 27,
portraying a warrior wearing a helmet
made from boars' tusks. This type of
helmet is mentioned by the poet
Homer.

Right Early/Middle Bronze Age double-
edged dagger. Note the rivets for the
handle attachment. Separate handles
riveted like this are intrinsically weak.

One of the clichés of Greek Bronze Age civilization is that Minoan Crete was peaceful, while the Mycenaean civilization of the Greek mainland was warlike. Such clichés oversimplify the human reality. In order to discover the reality of Minoan and Mycenaean warfare and conflict, we should first examine our own preconceptions about what 'warfare' means.

In his *History of Warfare*, John Keegan persuasively argued that western civilization's understanding of warfare was essentially derived from the ancient Greeks. The Greek way of war was the meeting of two opposing groups of armoured soldiers on a defined field of battle. Victory or defeat was measured by the holding of or retreating from this field of battle. With the additional 'nuances' of invasion, siege and conquest, through the imperialism of Alexander and the Romans, this rather formal expression of warfare dominated western civilization until the 20th century. Contemporary military technologies have rendered such warfare impossible without threatening the planet's, not just humanity's, very survival. Thus we witness the emergence of a more circumscribed expression of warfare as limited but pervasive regional conflicts, guerrilla actions, and 'peacekeeping' missions. This fragmentation of the previous rather monolithic meaning of 'warfare' does now allow us to perceive the expression of war and conflict in ancient and non-western societies as a more complex and varied phenomenon of violent interaction between communities.

MINOAN CRETE – EARLY HINTS OF CONFLICT

Hints of the social significance of violence emerge in the appearance of double-edged bronze daggers within the assemblage of
finds in the communal tombs of Early and Middle Minoan Crete
(3000–1800 BC). These occur in such large numbers that they are
used to calculate burial numbers and community populations.
The increasing complexity and wealth of these tombs is often cited
as evidence of emerging social hierarchy, part of the process of the
development of the complex 'palace' states, such as Knossos, which
characterize Minoan civilization.

The bronze daggers are of limited design. Double-edged, thin
blades reinforced by a midrib, they are mostly relatively short. Wooden
handles were attached by rivets to the shoulder of the blade. This
method of attachment creates an inherent weakness, because handles
will easily snap away if put under pressure. The shortness of the overall
dagger, however, meant that this was probably not a major problem.
Defining these daggers as tools or as weapons is also important to their
understanding. Anyone who regularly uses knives for commonplace

Right Crete, mainland Greece and the main sites mentioned in this chapter.

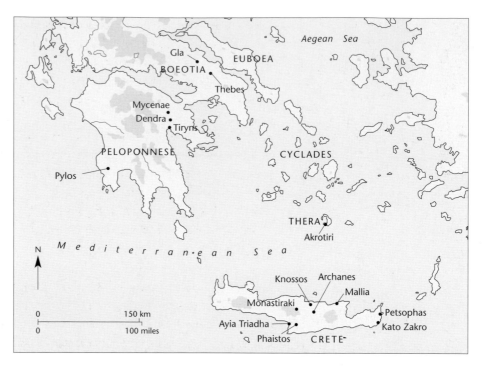

Below Male clay figurine offered at the peak sanctuary of Petsophas on Crete, dating to around 1800 BC. The model dagger with rivets, displayed prominently at the waist, resembles contemporary actual bronze daggers.

activities such hunting, skinning, whittling wood, preparing and eating food, will recognize that a double-edged blade is much more likely to cut you accidentally. By contrast the ability to cut in either direction makes them ideally suited to weapons.

That these daggers were not merely functional, but had a more complex symbolic dimension, is suggested by small clay figurines of men, with modelled daggers placed prominently at their waists. These clay figurines, mostly Middle Minoan in date (2000–1700 BC), were offered on mountain peak sanctuaries to memorialize participation in the rituals there. They portray worshippers rather than deities.

The prominent display of the daggers does suggest that association with a weapon was a significant symbolic element in the Minoan conception of masculinity. Judging by the figurines alone, this may have been limited to a particular elite social class, as it is often the best made and most fully painted figurines that have the daggers. But the sheer ubiquity of the daggers in the tombs does suggest that this association was more pervasive in Minoan society.

Beyond the symbolic there is more pragmatic evidence that Minoan Crete was less peaceful than conventionally thought. One element cited to 'prove' Minoan peacefulness is the lack of fortifications at Knossos and other palaces. This is true, but we should be wary of applying such a perception as a generalization about the whole of Minoan civilization. A change of settlement pattern to strategically located and defensible mountain refuge sites is well-known for Crete at the end of the Bronze Age, but scholars have variously argued for a similar choice for defensible settlements at the beginning of the Bronze Age, and even for small citadels in the dynamic run-up to the founding of the palaces in the Early Minoan III-Middle Minoan I period (2200–1900 BC).

Choosing defensible locations can be more the result of a perception of threat rather than actual threat. But we can glimpse the consequences of actual conflict at another key moment in Minoan history, the transition from Protopalatial to Neopalatial. The main event was an earthquake which destroyed the first palaces,

Type A and B swords from Mycenae, dating to the 16th century BC. The rounded shoulders of the Type A sword (*left*, 95 cm (37½ in) long), similar to earlier daggers, suggests the origin of swords arises from elongated daggers. The elongated tang of the Type B sword (*right*, 43.2 cm (17 in) long) eliminates the weakness of the handle attachment.

but social continuity was preserved in that they arose from the ruins to achieve the high-point of Neopalatial civilization. Possible conflict, however, at this troubled time is suggested by destruction and abandonment of the Protopalatial palace of Monastiraki in the Amari valley of western Crete. In the adjacent Ayios Vasilios valley, there is a clear break in settlement pattern at the same time. Both areas in the Protopalatial period are satellites of Phaistos, whereas evidence from the Neopalatial period suggests that Knossos was extending its interests in the area.

How should we interpret these sparse but persistent hints of conflict? Certainly this is not warfare as conventionally interpreted. Perhaps what we see here is a practice well known to anthropologists, intercommunity raiding. This sort of low-key conflict offers opportunity for masculine posturing, small territorial changes and resource exchange, but it minimizes actual casualties and destruction, and thus is rarely culturally destabilizing.

NEOPALATIAL CRETE – GROWING CONFLICT

Neopalatial Crete represents the high point of Minoan civilization, with its artistic treasures, the palaces, the frescoes, the sculpted stone vases, the miniature masterpieces of stone seals and gold rings. And yet it ended in violence and destruction. A growing militarism is apparent in the development of the first swords. Minoan and Mycenaean swords are given a standard characterization based on a typology of sword hilts. The Type A swords are the earliest. With their rounded shoulders and almost non-existent tang, they clearly resemble the earlier daggers. Indeed it is quite likely that they are essentially an elongation of the dagger shape. The earliest Type A swords are found in religious contexts, mostly famously a Middle Minoan II-III shrine at Mallia. This again emphasizes the symbolic nature of weaponry in Minoan civilization.

Once swords were developed, the Minoans rapidly developed their functional technology. Although the Type B sword, which was the first to remedy the weakness of the handle by elongating the tang, was probably developed by the early Mycenaeans, it has been convincingly argued that the main workshop of the Types C and D swords was based at Knossos. Even with their ornate handles, as blades these swords are highly functional. What also makes the two swords interesting is that they were designed for different fighting styles. The Type C handle favours a 'sabre' grip, which also allows the forefinger to be wrapped naturally around the 'horned' guard; this grip presents the point of the blade forward to the opponent, a more fencing style of

Type D 16th–15th-century BC sword with an ornate gold hilt, from the Zapher Papoura cemetery at Knossos. The blade is functional, suggesting the gold handle was added for the sword's final use as a grave offering.

Type C sword (*top*, replica) with characteristic horned guard. The design of the horned guard naturally allows for grip with the forefinger over the guard (technically known as 'fingering the ricasso'), presenting the point forward, and suitable for duelling and thrusting actions. This contrasts with the Type D sword (*above*, replica). The small handle and characteristic T-shaped guard favour a 'hammer' grip, which presents the edge forward, better for cutting actions and rapid changes of direction in a melee where there are multiple opponents.

(*Below*) Three gold seals showing combat scenes (all from Mycenae and dating to the 16th century BC).
(*Left*) The swordsman overcomes the better-protected shield-man by pushing the top of the shield and making an overhand thrust, a killing blow.
(*Middle*) The swordsman dominates a group of enemies, including a shield-man, and uses the overhand thrust.
(*Right*) Man and lion combat – the warrior uses an overhand thrust to attack the lion.

fighting. By contrast, the Type D handle is created for a 'hammer' grip, which presents the edge of blade forward – suggesting more cutting actions. Such form and function distinctions strongly suggest a social context in which specialized skill sets were valued and supported. This sort of formal one-on-one combat certainly suits the elitist, hierarchical nature of Minoan society in the Late Minoan I-II period (1600–1400 BC). Most of the swords are found in male tombs, which have come to be called 'Warrior Tombs', accompanied by daggers and spearheads, and also by a distinctive set of jewelry.

Although most of the pictorial art focuses on religious pageantry and ritual, there are some combat images, portraying both man-to-man and man-to-lion combat. It is significant how the sword is the dominant weapon, even allowing a bare-chested swordsman, portrayed in some detail, to defeat a more anonymous spearman with a tower shield. The consistent elevation of swords over other weapons is clearly indicative of a hierarchical perception of combat skill. The techniques too that we see in the images, a preference for long-range slashing and thrusting (which absolutely suits the design of the swords), also suggest a formal, fencing type of combat, dueling one-on-one rather than fighting in a unit. A favourite technique is a downward stab to the neck. As well as being a quick kill technique, by cutting major blood vessels, the neck is difficult to protect with armour and tends to be exposed.

Although not directly Minoan, the practice of raiding, hypothesized above, is portrayed on the famous 'Ship Fresco' from the West House at Akrotiri on the island of Thera. Among scenes of towns, a ship procession, and a storm at sea, is one which shows men armed with large tower shields, boars' tusk helmets and spears. They appear to be on a cattle rustling expedition.

The chronology of these 'Warrior Tombs' overlaps the period Late Minoan I-II. At the end of Late Minoan I (1450 BC) all the major sites, palaces, villas and towns, except for the palace of Knossos, suffered destruction by fire, from which they did not recover. These destructions were the result of human agency, war. Although the chronology of these destructions is archaeologically contemporaneous, in human terms this may have covered a generation. The interpretation of Crete in this period as a troubled island, suggests that as a result of the ecological damage wrought on Crete by the earlier eruption of the Thera volcano, competition for scarcer resources pushed the palace states into competition. This clearly took on a scale far greater than the raiding of earlier generations, apparently resulting in a systematic destruction of the infrastructure of all the states, except Knossos.

90

Above Miniature fresco from the West House at Akrotiri on Thera (15th century BC). This section of the larger 'Ship Fresco' shows a raiding party of warriors with 'tower' shields, boars' tusk helmets, and armed with spears and swords.

Knossos was excepted from this destruction, essentially because it was the only palace not to suffer a major destruction, and its administration survived intact for another generation or two, down to about 1375 BC. The nature of that survival, however, does suggest some changes. The 'Warrior Tombs' at Knossos, coupled with the appearance of the Mycenaean Greek language used in the Linear B script, strongly suggest that Knossian survival was assisted by the presence of Mycenaean warriors from the Greek Mainland. Earlier scholarship had thought Mycenaeans invaded Crete. It is much more likely that the evidence reveals a smaller group of military specialists, mercenaries in modern terms, who assisted Knossos and then took it over, by marrying into the Minoan ruling class – perhaps the elite women who are buried in the large, built tombs, at Knossos, Archanes and Ayia Triadha, which overlap the date of the 'Warrior Tombs'.

EARLY MYCENAEANS

This brings us to the Mycenaeans. The spectacular wealth of the Mycenae Shaft Graves in Late Helladic I (1600–1500 BC) is a stark contrast to the relative poverty of Mainland Greece in the previous Middle Helladic period. Various explanations have been put forward for this sudden wealth, for example, were these really Minoans, or were they Greek mercenaries returned from Egypt with their loot. Whatever the narrative behind the material, it is evident that this represents a group with military specialization far more sophisticated than the Minoans. There are dozens of swords, spears, daggers and knives in the graves. The bones

A 13th-century BC Linear B tablet from Pylos. The script, originally Minoan, records the early form of Greek used by the Mycenaeans. The tablets are palace accounts itemizing production, from wool and oil to horses, chariots and weapons.

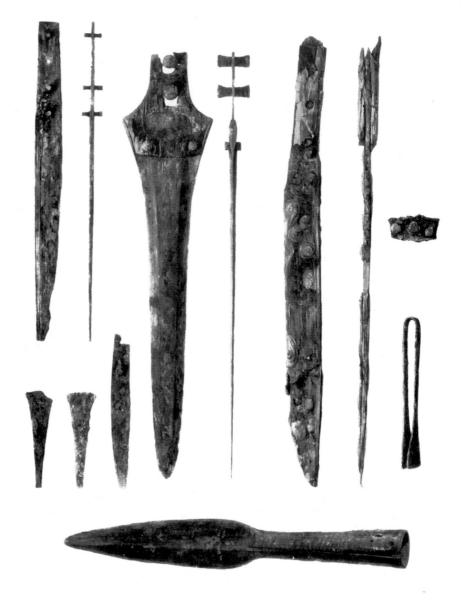

Decorated weapons, including daggers, knives and a spearhead, from Mycenae Shaft Graves. Each of the graves contained dozens of weapons, reflecting the warrior ethos of the people.

themselves tell a stark story. Not only are there fatal head wounds, there are also healed wounds on the sword-arms of the skeletons, indicating long fighting careers, and even training injuries – bruises on the leg bones from running with large body-shields. Two types of such large shields are shown on one of the Shaft Grave daggers, where warriors with both 'figure-eight' and 'tower' shields fight lions.

The images on the Shaft Grave treasures also celebrate military knowledge. Perhaps most telling is the fragmentary Siege Rhyton, which demonstrates that right from the beginning the Mycenaeans knew and valued the skills of siege warfare and group combat with specialist units of swordsmen, spearmen and archers, rather than just raiding and duelling – armies, not just bands of warriors.

That this cultural value was not limited to Mycenae itself, is indicated by finds elsewhere. Contemporary tombs have not just weapons, but also pieces of armour, including fragments of real boars' tusk helmets, and most famously the whole suit of armour, the Dendra corselet (see box).

The Dendra Armour

No discussion of warfare in Bronze Age Greece should neglect the full suit of armour found in an early Mycenaean tomb at Dendra near Mycenae. The suit comprises a simple corselet, breastplate and backplate. A large gorget covers the neck and lower face. The shoulders are protected by curved shoulder plates. Hanging from the waist is a 'skirt' of overlapping plates, which allow movement of the lower body and legs. It is crudely constructed of semi-cylindrical bronze plates, curved to fit the body, but without the elegant anatomical detail of the later Greek hoplite armour.

The problem with interpreting this armour is that it is unique in the archaeological record; we have no idea whether it is typical of Mycenaean armour, or was itself an unusual construction. Nothing like it has been found in other warrior tombs, nor is portrayed on images. Clearly it was special to the owner with whom it was buried, and represented considerable expenditure in terms of the amount of metal.

Modern interpretations focus on the armour's cumbersome appearance. Illustrative reconstructions place the warrior wearing this armour in a chariot, on the assumption that it was too heavy for its wearer to engage in personal combat. There have however been several modern attempts to replicate the armour accurately. Such experiments agree that the armour was made for a stocky individual, with the 'physique of a rugby player'. Though it is indeed difficult to rise from a prone position, and running tires the wearer quickly, the armour is not especially cumbersome to wear. It compares in mobility to medieval armour, and such comparison may give a clue to its real use.

'Tonlet' armour is a tournament armour design of the early 16th century AD, especially favoured for poll-axe duels. It has a distinctive skirt, and its curves are engineered to prevent an opponent's weapon getting a purchase with edge or point. As a functional comparison, it suggests that the Dendra armour was not battlefield gear, but rather was designed for duelling. Such an interpretation would certainly support the model of Mycenaean society as dominated by an aristocracy whose prestige was measured by personal skill at arms. In summary, the Dendra armour is more likely to have been used for personal combat than for chariot warfare.

Above The Dendra armour. The first European suit of armour known, its simple design offers protection from the thighs up to the neck.

Left Dr Barry Molloy wearing a replica of the Dendra armour, and using it for foot combat. Although heavy, it offers sufficient mobility for one-on-one foot combat, such as a duel, rather than fighting from a chariot.

Below Helmet from Spata in Attika made from boars' tusks, dating from the 13th century BC. Up to 30 boars may have been needed to provide the tusks. The danger of the boar hunt required combat skills appropriate to warfare training.

Above Fragment of a 16th-century BC silver rhyton (drinking vessel) from Mycenae, showing a siege. There appears to be some form of ranking coordination of the attacking force using swordsmen, archers and shield-and-spearmen. This indicates knowledge and use of battle tactics.

Above A 16th-century BC bronze dagger with Lion Hunt scene, found at Mycenae. Both figure-of-eight and 'tower' shields are portrayed. The shields are supported by body-straps. Note the two-handed overhand thrust action of the spearmen.

MYCENAEAN DOMINATION

After the elimination of Knossos, in the Late Helladic IIIb period (1350–1200 BC) Mycenaean civilization grew to dominate the whole of the eastern Mediterranean. At home in Greece, this is the time of the great walled citadels. With their huge 'cyclopean' masonry, they demonstrate considerable knowledge of architectural engineering. At Mycenae and nearby Tiryns in particular, the military dimension to this knowledge is revealed in the way that gates are set at angles to the main walls, so that the flanks of potential attackers would be exposed to fire from the defenders. Both those sites also incorporated within their layout access to nearby springs, for water in times of siege, and postern gates for the defenders to either flee or to mount surprise ambushes on attackers.

Regrettably we have no contemporary literary or historical texts, which would reveal the narrative to explain these cultural phenomena. Were the Mycenaeans constantly at war with one another? The Linear B texts preserved in the destructions of the main Mycenaean sites are, of course, primarily the administrative accounts of a highly organized economy. The Mycenaeans may have been warriors, but they were also bureaucrats. Amid the sheep, and the wool, and the olive oil, however, are the records of large numbers of weapons, armour, horses, chariots and chariot wheels. Given the rocky Greek terrain, it is debatable whether the Mycenaeans ever really fought with chariots. Only the Boeotian plain, dominated by Thebes and the massive fortress of Gla, has sufficient open land. Nevertheless these are indications of a huge arms build-up. Dare we say an 'arms-race'?

It is possible too that there was a decidedly military nature to Mycenaean social and political hierarchy. The highest officials named in the Linear B texts are the *wanakas* and the *lawegetas* (literally the 'leader of the people'). Both words survive into later Archaic Greek, the former as *wanax* meaning king, and the latter referring to the leader of the warhost.

Abroad this is also the period of Mycenaean economic and military adventurism. First as trading outposts and later as colonies, the Mycenaeans established the first Greek presence in what would later become the great Greek cities of Asia Minor,

Above A 16th-century BC gravestone from Mycenae with a carving of a chariot riding down an armed warrior on foot. The charioteer seems to be alone in the chariot; the foot warrior is carrying a sword, possibly single-edged.

Opposite above Reconstruction of the Mycenae citadel at its largest. The gate is set at right angles to the walls and has an additional rampart to the side, so that the flanks of any attackers would be exposed. This is a sophisticated use of fortifications.

Opposite below Aerial photograph of the citadel of Tiryns. The upper citadel on the right has the thicker walls to defend the palace. The thick double walls allow for protected access to water in case of a siege.

Ionia and Cyprus. If Hittite references to the Ahhiyawa accurately refer to the Achaians, i.e. the Greeks, there is certainly recognition of the military capability of the Mycenaeans, even if it was only an irritation to the Anatolian superpower. It is very likely that these Mycenaean military adventures in Asia Minor were the roots of the stories of the Trojan War, later compiled into Homer's *Iliad*.

MYCENAEAN DEMISE

Given this apparent military might of the Mycenaeans, their total collapse at the end of the Bronze Age seems surprising (Late Helladic IIIc, 1200–1050 BC). Again in human terms, it was rather drawn out over several generations. Various explanations have been advanced, from barbarian invasion to drought to internecine warfare, probably all of which may have been factors. Certainly the demise of Mycenaean civilization should not be seen as an isolated event. The 'main event' of the period was the migration of what the Egyptians called the 'Land and Sea Peoples'. This enigmatic dislocation and migration of populations overthrew the Hittite empire, and threatened Egypt from *c.* 1207 BC, until the Sea Peoples' defeat by Ramesses III in *c.* 1174 BC (see p. 44). They then settled in Palestine, and became known to the writers of the Bible as the Philistines. Philistine culture includes a strong Aegean component, suggesting that the Sea Peoples may have included dislocated Minoans and Mycenaeans.

Returning to the Mycenaeans, the nature of the threat clearly caused changes in the weaponry and tactics. The Warrior Vase from Mycenae shows a procession of warriors wearing horned helmets, armour of cuirass and greaves and carrying round shields. In all this is a set similar to the later hoplite panoply, which suggests the need to equip and field groups of soldiers in battle rather than only the

The Warrior Vase from Mycenae, c. 1200 BC. The armour of these later Mycenaean warriors has changed from that of their ancestors: it is lighter and the shields are smaller. Their depiction in procession suggests too that they fought as a unit, an indication of group warfare, rather than aristocratic duelling.

In this rendering of a fresco from the Palace of Pylos, Mycenaean warriors are shown in combat with 'barbarians'. The Mycenaeans, with boars' tusk helmets and greaves, are distinguished from their enemies who wear skins. Note the thrusting use of spears and short swords.

Top Bronze Type F sword from Trikala in Thessaly (36.6 cm (14½ in) long, 12th century BC). A sword design as functionally simple and brutal as a Roman sword. Note the integrated pommel and the recurved edge; this is a weapon for close-quarter melee battle.

Above Bronze Naue II sword from Antheia in Achaia (65 cm (25½ in) long, 12th century BC). This type of sword, with its distinctive guard, was probably introduced into Greece from central Europe. It became the dominant sword design in Europe from Ireland to the Mediterranean in the latter stages of the late Bronze Age and throughout the Iron Age.

elite warriors of earlier periods.

Supporting this suggestion is the fresco which decorates Hall 64 of the Palace of Pylos. The fragmentary scene shows helmeted Mycenaean warriors fighting enemies dressed in skins (which may be a way of indicating their 'barbarity'), in a melee of individual combats, rather than formal duels or ranks of warriors.

Appropriately the swords shown in the fresco are short, and are used to stab the opponents. As the Romans later discovered, shorter swords are better suited to the chaos of battle, because they can be more quickly manoeuvred to change directions, when one is threatened by multiple enemies. Fittingly, the actual swords of this troubled period (Types F, G and the Naue II) underwent rapid development. They are mostly shorter and a little broader than the earlier types, but the two most significant improvements are the replacement of the midrib by a flattened triangle (which makes the sword stronger), and the development of the recurved edge (which makes a leaf-shaped blade). The particular advantage of the recurved edge is that it improves the efficiency of the cutting action, especially the pull-cut (where one cuts by pulling back rather than thrusting forward). This again is an advantage when one fights multiple opponents in a melee. And it is these sword designs which look forward from the Bronze Age into the Early Iron Age and the warfare of Archaic and Classical Greece.

6 War in Archaic and Classical Greece

A fully armoured hoplite on a Greek amphora of c. 480 BC, found in Caere (Etruria). He wears an Attic helmet and linen or leather corselet; his shield emblem represents an unarmed figure blowing the *salpinx*, a trumpet used to give signals in battle.

The Greeks prided themselves on their distinctive style of waging war. The most characteristic Greek soldier, the hoplite, went into battle in heavy armour which enabled him to engage in far more intense close combat than was usual in the ancient world. This boosted the Greeks' self-image as a nation of exceptionally brave and strong fighters, surrounded by weak and cowardly barbarians who preferred the safety of long-range fighting with javelins and arrows. A further source of Greek pride was that they fought in a restrained manner, according to 'laws' which required, amongst other things, respect for the war-dead.

An image of Greek warfare as dominated by the hoplite pervades ancient literature and modern studies. One could easily come away with the impression that Greek warfare consisted of little more than hoplite armies fighting game-like ('agonistic') pitched battles – at least until the 5th century BC, when other kinds of warfare came to the fore. But this is a misleading impression, because it neglects the other types of military personnel, action and values which had always played their part alongside the hoplite.

THE GREEK CITY-STATES

After several centuries in which the Greeks lived in scattered villages, the 8th century BC saw the appearance of hundreds of small towns, the first use of writing since the fall of the Mycenaean kingdoms, and the first recorded wars in European history – other than the Trojan War and other epic struggles of Greek legend.

Throughout the Archaic period (700–480 BC), settlements grew larger, fortifications and monumental buildings appeared, and Greeks travelled across the Mediterranean and the Black Sea founding many new cities. Slowly, the characteristic Greek form of political organization, the city-state (*polis*), emerged. We cannot reconstruct the military history of this period in any detail because most of our evidence comes from much later sources and is patchy and unreliable. However, fragments of Archaic poetry, battle scenes in art, and archaeological finds do reveal the general nature of warfare at the time, and throw some light on the major conflicts. Best-known are the Messenian Wars of the 7th century BC, during which Sparta reduced its neighbours to serfs and made itself the most powerful state in Greece.

Around 550 BC international relations among the Greek city-states were first formalized by means of treaties of alliance and friendship, some of which survive in inscriptions. Sparta's bilateral treaties with subordinate allies covered most of the Peloponnese (the southern Greek peninsula), and amounted to what modern scholars call the Peloponnesian League. Sybaris built up a similar system of alliances among the Greek cities of southern Italy, but this came to an abrupt end when the city was razed to the ground by its neighbour Croton in 510 BC.

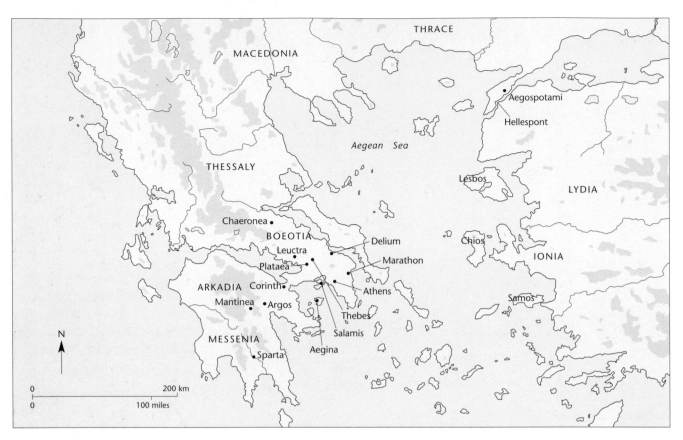

The major city-states, regions and places mentioned in the text.

Throughout the Archaic period, Greek cities on the coast of Anatolia (modern Turkey) suffered attacks by the kingdom of Lydia, which ultimately conquered much of the region. Not long afterwards, Lydia was itself overthrown by the Persians, who from the mid-6th century BC onwards created a vast empire with its centre in Iran. The Greeks in Anatolia were subjected in 546 BC, and by the end of the century Persian control extended also to some of the Aegean islands and into the northern Balkans.

A turning point in history, in the Greeks' own eyes, came at the start of the Classical period (480–338 BC) with resistance against Persian imperial expansion (as described by Herodotus). A failed attempt to throw off Persian control (the Ionian Revolt, 499–494 BC) was followed by the first direct Persian attack on mainland Greece, halted by defeat at the hands of Athens at the battle of Marathon in 490 BC. A much larger expedition followed in 480 BC, commanded by the new king, Xerxes. This led many, but by no means all, Greek city-states to join forces in an alliance led by Sparta. The allied fleet, dominated by the Athenian navy, scored a surprise victory at Salamis (see box opposite), after which the bulk of the Persian forces retreated. The allied army won another unexpected victory against the remaining Persian troops in the battle of Plataea (479 BC), and a series of Greek campaigns of retaliation in Persian-controlled territory ensued. Sparta soon lost interest, allowing Athens to make itself leader of a new anti-Persian alliance, the Delian League, which soon turned into an Athenian 'empire' with tribute-paying subjects. In a similar development, Syracuse established itself as the dominant Greek power in Sicily after leading campaigns against an expanding non-Greek power, here the empire of Carthage in North Africa, and achieving victory at the battle of Himera in 480 BC.

The Battle of Salamis

Despite its fame as 'the battle which saved western civilization', the clash between the Persian and Greek navies at Salamis in 480 BC is important more for its symbolic value than for its military impact on the Persian empire.

The course of the battle is impossible to reconstruct beyond a bare outline because each state in the Greek coalition told a different story, glorifying its own role and playing down that of its rivals. Thus the Athenians claimed that they opened the battle and that the Corinthians fled without fighting; others said that the Aeginetans began hostilities and that the Corinthians dominated the action. It was agreed, however, that the Greek fleet, stationed at Salamis to cover the evacuation of Athens, was persuaded with difficulty to make a stand here against the Persians, led by Xerxes himself, and that the Greeks managed to draw the enemy into the narrowest part of the gulf where the Persians could not exploit their vast numerical advantage. The sources put no figure on the losses but suggest that the Greeks did such damage that the remnants of Xerxes' fleet and the bulk of his army immediately retreated to Persia in panic and despair.

The Greeks were not in fact outnumbered by much. The Persians are said to have launched 1,207 ships, but 600 were lost in two separate storms, and at least another 100 in previous engagements. Thus the Greeks, with 380 ships, faced at most 500 enemy vessels. The havoc wreaked by storms is not surprising because it was mid-September, and in fact, even if Xerxes had won the battle, it would have been high time for his navy to return to dock for the winter. It is quite likely that the Persian retreat was always part of their plan. To the Greeks, however, Salamis seemed a miraculous victory, and it quickly became a symbol of their determination to defend their freedom against all odds and at any cost.

Above The course of the battle reconstructed.

Below An artist's impression of Phoenician and Greek triremes in action at Salamis.

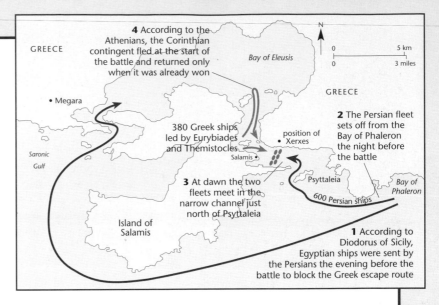

GREECE

4 According to the Athenians, the Corinthian contingent fled at the start of the battle and returned only when it was already won

Bay of Eleusis

N

0   5 km
0   3 miles

GREECE

• Megara

380 Greek ships led by Eurybiades and Themistocles

position of Xerxes

Salamis

2 The Persian fleet sets off from the Bay of Phaleron the night before the battle

Saronic Gulf

3 At dawn the two fleets meet in the narrow channel just north of Psyttaleia

Psyttaleia

600 Persian ships

Bay of Phaleron

Island of Salamis

1 According to Diodorus of Sicily, Egyptian ships were sent by the Persians the evening before the battle to block the Greek escape route

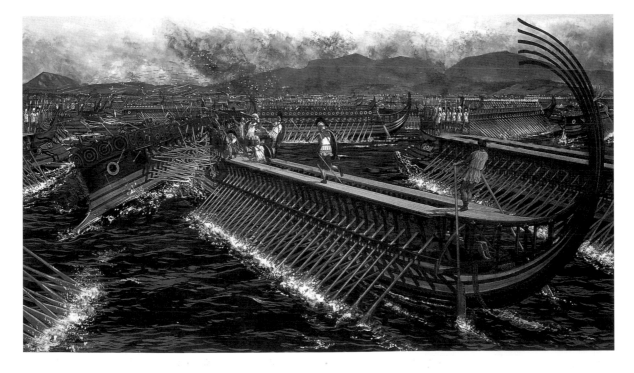

Bronze statuette of a hoplite, *c*. 500 BC, found at Dodona. The figure once held a raised spear, and realistically represents the sideways-on stance adopted by the hoplite in combat. His shield is of the 'Boeotian' rather than standard hoplite type (the scalloped indentation at the side is just visible), with a central armband and a handle at the far end.

Three pieces of decorated armour.
Left A 6th-century BC Corinthian helmet from Olympia.
Far left and below Ornate pieces of armour from Afrati in Crete, dating to *c.* 650–600 BC, which were apparently captured in battle and then hung up on the walls of a communal dining hall, with inscriptions naming the men who took the spoils.

Left An early 5th-century BC Athenian cup showing young men arming. Starting in the bottom left corner, we see them clipping on greaves, tying on a linen or leather corselet, and putting on a sword; the next figure looks at his helmet in alarm, perhaps because the crest is missing. Their shields lie or stand behind them.

Below The battle scene on the Chigi Vase, *c.* 640 BC. In the centre, a boy blows a pipe to encourage those fighting ahead of him, or summon help from the larger group running up behind. On the far right more soldiers are about to join the action; and on the far left even more soldiers are arming. All have two spears, apparently fitted with throwing loops.

Greek Shields

The Classical hoplite carried a circular, convex, wooden shield, c. 90 cm (3 ft) in diameter and 7 kg (15 lb) in weight, with a central armband through which the bearer slid his left arm up to the elbow, and a handle, usually made of rope, at the rim. For additional support, the hoplite carried the shield tilted backwards against his left shoulder. Its thickness and convexity made the shield hard to penetrate, especially if reinforced with a bronze facing, while its size ensured cover for almost the entire body: the lower half, which jutted forward as the top of the shield rested against the shoulder, provided some protection even for the shins. When a hoplite adopted his normal sideways-on stance, he stood right behind the centre of his shield and was exceptionally well protected, though his right flank remained vulnerable.

A minority of Archaic hoplites preferred the light 'Boeotian' shield and carried a pair of short spears suitable for both close- and long-range combat rather than the standard single thrusting spear. The shield was oval in shape, consisting of a wooden frame across which leather or wicker was stretched, with semi-circular indentations in the middle of each of the long sides (a less exaggerated form of the Dipylon shield, see box on p. 71). Originally it had a single central handle, but later versions copied the double-grip system of the hoplite shield, except that the handle was set near the bottom and the bearer carried it with arm outstretched.

In northern Greece, many soldiers were similarly equipped with a light shield of wicker or leather called a pelta. The Boeotian shield and pair of spears went out of use in the early 5th century BC, and it was perhaps only then that a sharp distinction developed between hoplites and pelta-bearing 'peltasts'. The term 'hoplite' is in any case not attested before 470 BC.

Their successes in these great conflicts did much to create the Greek idea that they were innately superior to their 'barbarian' enemies, and defenders of freedom against the slavery of totalitarian empires. Note that 'freedom' is not to be confused with democracy: even Athens, the most democratic state in the Greek alliance, enjoyed only limited popular participation in politics at the time, and most of the other allies were oligarchic states, ruled by wealthy elites. Syracuse was ruled by a series of powerful dictators.

For some time, Sparta and Athens shared the position of 'leader of the Greeks', but the ambitions of both sides led to a series of wars for hegemony, for which our main evidence comes from the contemporary historians Thucydides and Xenophon: the First Peloponnesian War (461–446 BC), the two phases of the (Second) Peloponnesian War (431–421 and 413–404 BC), and the Corinthian War (395–386 BC). For much of the 5th century BC, the Athenians were successful and confident enough to get embroiled in more distant wars as well, notably a failed attempt to support an Egyptian revolt against the Persians, and a disastrous expedition to Sicily, but Sparta ultimately gained Persian financial support, which enabled it to defeat Athens and its allies comprehensively. In the late 380s BC, Sparta was again the unchallenged hegemon of Greece, and more powerful than ever before. But its rival did not give up, creating a Second Athenian Confederacy in 377 BC, and new challengers for the leadership also emerged, most notably the Boeotians, Arkadians and Thessalians. After Sparta was decisively defeated at Leuctra in 371 BC, constantly changing alliances under changing leadership fought for hegemony but with less and less lasting success. The (second) battle of Mantinea in 362 BC left Greece without any recognized 'leader' at all.

Two hoplites attempt to rescue a wounded or dead comrade from his killer, on a Corinthian vase dating from around 600 BC. The central armband and peripheral handle typical of the hoplite shield are clearly shown. The fallen soldier wears a tunic but no cuirass; the nudity of the others may be a 'heroizing' artistic convention.

At this point, the political landscape was transformed by the rise of Macedon. The potential power of the main peoples of the Northern Balkans, the Macedonians and the Thracians with their great resources of manpower, gold and silver and their warlike traditions, had long been recognized by the Greeks, but it was not until Philip II of Macedon politically unified a large part of the region, won control over its gold mines, and transformed its military forces that this power was realized. Despite resistance by Athens in particular, Philip's influence in Greece extended further and further until his victory at Chaeronea in 338 BC made him 'leader of the Greeks', who were united in the new League of Corinth. Soon Athens, Sparta and other Greek states were reduced to minor players in international politics, but they continued to exist – and fight – as independent states until Greece became a province of the Roman empire in 146 BC.

A MOTLEY MILITIA: THE CITIZEN-ARMY

The great majority of soldiers who fought in Archaic and Classical Greek wars were amateur militiamen. Whether they made a living from agriculture, crafts or trade, Greek citizens in most cities were expected to provide their own equipment, take care of their own training, and serve in war to the best of their ability. The poorest men could not afford to buy expensive arms and armour, engage in regular training or abandon their livelihoods to serve on long campaigns, but nevertheless turned out with their javelins, bows and stones when a general levy was mustered in self-defence or for short campaigns just across the border. Ancient authors thought so little of this poorly armed and trained crowd that they rarely bothered to mention them, but masses of light-armed troops were present in many important battles and must have had some impact on their outcome (see box on the battle of Delium, pp. 114–115).

Citizens who could afford to buy at least a shield and spear, and ideally bronze body armour and a sword as well, served as *hoplitai* or hoplites, meaning simply 'men who have military equipment' (*hopla*) as opposed to the shieldless masses of 'light' and 'naked' men (*psiloi*, *gymnetes*). Greek art of the Archaic period shows uniformly heavily armoured soldiers, but archaeological finds reveal that in reality some pieces of body armour were used far more widely than others: helmets outnumbered greaves by 3 to 1 and cuirasses by 10 to 1. Most hoplites carried only a spear and shield (see box on p. 104), and wore no more than a helmet and short tunic.

The richest citizens were equipped with a panoply of splendid armour, including triple-crested helmets and shields with personalized blazons rather than the national emblems of their cities which widely served as shield devices for common soldiers. Affluent hoplites were attended by servants, usually slaves, and the very richest rode to battle on horseback, even if they fought on foot. In the Archaic period, such mounted hoplites were relatively common, whereas cavalrymen – soldiers who fought on horseback – were rare. But in the course of the Classical age more and more cities organized cavalry forces, and mounted hoplites were seen correspondingly less. Despite moves towards uniformity, the Classical hoplite militia remained a motley force, each individual's equipment determined solely by what he was able and willing to buy.

Training, too, was left largely to the men's own initiative. Wealthy men spent much of their leisure in private or public gymnasia and wrestling-grounds, where they ran, jumped, threw the discus and javelin, wrestled and boxed in order to cultivate general fitness, agility and stamina. Weapons-drill was not usually a part of the training programme. Some might hire a private fight instructor (*hoplomachos*), but others argued that this was a waste of money because skill in handling weapons came naturally. Less well-off men trained less frequently, and those who were too poor to find time for any training simply relied on fitness and strength derived from hard work. Formation-drill exercises were rarely possible: since men trained mostly on their own or in small groups, if at all, battlefield manoeuvres could be practised only during campaigns, after the troops had been assembled. Greek soldiers thus owed their military successes more to an exceptional

Bronze statuette of a mounted hoplite from southern Italy, *c.* 575–550 BC. The rider's bent left arm shows that he originally carried a hoplite shield, and marks on his helmet show that it was decorated with a transverse crest.

willingness to fight at close range and in close order than to any particular proficiency in the use of weapons or tactical manoeuvres.

The composition of a general levy depended on a city-state's military traditions and the distribution of wealth among its people. In Classical Athens, about 40 per cent of citizens of military age – between 18 and 60 years old – served as hoplites; 2 per cent as cavalrymen; the rest as haphazardly armed light infantry, and as rowers in the navy. Few states are likely to have had an equally large proportion of heavy infantry. In regions such as Thessaly a wide economic gap between the elite and the masses contributed to cities fielding larger numbers of cavalry and light infantry, and smaller forces of hoplites.

Only a minority of citizens could afford to serve for long periods of time, and a city could not commit its entire general levy to a distant overseas campaign or a long war of conquest. For such campaigns, a state called on volunteers or compelled its wealthier citizens to serve: those who met a specified property qualification might be obliged to equip themselves to a minimum standard and be available for service. The lowest ranking classes were under no such obligation but could volunteer.

Sparta was a partial exception to almost everything which has been said so far. The subjection of the inhabitants of nearby areas to the serf-like status of 'helot' made it possible to turn all Spartan citizens into a leisured elite of 'peers' (*homoioi*) dedicated to hoplite warfare. These citizens adopted a strongly egalitarian and communal lifestyle which involved far greater uniformity of equipment and a much more regulated daily regime than found elsewhere, with, for example, exercise and meals taken by public mess-groups. Spartan training was nevertheless fundamentally

Light-armed cavalrymen in target practice on a 4th-century BC Athenian mixing bowl. The target is a white shield on a stand; one rider has already moved past and left his javelin broken on the ground, the next is about to throw while winged figures hold out a wreath, symbolizing success.

Beardless young men, whose greaves and spears show that they are soldiers, carry home from battle the dead bodies of their older, bearded comrades. The scene is painted inside a 6th-century BC Spartan drinking cup. The fighting-cocks at the bottom symbolize competitive masculinity.

the same as the kind practised in other cities: general athletic exercise rather than specialist military drill. Nor is there is any sign of regular formation exercises: the Spartan army owed its famously superior cohesion and manoeuvrability to an unusually high level of discipline rather than training.

Despite the importance of citizen-soldiers in military practice and ideals, non-citizens were also widely employed. From at least the time of the Persian Wars onwards, half or more of the Spartan hoplite army consisted of *perioikoi*, inhabitants of subject communities who were free men but did not enjoy full citizen rights. Thousands of helots were made to serve as hoplites after being set free but given at best limited citizen rights. The Spartans also hired mercenaries, including the remnants of one of the largest Greek mercenary armies ever assembled, known as the Ten Thousand and led at the time by Xenophon, whose *Anabasis* gives a vivid account of the expedition. Indeed, in many a successful Spartan expedition only a single Spartiate citizen took part, as leader of many thousands of non-citizen troops.

Mercenaries were employed, alongside citizens, by most states in most wars in the 4th century BC, to the dismay of some contemporaries who worried that they might one day replace the citizen-soldier altogether. Such fears – which proved unfounded – may seem to suggest that the use of non-citizen troops was a new phenomenon of the late Classical period. But in fact, cities had always relied heavily on 'allies' to help them wage their wars, from Troy in Homer's *Iliad* to Sparta and Athens and their allies in the Peloponnesian and Delian Leagues. What changed in the 4th century was that Greece became so fragmented that troops from political allies were hard to come by, and cities resorted instead to mercenaries who served for pay rather than by virtue of friendship or treaty.

The same readiness to hire the military services of outsiders is in evidence in naval warfare. The small fleets of 50-oared galleys of Archaic Greece may have been manned by friends and dependants of their captains, but it was rarely possible on that basis to raise the crew of 200 men required for the trireme (*trieres*) which became the dominant Greek warship from the late 6th century onwards. Corcyraean crews consisted predominantly of slaves, while Spartan crews were a combination of helots and foreigners, and in Athens all kinds of men served as rowers, the single largest group probably being resident aliens, many of whom had migrated to Athens specifically to make a living as oarsmen. Only in a crisis were Athens' ships manned by general levies of citizens, and although these scored notable successes, above all in the battle of Salamis, their inferiority to professional crews was openly acknowledged.

RAVAGING AND RESTRAINT: THE CONDUCT OF WAR

In 341 BC, the Athenian politician Demosthenes complained that the Macedonians were fighting a new kind of war, which continued all year round, employed all kinds of soldiers and tactics, resorted to treachery, and destroyed entire cities. By contrast, he said, 'in the old days the Spartans and all the others invaded and ravaged enemy territory with hoplite citizen armies for four or five months – the war season – and then returned home. They were so old-fashioned, or rather civic-spirited, that they fought wars according to rules and openly.' These good old days turn out to be the decades either side of 400 BC, a time when in fact pitched hoplite battles were only rarely fought, hoplites never fought alone, and numerous cities and populations were wiped out by the warring states. Demosthenes' speech thus is not a reflection of how Greeks once actually fought, but of a Greek ideal nostalgically, falsely, projected back into the past. The Greeks waged 'total' as well as 'agonistic' wars from the beginning of their history.

Every campaign, from the smallest private raid to the greatest invasion, involved devastation of the enemy's agricultural land. Crops and trees were burnt or cut down, farmsteads and agricultural installations destroyed, livestock and people seized. Sometimes no more than token damage was done, as a challenge to the enemy to come out and fight – or else suffer loss of face. On other occasions, the damage inflicted was so severe that it forced the enemy to surrender. The latter was only possible when a large force invaded a small territory at the right time of year, took the enemy by surprise, and stayed for a long time. The element of surprise was vital, for if the enemy were forewarned they would evacuate the countryside, removing even the woodwork of the farmhouses. Invaders could do the most extensive damage by burning grain on the stalk just before the harvest in May or by preventing the ploughing and sowing in October and November, but these were of course precisely the seasons when most citizen-soldiers needed to be at home to look after their own farms. Those who were able and willing to serve abroad at these times were normally too few to do much damage. Not surprisingly, the Spartans with their huge forces of leisured citizen-hoplites, subjects and allies were able to use agricultural devastation to much greater effect than most, by means of large-scale, well-timed annual invasions as well as smaller-scale but permanent occupations of fortified posts in enemy territory as bases for raiding-parties.

In some campaigns the goal was nothing less than the utter destruction of the enemy and their city. This required even more time, manpower and resources than extensive devastation of the countryside. Unless traitors were prepared to open the gates, it was very hard to take a city, but that did not stop the Greeks from trying, and sometimes succeeding. We know of the destruction of ten cities during the Archaic period, and can infer that there were many more less successful or less destructive sieges, like the Spartan assault on Samos in 525 BC, abandoned after 40 days. For the same period we know of a mere handful of pitched battles. From the mid-5th century BC onwards, some states became rich and powerful enough to sustain sieges over months

Heracles stealing the cattle of Geryoneus, on an Athenian cup painted by Euphronius, c. 510 BC. This mythical scene is here represented in a realistic fashion, with the hero and his companions portrayed as a group of regular hoplites driving off the enemy's livestock.

Two scenes of siege. *Top* Hoplites fight hand-to-hand over a low fortification wall, on an Athenian cup of *c.* 500 BC; one attacker picks up a stone to throw at a defender. *Above* A theatrical version of the legendary siege of Thebes, on a Campanian amphora of *c.* 340 BC. The fortifications are a wooden stage set, and the hero climbing a scaling ladder with torch and axe has turned to face the audience.

and years, use labour-intensive tactics such as circumvallation and sapping, and invest in building battering rams, catapults and mobile siege towers. As first Athens, then Sparta, Syracuse in Sicily and other major powers acquired the capacity for siege warfare, something of an arms race developed, in which it was ultimately the Macedonians who triumphed. Many cities fell and some were literally razed to the ground. Their inhabitants became refugees if they were lucky, or else the men were massacred, and the women and children sold as slaves.

If the militia marched out to put a stop to the devastation of the countryside or to prevent the invader from attacking the city itself, a pitched battle might ensue. In the battles for which we have contemporary evidence (see box overleaf), there is little sign that combat was subject to regulations and restrictions, except that the winner was entitled to set up an inviolable 'trophy' (*tropaion*) on the battlefield and was obliged to hand over the enemy dead for burial at the formal request of the loser. None of these Classical battles were fought at an arranged time and place or subject to other agreed conditions. They often ended up being fought in relatively open and equal circumstances, but only because neither side had managed to manoeuvre itself into the position of advantage which it sought. Generals sometimes tried to outwit the enemy by means of surprise manoeuvres, ambushes, and deliberate misinformation. In naval warfare, a favourite trick was to attack when most rowers were away shopping for supplies in the nearest town: the Spartans pulled this off against the Athenian fleet at Aegospotami in 405 BC, thereby all but ending the Peloponnesian War. Fleeing enemies were not simply let go, but pursued for as long as possible and killed. The slaughter would not last long if terrain, weather or failing light made conditions too risky for the pursuers, but continued until no one was left alive if the routed army found itself trapped. At sea, the crews of captured warships were often enslaved or slaughtered.

For the Archaic period, apart from idealizing generalizations of the kind already cited, we have some traditions about wars in which specific restrictions were observed. These include the Battle of Champions between Sparta and Argos in *c.* 550 BC, one of several known attempts to decide a war through combat between two or more picked champions, and a ban on missiles agreed during the so-called Lelantine War (of uncertain date). Remarkable as these episodes are, they should be seen in context: each formed part of a long-running war which at other times was fought with maximum force. Restricted warfare, in other words, was not the norm even in earlier ages but merely a temporary – and in all known cases unsuccessful – expedient to put an end to unacceptably costly conflicts.

TACTICS AND COMBAT

Ancient authors provide few details of the tactics of Classical warfare, but the accounts of Thucydides and Xenophon show that hoplites fought exclusively hand-to-hand in a dense formation, the phalanx. Close combat involved pushing at the enemy with one's shield as well as stabbing and slashing with one's spear and sword.

Some scholars believe that such shoving was done in a concerted manner, every hoplite throwing his weight behind his shield and leaning into the enemy, or into a comrade ahead of him, until one side or the other gave way, and that this was 'the push' (*othismos*) which the sources mention as the crucial moment in battle. More probably, however, pushing was confined to the occasional banging together of shields in man-to-man combat, and the decisive moment was only metaphorically a 'push' (as it certainly was in naval battle). Similar doubts surround the density of the hoplite phalanx: some think that shields actually touched and formed an unbroken wall, but the evidence tends to point to wider intervals which allowed more room to wield spears and swords. Whatever the nature of the formation, it can hardly have reached the enemy in good order, given that citizen-hoplites had little or no chance to practice formation drills, and that the last few hundred metres of their advance into battle tended to degenerate into a wild dash. Only the Spartans and the Cretans did not run but marched in step.

Combat in the archaic period is even more difficult to reconstruct. It is usually assumed that hoplites fought in the Classical manner from the moment hoplite arms and armour were introduced. But there is strong evidence in art and martial poetry that, whereas in the Classical period hoplites, cavalry and light infantry each had their own station on the battlefield, in the Archaic period all mingled freely and fought in an undifferentiated mass. Moreover, some Archaic hoplites fought with missiles as well as hand-to-hand. This would have entailed a much more open, fluid formation, and battles which swung back and forth across the field all day, rather than being decided in a single clash as they were in the Classical period. In this light, it is significant that the Classical custom of marking a victory by setting up a trophy and surrendering the enemy dead at the end of battle is not attested in the Archaic period. This custom, and the Classical style of hoplite battle may have emerged only in the early 5th century BC. If so, it had existed for little more than a century when the Macedonians developed a still more dense and disciplined version of the phalanx which comprehensively defeated all Greek resistance.

Naval combat also underwent a drastic development. Sea battles did take place in Archaic Greece, and involved both

Flight and pursuit after battle, on an Athenian pot by the C-Painter, *c.* 560 BC. Most scenes show a soldier with a broken spear about to be killed by one or two of the enemy; in three scenes a retreating soldier is still putting up a fight. All wear tunics, greaves and helmets; no one wears a cuirass.

The Battle of Delium

	BOEOTIANS	ATHENIANS
COMMANDERS	Pagondas	Hippocrates
STRENGTH (excluding light-armed)	8,000	8,000
CASUALTIES (excluding light-armed)	c. 500	c. 1,000

The earliest hoplite battle of which a detailed contemporary account survives was fought between Athenians and Boeotians at Delium in 424 BC, as described by Thucydides. The campaign began with the Athenians occupying a sacred precinct at Delium to establish a fortified post there. They hoped to do so without fighting a battle, by distracting the Boeotians with a diversion: two towns at the other end of the country were to be seized by Athenian allies with the help of collaborators inside. This plan failed, but the Athenians nevertheless managed to take Delium before the Boeotians could counterattack. Both sides had 7,000 hoplites and 1,000 cavalry, but the Boeotians also fielded 10,000 light-armed troops, when the even greater mass of Athenian light-armed soldiers had already gone home. The Boeotians took advantage of the terrain and of the element of surprise: they only showed themselves after covertly drawing up for battle, then attacked from the top of a hill while the Athenian general was still in mid-harangue. Another surprise was sprung when the Boeotian cavalry moved to the left wing unseen by the Athenians, who fatally panicked at their sudden appearance. The Boeotians killed 1,000 men, and would have killed more in pursuit if darkness had not intervened. They refused the Athenians permission to recover their dead, except on condition that they evacuate Delium.

The Athenians had resorted to a strategic ploy to avoid battle, and when battle was forced upon them it was fought neither at an agreed time or place, nor on

• Delium

1 The Boeotian army advances downhill towards the approaching Athenians

3 The Boeotian heavy infantry continues to march downhill

4 The armies meet, and the Boeotian left and centre are pushed back

Ravine

PAGONDAS

2 The Boeotian cavalry and light-armed troops are prevented from advancing forward by ravines

HIPPOCRATES

Ravine

5 The Boeotian right, with its deep formation, slowly drives back the Athenian left

level ground or otherwise under equal conditions, nor according to rules of fairness or restraint. Perhaps the previous seven years of fighting in the Peloponnesian War had already driven the Greeks to abandon military tradition. But if this first reliably recorded hoplite battle followed almost none of the 'rules', one may wonder whether these were really ever followed in earlier ages, for which we have no contemporary record.

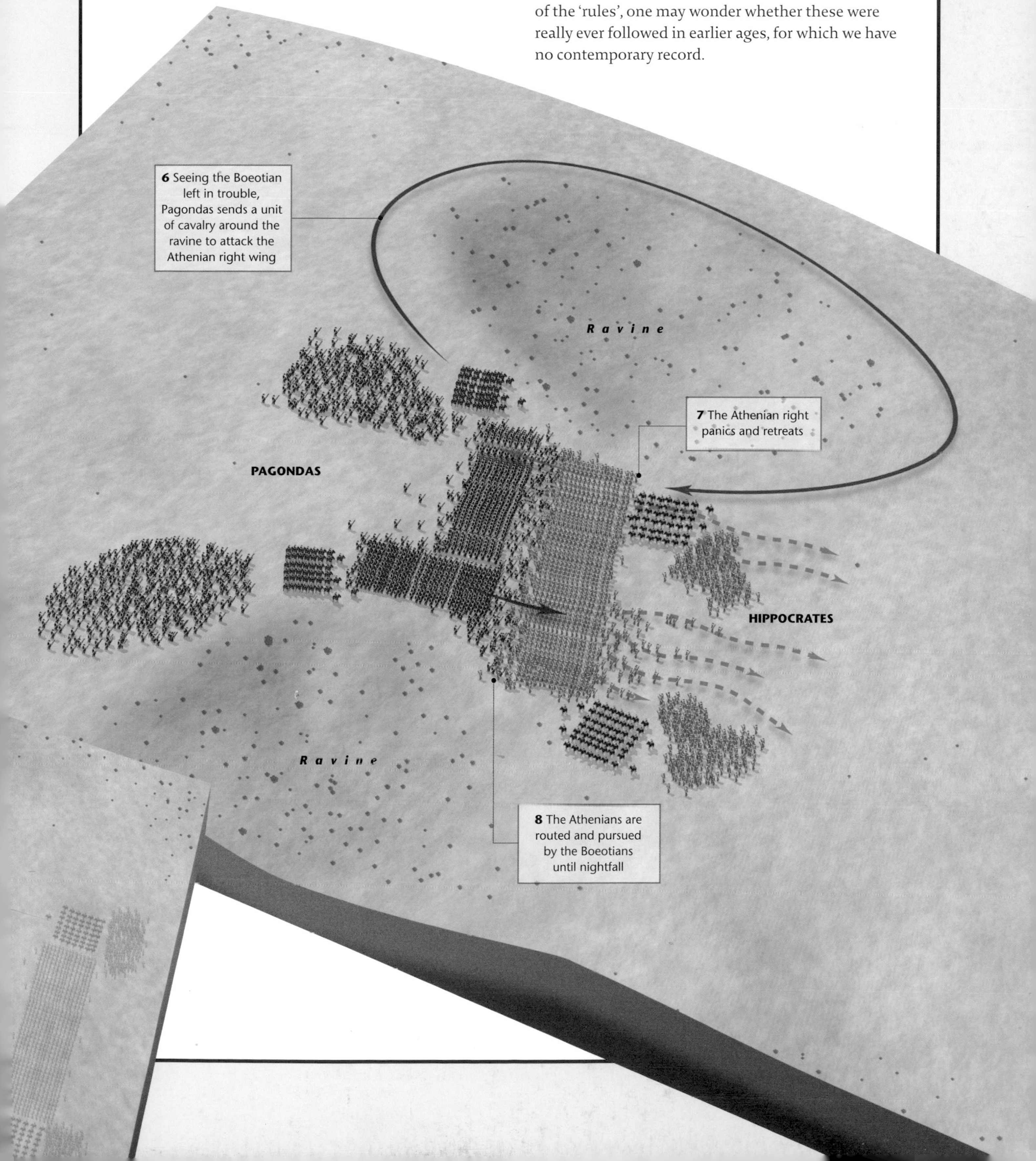

6 Seeing the Boeotian left in trouble, Pagondas sends a unit of cavalry around the ravine to attack the Athenian right wing

Ravine

PAGONDAS

7 The Athenian right panics and retreats

HIPPOCRATES

Ravine

8 The Athenians are routed and pursued by the Boeotians until nightfall

On this late 6th-century BC Athenian cup, a drifting merchant ship is attacked by a warship with oars at two levels (a bireme). Attached to the warship's bow is a bronze ram in the shape of a boar's head. On the other side of the vase the merchantman unfurls its sails in an attempt to escape.

ramming tactics and deck-to-deck fighting between hoplite crews, but early warships served primarily to transport soldiers, who did their own rowing, to enemy territory. The classical trireme, by contrast, was primarily designed for speed and manoeuvrability. Its widespread adoption meant a shift of emphasis from transport to battle, and from deck-to-deck fighting to ramming. For naval battle, triremes normally formed up in a single long line and engaged in one-on-one duels in which they circled one another, looking for a chance to outflank the enemy vessel, ram it, and quickly reverse before it capsized. This made high demands on the skills of rowers and sailors, especially helmsmen, and strongly encouraged the employment of at least semi-professional crews.

THE PRICE OF AMBITION: CAUSES, GOALS AND COSTS OF WAR

The fundamental cause of war, as the Greeks saw it, was 'wanting more' (*pleonexia*). The two things of which everyone wanted more were honour and wealth. Cities sought to win greater honour among neighbouring states and retaliated for acts of disrespect, and open-ended rivalry produced constant tension and frequent war. The greater a city's power, the higher its position of honour in the Greek world, and the greater its sensitivity to perceived slights. Wealth, in the form of booty, slaves and territory, was equally sought after, not only by cities which suffered shortages but also, and especially, by cities which already had an abundance of resources which they could mobilize with a view to acquiring even more.

Honour or greed might be satisfied by burning and plundering enemy country for a few days, but in the course of a long rivalry the stakes tended to become higher. The fiercest rivalries escalated to the point where only the complete annihilation of the enemy would bring satisfaction. These causes and goals of war were constant in Greek history, and were vigorously pursued throughout –

116

The reconstructed trireme *Olympias*. Triremes had a crew of 170 rowers, 14 soldiers and 16 sailors. The helmsman and look-out navigated, while a rowing-master and piper ensured that the oarsmen kept time. There was room on deck for another 30 soldiers, if necessary. In Athens, the captain was normally not a naval specialist, but a rich citizen appointed to cover some of the cost of maintaining ship and crew.

within the limitations of what could be done with amateur militias and an underdeveloped state apparatus.

These limitations were particularly severe in the Archaic period, when state control and finance were rudimentary. Almost all costs of war were met by the soldiers themselves, and the organization of armies and fleets relied heavily on personal relationships between leading men and their followers. Logistical support was non-existent and discipline precarious. From the late 6th century onwards, accelerating state-formation made it possible to create a denser hoplite phalanx, adopt the expensive trireme as the main weapon of naval warfare, develop siege engines and techniques, and generally pay citizens and mercenaries to wage longer, more ambitious wars. Even then Greek armies only achieved their famous successes against the Persian empire despite a constant struggle with fragile discipline, poor logistics and inadequate finance.

These weaknesses, together with the fierce internal rivalries which divided them, meant that the Greeks could not match the growing military power of Macedon, and were reduced to subject status in 338 BC. Athens made an attempt to catch up by creating a better-trained citizen-army, and some other states later followed suit. Most Greek cities, however, simply did not have the resources to compete with the new kingdoms, and had to be content with maintaining their traditional amateur hoplite militias, even if now largely for show.

7 Alexander the Great and Hellenistic Warfare

Alexander the Great, at the battle of Issus in 333 BC, is depicted in this Roman mosaic found at Pompeii. The design is probably modelled on a painting done in Alexander's lifetime. The entire work is shown on p. 123.

By the end of the day on 2 August 338 BC, the effects of the most radical programme of military reform in Greek history were plain to see. The field of battle at Chaeronea was strewn with the bodies of dead Greeks. Exhausted and disordered, they had fallen victim first to a cavalry charge, and then to the inexorable advance of the Macedonian line. The battle at Chaeronea was not simply a victory for a skilled tactician, it was a decisive victory for a revolutionary tactical system that effectively linked units fighting in a variation of the traditional phalanx with light-armed troops and the cavalry. The cavalry were commanded on this day by the son of Philip of Macedon who would become his successor as Alexander III of Macedon. He is better known now as Alexander the Great.

So rapid was the emergence of the new Macedonian system of fighting that the enemies of Philip and Alexander proved incapable of devising an adequate battlefield response. During the next 50 years armies from mainland Greece achieved what had been only a vague dream a decade before Chaeronea. They altered the geopolitical balance between the Mediterranean and the Near East, shifting the centre of political power away from the territory that is now Iraq and southern Iran to the Mediterranean coast. The course of military innovation that enabled this transformation continued to run throughout these years as Greek and Macedonian generals followed the pattern laid down by Philip by incorporating new peoples and fighting techniques into their armies. Within little more than 20 years of their first encounter with war elephants, for example, these generals had incorporated a redesigned version of this weapon – now part beast and part mobile fighting tower – into their tactical operations. These same years, as is the case in genuinely revolutionary periods, also witnessed extraordinary changes in other areas of Greek life as Aristotle's programme of classification was extended by members of the peripatetic school of thought that he had initiated, and was joined by novel philosophic systems developed by Epicurus and Zeno of Citium; Greek drama came to include more realistic representations of daily life, while other forms of poetry synthesized the human experience with mythic traditions, and the canons of Greek art became ever more fluid.

The years of military and intellectual expansion were also years of political instability. At the beginning of this period the kingdom of Macedon arose from chaos to world power. Indeed, when Philip took the throne in 359 BC it was not at all clear that Macedon had much of a future. Philip himself was but 23 years old; his older brother, Perdiccas, had just died in battle. After barely surviving his first 12 months, Philip moved rapidly to secure the resources that he would need to build an effective army, and to create the flexible military machine that would enable him to dominate his foes. In the course of his campaigns he showed not only that he was an extraordinarily innovative warrior willing to adapt new techniques of warfare – especially siege warfare – to his needs, but also that he was a skilled diplomat. Thus it was that, once he had secured control of Greece in the wake of the battle of Chaeronea, he formed a league of Greek states, the League of Corinth, to unite the mainland behind him in a war against the Persian empire, resurrecting the ideology of the great struggles of the 5th century BC to seek the 'freedom of the Greeks' under Persian rule.

Philip's campaign against Persia was cut short by his assassination in 336 BC. Alexander recognized that he needed to continue the struggle if he were to succeed in maintaining control over the mainland. Crossing into Persian territory in 334 BC, it appears that Alexander's initial plan was to secure the 'liberation' of the Greek cities of western Turkey. After annihilating the Persian army that was charged with halting his invasion at the battle of Granicus, and neutralizing the Persian fleet by capturing its bases along the Aegean, he was inevitably drawn more deeply into Persian territory. A massive victory over the Persian king Darius III at Issus in 333 BC (see box overleaf) appears to have convinced Alexander that he could conquer all of the Persian empire. After securing the rest of the Mediterranean coastline – an operation that was highlighted by his remarkable siege of the city of Tyre – he advanced into Iraq. Darius was able to raise one more army, but to no avail. In 331 BC,

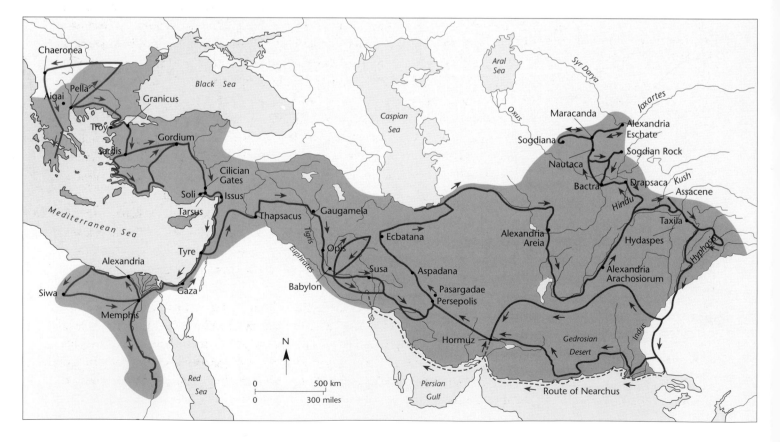

A Babylonian astronomical calendar that records the battle of Gaugamela on 1 October, 331 BC, the defeat of Darius and Alexander's occupation of Babylonia. One of the most interesting aspects of the text is that it mentions Alexander's title 'King of Asia' in the form 'King of the world' since 'Asia' was not a concept recognized by Babylonian astrologers. It also offers a different take on the battle in that it states that Darius' army deserted, a statement that might have been influenced by Alexander's propaganda.

Opposite above Bust of Alexander, found on the island of Delos, and now in the Louvre. As with other portraits, this one stresses the king's youth.

Opposite below The wide-ranging campaigns of Alexander. The tinted area shows the extent of Alexander's conquests at his death in 323 BC.

Alexander destroyed this army at Gaugamela near the modern city of Mosul; Darius fled onto the Iranian plateau, where he was murdered by a cabal of his own generals, one of whom, Bessus, claimed the throne for himself. The pursuit of Bessus led Alexander into Central Asia, where Bessus was finally surrendered to him for punishment by his own supporters in 329 BC. Now the undisputed ruler of the Persian empire, Alexander seems to have found it impossible to stop. Drawn ever eastward, he invaded Afghanistan, and began to found a series of cities in central Asia for veterans who could no longer follow his march. Their place was taken by fresh drafts from Macedon and, despite the opposition of many of his own generals, from the population that he had subdued. In 326 BC, Alexander entered India where he fought his last major battle at the Hydaspes river against the local king Porus, who employed a host of war elephants, a weapon previously unknown in Greek warfare.

Alexander continued to march through India for a year after the battle with Porus before his army declared that it had simply had enough. After brutal fighting on his way west, and further crises brought about by his failure to understand the geography of the region that he had selected for his return – the desert coast of southern Pakistan – he returned to the territory of the Persian empire at the end of 325 BC. The last 18 months of his life were spent planning new expeditions, and bringing a semblance of order to the administration of his empire: unlike many of his Macedonian followers, Alexander understood that the new empire needed to be governed in alliance with the peoples he had conquered. Whether he could have succeeded in forging a genuinely successful polity will never be known, for he died at Babylon in June 323 BC.

The destruction of the Persian empire, and the failure of Alexander's vision to mature, gave rise to various competing and experimental political orders until the deaths of Lysimachus and Seleucus, the last of the new kings who had served on the staff of Alexander, in 281 BC. Thereafter arose three major kingdoms: the Antigonid realm in Macedon; the Seleucid empire that controlled much of the former inland territory of the Persian kings; and the Ptolemaic kingdom in Egypt. The pace of innovation slowed, and was in some cases even reversed. Macedonian armies fell in rapid succession to those of Rome and Seleucid armies rapidly lost ground to the Parthians in the east, and failed even to control the emergent Jewish state in Palestine, while the Egyptian military seems to have imploded by 200. The later 3rd to 2nd centuries BC are characterized by the sacrifice of tactical efficiency to special interest groups, racial prejudice and the collapse of technological innovation into expensive technophilia. At the same time, original philosophic speculation gave way to dogmatic competition between increasingly well-defined schools of thought, immensely original efforts to organize knowledge gave way to librarianship and literary innovation gave way to generic specialization. The torch of innovation passed now to others.

The Battle of Issus

	MACEDONIANS	PERSIANS
COMMANDERS	Alexander the Great	Darius III
STRENGTH	32,000 foot 5,000 cavalry	35,000 foot 5,000 cavalry
CASUALTIES	c. 7,000	c. 25,000

The battle of Issus – famously depicted on a mosaic from Pompeii (shown opposite) – was fought in November 333 BC on a plain transected by the river known in antiquity as the Pinarus. The two armies,

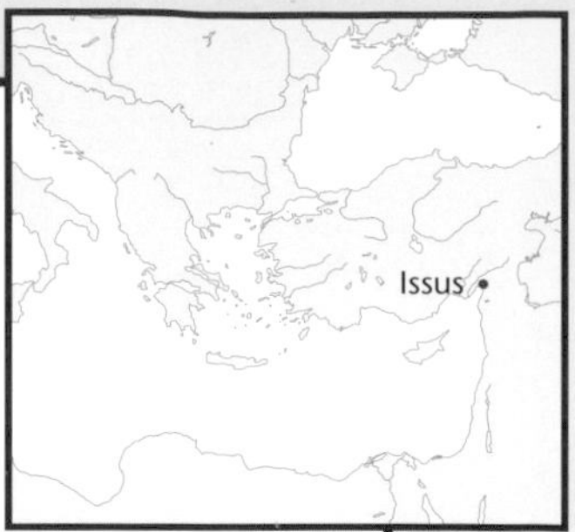

Key to the complex make-up of the two armies:
Macedonians (blue): **1** Companion cavalry; **2** Hypaspists; **3** Macedonian phalanx; **4** Cretan archers; **5** Thracian javelin-men; **6** Allied Greek cavalry; **7** Thessalian cavalry; **8** *Prodromoi*; **9** Paeonian cavalry; **10** Macedonian archers; **11** Agrianian javelin-men; **12** 300 cavalry; **13** Some of the Macedonian archers (ex 10); **14** Greek mercenary infantry;
Persians (red): **1** Persian cataphracts; **2** Slingers and archers; **3** Greek mercenary infantry; **4** Reserves; **5** Hyrcanian and Median cavalry; **6** Persian cavalry; **7** Javelinmen and slingers; **8** Detached infantry.

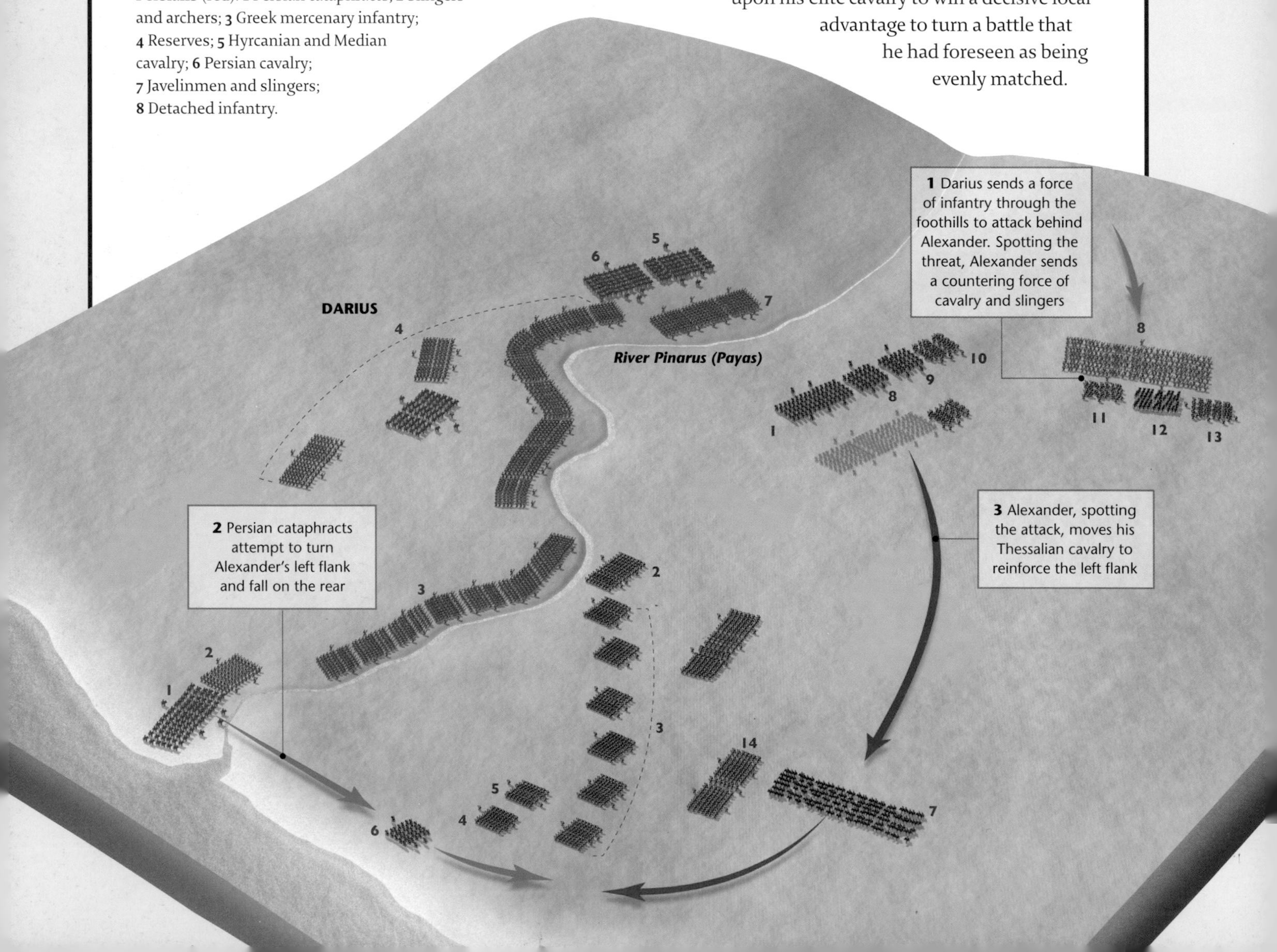

drawn up on a front of roughly 3 km (2 miles), were probably roughly equal in strength. The best estimate for Alexander's force is c. 32,000 foot and 5,000 cavalry, while the Persian army, despite the claims in the ancient sources that it numbered 600,000, must have been roughly the same size: it occupied the same front as Alexander's without significant tactical reserve, a crucial point in deciding the outcome. As the battle began, Darius shifted cavalry to his right flank to surround the Macedonian left. Alexander reinforced his left to hold this attack, ordering the phalanx to pin the Persian centre in place while he exploited a gap between the Persian centre and left with his Companion cavalry, driving directly at the position occupied by Darius. Having no reserves, Darius fled and his army collapsed. A crucial tactical aspect of the battle is that Alexander did not regard the phalanx as potentially decisive, but rather depended upon his elite cavalry to win a decisive local advantage to turn a battle that he had foreseen as being evenly matched.

Issus

DARIUS

River Pinarus (Payas)

1 Darius sends a force of infantry through the foothills to attack behind Alexander. Spotting the threat, Alexander sends a countering force of cavalry and slingers

2 Persian cataphracts attempt to turn Alexander's left flank and fall on the rear

3 Alexander, spotting the attack, moves his Thessalian cavalry to reinforce the left flank

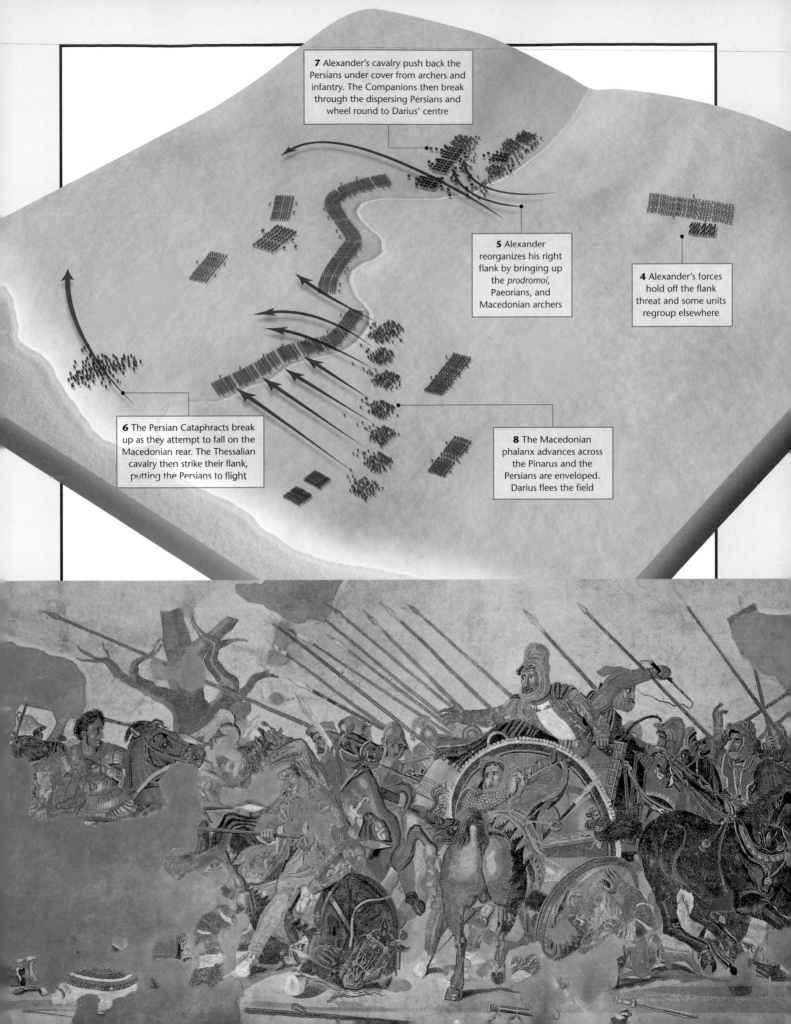

7 Alexander's cavalry push back the Persians under cover from archers and infantry. The Companions then break through the dispersing Persians and wheel round to Darius' centre

5 Alexander reorganizes his right flank by bringing up the *prodromoi*, Paeorians, and Macedonian archers

4 Alexander's forces hold off the flank threat and some units regroup elsewhere

6 The Persian Cataphracts break up as they attempt to fall on the Macedonian rear. The Thessalian cavalry then strike their flank, putting the Persians to flight

8 The Macedonian phalanx advances across the Pinarus and the Persians are enveloped. Darius flees the field

Below Ivory portrait thought to be of Philip II. The right eye appears to be damaged, and we know that Philip lost his right eye in battle in 353 BC. The bust was found in what is believed to be his tomb at Vergina in northern Greece.

Above The iron helmet found in the 'Tomb of Philip' at Vergina is similar to the Phrygian-style helmets that were in common use by the rank and file of Philip's army.

Right This iron cuirass, also found in the 'Tomb of Philip', is an elaborate variation on the linen corselets that were common in the Macedonian army.

PHILIP AND ALEXANDER

Philip II's creation of the new-style Macedonian army was remarkably rapid. Nine years after Philip had assumed the throne, Demosthenes the Athenian orator who spent much of his energy trying to rally Greek resistance to what he (rightly) perceived as the threat growing in Macedon, first uses the word *pezhetairos* in a speech. Although he seems confused about what the term meant, we know that under Alexander this was the word for the soldiers who formed the phalanx, and that under Philip the term was used to define a unit of the phalanx containing the biggest and bravest soldiers. Thus we may conclude that by 349 BC Philip had organized some sections of the army into what would become the classic Macedonian phalanx. Eight years later Demosthenes said that Philip could do whatever he liked 'not because he commands a phalanx of hoplites, but rather because he is accompanied by javelinmen, cavalry, archers, mercenaries and troops of this sort'. By 341 BC then, it would appear that Philip had succeeded in creating an army in which the tactical actions of diverse units were coordinated on the battlefield, and that the core of the army was the phalanx.

Although men with experience outside of Greece recognized that hoplites needed to coordinate with light-armed troops, the lesson seems to have been lost upon generals whose experience was solely of battle on the mainland. The shock of the destruction of a Spartan regiment by light-armed troops in 390 BC does not seem to have caused any serious rethinking of the hoplite-first tactics that had dominated Greek warfare since the 7th century. Philip, however, faced different battlefield conditions than did the average hoplite general. In his first years he had to contend with invasions by Illyrian armies from the north that seem to have specialized in light infantry tactics. His solution – the creation of an infantryman, armed with a 5-m (16-ft) pike (the sarissa) but otherwise lightly armoured who could stand toe-to-toe with the hoplites of traditional Greek armies – made it possible for him to exploit the manpower resources of his kingdom with greater effectiveness than had his predecessors. Philip also built upon the existing strength of the Macedonian

The basic tactical unit of the Macedonian phalanx was the syntagma, with 16 files of 16 men. When the syntagma entered battle the pikes of the first five ranks in each file would project beyond the shields of the soldiers in the front rank. This formation was immensely powerful in defence and on a flat plain, but challenged on ground that made it difficult to keep the ranks intact.

kingdom in cavalry: the children of the nobility were recruited into a special guard unit – the original Companions (*hetairoi*) – and trained with most of the other cavalry units to charge home against any formation other than a hoplite phalanx.

While we have no reliable descriptions of the battles in which Philip defeated the Illyrians, it is not unreasonable to assume that one factor in his success was simply that he had the ability to put more men in the field. Another was that the new infantrymen, trained to fight in a phalanx of 16 ranks, were able to control the centre of a battlefield against less well-organized forces, while his light infantry and cavalry could carry the fight into areas where a phalanx would not be effective; it was often a well-timed cavalry charge that decided a battle. Neither Philip nor Alexander seem to have regarded the phalanx as a decisive unit. Indeed, as accounts of the battles of Chaeronea (338 BC) and Issus (333 BC), as well the less well-known battle of Crannon against allied Greek states in 323 BC, suggest, the Macedonian phalanx was not more effective than the traditional hoplite phalanx. It was a cavalry charge that started the rout at Chaeronea; the phalanx did not defeat Darius' hoplites at Issus, and indeed lost to hoplites at Crannon.

One of Demosthenes' constant complaints about Philip was that he was able to disorganize his opposition through diplomacy. Put another way, what Demosthenes observed was that Philip understood that war was waged off the battlefield as well as on it, that he understood the psychology of his opponents. Descriptions of Chaeronea suggest that this was also true on the battlefield, for it seems that he exploited the inherent aggressiveness of his rivals and tricked them into launching attacks that served only to exhaust their men. Alexander's mastery of the psychology of battle is even more evident in his set-piece encounters with the Persians. The Persian command structure was severely hierarchical and if the commander could be neutralized or killed, then the whole force was likely to fall apart. In all three of his great battles with the Persians Alexander led an attack of the Companion cavalry directly at the enemy commander. Indeed, Alexander's concept of generalship appears to have been that once the battle line was set, the best thing he could do would be to take personal command of the decisive attack, relying on his own tactical sense rather than that of a subordinate. In all three battles he gave away the advantage of being able to pick the terrain to the enemy, ensuring that they would be tempted to fight on ground that they regarded as advantageous when his own strategy required a decisive encounter. At Granicus in 334 BC, for instance, he needed a victory for political reasons at home, and to remove the Persian army so that he could capture the bases of the Persian fleet on the coast. At Issus, he seems to have been out-generalled by Darius III, who had succeeded in placing the Persian army across his line of supply, while, at Gaugamela, he was operating at great distance from his bases. It was only at Hydaspes river, confronting an Indian enemy whose tactics were well beyond the experience of any Greek, that his effort to win with his cavalry failed. That battle was won by the phalanx, which could take on Porus' elephants.

If Philip and Alexander excelled at anticipating the responses of their enemies on the battlefield, they excelled no less in their capacity for siege warfare. Again it was Philip who showed the way for his son. It appears that Dionysius I of Syracuse was the first Greek to use the torsion catapult for his capture of the Sicilian city of Motya in 397 BC, but that weapon seems to have been so generally ignored on the mainland that Aeneas the Tactician, writing in the 350s BC, does not mention it as a threat to a city under siege. Philip, however, recognized the potential of a weapon that would enable the capture of a city by storm, and his ability to seize fortified areas in a very short period of time shocked his rivals. He appears to have deployed a full siege train including rams and towers (see box overleaf) as well as catapults against Amphipolis in 357 BC, and his catapult bolts have been identified amongst the remains of Olynthus, which he stormed in 348 BC. Alexander brought experts in siege warfare, *katapeltaphetai*, with him, and their extraordinary accomplishments at places such as Tyre show that they could construct massive weapons on the spot and improve their technology as the years passed.

Another characteristic of both Philip and Alexander was their willingness to incorporate conquered peoples within their own armies. In the case of Alexander, the incorporation of Persians directly into the Macedonian army caused a crisis between himself and substantial elements within his own army that remained unresolved at the time of his death. Although Alexander was committed to a policy of integration, his soldiers resented the notion that they should share their privileged

Scene from the sarcophagus of Abdalonymus of Tyre depicting Alexander in action against the Persians, reflecting both Alexander's tendency to fight in the front ranks at decisive moments, and his dependence on cavalry to strike decisive blows in battle.

Siege Engines

Prior to the lifetime of Philip basic siege techniques involved circumvallation to starve a place that could not be carried by direct assault into submission, or the construction of ramps to give attackers access to the walls. It was only with the invention of spear-throwing devices (*oxybeleis*) and stone throwers (*petrobaloi*) which worked through the application of rotational force to a latitudinal bar, that it became possible to attack the walls of a city from a distance. In the later 4th century BC (possibly already in the lifetime of Alexander) an enormous advance took place in the technology of these machines with the introduction of machines that derived their power from the rotational force applied to a longitudinal bar. These machines, known as *katapeltai* when using arrows and *lithoboloi* or *petroboloi* when hurling rocks, had an effective range of about 150 m (500 ft). Stone-throwers had the force to be able to destroy walls through bombardment.

Stone- and spearthrowers were also incorporated into siege towers such as Demetrius' *helepolis*, the 140-m (460-ft) high structure used for the siege of Rhodes in 304 BC. This tower was moved into position by a team of 200 men who operated a capstan that moved the eight iron clad wheels with which it was equipped. The development of siege technology in the late 4th century was such that while, prior to the lifetime of Philip, successful sieges were rare, 59 out the 79 sieges attempted between 317 and 303 BC were successful.

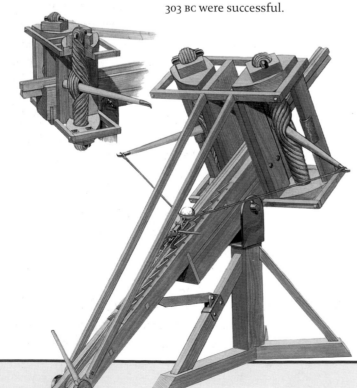

Above Demetrius' *helepolis* was a sort of proto-tank designed to enable close rank bombardment of the Rhodian city wall from 20 war machines on its nine floors ranging from *lithoboloi* on the lowest level to dart throwers on the top.

Left *Lithoboloi* such as the one depicted here were designed to hurl stones that ranged in size from 5 to 80 kg (10 to 180 lb). At close range these machines could destroy a city-wall. They do not seem to have been used for tactical purposes in open battle.

position with peoples whom they felt to be barbarians. Nor did the problem end with Alexander's death. Even though his immediate successors, pressed as they seem to have been to find soldiers to support their endless wars, used some units of non-Greek soldiers, they resisted the full-scale integration of their core units. It was only in 217 BC that Ptolemy IV, facing a severe manpower shortage, recruited large numbers of Egyptians directly into his phalanx. The Greek historian Polybius said that the result was disaster, leading to indigenous revolts throughout Egypt, and his view that this was a bad idea appears to have been widely shared. The result was that the Seleucids were never able to exploit the potential manpower resources of their vast territory, and that the Antigonids of Macedon never developed clear superiority in numbers over the states of southern Greece.

THE SUCCESSORS TO ALEXANDER

Coin of Ptolemy I, the friend and companion of Alexander who became the first Macedonian king of Egypt. As was typical of the Macedonians of his generation, he was a highly competent soldier; he was less typical in that he proved a highly competent ruler in peace as well as war.

Alexander died without an obvious heir. His half-brother, Philip III, was generally thought to be incompetent, and Alexander's wife, Roxane, was pregnant. Alexander's own ambiguous last word on the subject – heard either as *tôi Kraterôi* a recommendation for the general Craterus, a senior marshal who had recently been dispatched to western Asia with a large force of veterans, or *tôi kratistôi*, 'to the strongest' – did nothing to help. To complicate the situation further, Philip's longtime aid, Antipater, was still regent of Macedon, and could not be ignored. After full scale civil war was barely averted at Babylon, a compromise was reached by which Philip III and, the child of Roxane, if the child should prove to be male (as was in fact the case, and he became Alexander IV) should rule jointly, with effective government divided between Perdiccas, a general in Babylon, Craterus as 'representative' (*prostates*) of the kings and Antipater as regent for Europe. Other territories were distributed to various generals as satrapies, with Egypt going to Ptolemy son of Lagus, and some sort of superior command over western Asia being granted to Antigonus the 'one eyed' who was then holding satrapy of Phrygia.

Perhaps the only thing that kept this unwieldy compromise together for the 18 months that it lasted was the fact that a major revolt was breaking out in Greece. Athens took a leading role in the revolt, with an army vastly enhanced by a large force of mercenaries that had assembled on the southern tip of Laconia in the last year of Alexander's life. The assembly of this force stemmed from Alexander's effort to demobilize former Greek mercenaries of the Persian king serving various authorities in the west. The problem was that these mercenaries knew no other trade and did not wish to be disbanded so much as they wished a new master. Reinforced by professionals, the Athenian army defeated Antipater at Crannon and besieged him within the city. Craterus marched to rescue Antipater while a fleet assembled from Phoenicia destroyed the Athenian navy in battle off the island of Amorgos. This would prove to be the last battle in which the trireme was the main line warship.

With Craterus and Antipater in Europe, Perdiccas tried to assert his authority over 'the whole', as contemporaries called Alexander's empire. The result was civil war in which Perdiccas soon proved unequal to his ambition, dying in a mutiny. But he was not the only casualty of significance in this campaign. Craterus too had fallen, leading a cavalry charge against Eumenes of Cardia, who commanded Perdiccas' troops in Anatolia, and who would continue to resist the victorious alliance for three more

Grave monument of a soldier who died fighting at the battle of Corupedion in 281 BC, where Seleucus defeated Lysimachus; it was the last battle between generals who had fought with Alexander. This monument reflects the continued use of civic levies in royal armies.

years before Antigonus suborned his exhausted troops. War between the generals continued for 15 more years until Antigonus, who sought to secure his own claim to 'the whole', died in battle against Seleucus at Ipsus in 301 BC. Seleucus had taken over the eastern satrapies in 312 BC, and claimed the title of king six years later, after the last members of Alexander's family had been massacred by Cassander, son of Antipater and ruler of Macedon following his father's death in 319 BC. Seleucus' claim to the title followed a move by Antigonus, who was proclaimed king after a naval victory off Salamis on Cyprus in 306 BC, and the other major players of the time – Ptolemy, Cassander and Lysimachus.

The successors of Alexander showed that they had absorbed the traditions of Philip and Alexander, and that they were capable of expanding upon what they had learned. Battles in the decades after Alexander's death were largely determined by cavalry charges around the fringes of the phalanx, while new troop types were regularly integrated into the mix of armies that often contained a high proportion of non-Greeks trained in the latest tactics. The armies of Antigonus and Eumenes, for instance, employed eastern cavalry units, elephants and non-Greek phalanxes, brigaded separately from Greek units. The logistical support for their operations, and indeed those of all the other successors, were sufficient to support long, and often very rapid, movements, while technological innovation was the order of the day in both naval and siege warfare.

At the same time, great stress was also placed on the personal performance of the kings as warriors as well as generals. Thus in the battle at the Fort of the Camels on the Nile in 320 BC, where he took advantage of prepared defences to drive off the forces of Perdiccas, Ptolemy is said to have fought in the front rank and to have blinded an elephant, while in the battle where he defeated Craterus, Eumenes engaged in single combat with a particularly hated former colleague. Thrown from their horses they fought hand to hand, and when he had crippled his foe with a blow to the hamstring, Eumenes exulted over him in a way that recalled heroes in Homer before administering a death blow and stripping off his armour. Three years later, a cavalry charge led by Antigonus and his son Demetrius halted Eumenes' advance long enough for a successful flanking manoeuvre to capture Eumenes' camp. A similar manoeuvre was not so successful at Ipsus in 301 BC, where Demetrius pursued the wing of the Seleucid army that he had routed too far. Seleucus threw out a screen of elephants to prevent Demetrius' return while he encircled Antigonus' phalanx with the cavalry under his personal command, offering his enemies a chance to desert, which, ultimately, some portion did, to the ruin of the line as a whole. Antigonus himself was killed by a hail of javelins.

The ability to adjust to new situations was not simply a feature of land warfare. Neither Philip nor Alexander had any profound understanding of war at sea. Although Alexander made up for this by depriving the Persian fleet of its bases in Asia Minor, he had no use for fleets himself as anything but appendages to his land campaigns, and even then, he had minimal understanding of the constraints of wind and tide under which ships needed to operate. The same cannot be said of his successors, who raised naval warfare to new levels of technological and tactical achievement.

The crucial development of the early Hellenistic period was the replacement of the trireme, with three banks of oars with a single rower for each oar, by ships using

Right Antiochus I's victory over Celtic invaders of Turkey in 275 BC was in part due to his use of elephants, and this is commemorated by terracottas such as this one, showing a Celtic warrior being trampled.

Below A 3rd-century BC representation of an African war elephant on an Italian bowl; the Carthaginians adopted the use of war elephants under the influence of Greek practice.

Below right This 3rd-century BC plate, found in Italy's Ager Faliscus (a territory near Rome), depicts a female war elephant with her cub, and clearly represents an Indian mahout as well as two pikemen in the fighting tower.

The larger ships of the early Hellenistic period, of which the hepteres depicted here was one, show considerable technical advances over earlier ships. The upward slope of the oar benches towards the centre of the ship made it possible to accommodate more oarsmen in each bank.

A coin of Demetrius showing Victory on the prow of a warship, issued to celebrate Demetrius' victory over Ptolemy off Cyprus in 306 BC.

multiple oarsmen per bank. The earliest model for this sort of vessel, the tetreres, with four men to a bank, was evidently developed in Sicily during the early years of the 4th century BC, but was adopted very slowly in the eastern Mediterranean. The Athenian navy of 326/5 BC possessed only 50 tetrereis, and a mere seven pentereis (five men to a bank) out of a total of 417 hulls, and the (admittedly unreliable) record of Alexander's ship building in the last year of his life suggests that he too regarded the trireme as the basic battleship. But by 306 BC, when we get details of the ships used in the naval encounter off Salamis in Cyprus, it appears that the basic warships were the tetrereis and pentereis. Extensive use was made of bolt throwers mounted on the prows of ships, while ship-to-ship duels were decided either by ramming or boarding. The striking thing here is that, although the basic ship types had been available for nearly a century, the replacement of the trireme, and experimentation with variations on the tetreres/penteres (largely by Demetrius) took place in the 15 years after Amorgos.

Demetrius' naval innovations, which ultimately included the construction of pentekaidekareis and hekkaidekereis, essentially triremes with 15 or 16 oarsmen for each oar bank, were but one feature of a fertile technological imagination that excited awe even from his enemies. Even Lysimachus, who hated him, asked for, and was given, a tour of his camp and came away expressing admiration for the machines that he was able to construct, while the Rhodians, who successfully withstood a siege, asked that he leave his massive *helepolis* (siege tower) behind so that they could have it as a memorial of the greatness of the man they had defeated. His was an example that other kings sought to follow, though, in time, without his sense that technology needed to have practical application.

The personal involvement of the king in battle, and the linkage between royal power and military display did not end with the deaths of Demetrius (285 BC), Lysimachus and Seleucus (both in 281 BC). The image of the king as a warrior continued to inform the ideology of all three major royal houses, as well, ultimately, of the one that emerged in Pergamon in the decades after the death of Seleucus. Even though kings obtained new roles as patrons of the arts, and would continue the tradition begun under Alexander (if not, indeed, by Philip at the end of his life) of equating their power with that of the gods, the inherent militarism of their position served to intensify the already prevalent tendency in the Greek world to define status through the capacity for violence, and of individual city-states to wage war with their neighbours. Cities were filled with memorials of battle, and groups of states in areas such as Crete and Aetolia would join together to engage in collective acts of piracy to enhance their status in the world at large. For young men, the choice of a career as a mercenary was opened up by the insatiable demands not only of royal armies for new recruits, but also the needs of individual states for increasingly professionalized defence forces. The question of whether royal militarism was simply a reflection of a more general ethos of interstate violence, was itself a contributing factor to the development of this ethos, or, perforce became one as kings lacked the inclination to seek alternative ways of solving their differences, must remain, for now at least, an open question.

The militaristic ethos of the 3rd century BC gave rise to a far more sophisticated mercenary culture than had existed previously. While mercenary service was scarcely novel in the Greek world of this time, the terms that soldiers could demand appear to have improved dramatically. Kings and aspiring strongmen needed to be seen as good paymasters. Rare was the circumstance when rebellious mercenaries would simply be slaughtered. More common would be arrangements such as those reached by Eumenes I of Pergamon with a group of mutinous mercenaries, who received a generous settlement for agreeing to rejoin his service. It is in this period that we begin to sense that general practice was that mercenaries would sign on for four-month terms, after which they might be resigned or move on, while the ultimate privilege was to obtain a grant of land where the band could settle down once it had negotiated an end to its fighting days. The result was that by the end of the 2nd century BC Asia Minor was littered with new settlements that had the coincidental effect of spreading Greek culture into the hinterland. The urge to settlement is a sign of the hardships that drove men to abandon all that they had grown up with to seek a better life through war. It was not an easy choice, perhaps, but it is also one that is reflective of a world where military service was a ready alternative to trade, or the sort of civic colonization that had been characteristic of earlier periods of Greek history.

STAGNATION

High levels of military competence continued to be a feature of Hellenistic kingship in the generation that followed the death of Seleucus in 281 BC. Ptolemy II of Egypt waged a series of aggressive wars against his dynastic rivals, gaining some success against Antiochus I in the 'First Syrian War' (274–271 BC), a badly documented struggle stemming from claims that Seleucus had cheated Ptolemy I of territorial concessions following the defeat of Antigonus. In the next decade Ptolemy II attempted to overthrow the nascent Antigonid power in Greece with the aid of a league of Greek states – the Chremonidean War of 265–260 BC – and, to wrest still more territory from Antiochus in the 'Second Syrian War', an even more poorly documented struggle that lasted from 260 to c. 253 BC. Although these efforts proved futile, ending with the loss of some territory in Asia Minor to the Seleucids and of influence in Greece after Antigonid naval victories off Cos and Ephesus, they betray the continuation of the notion that a king should seek to rule 'the whole', and that the kings still had the logistical ability to make war on a vast scale. Ptolemy III's attack on the Seleucid empire in the 'Third Syrian War' of 246–241 BC was perhaps the most spectacular of all these efforts, as Ptolemaic armies reached Babylon before concluding a peace that left Ptolemy with some territorial gains in Asia Minor and control of Laodicea on the Lycus, the harbour that served the Seleucid capital at Antioch. But it was in the ensuing generation that the military rot set in across the Hellenistic world.

It is unfortunate that we have no detailed description of any of the wars of the 3rd century BC that would enable us to know why the Ptolemies and Seleucids abandoned the policy of including non-Greeks in their main line units. All we can know is that the main strength of both the Seleucid and Ptolemaic armies consisted of Greeks who held land in a semi-feudal arrangement through their assignment to *katoikiai*. *Katoikiai* consisted of soldiers who held an allotment of land (*kleros*) from the king, and owed military service in return for this grant. Although we cannot be certain of it, the system of *katoikiai* may have developed out of Alexander's settlement of groups of veterans in eastern cities during his long march to India.

The result of these grants was catastrophic: the military class failed to reproduce itself, meaning that armies became progressively weaker even though the *klerouchoi*, as the grant-holders were called, seem to have retained sufficient political influence to prevent the integration of native soldiers into their formations. By the end of the 3rd century BC it appears that the total Greek military establishment of Seleucid settlements was reduced to a total of roughly 55,000 men. Efforts to bolster the numbers through the recruitment of mercenaries and units of non-Greeks, serving as 'national contingents', were notably lacklustre. At the height of his power in 217 BC, Antiochus III could muster, in addition to his military settlers, no more than 12,000 mercenaries and 19,500 other troops, meaning that the total manpower directly available to the Seleucid king was less than 90,000 men. The Ptolemies were even worse off, for by 217 BC, only 5,000 Greeks were available for the phalanx, to which were added 3,000 members of the royal guard and 2,000 peltasts, and 700 household cavalry. The rest of the army, prior to the recruitment of 20,000 Egyptians for the phalanx, consisted of 8,000 Greek mercenaries, 2,000 freshly recruited Greek cavalry, 3,000 Libyans trained as peltasts, 2,300 Egyptian and Libyan cavalry that could be brigaded with the household cavalry (possibly reflecting earlier Ptolemaic concern with the declining number of Greeks at their disposal), 3,000 Cretans and 6,000 Gallic or Thracian troops, of whom 4,000 were *katoikoi*, as well as 73 African elephants.

More problematic than the failure to exploit the potential manpower resources of their kingdoms, was the fact that the armies of Antiochus III and Ptolemy V were less flexible than those that had contended for mastery after the death of Alexander. Polybius' account of the battle of Raphia in 217 BC suggests that there had been minimal development in tactical doctrine during the previous century. Antiochus placed himself on the left side of his line with the intention of engaging Ptolemy in hand-to-hand combat (something that did not happen), and simply pursued his enemies off the field after they had been disordered by the failure of their elephants. Ptolemy retreated under cover of his phalanx, and when his own left wing trounced the right wing of Antiochus, ordered what proved to be a successful attack by his own phalanx. Learning through observation of the dust cloud shrouding the battlefield that the rest of his army was in retreat, Antiochus withdrew to his camp, which Ptolemy made no effort to attack. It is perhaps ironic that Polybius tells us that both kings tried to inspire their armies by reciting the deeds of their ancestors. Both were young men with no accomplishments of their own, but in a war that was fought to resolve a quarrel that

The Battle of Cynoscephalae

The battle of Cynoscephalae – the name comes from a chain of hills near Volos in Greece – was contested between the Macedonians under Philip V and a Roman army under Titus Quinctius Flamininus in May or June, 197 BC. Each force numbered about 25,000 men. On the night before the battle, the armies encamped on the opposite sides of the ridge-line. In the morning, covered by a deep mist, light troops from each side mounted the top of the ridge and began to engage. At the news of the encounter, both generals mustered their main forces, with Philip reaching the top of the ridge before the Romans, though, in the process, his left wing became detached from the centre. When Philip's phalanx charged and began to press the Romans backwards, a tribune on the Roman right wing, noticing the gap between the Macedonian left and centre, detached 20 maniples, roughly 2,000 men, and attacked the Macedonian centre from the rear, causing the army to rout. The flexibility of a Roman army that allowed junior officers to have tactical discretion decided the battle; Philip's plan, which depended on his phalanx, left no place for tactical manoeuvres by other units once the battle began.

Above Titus Quinctius Flamininus, the victor at Cynoscephalae, was perhaps a better diplomat than general. His battlefield victory over Philip stemmed from the inspiration of a subordinate, but his diplomatic campaign in Greece before and after the battle was brilliant.
Below Plan of Cynoscephalae, showing the turning point of the battle.

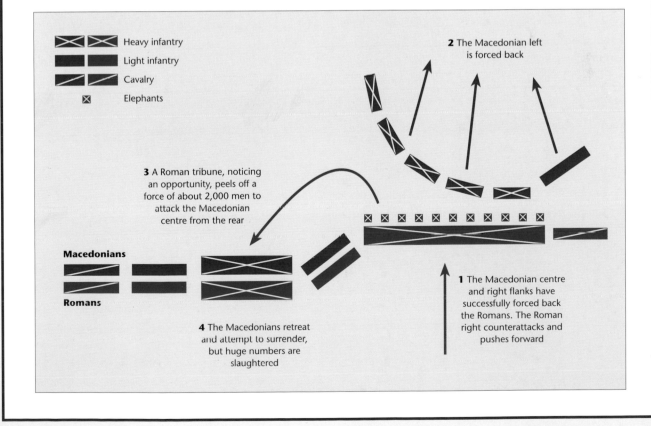

Heavy infantry

Light infantry

Cavalry

Elephants

2 The Macedonian left is forced back

3 A Roman tribune, noticing an opportunity, peels off a force of about 2,000 men to attack the Macedonian centre from the rear

Macedonians

Romans

1 The Macedonian centre and right flanks have successfully forced back the Romans. The Roman right counterattacks and pushes forward

4 The Macedonians retreat and attempt to surrender, but huge numbers are slaughtered

Legion versus phalanx: this picture shows the crucial difference between the tactics of the two units: the Romans placed far greater stress on the skills of their soldiers in single combat. Here the soldiers of the phalanx (on the right) attempt to maintain the stability of their formation, while Roman soldiers seek to work between the pikes of their enemies to make use of their swords.

went back to the respective founders of their dynasties, it is also a sign that the past had come all too much to dominate modes of thought in the present.

A feature of Antiochus III's career is that he seems to have learned from the experience at Raphia. In 189 BC he confronted a far more dangerous enemy than Ptolemy, a Roman army amongst whose commanders was none other than Scipio Africanus, the victor of the battle of Zama, fought against the Carthaginians in 202 BC. The battle took place near the city of Magnesia on the Meander and was the second of three major conflicts that revealed the complete inferiority of the contemporary form of warfare in the eastern Mediterranean as compared to that of Rome. Philip V of Macedon had gone down in defeat at Cynoscephalae in Thessaly in 197 BC (see box on p. 135), and his son, Perseus, would suffer a similar fate at Pydna in 168 BC. The battle of Magnesia in 189 BC was perhaps the worst of these great confrontations, for it matched an incompetent general in Antiochus III against one of the best soldiers of the age. The result of the contest was determined as soon as Antiochus lost control of his own battle plan. Having taken personal command of the cavalry on his right wing he managed to rout the Roman legion opposite him, but then, instead of turning on the Roman line, he pursued the defeated Romans to the camp, where they managed to rally and draw him into further assaults. The rest of his army collapsed as he was pressing his attacks. On the far left Antiochus had set scythed chariots in front of his own cavalry, and in the centre he had arrayed 22 elephants between battalions of the phalanx. The scythed chariots were thrown into confusion by light infantry allied with the Romans and managed to rout their own cavalry as they fell back. In the centre, the Romans did not even close with the phalanx, preferring instead to bombard both it and the elephants with javelins until the elephants routed into the troops to which they were adjacent. As a basic rule of war, elephants were never brigaded with other troops precisely because they could not be controlled. They were effective if they could charge home in advance of their own battle line to disorder the enemy, or as a screen for infantry against opposing cavalry. The point of these dispositions was that an army broken by elephants could not reform, while, if the charge failed it had best do so where the animals could not turn on their own men.

THE LAST CENTURY OF HELLENISTIC WARFARE

The Roman legion had long been a threat to the Greek army, and in the last two decades of the 3rd century BC Hannibal (see p. 147) had shown how an army could be shaped that could contend with the Romans. Why then did the military systems of the eastern Mediterranean not adjust? The answer may lie in the linkage between the warfare and the position of the king. The army of Alexander remained the model for later armed forces, just as the example of Alexander remained a model for the role of the king in battle. The perception that royal power depended upon the ability to display certain forms of military power caused kings to mount massive displays of their traditional power, and to invest in useless display pieces such as a tesserakontere, or ship with 40 rowers per group of oars that Ptolemy IV constructed in the latter half of the 3rd century BC. If being a king meant having an army that evoked the army of Alexander, then the pressure against reform was almost irresistible. Failure to adjust to changing circumstances doomed the Seleucids to a series of catastrophic campaigns against the new Parthian power that began to arise on the Iranian plateau in the course of the 2nd century BC, and helps explain why the small armies of the Maccabees in Palestine were able to carve out an independent state only a few hundred miles from Antioch. It may also explain why Perseus of Macedon, even though he had the examples of Cynoscephalae and Magnesia before him, tried to fight Rome with an army that was in no significant way different from that of his father, and why, in 146 BC, the Achaean league faced the Romans with an army of hoplites. The power of the tradition can be seen even later as Mithridates of Pontus, whose view of kingship seems to have embraced both Achaemenid and Greek traditions, equipped an army based on the phalanx for his first war with Rome in 89 BC.

Mithridates learned from his experience. Before he went to war with Rome for the third time in 76 BC, he made some attempt to retrain his forces with the aid of Roman drill instructors, and another army, raised by King Deiotaurus of Galatia in the middle of the century, was organized in Roman fashion from the start. But by then it was too late. The Roman general Pompey the Great brought the Seleucid regime to a formal end in 63 BC, when he organized the central lands of Seleucid Syria into the Roman province of Syria, and, 30 years later, Cleopatra of Egypt joined her fate to that of Mark Antony. The Macedonian kingdom had been dissolved after Perseus' failure in 167 BC, and Rome had acquired the kingdom of Pergamon through the last will and testament of its last king, Attalus III, to form the basis of their province of Asia. Macedonian-style armies would reappear, from time to time, thereafter – 10,000 phalangites were offered by the king of Commagene to the Romans at the siege of Jerusalem in AD 70, and the Roman emperor Caracalla created a Macedonian phalanx as part of his own fantasy about Alexander around 215 – but these were eccentricities.

The deadly verve and originality that characterized the art of war in the 4th and 3rd centuries BC had long since given way to a doomed form of Alexander-imitation that missed the point of what the real Alexander had attempted.

8 Armies of the Roman Republic

Two Latin hoplites in full panoply (save for their shields) from the late 4th century BC are represented on these bone plaques found at the city of Praeneste, about 40 km (25 miles) southeast of Rome.

The Roman Republic created the most potent military machine the ancient world ever knew and used it to create an empire equally unprecedented, stretching from the North Sea to the Sahara, and from the Atlantic to the Euphrates. The army that created this colossus was drawn from the farms of Italy, organized, trained, and led by aristocrats for whom war was the gateway to political power. Underlying their military triumphs, however, was a quietly spectacular political and diplomatic one: the amalgamation of Italy into a vast coalition of Roman citizens and allies, creating the deep reservoir of manpower that enabled the Republic to defeat Hannibal and then go on to conquer Spain, Northern Italy and the great Hellenistic powers within half a century. Yet this same army also became the instrument of the Republic's demise, first by enabling Caesar in Gaul to rival Pompey as a conqueror and then, when political tensions came to a head, by establishing Caesar's monarchy and, after his death, his son's.

WARRIORS AND WARBANDS

Early Italy was a world of warbands. Although we are accustomed to thinking of wars waged by states, it is not clear that state formation had advanced sufficiently during the 7th and 8th centuries BC to permit rulers to marshal formal armies. Rather, social bonds structured war-making. Groups of warriors clustered around prominent leaders – like the Etruscan heroes Caeles and Aulus Vibenna, the 'king' of Clusium, Lars Porsenna, or even the 6th-century BC Roman leader, Publius Valerius. Their service was based on personal loyalty, not citizenship or deference to a government. Occasionally these bands succeeded in establishing control of a city, as Mastarna, a follower of the Vibenna brothers, did at Rome after the latters' deaths – Roman tradition knew him as King Servius Tullius. But just as often they were stateless freebooters, *condottieri*. The exception was long thought to be the Greeks, who colonized southern Italy and Campania in the 7th and 6th centuries BC, bringing their distinctive style of fighting, the hoplite phalanx, with them, whence it spread to Etruria. However, the appearance of the phalanx in Greece is now thought to post-date this period. In all likelihood, therefore, Greeks, Etruscans, and Romans all fought with a variety of weapons in mixed bands, larger or smaller depending on the importance of the occasion and the prestige of the leaders involved. Some warriors will have appeared in full panoply, others with only part, and still others armed only with stones or javelins.

At Rome this situation began to change in the 6th century BC with a series of reforms traditionally attributed to King Servius Tullius. He established a new, 'Roman' army, one drawn from the whole citizenry. To ensure it was as large as possible, he changed the basis of citizenship from birth to simple residence. He also established a new citizen assembly, the *comitia centuriata* or 'assembly of the centuries', which was simply the army meeting as a deliberative body in its military units, the 'hundreds'. This assembly allowed the army to give its assent to any war the king intended to embark on and that its members would have to fight. In addition, Servius probably established a census intended, first, to establish the number of citizens and, second, to ascertain how many of them were able to equip themselves for war. The latter formed the *classis*; those with less wealth were *infra classem*, or 'below the *classis*'. Finally, a small group of aristocratic cavalrymen had their mounts provided at public expense. With this new army, Servius and his successor Tarquin the Proud were able to establish a hegemony over their neighbours.

Even after the monarchy fell and a Republic was established, Rome remained dominant in central Italy, as a treaty struck with the powerful city of Carthage around 509 BC reveals. Yet the 5th century BC brought major challenges as hill-tribes filtered into the fertile lowlands. Rome found itself in a fight for survival, and it is difficult to know how often its 'national' army took the field and how often the wars were waged by warbands under the command of clan-leaders, as in the case of the defeat of the Fabii, wiped out almost to a man by a neighbouring tribe. Yet the severity of the threat forced the Romans to bury their differences and work together, and gradually they prevailed – despite disasters like their defeat by a band of Gauls in 390 BC and the subsequent capture of the city. By the mid-4th century BC Rome had established itself as hegemon in central Italy, subdued its neighbours and incorporated them into its citizen body, and begun to establish the system of alliances with peoples and cities further afield that would be the cornerstone of its control over the Italian peninsula.

The extent of the Roman Republic and the sites and regions mentioned in this chapter.

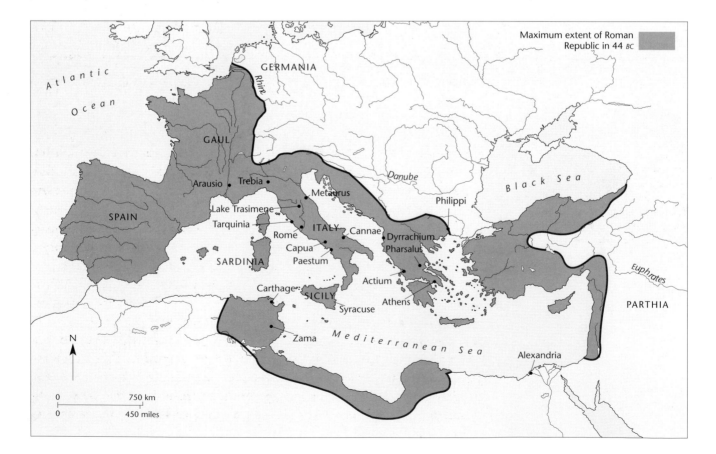

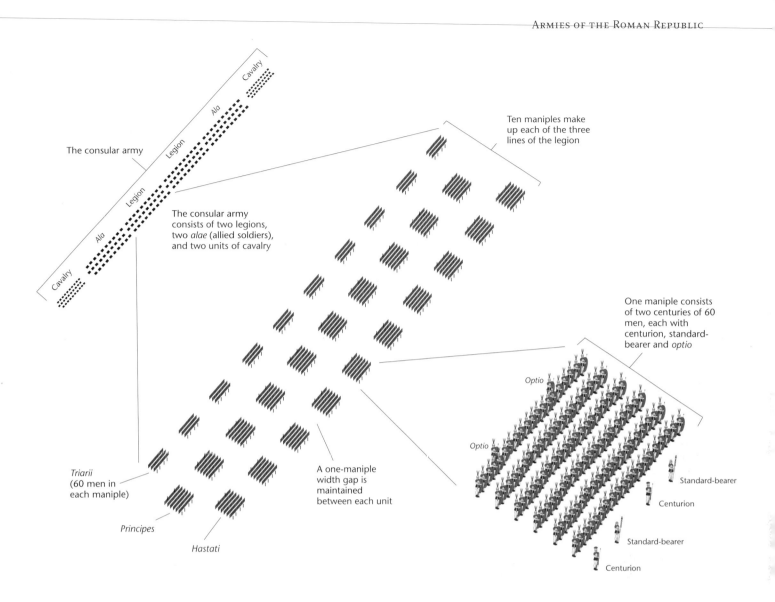

The consular army

The consular army consists of two legions, two *alae* (allied soldiers), and two units of cavalry

Ten maniples make up each of the three lines of the legion

One maniple consists of two centuries of 60 men, each with centurion, standard-bearer and *optio*

Optio

Optio

Standard-bearer

Centurion

Standard-bearer

Centurion

Triarii (60 men in each maniple)

A one-maniple width gap is maintained between each unit

Principes

Hastati

The Roman order of battle, manipular phase (*c.* 300–100 BC). Breaking the legion into maniples – discrete blocks of infantrymen capable of independent manoeuvre in battle – afforded the legions flexibility and resilience under the stress of hand-to-hand combat.

MANIPLES

The manipular army won Rome its empire. Its origins are poorly understood, but sometime in the latter part of the 4th century BC, Rome reorganized its forces into small tactical units called maniples, literally 'handfuls'. At this time, Rome was engaged in a long, hard struggle against the Samnites, tribes occupying Italy's south-central highlands. The ineffectiveness of massed formations against the looser fighting style of the Samnite warriors led Rome to adopt similar tactics. Rome broke the dense mass of its armies into squads of legionaries, the maniples, which were arrayed in three lines. Ten maniples, each containing 120 men, made up the first line, the *hastati*. Behind them were ten maniples of *principes*, likewise 120 men strong, and in the rear were ten maniples of *triarii* with 60 men (making 3,000 men in total). Maniples in each line were separated from their neighbours by a gap equal to their own fronts while maniples in the lines to the rear were positioned behind these gaps. How this formation, known as the *quincunx*, operated in battle is unclear: possibly the maniples of the first line somehow spread out as they moved into action. Or perhaps the gaps were maintained in combat, allowing the maniples of

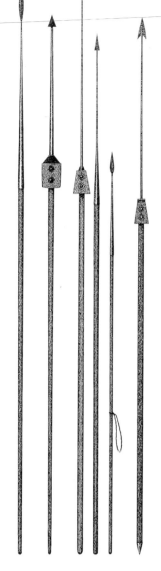

the first and second lines to fall back if they were hard pressed or the maniples of the second or third line to be brought forward to replace the *hastati* when they became exhausted.

Within the maniples, each soldier occupied about six feet of space, about double what fighters in close array had previously required, owing to changes in the legionaries' weaponry. Heavy infantrymen now fought with an oblong shield, the *scutum*, a short stabbing sword, the *gladius*, and throwing spears, *pila*, replacing the hoplite's long thrusting spear (except for the *triarii*, who alone retained it). Wielding swords and throwing spears meant each man needed more room to fight. A more open type of helmet permitted the greater field of vision this new order of battle required. The looser formation also permitted soldiers in the rear ranks of the maniple to step forward and relieve front-rank fighters and the latter to fall back more easily. This ability to keep fresh fighters in the 'killing zone' gave the legions a major advantage in battle (see box overleaf).

In addition to the heavy infantry, a legion (of 4,500 men) also comprised 1,200 light-armed troops, the *velites*, who carried smaller shields and throwing spears, along with 300 cavalry drawn from citizens rich enough to own horses. In addition to skirmishing at the outset of any battle, the *velites* and cavalry were critical in scouting, foraging and pillaging the countryside, and the comparatively high proportion of them within each legion gives a good indication of how prominent these sorts of operations were in the conduct of any campaign.

Beginning around 311 BC, the armies themselves were enlarged so that each consul commanded two legions. In addition, there was usually available a contingent of Rome's allies equal to or greater than the number of legionaries, so that armies with a paper strength of upwards of 18,000 men could be fielded. The allied contingents were marshalled in somewhat larger units, *cohorts*, and probably were armed and operated in battle similarly to the legions, although there is no direct evidence.

Above Roman *pila*. The tips pierced enemy shields and bent, making the shields useless. The pins attaching the tip to the shaft of later *pila* were designed to break, preventing re-use.

Right Roman cavalryman, late 2nd century BC. Prior to the Hannibalic war, Roman cavalrymen had fought without defensive armour apart from a light shield, but their ineffectiveness against Punic cavalry led to the adoption of mail armour, as represented here.

Opposite Samnite warriors from a 4th-century BC wall-painting at Paestum. The Samnites were among the toughest opponents the Romans faced during their conquest of Italy. According to some scholars, their small-group tactics forced the Romans to develop the manipular order of battle in response.

How the Romans Fought

The historian Polybius, an eye-witness to the manipular army in action, stresses the inherent flexibility of the legionary formation and of the individual soldiers it comprised:

'For though the Roman line is hard to break, yet each individual soldier and each company, owing to the uniform tactic employed, can fight in any direction, those companies, which happen to be in nearest contact with the danger, wheeling round to the point required. Again, the nature of their arms gives at once protection and confidence, for their shield is large and their sword will not bend: the Romans therefore are formidable on the field and hard to conquer.... Now, a Roman soldier in full armour also requires a space of three square feet. But as their method of fighting admits of individual motion for each man – because he defends his body with a shield, which he moves about to any point from which a blow is coming, and because he uses his sword both for cutting and stabbing – it is evident that each man must have a clear space, and an interval of at least three feet both on flank and rear, if he is to do his duty with any effect.... The Roman order... is flexible, for every Roman, once armed and on the field, is equally well equipped for every place, time, or appearance of the enemy. He is, moreover, quite ready and needs to make no change, whether he is required to fight in the main body or in a detachment or in a single maniple or even by himself. Therefore, as the individual members of the Roman force are so much more serviceable, their plans are also much more often attended by success than those of others.'

Roman legionaries of the middle Republic. Wealthier legionaries, like the *triarius* on the right (identifiable by his heavy thrusting spear), were permitted to wear a mail shirt (*lorca*) instead of the usual square metal 'heart protector' of the legionary on the left. *Velites*, like the soldier in the centre, wore little defensive armour and carried lighter shields.

Probably in the latter part of the 4th century BC, Rome also began regularly to pay its legionaries. The *stipendium*, as the payment was called, eliminated the necessity of soldiers furnishing their own food and other items while on campaign. However, this meant that a supply of food had to be made available to them, and soon, if not at the outset, Rome itself assumed responsibility for this. Roman armies did not 'live off the land', since grain crops in the Mediterranean are ripe and so usable as food only a few weeks of the year. While Roman troops regularly pillaged enemy territory and certainly utilized whatever food they obtained in this way, the primary goal was to deprive the enemy of it. Rome's logistical system instead depended on buying or requisitioning food from a variety of sources, both local and, as Rome's empire expanded to include such grain-producing areas as Sardinia, Sicily and North Africa, foreign. Allotments of food, charged against pay, were made to the legionaries every few days, and although Rome did not pay its allied troops (their own cities did), it did supply them with grain. In addition, at some point, probably by the late 3rd century BC at the latest, Rome began furnishing weapons and other equipment to soldiers who did not provide their own or who required replacements while on campaign, also charged against pay.

To lead Rome's armies was the job of the Republic's ruling class, the senatorial aristocracy. No bureaucracy or civil service managed the city's public business. This was the obligation of every Roman aristocrat, and his rewards were honour and glory in the eyes of his peers and fellow citizens, prizes that could only be gained thereby. At this time, the city's most pressing business was war, and so war was where aristocrats endeavoured to make their mark. They served in the cavalry and competed eagerly to win a reputation for personal courage (*virtus*) in combat. The greatest glory accrued from leading an army to victory, yet opportunities to do so were severely limited. Command came only with election to one of the city's two chief magistracies, the consulate or – very occasionally – the praetorship, ranking just below the consulate. Men elected consuls served for a single year, although in cases where military or other needs required more commanders than office-holders available in a year (which became common during the war with Hannibal – see below – and continued subsequently), their terms could be extended, in which case they became proconsuls or propraetors ('acting consuls or praetors'). Competition was keen, and the advantage generally went to the scions of established aristocratic families, particularly those who could boast a consular ancestor. These men were under intense pressure to equal if not surpass their ancestors' achievements, for each new generation had to renew its claim on aristocratic status by winning the Republic's highest offices.

These political pressures had a direct impact on the ways Rome waged war. Because the consulship was the pinnacle of an aristocrat's career and so many sought the office, rarely did any general, even a successful one, win re-election. Instead, a succession of different men held the office, men who, although possibly experienced in campaigning, usually had little or no experience in supreme command. Therefore, Rome needed a fairly simple tactical repertoire that could be mastered easily by men who may or may not have demonstrated any aptitude for command. A general of course was responsible for levying his army (although military tribunes did the actual picking of recruits), for arranging for supplies and transport, and for gathering the intelligence and conducting the diplomacy that would enable him to find the enemy and bring them to battle. These were not negligible tasks, but they required little in the way of specialized skill or knowledge. But once battle was in prospect, Roman armies always formed up in the same way – legions in the centre, allies on the wings – and once battle was joined the general's job consisted primarily of deciding when to move maniples up to or back from the 'killing zone'. Manoeuvre was limited simply to this. Yet these decisions were probably taken largely on the basis of information relayed by the tribunes or even the centurions, who were close to the fighting and had a much better sense of how their men were bearing up. Beyond that, a general's primary contribution was mainly to boost moral: to move among the maniples, let himself be seen sharing their dangers, cheer them on and give heart to waverers. Rome could afford inexperienced generals because the experienced and disciplined soldiery won her most of her battles.

Yet defeat was not unknown, and the history of Roman warfare is punctuated by some truly terrible disasters. What gave the Republic its staying power and enabled it to prevail in the end was the enormous reserve of manpower it built up in the course of the 4th, 3rd and 2nd centuries BC. Unlike the cities of Classical Greece, which were

The Carthaginians easily out-sailed the Romans in naval combats early in the First Punic War – until the Romans devised a way to turn sea fights into land battles. The *corvus*, mounted around a warship's mast and deployed to either side, let the Romans lock their ship to an enemy vessel and so bring their superior infantry into action. The coin of Pompey the Great (*inset*) was issued during the civil war and depicts a sea battle (Q. Nasidius was the official in charge of the mint at the time). Warships in this period fought by ramming one another, the *corvus* having been abandoned once the Romans became better sailors and able to manoeuvre on equal terms with enemy ships.

insular, exclusive places, Republican Rome found it easy to admit new citizens into the body politic and did so repeatedly until Roman territory embraced much of central Italy. At the same time, Rome enlarged its network of allied cities and peoples, both those who sought its protection and, often, those it conquered, as well as colonies with 'Latin rights' (a privileged category of allies) throughout the peninsula. All of these were required to supply a fixed number of troops for Roman armies. As a result, on the eve of the war with Hannibal, Rome could call on 250,000 citizens for infantry service and 23,000 potential cavalrymen along with 320,000 allied infantry and 31,000 cavalry. These reserves enabled the Republic to absorb crushing defeats and still battle back to victory, as its struggles with Carthage clearly reveal.

THE FIRST AND SECOND PUNIC WARS

Concern over control of the straits of Messene brought Roman forces to Sicily in 264 BC, initially to fight Hiero, the king of Syracuse. Once that crafty monarch had surrendered on easy terms, however, Rome found itself confronting Carthage, which had longstanding ambitions to extend its rule into the eastern half of the island from its domains in the West. In this First Punic War, Rome's legions quickly mastered the open country, leading to a long, grinding struggle to reduce Carthage's coastal strongholds by siege. Since these positions depended on re-supply by sea, the key battles took place there. The Republic scored notable victories when it equipped its ships with the *corvus*, a ramp with a large spike at the end that embedded itself in an enemy vessel when the plank was dropped, enabling the legionaries aboard to swarm across and capture it. Yet defeats and storms cost Rome dearly in men and ships, and the city's attempt to land an army in Africa and attack Carthage directly ended in disaster when its legions were crushed and their general captured. In the end, though, the Republic's greater staying-power enabled it to rebound from these reverses better than Carthage, and following the destruction of the latter's fleet off the Aegates Islands in 241 BC, Carthage was forced to capitulate.

Roman manpower would prove even more critical in the rematch during the Second Punic War 23 years later. Although the discipline and courage of Roman and Italian soldiers had down to that point amply compensated for the Republic's inexperienced generals, this system met its match in Hannibal. He was everything Roman generals were not. Trained by his father and brother-in-law in military leadership during their conquest of Spain and brought up amid their soldiers, he combined a mastery of the arts of command with the ability to inspire utter devotion among his men. These talents he placed at the service of a strategy as brilliant as it was bold. Realizing that the heart of Rome's military strength lay in its network of alliances, he aimed to strike at it by marching into Italy and offering freedom to the Republic's allies. To convince them to cast their lot with him, he would prove that he could protect them from reprisals by defeating the Romans in battle. As Rome lost manpower, Hannibal's strength would increase until he had overthrown the Republic's dominance in Italy. And unhappily for the Republic, Hannibal possessed the tactical genius to almost bring it off. After a brutal march to Italy, Hannibal won three major victories in quick succession – at Trebbia River (218 BC), Trasimene (217 BC), and Cannae (216 BC). This last was crushing (see box overleaf).

Rome had nothing left to fall back upon but its superiority in numbers. Yet Cannae had provoked a wave of defections, and Roman strategy in its aftermath focused on preventing more. The Republic began to field one army after another: one was already in Spain to prevent reinforcements reaching Hannibal; another went to Sicily after Syracuse had gone over to Carthage; others operated in Italy, visiting harsh reprisals on rebels and holding waverers in line. By 212 BC, Rome had mobilized 25 legions, some 80,000 men. This strategy presented Hannibal with an insoluble dilemma. To protect his existing allies required his presence, but to win new allies he also needed to be on hand elsewhere. Roman sympathizers within allied cities, as well as long-standing rivalries between those allies that did revolt and their immediate neighbours proved serious obstacles to the widespread rush to join his cause that Hannibal had counted on to remedy his inferior numbers. He could not be everywhere at once; Rome could. After the fall of Capua in 211 BC, to a Roman siege which Hannibal had proved powerless to break, the tide decisively turned. With the defeat of a relief force from Spain led by Hannibal's brother at the Metaurus River in 207 BC, all hope of a Carthaginian victory in Italy was lost and the focus of the struggle shifted to Africa and to the greatest of Rome's generals in this era, Publius Cornelius Scipio Africanus.

A bust of Scipio Africanus. Rome's greatest general until Caesar, Scipio Africanus brought the manipular army's tactical development to its highest pitch during the Second Punic War. Later he accompanied his brother during the latter's command against the Syrian king Antiochus III and defeated him at the battle of Magnesia in 189 BC.

The Battle of Cannae

	ROMAN REPUBLIC	CARTHAGE
COMMANDERS	Terentius Varro, Aemilius Paullus	Hannibal
STRENGTH	50,000–86,000	50,000
CASUALTIES	c. 30,000–50,000 c. 10,000 captured	5,700–8,000

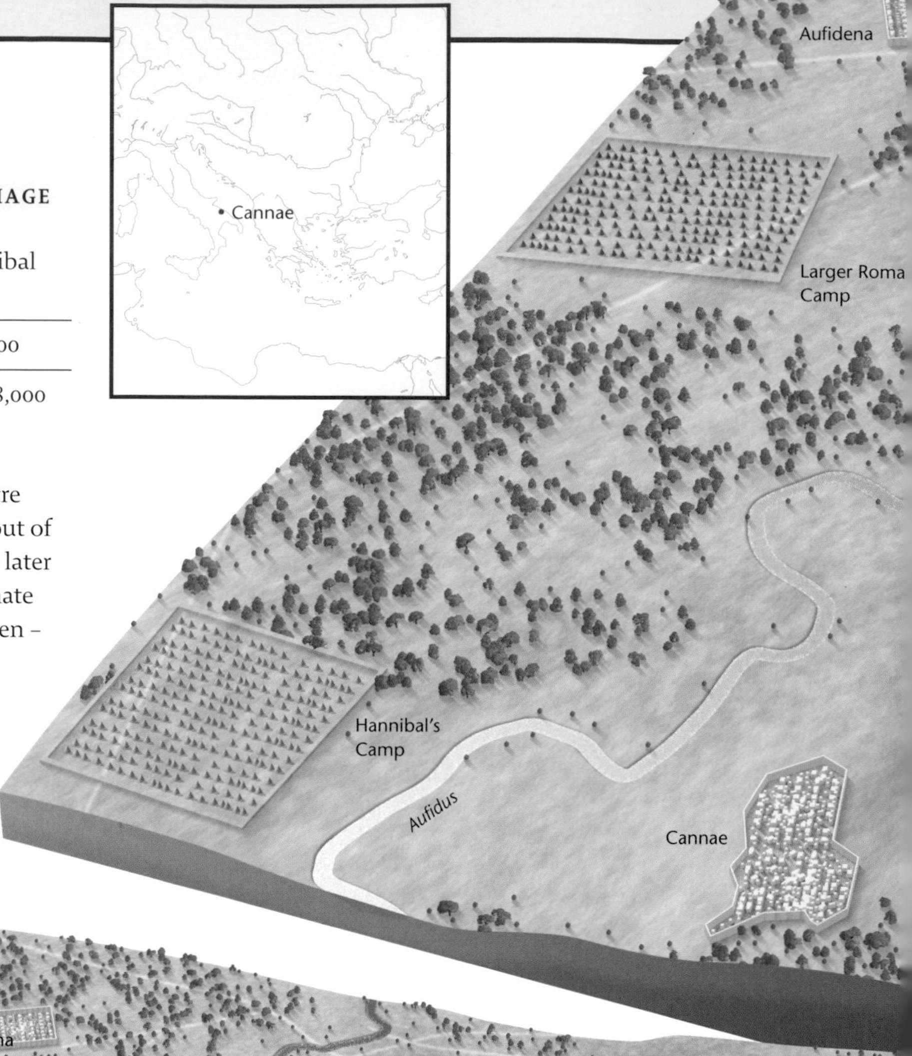

At the battle of Trasimene, the legions in the centre had succeeded in breaking through despite the rout of their flanks. Roman strategy at Cannae, two years later in 216 BC, sought to build on that success. The senate augmented its forces – to 50,000 or even 86,000 men – and, more crucially, abandoned the *quincunx* formation. The number of files within maniples was decreased and the ranks increased while the distances between maniples were reduced. The army thus formed a dense mass much deeper than normal. The plan was to use the weight of this formation to burst through the Carthaginian lines and win the battle before the flanks gave way. It didn't work. Hannibal drew up his forces in a wide, convex line with his Spanish and Gallic troops in the centre, totalling around 24,000 men. Their role was to engage the massive infantry

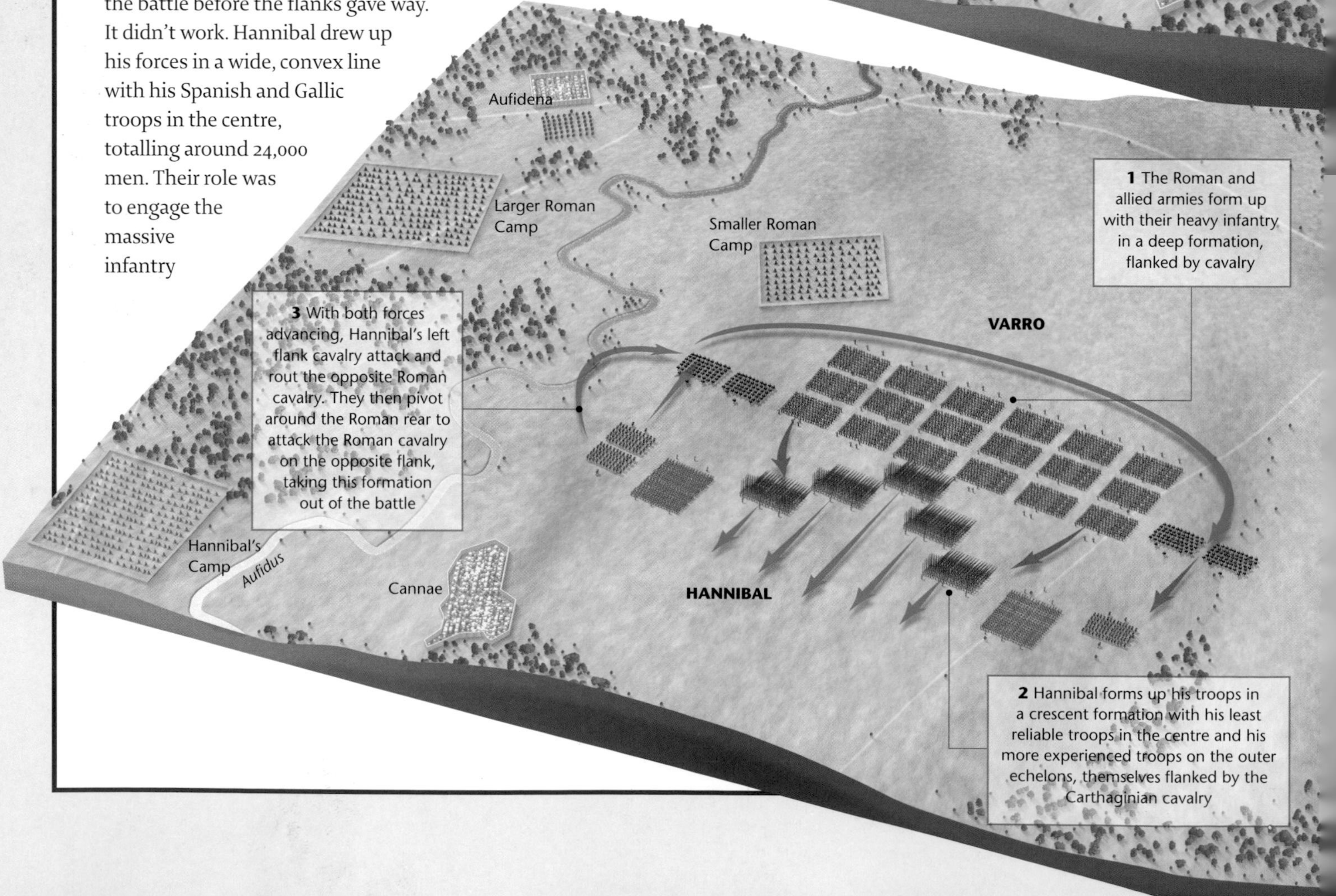

Larger Roma Camp

Hannibal's Camp

Aufidus

Cannae

Aufidena

Larger Roman Camp

Smaller Roman Camp

Aufidena

1 The Roman and allied armies form up with their heavy infantry in a deep formation, flanked by cavalry

VARRO

3 With both forces advancing, Hannibal's left flank cavalry attack and rout the opposite Roman cavalry. They then pivot around the Roman rear to attack the Roman cavalry on the opposite flank, taking this formation out of the battle

HANNIBAL

Hannibal's Camp

Aufidus

Cannae

2 Hannibal forms up his troops in a crescent formation with his least reliable troops in the centre and his more experienced troops on the outer echelons, themselves flanked by the Carthaginian cavalry

Cannae

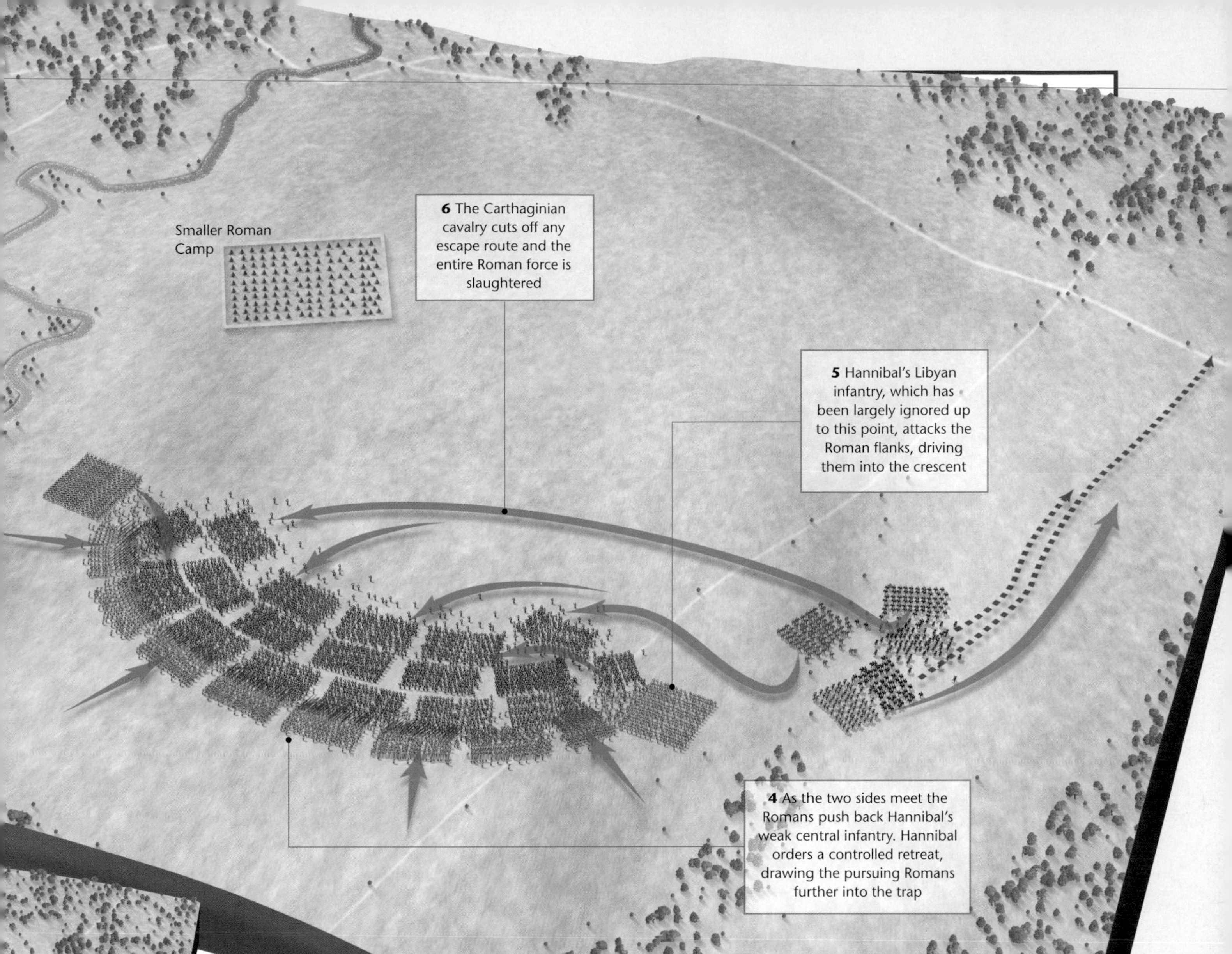

Smaller Roman
Camp

6 The Carthaginian
cavalry cuts off any
escape route and the
entire Roman force is
slaughtered

5 Hannibal's Libyan
infantry, which has
been largely ignored up
to this point, attacks the
Roman flanks, driving
them into the crescent

4 As the two sides meet the
Romans push back Hannibal's
weak central infantry. Hannibal
orders a controlled retreat,
drawing the pursuing Romans
further into the trap

force of the
Romans, giving ground
gradually and sucking the Romans into a
trap. As the battle progressed, the weight of
Roman infantry first pushed the formation flat
and then concave, allowing 10,000 Libyan spearmen
deployed on the two flanks to hem the legions in.
The trap was shut by the 2,000 Spanish and 4,000
Gallic cavalry originally deployed on the left, which
had first routed the Roman cavalry opposite, then,
with extraordinary control and discipline, had reformed
to ride behind the Roman lines and defeat the Roman
allied cavalry on the right, before turning back to attack
the legions in the rear. The result was a slaughter:
30,000, possibly as many as 50,000 Roman and allied
dead, as against 5,700–8,000 Carthaginians.

Hannibal Barca, a bold
strategist and master tactician.

The practice of placing inexperienced generals in command meant that manipular armies rarely realized their full potential, which lay in their manoeuvrability. Roman generals for the most part simply lined their armies up, sent them into battle, and let the soldiers do the rest. Yet the manipular legion made up of 30 discrete blocks of soldiers was capable of much more, and under the pressure of the struggle against Hannibal, Roman commanders finally began to exploit its possibilities, best seen in the career of Scipio. In 210 BC the senate sent this young man of 26 to Spain to pin down the Carthaginian forces following a major defeat there. Over the next five years he was able to exploit the full potential of the manipular legion, culminating with the battle of Ilipa in 206 BC. There Scipio and his Carthaginian opponents faced one another across a plain, and each morning Scipio drew up his forces with his Roman legions and Italian allies, the mainstay of his army, in the centre and his Spanish allies on the wings. The Carthaginians countered by opposing their best troops to the Romans and their lesser forces on the wings. Yet neither side attacked for several days. Finally, Scipio marched out earlier than usual and placed his Roman and Italian forces on the wings and his Spanish troops in the centre. The Carthaginians, surprised, hastily formed up as usual, so that Scipio's best troops faced their worst. Instructing his Spanish allies to move forward slowly and avoid engaging with the Carthaginian centre, Scipio marched his maniples to the left and right of his line, then forward towards the enemy in column, then wheeled them back into line of battle, bringing them into contact with the flanks of the Carthaginians. The result was a complete rout before the Carthaginian centre could strike a blow: with their flanks crumbling they had no choice but flight. This showed what the manipular army could do, but once Scipio had gone on to Africa and finally defeated Hannibal at Zama in 202 BC, the need to let other men have their turn at the consulship meant that Scipio had to step aside; he held the consulship only once again. His knowledge, skill and talent for command lay fallow. Lesser men led Rome's armies, and tactics returned to their previous rudimentary level.

Yet the system worked well enough to enable Rome to conquer the entire Mediterranean. In the decades after Zama, Roman armies pacified Cisalpine Gaul, conquered Spain, North Africa, Greece and Asia Minor, often fighting on several fronts simultaneously. Progress was not always smooth, but the Republic's vast reserves of soldiers enabled it to renew the fight as often as necessary. In the end, Rome always won.

THE AGE OF THE COHORT ARMY

In 105 BC, at Arausio in what is today southern France, four legions were annihilated by a massive force of migrating Germans. In response, the Romans realized that their maniples were incapable of withstanding the Germans' massed attack and needed to be toughened. Three maniples were combined into a cohort, ten of which now made up a legion. To add even more mass, the *velites*, *triarii* and cavalry were eliminated and all legionaries armed alike with *scutum*, *gladius* and *pila*. Thereafter cohorts became the basic tactical unit. Seven-time consul Gaius Marius is usually credited with the change, but there were precedents: Roman legions had long fought in cohorts when the situation required it – Scipio formed his men in cohorts at Ilipa for example. These larger units not only proved better able to withstand the German onslaught but far

Opposite above The Roman order of battle, cohort phase (from *c.* 100 BC). Tougher and more capable of independent manoeuvre than maniples, cohorts were the tactical building blocks of Roman armies. Interestingly, the centuries continued to exist as the basic administrative units of the legions although they had long ceased to play any tactical role in combat.

Opposite below A coin issued by the Italian confederation during its revolt against Rome, 91–89 BC. Like Rome, the Italian confederation issued coined money in order to pay its troops, enabling them to meet their expenses while on campaign, which in turn enabled a much larger segment of the male population to go to war. The obverse shows the head of the goddess 'Italia'; the reverse shows an oath-taking scene: the kneeling figure in the centre is about to sacrifice a pig; the figures on either side of him with their hands extended are swearing the oath and represent the individual peoples who came together to throw off Roman rule.

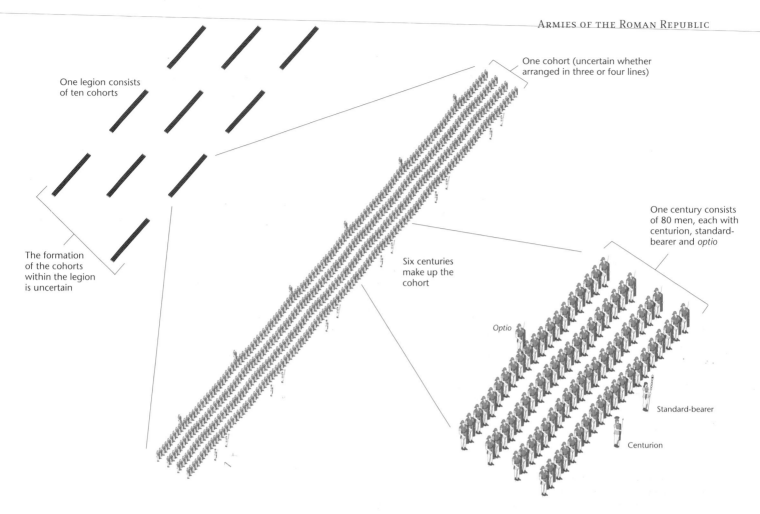

One legion consists of ten cohorts

The formation of the cohorts within the legion is uncertain

One cohort (uncertain whether arranged in three or four lines)

One century consists of 80 men, each with centurion, standard-bearer and *optio*

Six centuries make up the cohort

Optio

Standard-bearer

Centurion

more adaptable than the maniples. Cohorts still fought in *quincunx* formation in pitched battle, but could also be marshalled in detachments smaller or larger than a legion as needed. The Romans at last found a way to utilize regularly the inherent flexibility of their legions.

The men who served in the legions of the late Republic were conscripted from the same class of small farmers as before. Although poverty was becoming an increasing problem in the 1st century BC, and although the property requirement had gone by the board in the German crisis (and then in the exigencies of the Social War in 91 BC, when Rome's Italian allies rose in revolt), the legions were not composed mainly of desperate, impoverished men with no stake in the system, as some scholars have claimed. Nor were the soldiers becoming in any sense 'professionals'. They looked upon military service as a duty and an opportunity for enrichment, just as before, and they expected eventually to return to farming. Only a small cadre of mid-level officers showed any sign of developing into a class of professional soldiers. These were the *viri militares* or 'military men' – long-serving centurions or officers termed *legati*, 'legates', who were appointed by generals to subordinate positions of command. They were the repositories of the technical know how that enabled lessons once learned to accumulate into a common fund of military knowledge that allowed armies of conscripted farmers to perform

Opposite A Roman legionary, probably from the 2nd century BC. He carries a long, thrusting spear, indicating that he is a *triarius*, and wears a mail shirt, which was the prerogative of members of the first census class, the wealthiest category of citizens below the aristocracy.

Above Reverse of a coin struck in 101 BC depicting a triumphing general riding in a four-horse chariot. The date of the coin and other evidence make it quite likely that the general depicted here is Marius, celebrating his triumph in this year over the Cimbri and Teutones.

Right The Romans, like the Greeks, erected trophies on battlefields to mark their victories. This coin, struck for Julius Caesar in 48 or 47 BC, shows on its reverse a suit of armour and weapons taken from the enemy and hung on a tree trunk, symbolizing Caesar's conquests in Gaul and portending his victory in the civil war.

spectacular feats of military engineering and logistics as well as operate at a level of tactical sophistication on the battlefield far beyond that of any of Rome's enemies.

The biggest change, however, was the entry of the military into the political struggles of the aristocracy. Political competition had been notably free from serious violence during the middle Republic, but that changed in 133 BC when a group of enraged senators lynched one of their number whom they feared was aiming at tyranny. Intermittent violence continued to mar the political process for half a century until a watershed was reached in 89 BC. After Marius had used riots and murder to transfer command of a war then in prospect against Mithridates of Pontus, promising easy glory and loot, from the consul of that year, Lucius Cornelius Sulla, to himself, Sulla responded by marching on Rome with his army. He drove Marius into exile and repealed the laws that had deprived him of command, then went east to fight Mithridates. But Marius raised his own army and besieged and captured Rome. And although Marius died soon thereafter, when Sulla returned civil war erupted between him and Marius' supporters. Sulla emerged the victor, and wreaked terrible vengeance on his opponents through murder and massive confiscations of land. This last was essential. Sulla's army had preserved his life and allowed him to triumph over his enemies. They demanded rewards, and substantial allotments of farmland, the basis of all wealth in the ancient world, were to be their recompense. Sulla then retired after re-establishing the senate in power and died soon thereafter. But a precedent had been set, and the prospect of political strife spilling out onto the battlefield cast a long shadow over the last generation of the Republic.

In these years the military challenges confronting Rome also grew beyond the capabilities of the rotational system of command. Beginning with the German crisis, the Romans faced a series of wars that called for the appointment of commanders for extended periods of time: Marius in Gaul, Sulla in the East, Pompey the Great in Spain, then against the pirates who had infested the Mediterranean, and finally against, once again, Mithridates of Pontus. At the same time, the *pax Romana* throughout much of the rest of the Roman world meant that military opportunities elsewhere were rare. This development culminated with the eight-year command of Julius Caesar in Gaul (58–50 BC). The area was in fact peaceful when he began his tenure, but the glory, power and wealth that Pompey had accumulated owing to his spectacular military successes raised the stakes in political competition enormously. Although Pompey and Caesar were political allies for many years, Caesar knew that to take his place at the forefront of his aristocratic peers he would need achievements to match Pompey's, and Gaul was to supply them. The wars he instigated there in his first year in command and the victories he won set in motion a chain reaction wherein tribes throughout Gaul saw in Caesar and his legions a new factor in the regional balance of power, one that could alter it decisively for or against them. Opportunities therefore abounded for an aggressive imperialist and opportunities were all Caesar needed. The Roman military system reached its apogee in Gaul as eight years of hard campaigning turned Caesar's legions into arguably the finest fighting force the ancient world had ever seen. And those same eight years saw Caesar perfect his enormous natural gifts for command. Together, the two were to carry Caesar not only triumphantly through Gaul but to monarchy at Rome.

A modern reconstruction of Caesar's siege works at Alesia. Note the various mantraps in the foreground, christened 'tombstones', 'lilies', and 'spurs' by the legionaries. As much as their fighting abilities, the legionaries' skills as combat engineers gave Rome a decisive advantage over its enemies, even in the face of apparently insuperable odds, as in their victory over Vercingetorix and the Gauls here.

Caesar had initially seized upon the Helvetii's attempt in 58 BC to migrate west from their homes in modern Switzerland as a pretext to attack and destroy much of the tribe on its march. His success here and his willingness to inject Roman arms into inter-tribal disputes in Gaul led him later that same summer to attack Ariovistus, the leader of a powerful group of recent immigrants from Germany. Victory in this struggle led to invitations in 57 BC from tribes further north for assistance against the Belgae, the strongest coalition in the northeast. They responded by attacking Caesar's army as it was making camp at the Sambre River where, after a desperate struggle, Caesar won decisively. He spent the remainder of the year reducing the Belgic strongholds and then in 56 BC campaigned in the northwest against the Veneti while a lieutenant pacified Aquitania in the southwest. With Gaul apparently fully subjugated, Caesar began to look further afield. Realizing that tribes across the Rhine posed a threat to Roman control of Gaul, he bridged that river in 55 BC and made a demonstration in force to deter German intervention in Gallic affairs. That same summer he built a fleet and crossed to Britain, which was poorly known among the Romans and reputed to be fabulously wealthy. His victories there in that year and the following were indecisive, few riches were found, and on each occasion storms wrecked much of his fleet, so that Caesar managed to return to Gaul only with difficulty. Far more ominously, the Gauls, many of whom had cooperated with Caesar in the hope of enlarging their own dominions, were realizing that Caesar's victories meant permanent subjugation to Rome. A serious revolt broke out in the winter of 54/53 BC during which a legion and five cohorts were destroyed and another legion rescued only with great effort. The following year was relatively quiet, but in 52 BC a major revolt broke out led by Vercingetorix (see p. 163). Eventually Vercingetorix was compelled to surrender, and with that, the revolt was over – but the political situation in Rome was reaching the point of open conflict.

Events in 50 BC brought tensions between Caesar and Pompey, backed by hard-liners in the senate, to a head, and Caesar appealed to his army to defend him. He had plausible grounds for defying the government: his own honour and achievements were being slighted; his enemies were violating the ancestral

Top Gnaius Pompeius Magnus – Pompey the Great. A brilliant general and strategist, his youthful exploits earned him his nickname and invited comparison with Alexander. His achievements dramatically raised the bar for military glory at Rome and kindled Caesar's desire for equally spectacular conquests in Gaul.

Above Gaius Julius Caesar. In the civil war, Caesar found himself outmatched time and again by Pompey. Only Caesar's charismatic leadership, his brilliance as a tactical improviser, and the discipline and devotion of his battle-hardened veterans enabled him to snatch victory from all but certain defeat at Pharsalus.

constitution. But he had also lavishly rewarded his men for their conquests in Gaul, and Sulla's precedent undoubtedly justified their presumption that victory in a civil war would be of material benefit to them as well.

The struggle that followed pitted Rome's two greatest military minds against one another. Caesar relied on his veteran army, their proximity to Italy, and his own daring. Pompey depended on his far greater, if scattered, resources in men and treasure, and a more deliberate, controlled style of war. Caesar struck first, racing into Italy in January and February of 49 BC hoping to cut Pompey off from his forces in the East and end the war swiftly. Pompey had certainly foreseen that move, and evacuated the peninsula despite the complaints of his senatorial allies that he was abandoning everything they were fighting for. But Pompey needed time to gather his resources for the fight, and so denied Caesar the ability to pursue him by taking with him or destroying every boat he could find. Caesar, knowing that when he followed Pompey to Greece he would leave his base in Gaul vulnerable to Pompey's lieutenants in Spain, turned west and in a single, lightning campaign defeated them. With his rear secure he crossed into Greece early in 48 BC and found Pompey at Dyrrachium. Hoping to starve Pompey into surrender, Caesar began to invest his position, but Pompey controlled the sea and so could keep his army fed while Caesar's men went hungry because the grain in the region had not yet ripened. They endured every privation for him, but Caesar had overreached. Pompey, awaiting his chance, found a weak point in Caesar's siege works and pounced. Caesar's position was utterly compromised, and he had no choice but to retreat with Pompey in hot pursuit. Pompey would probably have preferred to play a waiting game, but he could not wait. Political pressures, in the form of complaints from his senatorial allies in his camp, eager for a decisive victory and carping that Pompey was prolonging the campaign to extend his command, pushed him to a decisive encounter, and that was all the opportunity Caesar needed. As the two sides stood ready for battle, Caesar, realizing Pompey had massed his superior cavalry forces for a decisive blow against Caesar's right flank, quickly withdrew cohorts from his third line into a fourth, and sent this against Pompey's cavalry. Caesar's cohorts drove them from the field, and then swung left to attack Pompey's rear. Once the infantry engaged, Pompey's levies stood no chance against Caesar's battle-hardened veterans.

Pompey fled to Egypt and was murdered, but three more years of hard campaigning stood between Caesar and unchallenged rule. Yet it proved ephemeral, and his assassination brought only momentary peace. The perpetrators were destroyed at Philippi in 42 BC by Mark Antony and Octavian, Caesar's adoptive son and heir. These two eyed each other warily over the next decade as each sought to gird himself for the final struggle, Octavian by consolidating his power in Italy and the West, Antony, in alliance with Cleopatra of Egypt, by conquering Parthia in the East. The climax came at the battle of Actium – with a whimper: Antony and Cleopatra's naval forces, outnumbered and outmanoeuvred, disintegrated in flight, and their legions surrendered without a blow. Octavian had fought his way to the top, and as the emperor Augustus would remake the Roman army at last into a professional fighting force, one that tactically looked much like the Republic's citizen legions but whose loyalty to Augustus formed the bedrock of Imperial power.

9   Celtic and Iberian Warrior Cultures

Λ 1st century BC bronze statuette of a Gallic warrior or a god, found in the sanctuary at Saint-Maur-en-Chaussée, France. The belted tunic, trousers, oval shield and torc are typical elements of a warrior's outfit.

From the 5th to 1st centuries BC, much of western Europe was a patchwork of chiefdoms and tribes. These appear to have possessed a relatively homogeneous material culture, which archaeologists call La Tène (after a major discovery of artifacts at the site in Switzerland) and which has been identified with peoples known by the Greeks and Romans as Celts (*Keltoi/Celtae*) or Gauls (*Galatai/Galli*). In Spain, indigenous Iberian material culture was distinctive, although there was a strong Celtic presence in the north-central part of the peninsula (Celtiberia).

During the 4th century BC, 'Celtic' societies developed along the Danubian plain, while later Greek and Roman writers also remembered a wave of Gallic migrations into Italy, beginning in the 5th century BC. It is unclear what caused such migrations, although overpopulation and the attractions of land and booty probably played their part. A number of major tribes settled in the Po valley and along the Adriatic coast to Ancona. From here, warbands launched forays against the rich lands to the south: one force led by Brennus famously sacked Rome in 390 BC. However, despite several Gallic forays into central Italy, Rome emerged as the strongest power in Italy. In the wars of the early 3rd century BC, Gallic tribes allied with the Etruscans, Samnites and Umbrians, but failed to prevent the Roman conquest of Italy. At the battle of Sentinum in 295 BC, a large force of Gauls and Samnites, perhaps totalling as many as 40,000 men, engaged a Roman army of similar size. According to later accounts of the battle, the Gallic cavalry and chariots broke the Roman cavalry, but the Samnites were also routed, and the Gallic infantry, during a prolonged exchange of missiles, became surrounded and were defeated.

North of the river Rubicon, in what the Romans termed Cisalpine Gaul, the tribes remained powerful and independent. In 225 BC, provoked by Roman expansionism, a confederate army of tribes, supplemented by transalpine warriors – the Gaesatae ('Spearmen'), who were probably mercenaries – marched into Etruria. They were surrounded by two Roman armies at the battle of Telamon and destroyed (see box on pp. 160–161).

THE PUNIC WARS

During the First Punic War (264–241 BC), Carthage had employed both Gallic and Iberian mercenaries to campaign in Sicily against Rome. After the Carthaginian defeat, Gallic mercenaries, amongst others, became embroiled in the bitter four-year revolt against their paymasters ('The Truceless War', 241–237 BC). The Carthaginian general Hamilcar Barca crushed the revolt and then embarked on the conquest of southern Spain from 237 BC. The Barcid family established themselves as overlords, recruiting many of the local tribes into their army and exploiting rich Spanish silver

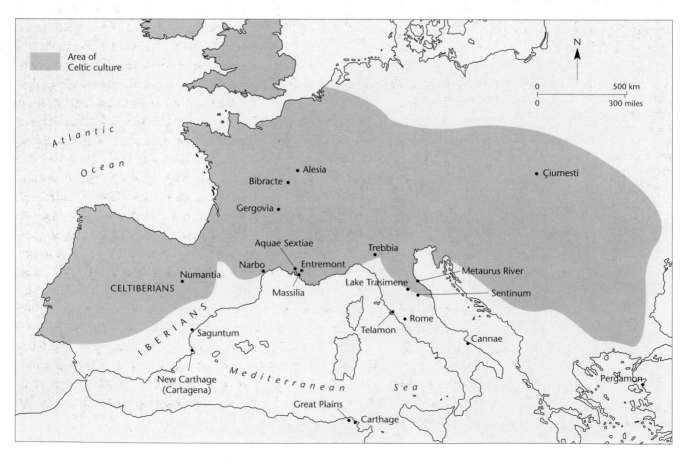

mines around New Carthage (Cartagena) to bankroll their conquests and pay their warriors. In 219 BC Hamilcar's son, Hannibal, besieged the Iberian city of Saguntum, a recent ally of Rome. It was the spark that began the Second Punic War (218–202 BC) in which Spanish, Celtiberian and Cisalpine Gallic warriors played a major role. Both sides drew on Iberian allies and employed Celtiberian mercenaries as they waged campaigns for the control of southern Spain. It was the defection of 20,000 Celtiberians that led to the destruction of two Roman armies under Publius and Gaius Scipio in 211 BC. Iberian allies were fickle and frequently changed sides depending on the fortunes of the war. In Italy, overwhelming Punic victories at the battles of Trebbia and Trasimene were followed by Rome's heaviest ever defeat, at Cannae in Apulia (216 BC – see box on pp. 148–149). Hannibal's allies in Cisalpine Gaul also destroyed a Roman army in the same year; the head of the general, Postumius, was turned into a gilded sacrificial bowl. Despite these victories, Hannibal was not easily able to exploit the manpower of his allies during the latter stages of the war. When, in 207 BC, his brother Hasdrubal brought a large army into Italy from Spain, augmented by many thousands of Gauls gathered on the march, he failed to rendezvous with Hannibal and his force was destroyed at the battle of the Metaurus.

Above Vase from San Miguel de Liria depicting Iberian warriors throwing javelins (possibly the *saunion* or *soliferrum*, a solid iron spear mentioned by Classical writers) and with highly decorated oval shields. Their patterned tunics may represent mail or scale armour.

Above A 3rd-century BC carved relief found at Osuna of an Iberian warrior with oval body shield (*scutum*), heavy cutting sword (*falcata*) and crested helmet with extended neck-guard, probably of sinew or leather. Polybius describes the tunics of such warriors as white with red (or purple) borders.

Opposite The main sites mentioned in this chapter.

Eventual victory over Hannibal in 202 BC allowed the Romans to direct their attention to the reduction of the chief tribes of the Po valley (Boii, Cenomani and Insubres). Major Roman armies campaigned each year in the region between 201 and 190 BC; the intensity of warfare was such that it was claimed that only old men and young boys survived Scipio Nasica's final victory over the Boii. The Romans paraded vast amounts of booty from their campaigns and the region south of the river Po was heavily colonized and Romanized by Latin settlers in subsequent years. To the north, however, despite increasing urbanization (e.g. Milan, Verona), the material culture in the countryside retained La Tène influences.

ROME AND THE IBERIANS

Carthaginian Spain had been conquered by Scipio Africanus, whose charisma and military achievements (such as the spectacular capture of New Carthage in 209 BC) drew tribal chieftains to his standard. The Romans divided the region into two provinces (Nearer and Hither), but tension between governors and tribes often erupted into violence. Furthermore, independent tribes beyond the provinces, in Celtiberia and Lusitania, often warred with the Romans. Indeed, violence appears to have been endemic, but it usually amounted to little more than hit-and-run raids. However, some conflicts were bitter and fierce, such as the 'Fiery War' the Celtiberians waged against Rome in the 150s BC, and were marked by atrocities and massacres. Charismatic leaders, such as the Lusitanian chieftain, Viriathus, sometimes united the tribes, but because of the fractious nature of tribal politics, when they were killed, coordinated resistance tended to collapse. Viriathus, for example, who had survived a treacherous massacre of Lusitanian tribes committed by the Romans in 150 BC, successfully engaged large Roman forces in the field and harassed others through constant raids and ambushes. On several occasions he extracted treaties from Roman generals (although the Senate in Rome repudiated them). He was a cunning tactician who exploited his knowledge of local terrain and the swiftness and ferocity of his Iberian cavalry and light infantry. He reputedly slept little and always in his armour, and he was generous in distributing booty to his followers and allies. However, despite eight years of success, he was finally assassinated by two of his own followers who had been corrupted by Roman bribes.

The Battle of Telamon

	ROMANS	GAULS
COMMANDERS	Atilius Regulus, Aemilius Papus	Concolitanus, Aneroestes
STRENGTH	70,000 infantry 5,400 cavalry	50,000 infantry 20,000 cavalry and chariots
CASUALTIES	Unknown	40,000 killed 10,000 captured

Polybius records a major incursion of Gallic warriors into central Italy in 225 BC. Some 50,000 infantry and 20,000 cavalry and chariots, drawn from the Cisalpine Boii, Insubres and Alpine Gaesatae, advanced into Etruria, where they plundered the region and advanced to a point only a few days' march from Rome itself. Having mauled one Roman army, they then headed for home laden with booty. At Telamon, however, they were intercepted by two Roman forces, which came at them from opposite directions.

The Gauls were forced to deploy their army facing both ways. Polybius emphasizes the elements of display and intimidation in their deployment: the din of many war-horns, trumpets and war cries, and the physique and gestures of the elite Gaesatae, who went naked into battle ahead of the rest. The battle opened with a struggle between the Gallic cavalry and the forces of Atilius for a hill that controlled the vital

escape route homewards, but although the Roman general was killed and his head brought to the Gallic king, Concolitanus, the cavalry failed to take this objective. In the opposite part of the field, the Gaesatae were unable to cope with the Roman light infantry and were forced back into the ranks of the army. In the protracted hand-to-hand fighting that followed, the Gauls' courage and desperation enabled them to endure

Telamon

Mediterranean Sea

Town of Telamon

Defile

1 A large force of Gauls commence a fighting retreat loaded with booty after attacking central Italy and threatening Rome. They are pursued by a cautious Aemilius Papus

Via Aurelia

sustained pressure until the Roman cavalry finally drove off their counterparts and fell upon their flanks. Polybius reports that 40,000 Gauls were killed in the battle, including Concolitanus. Another Gallic king, Aneroestes, and his retinue committed suicide rather than be taken.

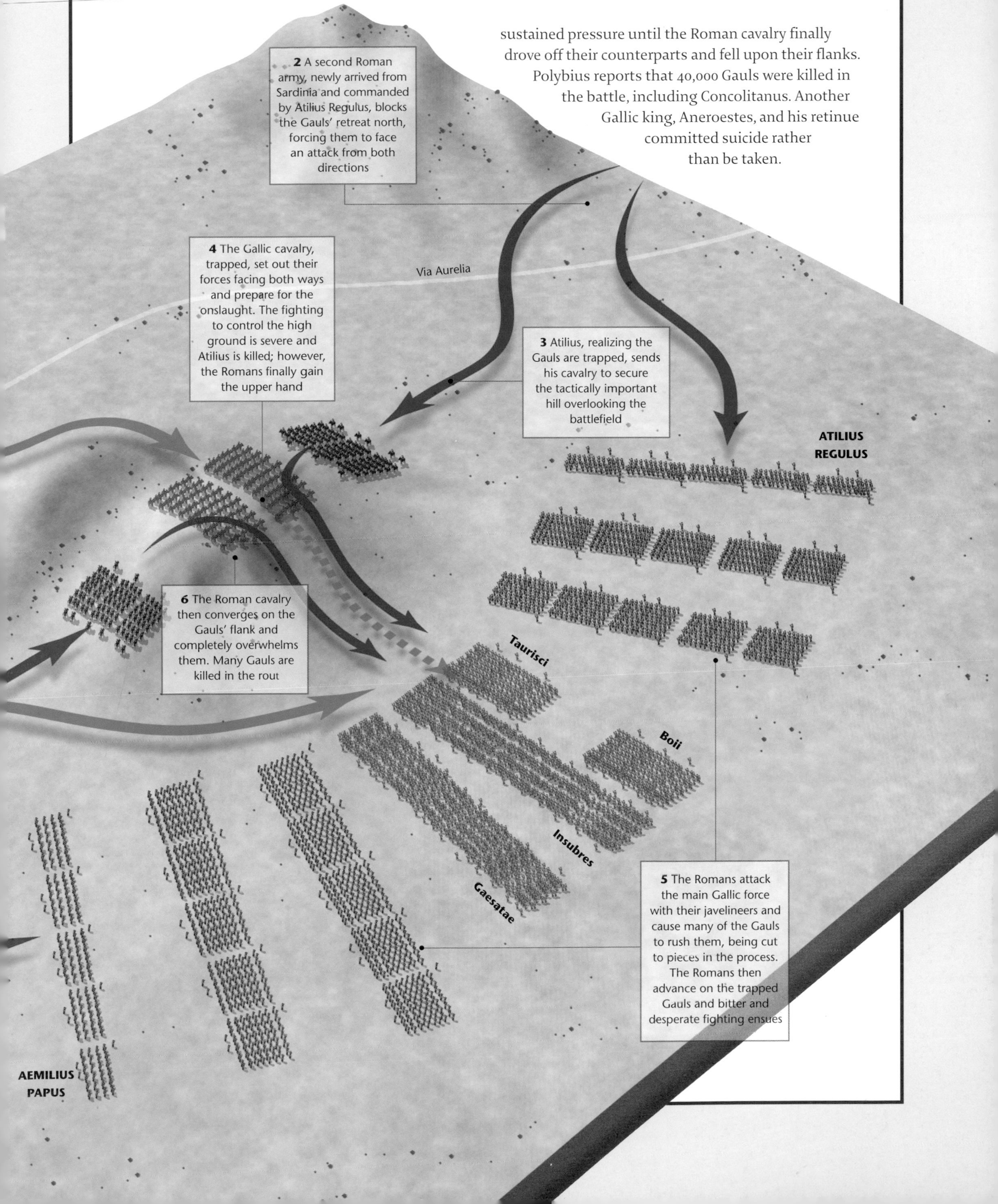

2 A second Roman army, newly arrived from Sardinia and commanded by Atilius Regulus, blocks the Gauls' retreat north, forcing them to face an attack from both directions

4 The Gallic cavalry, trapped, set out their forces facing both ways and prepare for the onslaught. The fighting to control the high ground is severe and Atilius is killed; however, the Romans finally gain the upper hand

Via Aurelia

3 Atilius, realizing the Gauls are trapped, sends his cavalry to secure the tactically important hill overlooking the battlefield

ATILIUS REGULUS

6 The Roman cavalry then converges on the Gauls' flank and completely overwhelms them. Many Gauls are killed in the rout

Taurisci

Boii

Insubres

Gaesatae

5 The Romans attack the main Gallic force with their javelineers and cause many of the Gauls to rush them, being cut to pieces in the process. The Romans then advance on the trapped Gauls and bitter and desperate fighting ensues

AEMILIUS PAPUS

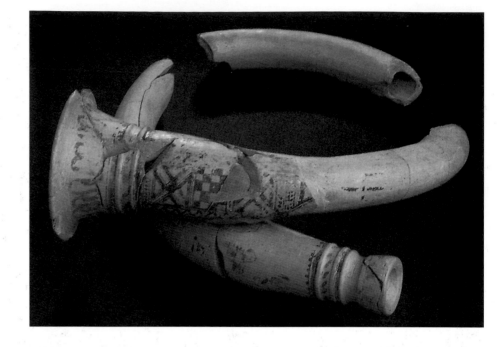

Right Celtiberian war-horn made of terracotta from Numantia. Sound was a powerful tool for intimidating the enemy and encouraging friends; such instruments helped to bend the din of battle to the warriors' advantage.

Below War-horn end-piece (for amplification) in the shape of a wolf head, found at Numantia. Animal- and monster-headed horns are commonly represented in Gallic and Iberian art, and may have been intended to emulate the roar of fierce beasts.

Viriathus had drawn the Celtiberians back into war with Rome and, for almost ten years, Roman armies failed to make significant headway against them. Celtiberian independence, however, was dealt a crushing blow at the siege of Numantia in 133 BC, where the fierce resistance of around 8,000 warriors was contained behind an extensive system of siege works, maintained by a Roman army and local allied tribes totalling 60,000 men. Archaeological excavations have revealed seven of the camps and parts of the circumvallation. The resistance of the Numantines was broken through starvation; many had resorted to cannibalism in the final stages. Those survivors who did not kill themselves surrendered. But even after the fall of Numantia, Roman campaigns to subdue the peninsula continued sporadically until Augustus.

CELTS OF NORTHERN AND CENTRAL EUROPE

In Gaul, most tribes initially appear to have been loosely organized. Most settlements were small and dispersed, suggesting relatively egalitarian communities with limited concentrations of power in the hands of local elites. During the 3rd and 2nd centuries BC, however, some tribes became organized enough to mint limited amounts of gold and silver coinage. By the end of the 2nd century BC, major population growth and increasing economic and social differences in the population were evident, at a time of increased contact with the Mediterranean. Some tribes developed magistracies and councils of noblemen, although the personal relationships of powerful men within and beyond tribal boundaries were a significant element in tribal politics. Urbanized hill-towns (*oppida*), with strong outer defences, developed. These acted as tribal capitals and centres of manufacture and commerce, as indicated by excavations of the *oppidum* of the Saluvii at Entremont or that of the Aedui at Bibracte (Mont Beuvray).

Part of the defensive system excavated at Entremont in southern France, the capital of the Saluvii. Stone walls 3–5 m (10–17 ft) thick, possibly standing 6–7 m (20–23 ft) high, were regularly punctuated by massive towers 9.5 m (31 ft) across, and were designed to encircle a densely settled high plateau. Most *oppida* were constructed with elaborate defensive systems (though not always of stone), demonstrating the communal organization and identity of tribes.

Tensions between the Greek colony of Massilia (Marseilles) and local tribes attracted Rome, which looked to secure its overland route from Italy to the provinces of Spain. From 124 to 121 BC, the Saluvii, Allobroges and Arverni were defeated, and the establishment of Roman bases at Aquae Sextiae (Aix-en-Provence) and Narbo (Narbonne) heralded the creation of the province of Gallia Transalpina (Provence). This province projected inland along the Rhône and gave Italian merchants access to the interior, where a significant trade in wine and slaves appears to have developed.

When an Alpine confederation, the Helvetii, decided to migrate in 62 BC, it caused fears that Transalpine Gaul might be overrun and enabled Julius Caesar to obtain a long command which allowed him to conquer Gaul. After seven years of successful campaigning, Caesar faced a major uprising led by Vercingetorix in 52 BC. Vercingetorix, through the strength of his character, the discipline he instilled in his army and the skilful martialling of the resources of a pan-Gallic alliance, conducted an effective campaign to harass Caesar's sources of supply and to defeat him at Gergovia. He had even detached Caesar's staunch allies, the Aedui. However, after defeat in battle, his army of 80,000 was forced to fall back to the *oppidum* of Alesia, where Caesar constructed extensive siege works 22 km (14 miles) long. Despite the efforts of a vast relieving army sent by the tribes, Caesar's lines held and eventually Vercingetorix surrendered in order to save his men from starvation. The mopping up of rebellious tribes continued for the next few years, but, thereafter, Gaul was absorbed into the Roman empire.

The Classical View of Warriors

Most classical writers emphasized the desire of warriors for personal glory in displays of martial prowess. Although often biased and stereotypical, such accounts, such as this one from Diodorus, nevertheless reflect an awareness of the fundamental values and interests of such fighters:

'...when they enter battle, the Gauls use two-horse chariots that carry a charioteer and the warrior. When they encounter cavalry in battle they throw their javelins first and then dismount their vehicles and enter the melee with their swords. Some in particular have such a disdain for death that they fight without armour and with little more than girded loins. They also bring their followers into war, poor men, to serve them as charioteers and shield-bearers. When they have deployed for battle, they are accustomed to step in front of the battle-line and challenge the best of the enemy to single combat, brandishing their weapons before them to intimidate their opponents. And when anyone accepts their challenge, they then burst into a song of praise about their ancestors' great deeds and boast of their own glorious achievements, all the while reviling and belittling their adversary, and attempting through words to strip his spirit of its courage before engaging. When their enemies fall, they cut off their heads and attach them to the necks of their horses; and turning over the blood-stained weapons of their opponents to their followers, they carry them off as booty, singing a paean over them and a victory hymn, and they fasten these first-fruits of battle to their houses by nails...'

Roman silver denarius minted by L. Hostilius Saserna (in 48 BC) to commemorate Caesar's victories, depicting a portrait of a Gallic warrior (possibly Vercingetorix) with a two-horse war chariot on the reverse.

WARRIORS AND WARFARE

Most Gallic and Iberian armies appear to have consisted of warbands led by chieftains and other powerful men. Vercingetorix was the son of a man who had been king of the Arverni, and his personal warband was drawn from a mix of his own tribesmen, clients and those attracted to his service from elsewhere (who Caesar disparagingly calls 'outcasts and desperate men'). Full-time warriors, who acted as the entourage and bodyguards of the leaders, formed the core of most warbands, while others who

Left Reconstruction of a typical Gallic spear-armed warrior and a nobleman in mail, from the 3rd century BC. The decorated wooden shields have a reinforced central spine with a central boss of iron. The Montefortino helmet was popular in northern Italy and was also adopted by Roman soldiers of the period. Long slashing swords needed room to be used effectively, but thrusting spears may have allowed denser formations to operate in pitched battle.

Opposite Sculpture of a warrior from Vachères, France. His short hair suggests Roman influence, although he also wears a torc. Most warriors could not afford to be equipped in mail, so this statue probably represents a Gallic nobleman or an auxiliary serving in the Roman army.

165

Silver coin issued by Dubnoreix (Dumnorix) of the Aedui, emphasizing martial qualities. The figure is dressed in a mail shirt and sword and holds a severed head in one hand and *carnyx* (war trumpet) and a boar in the other. The boar may represent physical strength and ferocity, hunting prowess or Dumnorix's generosity in feasting his followers.

chose or were obliged to follow would also march out on campaign. The ability of leaders such as Viriathus and Vercingetorix to retain and attract followers was based not only on their martial reputation and charisma, but also on their capacity to reward their warriors. The ability to dispense food and drink, especially wine, to followers at feasts seems to have been an integral aspect of the power of the leader. The position of Dumnorix of the Aedui, for example, appears to have rested on his control of the wine trade.

At times of major conflict or upheaval, more general levies of manpower, drawn from the wider tribal population, swelled armies to tens of thousands. Generals of such armies might be chosen by a popular vote of the tribe, or by its warriors. Ambiorix of the Eburones claimed that he had been compelled by the tribe to launch the attack on Caesar's legates, Sabinus and Cotta (in 54 BC), and that the terms of his own *imperium* ('command') meant that the multitude had as much jurisdiction over him as he over them. Some tribal armies appear to have been accompanied by their women and come to resemble migrations, which, in rare cases, they actually were. Such migrations appear to have involved considerable organization: the Helvetii apparently spent two years readying themselves for their march and even drew up written lists (using Greek writing) of participants and supplies.

Although some Gallic tribes and alliances were capable of bringing many thousands of warriors into the field, logistical support remained undeveloped and campaigns were relatively brief. Wars generally appear to have concerned the attempt to assert the power of one group over others through the devastation of enemy territory, or in seeking pitched battle where martial prowess could be demonstrated and the enemy subdued or destroyed. Confederate armies usually deployed by tribe, probably subdivided into clans or warbands led by individual clan chieftains. Such armies were potentially fractious; quarrels on a number of occasions undermined the progress of campaigns, or led forces seemingly to go their own way (as happened during an invasion of Greece in 279 BC).

The need to feast warriors appears to have fuelled raiding, with successful leaders attracting greater numbers of followers, who then needed to be repaid for their services in hospitality and booty. Raiding was also the primary way for men to demonstrate their prowess and enrich themselves. For youths, it might initiate them into the activities of warfare and realize their manhood. A successful raid enhanced the honour of the individuals, the warband and the community, and, in turn, humiliated the enemy, who might seek revenge in a similar fashion. This appears to have created a situation of almost constant, but relatively low-level, warfare.

The Greeks and Romans often portrayed Gallic warriors as being filled with impetuous and reckless fury and incapable of rational action. Despite such derogatory stereotypes, it is clear that an emphasis on 'fierce virtues' was an integral part of the self-definition of the warrior in these societies. The personal *virtus* ('manlihood') of the warrior was realized through war-like activities which brought prestige and respect. Much of this manifested itself in forms of martial display designed to intimidate enemies and show off the prowess of the warrior (see box on p. 165). Greek and Roman sources emphasize such things as war-dances, the yelling and shouting of warriors, the sound of their war trumpets, the wearing of golden torcs and ostentatiously decorated helmets, hair-styles and even the nakedness of some warriors. Their collection of trophies from slain enemies, often severed heads (or right hands) or equipment, demonstrated the prowess of the victor. Some of these elements were represented on the coins minted by Dumnorix to advertise his martial credentials to his followers and the wider community.

Tribes, too, appear to have been concerned with their reputation for military prowess and bravery; at least, this is the view that Caesar gives when explaining the motivations for several Gallic tribes and confederations to go to war. The Nervii, for example, were thought of as the bravest of the Belgae, who imagined themselves to be the bravest of all Gauls because of their past military achievements.

Below The ritual and social importance of the heads of the deceased in Gallic culture is evident at Roquepertuse, where the gates of a sanctuary had niches for the display of human skulls.

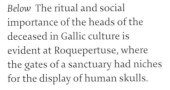

Above These remains of a life-size statue of a cross-legged warrior with a pile of trophy heads around his knees were found at Entremont (reconstructed, *right*). The torso also wore a sculpted clasp with a decapitated head decoration. The statue appears to have sat in the public meeting space of the *oppidum*, representing, perhaps, an ancestral or tribal hero.

Classical writers observed that the Gauls believed in an afterlife, so that death in battle held little fear for them, and indeed was a 'beautiful death' that warriors hoped to obtain. In Iberia, according to Strabo some tribes regarded 'those slain in war as noble, heroic and full of valour'. Certainly the martial identity or aspirations of the deceased were often marked in the form of the deposition of weapons in graves in these cultures. Such items, particularly swords, were sometimes even 'killed' (bent or broken, rendering them unusable), suggesting the close personal connection between the warrior and his arms and their role in the creation of his identity.

Weapons, then, performed an important social function. They affirmed the martial identity of the warrior, both in war and in peace, and suggested his excellence in weapon use and martial valour. Fine weapons and armour also indicated his social status and economic resources. Some examples of equipment have been discovered in 'warrior' graves, such as those at Çiumesti in Romania, which demonstrate the high quality of the workmanship and technological sophistication, but such items would have been time-consuming and expensive to make; it is probably the case that no more than a quarter of warriors possessed a sword. The majority appear to have used flat wooden shields and spears, while few wore metal armour, or, indeed, any armour at all. Such limited armament probably accounts for the lack of staying power in battle that Roman and Greek authors often noted.

Chariots were probably owned and used by the elite, primarily as status symbols. Although present at the battles of Sentinum and Telamon (in 295 and 225 BC), their use declined in continental Europe during the 3rd and 2nd centuries BC as they became supplanted by true cavalry. Caesar's men were unnerved by the unfamiliar sight and tactics of the British chariotry during his invasions of southeastern England (55–54 BC). Most tribal cavalry also consisted of nobles and their followers, who had the leisure time to become excellent horsemen. Certainly, Gallic and Iberian cavalry could be extremely effective in battle and on campaign, as their role at Cannae demonstrated (see box on pp. 148–149).

The emphasis on honour and prestige meant that the fighting style of Gallic and Iberian warriors in battle was individualistic. Slashing swords, which needed space to be swung, indicate such individualism in combat. Warbands appear to have fought with no regular order as such; the bravest and most eager to impress placed themselves at the front, as the naked Gaesatae did at Telamon. Their charge was ferocious and terrifying, but if it could be withstood or frustrated then the warriors often had limited endurance. At Sentinum, after the initial charge of the Gauls had been driven back, they rallied into a defensive wall of shields, but collapsed under a sustained

Weapons were sometimes buried in graves, such as these from a 3rd-century BC burial at Batina, Croatia, or deposited at sacred shrines, woods or in water. Some swords in particular were bent into an unusable shape. The spearhead (*top*) seems designed primarily for thrusting (see reconstruction on p. 165), though other types, for throwing, have also been discovered. The scabbard (*centre*) probably consisted of a leather or wooden sheath (since decayed), with a metal base to prevent wear and accidental injury.

Right High-quality craftsmanship and an ethos of ostentatious display in war are evident in this elaborate 3rd-century BC helmet topped with a raven, found at Çiumesti in Romania. The articulated wings probably moved as the wearer walked or ran and would have attracted the attention of both friend and foe.

Below This detail from the 2nd-century BC silver Gundestrup cauldron represents spear-armed and helmeted cavalry, shielded spear-infantry and *carnyx*-blowers. The scene is difficult and controversial to interpret, but may represent warrior initiation by plunging into a cauldron.

Above Gallic warriors with shields, spears and torcs represented on a fragment of a 2nd-century BC Roman triumphal monument from Civita Alba near Sassoferrato in Italy. One warrior is represented naked: perhaps this might have been for ritual reasons or to show off his physique and demonstrate disdain for the enemy, although the Roman sculptor and viewers of the monument may have interpreted it as barbarian vainglory.

bombardment of Roman javelins. However, it was the expectation that Gallic warriors would quickly tire and fall back that lured the Romans into the trap laid for them by Hannibal at the battle of Cannae. Many of Hannibal's 8,000 losses at the battle were Gauls and such a high casualty rate for the victors (20 per cent overall, 25–30 per cent of the infantry centre) is testament to their tenacity and to the ferocity of the fighting. Other warbands also notably fought with grim determination: 4,000 Celtiberian mercenaries, for example, fought to the last man at the battle of the Great Plains (203 BC). It was this desperate bravery in defeat that many Greeks and Romans admired and it inspired artists of Pergamon to sculpt the famous statues of suicidal and dying Gauls, iconic representations of the self-destructive bravery of the warrior's ethos.

Opposite Galatian tribes had established themselves in Asia Minor in the 3rd century BC and had both raided local Greek states and supplied them with mercenaries and allied forces. This Greek sculpture of a naked Gaul committing suicide in defeat (from a statue group in Pergamon) presents an idealized view of the physique and defiant spirit of these people.

10 Parthian and Sasanian Warfare

This magnificent silver plate shows a Sasanian king hunting lions from horseback. He is possibly the 5th-century AD king Bahram V Gur, who was long famed for his exploits in the field. The king wears flowing riding overalls over his trousers. These are typical of Sasanian riding dress, and highly decorated examples have actually been discovered in burials of Sasanian soldiers in Egypt.

'They are really formidable in warfare.... The Parthians make no use of a shield, but their forces consist of mounted archers and lancers, mostly in full armour. Their infantry is small, made up of the weaker men; but even these are all archers. The land, being for the most part level, is excellent for raising horses and very suitable for riding about on horseback; at any rate, even in war they lead about whole droves of horses, so that they can use different ones at different times, can ride up suddenly from a distance and also retire to a distance speedily.'

(Cassius Dio on the 3rd-century AD Partho-Sasanians)

After 323 BC, the vast Achaemenid empire fragmented into the warring kingdoms of Alexander's successors. Most of the Near East fell to the rule of Seleucus, but after little more than a century of Hellenistic rule two Iranian dynasties, first the Parthian Arsacids and then the Persian Sasanians, reasserted their control. In total they ruled Iran for more than 800 years and proved to be formidable adversaries for the Roman and Byzantine empires.

The origin and early history of the Parthians is little known, but around 238 BC, Iranian nomads called the Parni seized control of the Seleucid satrapy of Parthia, to the east of the Caspian Sea. Under their ruler Arsaces, and the later kings of the Arsacid dynasty, the Parthian empire expanded until by the end of the reign of Mithridates I, in 138 BC, the Parthians ruled a diverse, multicultural empire which included most of Iran and Mesopotamia. By 113 BC, the Euphrates frontier was secured by Mithridates II, who henceforth adopted the ancient Achaemenid title of 'king of kings'. The continuity between the Parthian dynasty and their Achaemenid predecessors was tenuous but Classical writers such as Tacitus were certainly not averse to making such comparisons, seeing behind Mithridates' policy the intent that 'whatever was possessed by Cyrus, and afterwards by Alexander, was his undoubted right, and he was determined to recover the same by force of arms'.

In fact, Parthia was rarely the aggressor and following the fall of the remnant of the Seleucid kingdom to Rome, it was due to provocation by Rome and struggles over influence in Armenia and Syria that hostilities were to continue intermittently for several centuries. The total annihilation of the Roman triumvir Crassus' army at the battle of Carrhae by a Parthian force in 53 BC gave the Romans a painful lesson in fighting an all-mounted army in good terrain, but Parthia was a tempting target, riven by dynastic disputes and wealthy through the trade in luxuries, particularly silk from Han China. However, Roman expansion was successful only in the annexation or destruction of friendly or neutral buffer states, and achieved no positive results – rather it damaged the authority of the largely peaceful Arsacid dynasty and stimulated the formation of hostile nomadic confederations on the desert frontier.

The weakened Parthian state fell after a prolonged struggle to Ardashir, the king of Persis, who claimed descent from the house of Sasan. Artabanus IV, the last Parthian king, was killed in battle against Ardashir at Hormuzjan in Media in AD 224. The Sasanian dynasty was to rule Iran and Mesopotamia for a further 400 years and their culture and religion heavily influenced Rome, Byzantium and the west, especially in relation to the ideology of kingship and in techniques of mounted warfare. The Sasanian kings styled themselves closely on the Achaemenids, and one of their reliefs carved beneath the Achaemenid royal tombs at Naqsh-i Rustam was to commemorate the resounding defeat of no fewer than three Roman emperors. Following centuries of intermittent but intensive warfare over Armenia and Mesopotamia the Sasanians finally all but conquered the east Roman (Byzantine) empire between AD 602 and 622 before, exhausted, Iran and the Near East became part of the Islamic world in the later 7th century.

Parthian leaded-bronze belt-buckle decorated with a horseman wearing a *bashlyk*, or cap, and armed with a composite bow in his right hand and an *akinakes* or short-sword, with ring-mounts, hanging from his belt. This type of light horseman supported the cataphracts; they were able to shoot equally well in attack, or while retreating from the enemy (the famed 'Parthian Shot') often as part of a mock flight designed to break up the enemy formation.

KING AND STATE

The Arsacid Parthian kings were overlords of a considerable number of semi-autonomous dynasts, some of whom also had the right to call themselves 'king'. Pliny the Elder noted no fewer than 18 dependent principalities between the Caspian and the Red seas. In addition the Arsacids administered extensive royal lands and provinces via appointed officials. We have few details of this hierarchy other than their titles but this structure appears in a more developed, and better known, form in the Sasanian period in royal inscriptions, headed by the king, the princes, the magnates and nobles (*Shahrdaran, vaspuhran, vuzurgan* and *azadan*). The 10th-century writer al-Masudi even describes a surviving Sasanian handbook, part of an *A'in-nama*, or 'book of rules', 'in which are mentioned all the officers of the Persian king amounting to 600 and classed according to their respective ranks'.

Right The main sites and regions mentioned in this chapter.

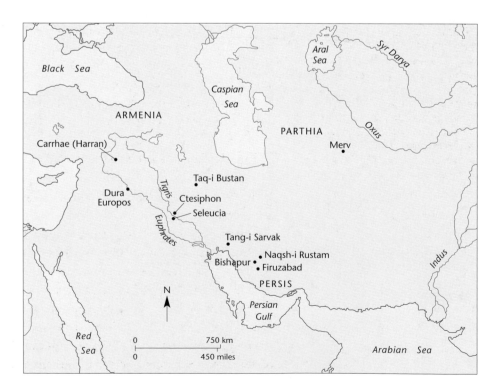

Rock reliefs at Bishapur in southwest Iran show the capture of Roman emperors and commemorate two great Sasanian victories. This scene shows King Shapur I riding over the dead body of the emperor Gordian III. His successor, Philip the Arab, kneels before Shapur and agrees treaty terms (in AD 244). The king holds another Roman emperor by the hand. This is Valerian who he captured in AD 260. The same scene, minus Gordian, is also famously represented at Naqsh-i Rustam.

The army came under the office of the *spahbed*, and the cavalry under the *asbed*. The Sasanians themselves ascribed their institutions to the reforms of Ardashir I, but the less bureaucratic and centralized appearance of the Parthian state is at least partly a result of the more limited evidence available. However, the Sasanian empire does show far greater royal control over the military and civil administration, so, for example, the local dynasts were replaced by members of the Sasanian royal family. There was also considerable direct royal intervention in extensive construction projects – the founding of new cities, and in complex systems of border fortifications and massive irrigation schemes – as part of elaborate schemes for defence in depth and economic development.

PARTHO-SASANIAN ARMIES

Both states mustered royal armies based around professional royal guards, mercenaries and conscripts, supplemented by the private forces of the magnates and the lesser nobility, and troops from foreign clients (particularly the Lakhmid Arabs of Al-Hira on the Mesopotamian frontier) and allies. Below the kings were ranked the great landed families, the magnates, from whom the army commanders were appointed. Ranked below the magnates were the lesser nobility, called variously in Greek, Latin and Middle Persian sources the *azadan*, or 'free-men'. This lesser nobility formed the formidable fully armoured cavalry of Parthian, Armenian and Sasanian armies, known simply as the *asavaran*, or 'horsemen'.

175

The Arsacids mustered their armies from the retainers and peasants under obligation to provide services to the crown and the land-owning aristocracy, the nobles and the magnates. According to the Gallic historian Trogus (whose account survives only in a later summary by Justin) the nobility instructed their retainers: 'in the arts of riding and shooting with the bow with the same care as they teach their freeborn children'. These retainers provided the famed lightly equipped horse-archers of Parthian armies, who skirmished in support of the heavy cavalry (known as cataphracts, see box opposite) and broke up the enemy's formations with feigned flight, all the while shooting showers of arrows from powerful composite bows. Plutarch wrote that the Parthian commander at the battle of Carrhae, a magnate of the powerful Suren family, had 1,000 cataphracts as his personal bodyguard, and 'many more light armed'. Parthian royal armies could be very large, as we see after the battle of Cremona in AD 69, when Tacitus says Vologeses I offered Vespasian 40,000 allied Parthian cavalry. Sasanian armies are frequently attested in numbers of 20,000 and above.

The lightly armed retainers of the Parthian period appear to have become more heavily equipped over time (Dio comments on late Parthian/early Sasanian 'mounted archers and lancers, mostly in full armour') until, by at least the reign of Khosrow I Anoshirvan (AD 531–579), all Sasanian cavalry had in theory standardized on the fully armoured, bow-armed, cataphract lancer. Sasanian kings strove to regularize paid service in the royal army and also encouraged the development of the *dekhan,* or minor nobility, to bolster the ranks of *asavaran.* Unlike the Parthians, the Sasanians were also masters of siegecraft, in attack and especially in defence.

This detail of a late Sasanian rock relief from Taq-i Bustan in northwest Iran, usually dated to the reign of Khosrow II (AD 591–628), shows a king hunting deer on horseback in a prepared enclosed area with a viewing stand. He is accompanied by attendants on horseback, and by musicians, but most noticeably also by attendants on elephants, which the Sasanians used extensively in warfare (see p. 179).

Cataphracts

Increasingly heavily armoured horsemen armed with lance, bow, mace and sword, riding armoured horses, appear in Iran from the end of the Achaemenid period. These are known as 'cataphracts' from the Greek *hippeis de kataphraktoi*, or 'fully covered' horsemen. The late Roman name for them, *clibanarii*, came from the Persian and punned on the similarities of the name for a piece of armour and an oven, evoking something of the sensation of wearing such a panoply in the heat of the Near East.

Surprisingly, depictions of this most striking of horsemen are rare, and few pieces of cataphract armour have been found. The most widely known image is a graffito from the site of Dura Europos in Syria, but the best early depiction of a Partho-Sasanian cataphract is actually on a rock relief at Tang-i Sarvak in southwestern Iran. It probably shows a prince of Elymais in full armour, charging with a lance against a (now missing) mounted opponent. The close-fighting weapon was the two-handed lance, which, according to Plutarch, had impetus enough to pierce through two men at once.

Above This rock relief, from Tang-i Sarvak in southwestern Iran, probably shows a local king of Elymais of the late Parthian/early Sasanian period. He is wearing full cataphract armour, except for his head which is left bare for the portrait. His horse also has a full lamellar trapper and a round pectoral on the breast. At the rider's waist are two quivers of arrows and a bowcase, while a pointed hammer or mace is attached to his right wrist by a lanyard.

The Sasanian rock reliefs at Firuzabad and Naqsh-i Rustam of the 3rd and 4th century AD show similar scenes of charging lancers.

Parthian and Sasanian representations and the surviving leather-scale horse armours from Dura Europos show that the trapper only covered the body and left the legs completely free. This is for the practical reason that the legs would be easily bruised or damaged by a heavy trapper and they also needed freedom of movement. Cataphracts, though usually deployed in slow dense formations, could manage a surprising turn of speed when required.

Right Similar trappers to that shown in the Tang-i Sarvak relief, of bronze and leather scale (here posed on a modern horse), have been found at the site of the Roman frontier town of Dura Europos in Iraq, destroyed by the Sasanians in the 250s. The trappers had been damaged in antiquity and were possibly awaiting repair. The plan view (*above*) shows the space left for the saddle and the lappets originally at each corner but now preserved only at the front. Parts of the separate neck armour were also found.

Opposite The late Sasanian rock reliefs at Taq-i Bustan, near Kermanshah in northwest Iran, are usually dated to the reign of Khosrow II (AD 591–628). The upper register at the back of the arch shows the king invested with the symbols of kingship, while below he is shown as a fully equipped armoured rider on a horse with a frontal trapper, armed with lance, shield and bow. The shield is attested for later Sasanian horsemen in Byzantine and Arabic accounts, but is not shown in the earlier reliefs of the dynasty.

Below A Sasanian iron helmet from the countermine tunnel under Tower 19 at Dura Europos. Helmets of this type seem to have inspired later Roman designs. It is made from two half-shells riveted to a strip with an added protective ridge over the apex. Originally there was a separate 'T-shaped' brow-ridge and nose-guard of which only the ends survive. There is a tubular plume-holder on the crown and the remains of a mail coif or camail attached to the rim. Some surviving Partho-Sasanian helmets seem to have had decorative cloth covers.

Sasanian horsemen were renowned for their fine panoply. The dazzling sight of *asavaran* in the field becomes a Roman literary cliche: according to Libanius, the Persians were 'a well-disciplined force with the glitter of gold in their armament', and in Julian and Libanius it is boasted that Constantius II's cataphracts were more perfectly equipped than the Persians – clearly the highest praise possible. Libanius' comment however is significant in other ways. For Classical writers, Persian troops were barbarians and so by definition could not have the battle-winning virtues of discipline and order. Ammianus Marcellinus, a Roman eyewitness from Emperor Julian's disastrous campaign into southern Mesopotamia, expands on this dramatic change in appreciation of 'barbarian' armies: 'their military training and discipline, and their constant practice of manoeuvres and arms drill, which I have often described, make them formidable even to large armies. They rely especially on their cavalry, in which all their nobility and men of mark serve. Their infantry are protected like *mirmillones* [gladiators] and obey orders like slaves....'

The weaponry and training regimen for the sons of Sasanian *asavaran* are shown in later 9th- and 11th-century Arabic and New Persian texts (primarily al-Tabari, Bal'ami and in the 11th century *Shahnameh* of Firdowsi) which ultimately derive from the late Sasanian royal annals, the 'Book of Kings', an official history composed in the 5th to 6th centuries AD. The ethos of the military elite, as expressed in art, tales and fable, emphasizes an all-round excellence in war and peace. The 6th-century 'Deeds of Ardashir', a late revision of a contemporary text, gives the earliest indication of such training, where the 15-year-old Ardashir, having acquired proficiency in learning and riding, is summoned to the Arsacid court of Artabanus IV. Firdowsi explains how youths were to be instructed and then sent to court to be mustered for the army in the time of Ardashir I: 'When he saw the increase of his army at the capital, he sent officials to all regions demanding that those parents who had sons should not permit them to grow to manhood without proper training. All should learn horsemanship and methods of warfare with axe, bow and sharp lances.' Al-Tabari also notes an 'instructor of the horsemen' in an account of the Sasanian royal guard.

The late Sasanian tax and army reforms promulgated by Khosrow I, as preserved in Arabic and New Persian sources, all agree in their summary of the muster requirements that 'the cavalrymen were to present themselves before him for inspection on their mounts and with their weapons, and the infantrymen with their requisite weapons'. The low-status infantry, as usual, receive little attention, but the required cavalry equipment was: horse armour, mail coat, breastplate, arm and leg armour plates, sword, lance, shield, mace and, fastened at his waist, a girdle, battle-axe or club, a bow case containing two bows with their strings, 30 arrows and finally (Firdowsi also adds a lasso) two plaited bowstrings, 'which the rider let hang down his back from his helmet'. Soldiers who appeared at the inspection received a cash payment.

That the Arsacids and Sasanians had a sophisticated organizational structure (based on a decimal system) is also hinted at by the use of unit standards. While poking fun at gullible historians, Lucian notes that the Parthians used 'dragon' standards,

Right and below Roman representations of Parthians and Sasanians are usually generic, representing an eastern 'type' rather than contemporary reality. However, they give some idea of the appearance of Partho-Sasanian infantry, as here on the Arch of Septimius Severus (showing the Roman capture of Seleucia-on-the-Tigris during Severus' second Parthian campaign of AD 197–8). The Parthian defenders have hexagonal or clipped-oval shields. Sasanian pointed-topped wicker siege-shields have been found at Dura Europos, identical to Mesopotamian designs used from the 3rd millennium BC.

one for each unit of 1,000 men. Tacitus also writes of Parthian horsemen 'ranged in squadrons (*turmae*) with their national insignia' (which in 1,000-strong Roman cavalry units would be about 40 to 50 men), while the badly weathered scenes showing the capture of Edessa (in AD 197) on the Arch of Septimius Severus appear to show a Parthian 'dragon' standard and a banner shaped like that of the Achaemenid kings.

In addition to the forces provided by the dependent kings and nobility, Tacitus records that the Parthian kings maintained both professional ('mercenary') bodyguards and permanently embodied guard cavalry ('the king's customary escort') and describes them being used for fast-moving operations while the main army was mustered. Several names for such Sasanian units, said to be 3,000 to 10,000 strong, appear in Persian, Latin, Greek, Syriac and Arabic sources. *Pushtighban* is used as a general term for 'bodyguard' in Middle Persian, and known names for the commander of the Sasanian bodyguards are *pushtighbansalar*, and *hazaruft* (*chiliarch*, 'commander of 1,000'). Bal'ami gives the name of the king's personal guard as the *gyan-abesp_aran*, the 'sacrificers of their lives', possibly a nickname acquired after a battle reported by Socrates Scholasticus in AD 422, where the royal guardsmen, called the 'Immortals' in Greek and Latin sources, died to a man. In the last battles against the armies of Islam, al-Baladhuri also mentions a 4,000-strong infantry guard recruited from Daylam in northern Iran, and highly efficient

Daylamite infantry is earlier mentioned by Agathias and Procopius. Parthian use of guard or conscript infantry is little known, though, for example, Josephus describes the king of Parthia 'with a great army of footmen and horsemen', and Parthian infantry with clipped-oval or hexagonal shields are shown on the Arch of Septimius Severus. Elephants were used extensively by the Sasanians in battle (and by at least one Parthian king as a mount). Crewed by *asavaran* according to al-Tabari, they formed behind the cavalry interspersed with infantry, 'like towers on a wall'.

BATTLEFIELD ORGANIZATION

Sasanian armies formed a single line of battle divided into a central division with two wings. The 6th-century Byzantine military manual attributed to the emperor Maurice, the *Strategikon*, claims that these were of equal size, with around 500 elite troops added to the centre, but the excerpts of a Sasanian military handbook in the *A'in-nama* do not quite support this. Here, it is stated that the army was to be arrayed so that the right was the attacking wing, and the left wing (of horse-archers capable of shooting to either side) was made stronger but held back in reserve in case of an enemy advance. The centre was to be sited on high ground with the infantry behind the cavalry in support against enemy charges. The *Strategikon* confirms that Sasanian armies preferred to deploy in rough ground. Also, the battle-line was to be aligned so that the men had the sun and wind to their back (important for effective archery). In accord with their warrior ethos, battle might open with challenges and single combats. The Byzantine chronicler Malalas even records a tale that Sasanian King Bahram V proposed that a single duel should decide the outcome of an entire war, with peace and tribute for 50 years as the prize.

This cameo gem, perhaps made by a Roman artist for a Sasanian king, probably shows the capture of the Roman emperor Valerian by Shapur I. The large decorative pom-poms attached to the harness are characteristic of a Sasanian horseman's panoply.

Sasanian horse formations were both dense and deep. John of Ephesus writes of the advance of a Persian battle-line in AD 577 as 'approaching in long files, firm as a wall'. The *Strategikon* describes the Persians forming their battle-array with two close-ordered front ranks of cataphracts, with everyone else falling in behind them in irregular depth. This hints at a similar separation between heavy and light-armed horsemen acting in close cooperation as described for the Parthian army at Carrhae – though there the cataphracts were hidden behind the lighter archers to maintain a tactical surprise.

After the collapse of the Sasanian kingdom, the skills of Iranian horsemen continued to be prized, entering into Arabic *furusiyya* literature on military horsemanship, and preserved as a living tradition into the early modern period: 'My skill in riding and archery is such, that the other [man] must be taken for fortunate, who can escape my arrow [hiding] behind [the head of his] horse. And my skill in levelling the lance is such, that the horseman must be taken for fortunate, who comes for an encounter and a combat with me on horse with lance and sword... And in throwing/wielding the mace I strike so unerringly, as if it were the face of a battering-ram...' (Husrav ud redag, *Khosrow and his Page*, a probably contemporary Middle Persian tale set in the reign of Khosrow I Anoshirvan).

11 Imperial Roman Warfare

A mail-armoured cavalryman
represented on Trajan's Column in
Rome. These formed the bulk of the
auxiliary cavalry regiments,
predominantly made up of Spanish,
German, Gallic and Thracian troopers.
This scene is one of the few on the
Column which accurately depicts a
horseman with a long cavalry
sword (*spatha*).

The period following the establishment of sole rule over the Roman empire by
Augustus up to the establishment of a 'college' of emperors by Diocletian,
conventionally known as 'the principate' (27 BC – AD 284), has often been seen as the
apogee of Roman military organization, efficiency and strength, unequalled again
in western states before the later 17th century. The empire's armies did sustain some
heavy defeats in this period, but always resiliently returned to win the wars. Certainly
the establishment of an army of career soldiers with a culture of peacetime training,
an ethos of service, loyalty to standing military formations, and highly sophisticated
logistical and communication systems, was a tremendous achievement, providing
a model which influenced the rest of world history. The volume of evidence for the
activities of the 'principate' armies in terms of literary texts, inscriptions, excavated
installations, military iconography and archaeological artifacts is quite extraordinary,
unparalleled until the early modern age; the torrent of information tails off in the 4th
century AD. This chapter examines the role of the emperors in these developments
and the nature of the constituent citizen and non-citizen forces, before examining
armies in the field facing a great variety of barbarian enemies.

EMPERORS AND ARMIES

The victory won for Octavian (named Augustus from 27 BC onwards) at Actium in
31 BC was so complete that he had the opportunity to end the century-long cycle of
civil war. He went about achieving this in many ways, but with regard to the army
the decision was made to retain a professional army of a finite number of legions,
rather than return to a citizen militia system. This had many advantages. A limited
army of standing legions could be more easily planned for in terms of pay,
equipment, recruitment of men and officers, available force, and shedding of
veterans. Legionaries eventually served for 20 years, and, before the early 3rd century
AD, they could not legally marry during their service. They were paid by Augustus
alone, using coins with his portrait on them to concentrate the recipients' minds
on their patron. A treasury was established to fund land-acquisition for veterans
using capital ostentatiously supplied by Augustus. New colonies were founded in
Italy, but it also became acceptable to plant them in the provinces, closer to where
soldiers had served. Loyalty to the Augustan line was further enhanced by the spread
of an informal cult of the emperor's spirit, and by the deification of deceased
members of the family. Soldiers joining the army swore an oath to emperor and
state. Every legion and auxiliary regiment carried portraits of the emperor on their
standards and erected statues in the shrines of military installations.

The emperors ostensibly ruled through the traditional institutions of the
Republican state, and this involved a continuing senatorial role in army command.

The cenotaph of Marcus Caelius, a centurion of *legio XVIII* (rendered as *XIIX*), found at Bonn (Germany). Caelius was killed in the Varus disaster of AD 9 and the numbers of the three lost *legiones XVII-XIX* were never used again in legionary titles. His bones lay out in Germania and the sculpture was erected by his two surviving freed slaves.

Thus they needed senators to command whole armies and individual legions of Roman citizens, both for their social cachet and administrative experience. The danger was that emperors and usurpers came from precisely this class, so, whilst the avenues leading to military glory could not be blocked, they had to be carefully supervised. Military ambition was institutionally curbed by making it clear that all the governors of provinces with substantial military forces were the emperor's delegates, thus any victory they might win against Rome's enemies was quite logically attributed to the emperor. Only emperors received formal acclamation as a victorious general by the army or were allowed the traditional triumphal procession through the streets of Rome.

Increasingly the second class within the Roman elite, the equestrians, were relied upon as military administrators, especially in the most politically sensitive posts such as commander(s) of the Praetorian Guard (see below). From the mid-2nd century AD onwards, the governors of newly formed provinces and the commanders of newly raised legions were equestrian *praefecti* rather than senatorial *legati*. Equestrians commanded all the non-citizen units of the army, including the naval forces. By the mid-3rd century senators had been excluded from all military commands, a process culminating in the complete separation of military command from civil (legal and financial) administration. A by-product of this process was to create a truly professional officer class. Promoted up through the ranks, some men eventually reached the very top as emperors, and the most prominent came from the Danubian provinces, collectively forming the region of Illyricum, hence these soldiers were known as '*Illyriciani*'.

Measures to protect the ruling emperors were remarkably successful, at least up to the end of the Severan dynasty in AD 235. However, at the centre of power emperors needed everyday protection, crowd control in Rome, secure communications with the provinces, and escort troops for when they travelled and took the field in war. The traditional bodyguard of Republican commanders was made permanent and expanded by Augustus, and in AD 23 Tiberius concentrated this Praetorian Guard in a custom-built fortress. Ten cohorts, each of 480 infantry and 120 cavalry, remained the normal strength until AD 193. All members were citizens recruited from Italy, serving for 16 years with higher pay than legionaries. The early emperors also had a fiercely loyal cavalry bodyguard of German tribesmen. These were disbanded in AD 68–69 and only reconstituted by Trajan who formed the Horseguards, 1,000 horsemen promoted from the provincial auxiliary regiments. Apart from escort duties, these troops formed a political counterbalance to the praetorians. Finding the Italian praetorians unreliable, in AD 193 Septimius Severus replaced them with promoted soldiers from his loyal Danubian legions. He also doubled the size of the praetorian cohorts to 800 (probably with 240 cavalry each), and of the Horseguards to 2,000. For most of their history these guard units served the emperors loyally until they were finally disbanded by Constantine in AD 312.

Individual soldiers identified with their own formations, and to some extent with the regional army that their formation belonged to. Legions increasingly recruited locally from populations outside Italy, and from the time of Hadrian (AD 117–38) they seldom shifted to new bases. Thus, it is helpful to think of 'the Roman army' as a series of regional armies, with diverging cultural features such as accent, jargon, architectural style, metalwork decoration and localized cult practices. These

M·CAELIVS
M·L·
RIVATVS

M·CAELIVS
M·L·
THIAMINVS

M·CAELIO·T·F·LEM·BON
O·LEG·XIIX·AN·LIII
CIDIT·BELLO·VARIANO·OSSA
NFERRE·LICEBIT·P·CAELIVS·T·F

divisions became especially evident in civil wars. From the Augustan period the soldiers also manifested their pride in personal service achievement by erecting gravestones bearing inscriptions recording name, unit, age at death, years of service, rank and military decorations. Many such gravestones were figural, depicting the deceased standing with military equipment and the insignia of rank.

The 'conflict landscapes' around Roman battlefields are now being systematically studied, but Republican armies have left little specific archaeological trace except when protracted sieges made a structural impact with fieldworks. However, from the Augustan period onwards Roman armies burst into archaeological visibility. New installations were constructed along, and in support of, the imperial frontiers for armies, individual legions, grouped formations, single auxiliary regiments and even smaller detachments. As the frontiers settled down, notably from the later 1st century AD, more resources were put into policing them with forts, small fortlets, towers and even linear barriers. This created thousands of sites containing a wide class of artifacts which reveal political, social, economic, technological and ritual aspects of Roman military activities. Individual military formations have left a 'footprint' which may be traced through their architecture, inscriptions, writing tablets, papyri, graffiti, stock-keeping stamps, equipment variants and regimental badges.

A relief from a triumphal arch erected to celebrate the conquest of Britain in AD 43, now in the Musée du Louvre, Paris. It depicts legionary troops in highly classicizing armour standing beneath their legionary eagle.

The Roman fort at Housesteads, Northumberland. Exposed within are a central headquarters, a courtyard residence for an equestrian class commander, granaries and barracks. Originally designed to house a large auxiliary infantry regiment, the plan is a scaled-down version of the legionary fortress, in turn derived from the planned layout of colonies in northern Italy.

THE IMPERIAL LEGIONS

Through discharges, amalgamations and new creations Augustus reduced 60 Civil War legions to an establishment of 27 legions, reduced to 24 (120,000 men) when three were destroyed by German tribes in AD 9. Thereafter, legions were very occasionally lost in warfare or cashiered for disloyalty, and new ones sometimes raised by emperors in connection with planned wars and territorial expansion. Elements of some still existed in the 7th century AD. Thus, the number rose to 29 under Vespasian, 30 under Trajan, and 33 (165,000 men) under Severus (AD 193–211). They were distinguished by number, and titulature based on such considerations as the name of the patron who raised them, the circumstances of formation, where they were raised, where they had served with distinction or were intended to serve, the name of a tutelary deity, or a martial epithet. These were composite titles so that, for example, when the second legion raised by Severus for his wars in Parthia was honoured for its loyalty by his son Caracalla (Marcus Aurelius Antoninus) it was known as *legio II Parthica Antoniniana* ('the second Parthian legion of Antoninus').

Each legion comprised 10 cohorts, each of 480 men, divided into 6 centuries of 80 citizen soldiers. Some legions at points in the 1st to 2nd centuries had a first cohort of 5 double-strength centuries with a total of 800 men. A small force of 120 horsemen per legion acted as scouts, couriers, escorts and battlefield cavalry. Their number may have increased in the 3rd century. Detachments of one or more cohorts could be sent off on specific tasks, or contributed to a field army during wartime. Such detachments might be away from their parent legion for long periods, or even never return at all. Artillery was also integral to the legionary organization (see box on p. 190).

These legions fulfilled many functions. One avenue of promotion for soldiers was the acquisition of skills, and there were scores of specialisms developed within the

187

Gravestone of Marcus Favonius Facilis, a centurion of *legio* XX, found at Colchester in Essex. Facilis very likely took part in Claudius' invasion of Britain in AD 43. He is depicted with the vine-wood stick (*vitis*) as insignia of rank, but does not wear military decorations. The stone was probably damaged in the Boudican Revolt of AD 61.

Opposite The plateau of Masada in Palestine, looking obliquely south. Visible as a lighter diagonal ascent on the right is the Roman siege ramp, used in the final assault against the Jewish rebels who held the stronghold. The Jewish King Herod's fortress-palace was occupied by Roman garrisons at various periods before and after the First Jewish War of AD 66–73. At *upper right* is a two-phase Roman siege camp (Camp F), built around AD 73 as part of the works encircling Masada, and located off the main photograph to the lower right. At *upper left* are stone artillery projectiles, found on the plateau.

legionary ranks. There were no separate organizations of engineers or pioneers. Thus legions built all their own military installations in timber and stone. Camps, roads, bridges, causeways, tunnels and harbours were constructed. The vast majority of military equipment was manufactured and repaired by soldiers in legionary workshops. The most important level of expertise and continuity of trained practice was that of the centurionate. Legionary centurions formed a pool of talent which could be detached for special duties: individual centurions administered ports, quarries, markets, imperial estates and local justice, and were seconded to command ad hoc military formations or regiments awaiting the appointment of higher-ranking officers.

Closely related to skills in building were the techniques demanded by ancient siege warfare. The legions already contained the artillery for such work, and had the capabilities to build all the 'machines' needed to breech or cross fortifications: siege towers, battering rams, mobile sheds, mantlets and linear barriers of containment. The Romans had inherited Hellenistic-period methodologies and technologies, improved both substantially, and applied them to great effect. In the eastern provinces they also had access to large numbers of bowmen who provided the necessary archery support. Roman-period sieges are very visible in the archaeological record for their major earth-movements and expenditure of missile artifacts. All the following occur archaeologically: siege-ramps for filling ditches and allowing wooden, wheeled towers access to fortifications; mines under walls dug by both attackers and defenders; artillery platforms for shooting over defences; contravallations to keep defenders in, and circumvallations to keep relieving enemy forces out; and attackers' defended camps. For example, the details of 1st-century AD sieges at Gamla and Masada (Palestine) and 3rd-century sieges at Cremna (Turkey), Dura Europos (Syria) and Hatra (Iraq) have been recovered through excavation. Indeed, it was in the eastern theatre that Roman siege techniques were tested and developed, in wars such as the First Jewish War (AD 66–73) and the conflicts with Sasanian Persia (AD 250s onwards), dominated by assaults on cities.

Dura Europos, a frontier town in Syria, was besieged by the Sasanian Persians around AD 253. The archaeology of the site reveals a desperate and cunning defence against overwhelming odds with no hope of relief because the Roman field armies had already been defeated in the field. Both attackers and defenders drove mine galleries under the walls to collapse towers and to destabilize assault-works. One mine collapsed entombing Roman soldiers and a Sasasian warrior with all their equipment; another 'unzipped' the wall-blocks of a corner tower making it untenable for archers; a third demolished another tower preserving the Roman shields, horse-armours and other equipment in its ground floor armoury. The site was strewn with artillery missiles, arrows and wicker mantlets. Presumably the Romans were allowed to surrender when the walls were untenable because, although the town was depopulated, there was no evidence of a sack.

Legions were always intended to form the main line of an army in order of battle. The arms and armour of legionary infantry evolved in part symbiotically with battlefield function, in part according to cultural influences. However, the main theme remained constant: the majority of legionaries were close-order, armoured swordsmen with missiles. From the time of Augustus to at least the mid-3rd century many legionary troops wore articulated, segmental steel armour protecting torso

Roman Artillery

The Roman imperial army did not simply inherit Hellenistic artillery technology, but developed it in both battlefield and siege functions. The 4th century AD writer Vegetius stated that each legion should have one bolt-shooter per century and one heavy stone-thrower per cohort, a total of 65 pieces. This accords well with Josephus' assertion that the three legions besieging Jotapata in AD 67 deployed 160 artillery weapons. The vast majority of catapults were two-armed, rather like crossbows, but powered by twisted sinew bundles. Their metal frame-fittings, especially the 'washers' which contained the sinew, are characteristic archaeological finds which, together with missiles, reveal calibre and design. The heaviest threw stones of up to 118 kg (260 lb) in weight, but more usually around 26 kg (57 lb), for use in demolishing gate structures, wooden siege engines, and for sweeping away the parapets protecting wall-top adversaries. The lightest shot arrows or bolts over a range of 400 m (1,300 ft) or more with extreme accuracy, sniping at individual enemies, or, using fire-heads, to burn besieged internal buildings and wooden siege-machines. An intact frame was recently found at Xanten in the German Rhineland. It comes from a small, sinew-powered, hand-held, single-operator weapon. Heavier bolt-shooters are first seen on Trajan's Column mounted on a cart for use in support of the advancing battle-line and these were current through to the 6th century.

Above Reconstruction of a torsion artillery-piece of a type current from the 1st century BC to 1st century AD.

Left Reconstruction of the Xanten hand-held, arrow-shooting, torsion weapon, a *manuballista* of a type probably more widely employed in the legions than has hitherto been envisaged.

Above View of the Palmyrene (West) Gate in the desert wall of Dura Europos. This was the most heavily defended portal of the city's defences, facing the open desert plateau, with two projecting rectangular towers and a walled forecourt. It was so strong that it was avoided by the Sasanian besiegers in the mid AD 250s.
Below Reconstruction of two 1st-century AD legionaries, both wearing segmented plate cuirasses and armed with sword, spear and shield.

and shoulders (the so-called '*lorica segmentata*'). Mail and scale cuirasses were also employed. Helmets developed with low, wide neck-flanges to protect neck and sides of the head. The shield varied in shape but was always large to cover the bearer from knee to chin, and curving on its narrow, lateral axis. Legionary shields were painted with Jupiter's thunderbolts and zodiac signs as formation badges.

During the 1st to 2nd centuries AD, legionary weaponry consisted of a short, double-edged sword worn on the soldier's right side so as to avoid encumbrance by the curved shield. This was a sword equally designed for cutting and thrusting, based on Republican forms. Republican heavy javelins (*pila*) also continued in use. Lighter javelins (*lanceae*) were used by some legionary soldiers and careful analysis of the literary sources suggests that integral, javelin-armed light infantry were always present within the legions. There is abundant evidence for archery playing a part in the general training of all Roman troops, especially for battlement defence, but integral archers are also attested within the legions at various dates. In the 3rd century a large, dished oval shield form became prominent and segmental cuirasses seem to have declined in use. The short sword was generally replaced by longer sword types (*spathae*) carried on the left side.

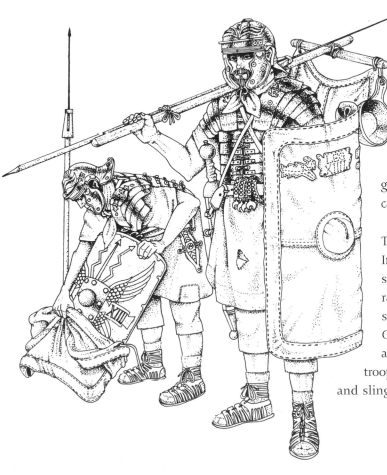

THE AUXILIARY FORCES

In all periods the heavy infantry of the legions required support forces. The Roman empire encompassed a great range of military cultural traditions. These produced specialists such as spear-and-shield cavalry (Spaniards, Gauls and Thracians), light skirmishing cavalry (Moors and Dalmatians), light infantry (Numidians), mountain troops (Spaniards), archers (Numidians, Thracians, Syrians) and slingers (Spaniards). Allies and mercenaries had been

191

Above Sculpture depicting two 1st-century AD legionary soldiers on a pedestal from the headquarters of the legionary fortress at Mainz in Germany. Carved by soldiers, such basic yet accurate reliefs are a valuable parallel iconographic source to the products of metropolitan workshops, such as Trajan's Column.

Opposite Gravestone of the Thracian auxiliary cavalryman Longinus, found at Colchester in Essex. The rider wears a scale cuirass rather than the mail armour more commonly depicted in funerary art. His face was presumably damaged in the Boudican Revolt but the missing broken part was recently rediscovered and restored.

employed during the Republic, but something more regularly available was needed to serve alongside the imperial legions. So the emperors created permanent 'auxiliary' regiments of infantry, cavalry and mixed, part-mounted formations. Cohorts of 480 or 800 men (to which 120 or 240 cavalry were often attached) were divided into centuries under centurions. Regiments made up entirely of cavalry were termed '*alae*' ('wings') and they too came in greater and lesser strengths, and were organized into *turmae* (troops) under decurions. Thus there were six types of auxiliary regiment based on the praetorian and legionary models. Entirely predictably the evidence of excavated barracks in forts thought to hold one regiment, and of unit-records on papyrus, demonstrates that these strengths were nominal and that internal regimental organization could vary widely. However, army commanders could have relied on the notion that auxiliary cohorts came in two orders of size, around 500 and around 1,000.

Each regiment was commanded by an equestrian and a hierarchy of seniority, or career-track, developed, especially from the AD 60s when the larger units first appeared. Cavalry was senior to infantry. Like the legions, these formations were raised for specific campaigns, amalgamated and lost. And like the legions their titles might reflect their creator, but titles based on the origin of the troops were more finely tuned, being designated by people, individual tribe, or, in the case of oriental regiments, by city. Further titles designated weapons specialisms such as cavalry lancers, cataphracts or archers. Regiments were rewarded for loyalty and actions in battle with military decorations and further titles such as *torquata* ('awarded torques') or *pia fidelis* ('faithful and loyal'). Most regiments were made up of non-citizens but some were rewarded with block grants of citizenship. Thus the accumulated titles of one regiment could become quite complex. For example, a cavalry regiment of the large size, first raised by Petrus from Gauls and honoured three times, was styled *ala Gallorum Petriana milliaria civium Romanorum bis torquata* ('the Petrian wing of Gauls, twice awarded torques, 1,000 strong, citizens of Rome'). Petrus was one of a number of Roman citizens who personally raised early cavalry units. Auxiliaries served for 25 years for less pay and reward than legionary troops, but, before AD 212 (when the free population was made citizen), the long-term attraction of enlistment included the advantages of citizenship granted at the end of service.

Above Fragmentary bronze sheet, one half of a discharge diploma from Malpas in Cheshire, issued to Reburrus of *ala I Pannoniorum* in AD 103.

The full establishment of auxiliary regiments can be estimated from period to period by examining formation titles, by tracing individual unit histories through their archaeological footprint, and through the bronze sheet documents ('*diplomata*') issued to soldiers on their completion of service. More than 400 of these have been recovered and crucially they list the names of all the regiments discharging men in a province at the same time. Thus, around AD 155, there were 81 large and small cavalry regiments and some 247 infantry and mixed regiments of various sizes, suggesting a paper strength of approximately 180,000 auxiliary soldiers for the whole empire.

The auxiliaries provided the bulk of the army's cavalry, scouts, skirmishers, light infantry and missile troops. They did the lion's share of policing on the imperial frontiers. It is likely that most did not have the skills for constructing installations until well into the 2nd century AD, but thereafter they built their own fortifications and other architecture, and cavalry regiments were just as active as other formations. Auxiliaries seldom, if ever, operated artillery.

In terms of equipment, both infantry and cavalry were universally armoured with scale or mail cuirasses. The Roman forces may have represented one of the most widely armoured armies in history, irrespective of personal wealth and status, principally because the equipment was available in quantity and at subsidized cost. Increasingly auxiliaries became involved in metalworking, equipment manufacture and repair. Infantry helmet forms were similar to those worn by legionary troops; cavalry wore different types which emphasized protection to the lower neck. In the later 2nd and 3rd centuries infantry and cavalry helmets came closer together in design and protection, partly denoting a more upright fencing stance for the infantry who were now using the longer swords. All auxiliaries used flat, oval or rectangular shields with a central grip-boss, but little is known about their painted decoration. In the 3rd century they used the same dished

A bronze cavalry-type 'sports' helmet for use in weapons-training displays, from Ribchester in Lancashire. The mask protected the face and eyes from wooden-headed practice javelins, and the owner's horse would have worn a similarly protective chamfron with eye-grills. The helmet bowl is covered in embossed decoration, and the mask takes the form of an idealized Greek male face.

oval shields as the other troops, and the same sword forms throughout. They replaced *pila* with spears (*hastae*) and light javelins. Cavalry also used these shafted weapons and wielded the long *spatha* for its necessary reach from horseback. Double-handed lances were adopted from the steppe nomad Sarmatians (see Chapter 13) for a few *alae* around the time of Trajan's Danubian wars. Composite bows were used by Levantine archers. Finds of sling-bullets suggest that many auxiliary units were trained as slingers without having a specific unit epithet. All cavalry, except the lightest Moorish irregulars, used the horned 'Thraco-Celtic' saddle which gave the rider a tremendously secure seat.

Apart from the auxiliary regiments, there were also transient formations raised for specific campaigns, or supplied by friendly states to supplement Roman armies. Moorish skirmishing light cavalry were always desirable for use against steppe nomads on the Danube, or Parthian horse-archers in the east. Likewise, Syrian archers, both foot and horse, were highly valued for use against unarmoured Germanic tribes and eastern horse-archers. Both groups often took on a more permanent existence as formations designated as *numeri* – an unspecific term used for any formation when other classifications, such as legion or cohort, were inappropriate.

A further, non-citizen component of the Roman forces was made up by the fleets. The battle of Actium in 31 BC was the last great fleet action of the Roman period. Thereafter the Mediterranean was a Roman lake. Augustus established two 'imperial' fleets, at Misenum on the Bay of Naples and at Ravenna at the head of the Adriatic Sea. During the 1st century AD further fleets were established in the English Channel, along the Rhine and Danube, in the Black Sea, and in the eastern Mediterranean. These transported and supplied armies in an ancillary role, transported the emperor and his entourage, acted as a mode of swift communication, and patrolled the northern river frontiers using ship-mounted artillery. Fleet troops also operated on land as skilled manpower for architectural and engineering projects, worked the awnings over entertainment buildings in Rome, and sometimes were either drafted into newly raised legions or acted as combat troops in their own right.

EMPERORS AND ARMIES AT WAR

Augustus added huge areas to the Roman empire but under his successors expansion slowed. Initially legions were concentrated at major bases on or behind the frontiers, poised for future advances. During the 1st century AD the army group on the Rhine was most numerous and politically dominant. Conflicts with eastern Germans, Dacians and Sarmatians in the Danubian theatre became paramount in the 2nd century with Trajan's Dacian Wars (101–2 and 105–6 – see box opposite), wars against the Marcomanni and other Germans under Marcus Aurelius (168–75, 178–80), and thereafter with the rise of new enemies such as the Goths. The result was that the balance of legionary

Trajan's Column

Trajan's Column in Rome is the monument to the skills and achievements of the Roman army par excellence. Its 200-m (650-ft) long helical frieze depicts 2,600 human figures engaged in Trajan's Dacian Wars across the Danube (AD 101–2, 105–6): Roman soldiers march, build, fight and triumph under the guidance of the emperor, and they bring barbarians under the emperor's power. Reliefs on the pedestal originally depicted more than 600 items of barbarian equipment as spoils of victory.

Verifiable historical events on the column are few, and the scenes of imperial speeches, sacrifices, victories and enemy submissions are stylized and formulaic. Citizen soldiers are depicted for ease of visual recognition in pursuance of propaganda themes in segmental armour and rectangular shields. They alone exercise the technical skills of building installations and operating artillery. Non-citizen auxiliary infantry and cavalry wear ring-mail armour, carry oval shields, and do most of the fighting, exactly coinciding with elite definitions of a glorious victory – won without the loss of *Roman* blood.

The Column still provides some independent information unavailable from other sources, notably concerning military standards, tents, the range of Roman forces present (citizen and non-citizen troops, marines, oriental archers, slingers, German irregulars, Moorish cavalry) and the varied barbarian types encountered in the wars. The Column reliefs were the first and last ever attempted on such a scale with such a level of sculptural detail.

Detail of the helical frieze of Trajan's Column, from bottom to top: genre scenes depicting barbarian submission and Roman army supply wagons; Roman fieldwork construction and troops advancing to battle; Trajan gazing over a major battle as severed barbarian heads are presented to him, and the army advances to the assault.

numbers shifted eastwards, and the Illyrian army became the military and political elite. The eastern frontier was the only one facing an urbanized enemy which posed a serious threat to Rome's territories. Wars against the Parthians were mainly aggressive campaigns seeking glory after the Alexander model, but in actuality involved multiple urban sieges. From the 230s a new, Sasanian Persian dynasty was a far more dangerous neighbour which inflicted some heavy defeats on Roman armies (see Chapter 10). The eastern theatre became a region of well-fortified cities and a 'school of war' in the Renaissance sense. Apart from short civil wars in which Roman armies exercised their military skills on each other (AD 68–69, 193–97, 217–18, 235 onwards), there were periodic internal revolts against Roman rule which were always unsuccessful once Roman armies assembled to crush them.

Between major wars and large-scale barbarian incursions the army had to police the frontiers against low-level threats. Thus, for reasons of political security and ease of supply, bases were reduced to holding just one legion, and most were positioned on navigable waterways. Legionary detachments and auxiliary regiments, or part-regiments, were spread out along river lines and linear barriers to man smaller installations. In the field the ability of Roman armies to bridge major rivers, to clear forest, build roads and to communicate over long distances by signal towers and other means, gave its campaign forces great advantages in strategic mobility over most barbarian adversaries. Theoretically, baggage trains were kept to a minimum, being integral to military formations; there was no separate transport organization or provision. Pack-mules were common throughout the empire, the remains of many having been found at one excavated site associated with the AD 9 Varus disaster, where three legions and

The maximum extent of the Roman empire and the main provinces and sites mentioned in this chapter.

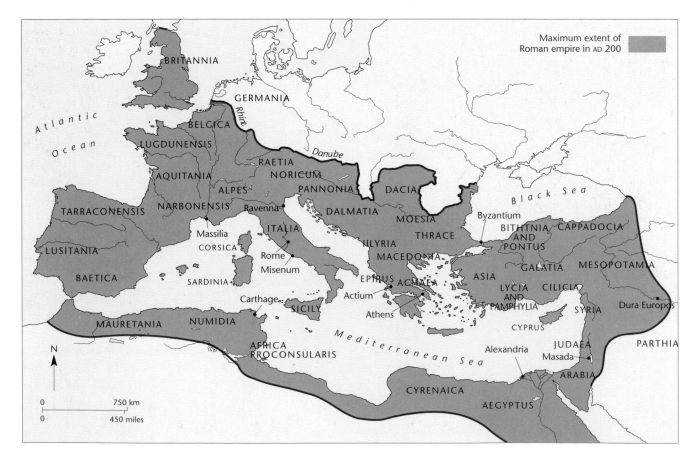

Trajan's Column, from bottom to top: the army marches across the River Danube at the start of the First Dacian War in AD 101; Roman soldiers construct bridges and fortifications.

attendant auxiliaries were destroyed by German tribes near modern Kalkriese in Germany. They carried tents, grain milling-stones and spare equipment. In the eastern provinces troops took full advantage of the availability of pack-camels, principally dromedaries. Bulk food, drink and equipment, notably artillery, were carried in two- or four-wheeled wagons drawn by mules, horses or bullocks.

The big picture of legionary and auxiliary establishments (140,000 and 180,000 strong in c. AD 155) does not help to reveal the Roman armies at war because so many formations policed frontiers in peaceful regions, or fulfilled rear-echelon functions in theatres of war. However, there are several examples which illustrate the composition of armies campaigning in the field. During the Pannonian War of AD 6–9, waged in the western Balkans against resurgent Pannonian tribes, the future emperor Tiberius gathered a huge campaign army together. It consisted of 10 legions and 10,000 additional legionary veterans, more than 70 auxiliary cohorts, 14 cavalry regiments, plus some irregular troops. At more than 102,000 soldiers this was an extraordinarily large gathering under Augustus' designated successor. During the First Jewish War (AD 66–73) Vespasian and Titus together commanded 3 legions, 23 auxiliary cohorts and five *alae*, plus 4,000 cavalry and 6,000 infantry archers supplied by neighbouring kings, amounting to 60,000 troops in total. A text written by an unknown author (known as 'Pseudo-Hyginus') in the 3rd century AD, which described the layout of a campaign base, enumerated an army of 4 praetorian cohorts with 400 attached cavalry, 450 Horseguards, three legions, 1,600 detached legionaries, four large *alae*, five small *alae*, 600 Moorish and 800 Pannonian irregular cavalry, 200 scouts, 1,300 fleet personnel, 12 assorted auxiliary cohorts, 3,300 Palmyrene archers and other irregulars, and 200 special service troops. Although a literary exercise, internal evidence suggests that this was an army envisaged in the Danubian theatre, perhaps at the time of Hadrian or Marcus Aurelius, with a strength of approximately 37,000 men.

The Battle of Mons Graupius

	ROMAN EMPIRE	CALEDONIAN CONFEDERACY
COMMANDERS	Agricola	Calgacus
STRENGTH	c. 20,000	c. 30,000
CASUALTIES	360	10,000

In AD 83/84 the governor of Britannia, Julius Agricola, met the Caledonian tribes in the northernmost set-piece battle ever fought by a Classical army. Perhaps the best part of three legions were drawn up in front of their camp. In front of them were 8,000 auxiliary infantry flanked by 3,000 cavalry. The auxiliaries swept forward, the infantry pushing back the Britons on the lower slopes opposite, the cavalry defeating chariot-warriors.

When the mass of British infantry counter-attacked, Agricola committed his cavalry reserve and the enemy then dispersed, the legions having played no active part. Caledonian losses were claimed at 10,000, and the emperor Domitian celebrated a

Mons Graupius

2 The Caledonian infantry counter-attack, rushing the auxiliaries making up the Roman front line

CALGACUS

1 The Caledonians' chariots, having been drawn up in front of the infantry, are dispersed by the Roman cavalry

AGRICOLA

triumph, but it is unclear how decisive a victory this really was. Clearly much of the tribal army was able to withdraw through difficult country. Although it lingered in Ireland, this was the last showing of the war-chariot which had dominated Bronze Age and Early Iron Age battlefields everywhere before larger horse breeds were available for cavalry. The site of the battle has been much sought-after, and one possibility is the valley northeast of the Hill of Bennachie (Aberdeenshire).

6 The Caledonians withdraw across difficult country and night ends pursuit

5 The Roman legions in reserve play no part in the battle

4 Up to 16 auxiliary cohorts make up the frontline. Pushing uphill, four Batavian and two Tungrian units lead the decisive assault on the Caledonian centre

3 Agricola commits his cavalry on both flanks, breaking up the Caledonian attack

Unfortunately, accounts of battles in surviving historical texts are brief and stylized. For example, according to Tacitus, at the battle of Mons Graupius in AD 83/84 auxiliary cavalry and infantry advanced so effectively that they alone swept away the Caledonian forces, leaving legionary troops to spectate (see box on p. 198). Exactly contemporaneously, the sculptures on Trajan's Column in Rome show auxiliaries fighting and citizen troops in reserve. The latter engage in battle on only a very few occasions, mainly in sieges which were linked with Roman technical expertise, therefore with superior Roman civilization. The concern here is that Tacitus' account (and also Trajan's Column) may have simply conformed to the elite ideal of military victory.

However, the Roman historical and technical literature suggests how Roman armies would actually have been drawn up to offer battle against barbarian adversaries. The basic method was to dispose the legionary cohorts present in three rows to form the main battle line, as was described by Julius Caesar. Auxiliary support troops would have been positioned on the army's wings and in reserve. The legionary armament of short sword and *pila* had proved to be effective during the Republic against the armoured, close-order, pike-armed or spear-armed infantry of Hellenistic and Carthaginian armies. Equally, the cohort formation was able to withstand the wild charges of northern barbarian infantry. The latter continued to be the significant adversaries in Britain, Germany and the Danube lands. A tactical scenario may be envisaged whereby oncoming barbarian warriors were first hit at long distance by artillery accurately picking off prominent leaders; then by archers and slingers, bringing down large numbers of unarmoured men. Close in, showers of heavy *pila* would have punched through shield-boards and armour. The legionary line would have counter-charged to meet a barbarian formation already losing its momentum through fallen bodies, tripping and disorganizing men coming on behind. Crashing into the barbarians, the well-armoured legionary line, in a loose formation with a frontage of about 1 m (3 ft) per man, fenced using shields in combination with lightning sword thrusts at vulnerable targets. If the Roman line held and the barbarian momentum was lost then the legions advanced cutting into the warrior mass until it disintegrated in flight. If the Roman line was pushed back, or, worse, overrun, then the next line of cohorts came into play.

Just how Roman armies dealt with steppe nomad, Parthian and Sasanian armies in the east may be judged from Arrian's *Order of Battle Against the Alans*. Arrian, a 2nd-century AD general, historian and philosopher, meticulously described the composition of his army in Cappadocia (eastern Turkey) during the reign of Hadrian, when an invasion was threatened by the Sarmatian Alans. Arrian's force consisted of one full legion plus 2,000 detached legionaries, cavalry scouts, three *alae*, the equivalent of 5 mixed auxiliary cohorts, and 1,000 irregular troops, a total force of some 13,000 men. When the army arrived at the chosen ground it was to draw up with the legionary troops in the centre. Their flanks were to be protected by hills topped by artillery, auxiliary infantry and irregular troops, including archers. The cavalry was to have been held in reserve. Most of the auxiliary cohort cavalry and infantry were archers, as was a significant proportion of the irregular troops.

The legionaries were to be drawn up in close files with a frontage of 45 cm (18 in) per man, shield-to-shield, in a deep formation of eight ranks, the first four armed with *pila*, the rear four with lighter javelins (*lanceae*). The whole line would be backed

Gravestone of a javelinman (*lancearius*) of *legio II Parthica*, dating to the first half of the 3rd century AD, from Apamea in Syria. A bundle of short, light javelins is clearly represented in the soldier's right hand.

by auxiliary infantry archers. When the Alans charged the Roman centre they would have passed through a storm of missiles. In the unlikely event of their horses reaching the Roman line, they would meet an impenetrable forest of points and a continuing rain of javelins and arrows. Once the enemy was repulsed then the javelin-armed infantry and reserve cavalry would pursue cautiously so that the pursuers could be supported in turn, should the Alans wheel back into the attack. The troops on the wings, especially archers, were to prevent the line being outflanked by barbarian counter-moves. Arrian was clearly focused on the dangers posed to a predominantly infantry army by the mobility and tactical flexibility of steppe nomad cavalry. In any case Roman armies in the east contained a much higher proportion of archers than those in the west for reasons of regional cultural tradition and because of the formalization of auxiliary regiments.

Such a tactical plan was probably usual for the eastern frontier where Roman armies faced not only steppe nomads but also the armoured cavalry armies of the Parthians and Sasanians. Gravestones found at Apamea (Syria), dating to the first half of the 3rd century AD, belonged to *legio II Parthica* soldiers and list various legionary specialisms including bolt-shooters, archers, javelinmen and close-order infantry. The *II Parthica* is likely to have drawn up in a deep formation similar to Arrian's order of battle, perhaps specifically when trained for war in the east. *Pila* continued to be manufactured in western legionary fortresses together with archery equipment. This evidence has been taken to suggest that from the time of Hadrian there was a shift in legionary tactics from flexible, multiple lines of cohorts to a single, deep, monolithic 'phalanx'. This both simplifies the evidence, drawing lines of development between too few fixed points, and insufficiently appreciates the specific eastern tactical context of the sources.

The Roman armies have always been held up as models of military excellence. This was partly because they had a philosophy of continuous training. All armies are as good as their last performance and without frequent wars their actual combat experience becomes dissipated over time. Very few armies before the modern period went beyond the initial weapons and formation training of recruits. The Romans held inspections and reviews and practised manoeuvres involving not just individual regiments but also whole legionary battle-groups. This lay behind Josephus' famous dictum that Roman exercises were bloodless battles and their battles were bloody exercises. The dangers of laxity, luxury and lethargy were well recognized and institutionally guarded against. Certainly Rome sustained some signal defeats at the hands of seemingly less-developed adversaries. However, the successful methods of waging war with citizen infantry developed during the Republic were brought forward, and a truly professional army developed under Augustus and his successors. The constituent military traditions of the empire were fully exploited through the non-citizen auxiliaries, and technologies and tactics evolved according to changing enemies and circumstances. How else may the long record of Roman military success be explained?

12 Rome and the Barbarians

Mosaic from the church of Santa
Maria Maggiore, Rome, dating to the
mid-5th century AD. This Biblical scene
shows the destruction of Pharaoh's
army in the crossing of the Red Sea.
The soldiers are modelled on
contemporary examples, although
the chariots are anachronistic.

The late Roman empire was surrounded by barbarian enemies in Europe, Africa and the east. In Europe, there were three northern frontiers, in Britain and the North Sea, along the Rhine and upper Danube, and on the middle and lower Danube. Here were groups of barbarians, occasionally allying into large confederations under competent leaders. Enemies faced in Britain included Picts, Scots and Saxons, on the Rhine various groups of Franks and Alamanni, and on the Danube Goths, Sarmatians and later Huns. In North Africa, Egypt and the Levant, threats came from various tribes of Moors, Blemmyes and Saracens. Roman policy in Africa and Europe was short term and aggressive. The barbarian threat could not be eradicated, so they were best kept off balance by a combination of political activity and pre-emptive strikes. Sometimes the barbarians were lucky and won victories, but any exploitation could only come if the Romans were distracted by domestic politics. Nonetheless, it must also be recognized that centuries of exposure to Roman military methods had made these enemies far more dangerous than those barbarians faced by the early empire. But the empire's major enemy was in the East: Persia. In Mesopotamia, the Caucasus and the central Anatolian mountains, the Romans faced an organized state which could field large armies. In AD 260, the emperor Valerian was even captured near Edessa. Relations with Persia were more formal, and states of war and peace existed, mediated by written peace treaties. So, even as the western empire collapsed under pressure from barbarians in the 5th century, Persia remained the major enemy.

BARBARIAN PROBLEMS

Throughout the 3rd and 4th centuries, the Romans were generally able to maintain superiority on their borders. Some battles were lost, but battles had been lost before, and at the end of the 4th century the Rhine and Danube were still the Roman frontiers in Europe. However, failure to defeat the Goths at the battle of Adrianople in 378 (see box on pp. 206–7) eventually led in 382 to the settlement of Gothic groups in the Balkans. The subsequent use of these Goths by the Romans in the civil wars against first Magnus Maximus in 388 and then Eugenius in 394 allowed the creation of a Gothic political identity. The Goths became an established part of the military and political landscape, a power to be negotiated with inside the borders of the empire. At the same time foreign threats continued. Thus, Roman problems with the Goths in Italy, leading to the sack of Rome in 410, took place against a backdrop of the crossing of the Rhine in 406 by groups of Vandals, Alans and Suevi and the loss of control of Britain. The Goths were then settled in Aquitaine in 418, where they were used against these Vandals, Alans and Suevi who had settled in Spain.

Porphyry statue of the four Tetrarchs (Diocletian, Maximian, Galerius, Constantius I) from Venice. The emperors are shown clasping each other's shoulders to symbolize imperial unity. They are dressed as soldiers, though wearing the typical undress cap (known as a Pannonian cap) rather than helmets.

It was not until the 450s that the Goths in Gaul began to develop any sense of independence. By that point, other problems were more important, in particular the Vandals who had occupied North Africa, the Burgundians who were occupying some of the Rhineland, and the Huns. The Huns provide a good example of the weakness of Rome's enemies. Though able to reduce the Balkans to a state of devastation in the 440s, the power of the leader of the Huns, Attila (see Chapter 13), was personal and could not survive setbacks. He was stalemated in Gaul at the battle of Châlons in 451, and he invaded Italy in 452 with little effect. Once Attila died in 453 his empire collapsed. But the frontiers were long and continuing problems beset the Romans, with a Vandal sack of Rome in 455, and the emergence of new Gothic groups on the Danube. Final western military collapse came only with the murder of the emperor Majorian in 461, but the eastern empire continued, and in the 6th century Justinian was able to launch a successful reconquest of Africa, Italy, and parts of Spain.

Imperial politics were also a large part of the story of Rome and the barbarians in late antiquity. When Diocletian seized imperial power in AD 284, he faced numerous problems. Political instability was perhaps the most critical. Diocletian's response was to create the Tetrarchy, a group of four cooperating emperors, who were able to stabilize the majority of the internal and external crises faced by the empire. The system collapsed under pressures of succession in the early 4th century, but established the principle of a college of emperors which was recreated in the reign of Constantine I (306–337), though with family rather than friends. Civil wars between the sons of Constantine followed, leading to the sole rule of Constantius II from 350, but by now it was clear that more than one emperor was necessary, and Constantius appointed his cousin Julian as junior emperor. Constantius died in 361, and Julian died fighting in Persia in 363. After the brief reign of Jovian, the next emperor Valentinian I shared power with his brother Valens. Though there was still one empire (with a single legal system and currency), from this point the eastern and western parts started to diverge, a process that accelerated in the 5th century. The last Roman emperor in the west was deposed in 476, but the eastern empire carried on.

THE LATE ROMAN ARMY

The late Roman army was like any other, with good and bad soldiers, officers and generals. On some days it was lucky, on others unlucky. Its mission was to defend the Roman state, a task which changed greatly between 284 and 500. The story of the empire's collapse in the west is now rarely seen as a military story, more of failures of leadership and politics.

But if the empire that had to be defended was drastically different in 284 and 500, what of the army? Rather than focusing on the failures of the army, or on selected anecdotes, a more useful approach is perhaps to ask whether the empire could have afforded a defensive system that kept all barbarians outside at all times. Contemporary writers may have wished this (and are often echoed by modern historians writing about the Roman empire), but whether they would have paid the necessary taxes seems unlikely. When the senior imperial financial official Ursulus saw the ruins of Amida (in modern Turkey) in 360, sacked by the Persians the year before, he remarked 'behold with what courage the cities are defended by our soldiers, for whose abundance of pay the wealth of the empire is already insufficient.' His comments were remembered by the troops, and at Chalcedon a year later he was condemned to death in the purges at Julian's accession. So our questions should be formed along the lines of how well did the army perform, given the resources available and the challenges it faced. During this period there was little change in the army itself, which is important as it suggests that the Romans themselves were satisfied with their military structures.

The evidence is best for the late 4th century, when we have the detailed histories of Ammianus Marcellinus, an officer who had served in Persia and on the Rhineland. Recruiting is an interesting issue. Older studies have argued for a shortage of manpower, though a better emphasis might be on difficulties in recruiting. The problems in extracting manpower from a reluctant population were the same in 500 as they were in 284, and no different in Gaul than in Egypt or on the Danube frontier.

In the mid-4th century, Flavius Abinnaeus was the commanding officer of a cavalry regiment based at Dionysias in the Egyptian Fayum. A small archive of Abinnaeus' personal and business papers is preserved. They tell us what soldiers were up to on a daily basis around the village of Dionysias. Besides collecting taxes, the most recorded area of legitimate activity was recruiting, but getting recruits from villages was not always easy. In one case, an official could not find any recruits in a village despite spending three days there; eventually the villagers produced money in lieu of a recruit, though far less than the official cash value of even one soldier. Other soldiers were less patient and more violent: another recruiting mission press-ganged men, looted houses and drove off some cattle. Reluctance to supply men was for various reasons, though the fact that many men who went to become soldiers did not return was probably central. Abinnaeus received one letter asking that the writer's brother-in-law be posted to the border troops so that he would serve in Egypt, rather than to the field army when he could go anywhere in the empire. However, focusing on manpower alone may miss the point. As Synesius, responsible for administering some of the defences of Cyrenaica in the early 5th century, put it, 'for war we need hands, not a list of names'.

A colossal bronze statue (5 m (16½ ft) high) of a late Roman Emperor from Barletta, Italy, though supposedly originally from Constantinople. Although dressed as a general, the identification of the emperor is uncertain; Valentinian I, Theodosius II, and Heraclius have all been suggested. The cross is a later addition.

The Battle of Adrianople

	EASTERN ROMAN EMPIRE	GOTHS
COMMANDERS	Valens	Fritigern, Atlatheus, Saphrax
STRENGTH	15,000–30,000	c. 20,000
CASUALTIES	c. 20,000	Unknown

On 9 August 378, a force of Goths defeated a Roman army at Adrianople (modern Edirne in Turkey). Thousands of Roman soldiers fell, and the emperor Valens was killed. Although the story has been told many times before, all accounts are based on the account of Ammianus Marcellinus.

We can say little with any confidence about the numbers of Romans or Goths involved or about how many died. When the two forces met, neither was in a hurry to fight: the Goths were waiting for dispersed cavalry to arrive, the Romans were still coming out of their marching formation. The Roman left flank cavalry were still trying to deploy when two Roman regiments – the *Sagittarii* under Bacurius and the *Scutarii* under Cassio – engaged the Goths, dragging the rest of the Romans into battle. At this point, some of the

Gothic cavalry arrived and were able to strike the Roman left flank, still coming out of march order. Instead of the battle being an ordered affair, in which Roman advantages could be deployed, it developed into a disorganized struggle in which the Goths gradually became victorious.

As the Romans fell back, Valens, surrounded by the regiments of *Lanciarii* and *Mattiarii*, became isolated; Roman reserves had already been committed to the developing clash in the centre. Then Valens was wounded by an arrow and took refuge in a farmhouse. The Goths, not knowing who was inside and facing fierce resistance from Valens' bodyguards, fired the house. As darkness fell, the Romans had lost the emperor, two generals, and 35 tribunes; Ammianus estimated that only a third of the army escaped the defeat.

Although Adrianople was a disaster, with the important exception of Ammianus, contemporary writers do not treat it as the end of an era. Moreover, the failures were not structural. The errors which led to defeat here lay at various levels. Most critical was the impatience of Valens who wanted to defeat the Goths before the arrival of a western reinforcing army. Because of

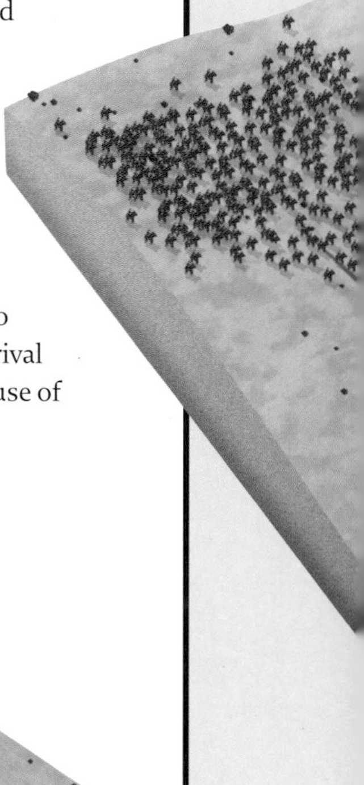

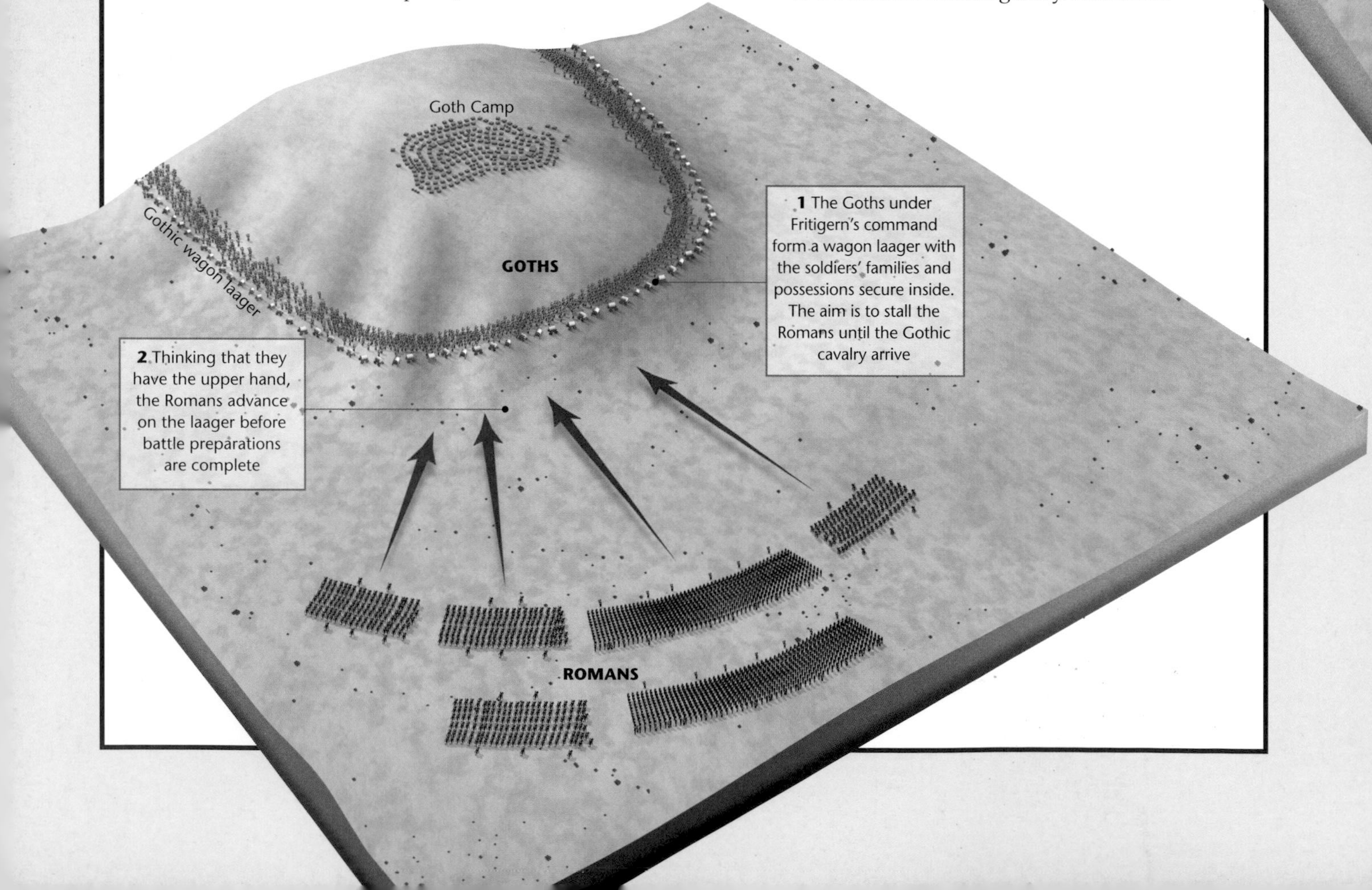

Goth Camp

Gothic wagon laager

GOTHS

1 The Goths under Fritigern's command form a wagon laager with the soldiers' families and possessions secure inside. The aim is to stall the Romans until the Gothic cavalry arrive

2.Thinking that they have the upper hand, the Romans advance on the laager before battle preparations are complete

ROMANS

his impatience, there was pressure to read an intelligence report in an optimistic fashion, committing the army to battle prematurely. And when the force was on the battlefield, combat began before the army had come fully out of the line of march, the result of two aggressive tribunes. Certainly things went wrong on 9 August 378, but the Roman army had little reason to reform itself after Adrianople.

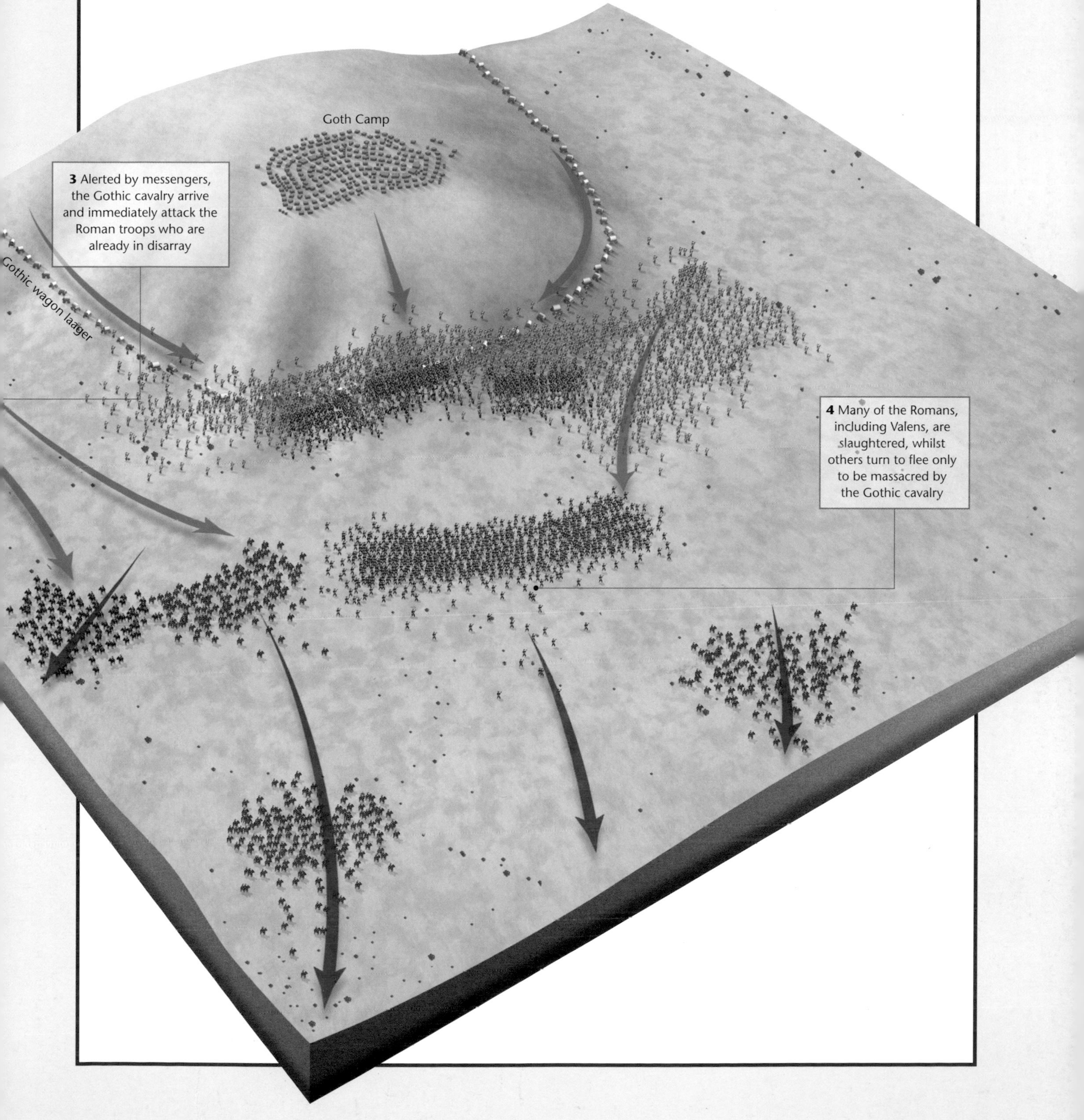

Goth Camp

3 Alerted by messengers, the Gothic cavalry arrive and immediately attack the Roman troops who are already in disarray

Gothic wagon laager

4 Many of the Romans, including Valens, are slaughtered, whilst others turn to flee only to be massacred by the Gothic cavalry

Silver Missorium (presentation plate) of Theodosius I. This large plate shows Theodosius in the centre, with his sons Arcadius and Honorius at his side. They are surrounded by imperial bodyguards, distinguished by their long hair and torcs. This plate has been folded at some point in its history, hence the large crack across the centre.

Some of the men in the garrison of Egypt would have been native Egyptians, posted not far from home. But others would have had the fate feared by Abinnaeus' correspondent and been sent a great distance. In the 380s, the emperor Theodosius I transferred some recently recruited Goths to Egypt, while an Egyptian regiment was sent to the Balkans to replace the Goths. The transfer took place overland, but when the two regiments crossed paths at Philadelphia in Lydia, there was a riot in the marketplace and a number of men were killed. Besides this regiment of Goths, there were many other imported units in Egypt. In Alexandria in the mid-5th century, part of the city garrison was a regiment of Isaurians, a tough mountain people from southern Anatolia. This was under the command of a certain Conon from Cappadocia. When Conon's son Saba visited, Conon offered him a senior non-commissioned officer post in the regiment.

Such units of Goths or other barbarians were recruited for various reasons. One was because of the problems of recruiting from landowners reluctant to lose tenants. Since soldiers did not pay taxes, the government was also concerned about diminishing the number of taxpayers. These recruits could sometimes cause problems, like the anonymous Gothic soldier who married Euphemia in Edessa in 396. Already married, he made Euphemia his slave. After she escaped, he was eventually arrested, tried and executed. Such problems were not confined to non-Romans, but were also caused by soldiers recruited from within the empire. Although we have more details of the problems caused by Abinnaeus' regiment of native Egyptians, his men seem no better or worse than any others.

MILITARY STRUCTURES

These regiments were part of a complex combination of border troops and mobile field armies. Until the mid-3rd century, most regiments were based in forts on the frontiers and came under the command of provincial governors. When the Roman army launched an offensive, expeditionary forces were created from troops drawn from the whole empire, usually led by the emperor himself. But by the mid-3rd century, the frequent military crises (whether involving internal or external enemies) kept the emperor in the field continually and the troops with him became a field army known informally as the *comitatus* ('accompanying'). During the Tetrarchy, each emperor had his own *comitatus*, but Constantine's defeat of his civil war rivals by 324 allowed the recreation of a single field army attached to the emperor. Initially, Constantine led this field army himself, but by the end of his reign, it was commanded by two new general officers, the *magister peditum* (master of foot) and

Above The tetrarchic fort of Mobene at Qasr Bshir in Jordan. The well-preserved fort covers 57 × 54 m (185 × 175 ft) with walls 1.5 m (5 ft) thick. The name and date are known from an inscription recording that the construction was ordered by the provincial governor Aurelius Asclepiades.

Right Sardonyx cameo, probably representing Constantine I.

magister equitum (master of horse). Despite their titles, both officers commanded forces of infantry and cavalry. As before, the troops on the borders were under the command of provincial governors (who were now known as *duces* and had military authority only). At the end of the 4th century, there were two ducates in Britain, twelve on the Rhine and Danube, seven in Africa and eight in the east.

In 337, Constantine's sons divided both the empire and the field army, creating separate field armies in Gaul (Constantine II), Illyricum (Constans), and the east (Constantius II). In 353 when Constantius II became sole emperor, the central imperial army was restored, and soon became known as the praesental army. However, the regional armies in Gaul, Illyricum and in the east continued to exist. The system of regional field armies supported by praesental armies remained intact beyond the 5th century, although the number of regional field armies and the structure of the praesental armies did change. Thus with Valentinian and Valens' division of the empire in 364, the central field army was divided and two praesental armies were created. The western praesental army was based in Italy, the eastern praesental army at Constantinople. The Illyrian field army was assigned first to western control, but after Valens' death at Adrianople in 378, it was transferred to the eastern empire. A second Danubian field army was created in Thrace during the 370s to reinforce the Illyrian army. Although Roman control of the Rhine weakened, some of the Gallic army continued to exist into the 460s, outlasting direct imperial

Off-Duty Officers

Soldiers did not fight all the time. Paintings from a temple of the imperial cult at Luxor in Egypt show early 4th-century cavalry officers relaxing. Other leisure activities were more strenuous, as represented by the hunt scene from the well-preserved villa at Piazza Armerina in central Sicily. Hunting was encouraged by the army, as good training for problems in moving men and horses cross-country. It was also a traditional occupation for aristocrats. In the hills above Antioch in the late 4th century, the holy man Macedonius once encountered a general out hunting, 'accompanied by dogs and soldiers'.

At other times, soldiers sought out holy men. In mid-5th-century Egypt, when a dux ('duke' – probably the dux Thebaidis Maximinus who campaigned against the Blemmyes in 453) visited Shenute, the ascetic was on a retreat in the desert. The soldiers waited in the monastery for several days until the monks summoned Shenute, worried by the speed at which the troops were eating the monks' food. When Shenute did emerge from isolation, he gave the officer one of his belts, which assisted him in fighting against the Blemmyes. And when Symeon the Elder Stylite died in 459, it was the *magister militum per Orientem* (general of soldiers in the East) Ardabur with a military escort who returned the body to Antioch.

Two soldiers conversing on an early 4th-century hunting mosaic from Piazza Armerina in Sicily. Both wear typical non-battle outfits, with shields and weapons but no body armour or helmets. The use of decorated patches on the shoulders, thighs and cuffs of tunics and cloaks may have indicated rank.

The insignia of the western *magister officiorum* from the *Notitia Dignitatum*. This document comes from the early 5th century, though the illustrations themselves are tracings of Carolingian copies of the original. The *magister officiorum* was responsible for arms factories (here represented by weapons and armour) and the regiments of *scholae palatinae* (represented by the units' shield patterns).

control of Gaul. And in Italy in 489 there was still a praesental army able to resist the invasion of Theoderic's Goths.

Most of the infantry in both field and border regiments were formidably armed and equipped, in contrast to their enemies, as well as being trained. Defensive equipment was usually a mail shirt, helmet and large shield. When deploying for battle, Romans fought in close formation. Combat began with a missile barrage, first of long-range archery from rear ranks, followed up by various hand-hurled missiles, and then a charge to hand-to-hand combat. The primary weapon was the spear, but a long sword was an effective secondary weapon. The heavy infantry could also lighten their own equipment for special missions. Cavalry regiments had differing types of equipment, depending on their role. Shock cavalry wore mail armour, and sometimes the horses were also armoured. Spears and lances were used for combat. An effective horned saddle compensated for the lack of stirrups, allowing charges to be deadly. Other cavalry were lighter armed, either with bows or javelins.

Recruits joined their regiments for professional careers of 20 years or more. The mobility of Roman armies and long careers meant that the range of experience of many

Silver-gilt helmet sheath from Deurne in the Netherlands, originally found in a calfskin bag. This would have covered an iron helmet. It is inscribed with *VI Stablesiani*, the name of a cavalry regiment. Associated coins suggest it was buried in the early 4th century.

late Roman soldiers was enormous. Aurelius Gaius' tombstone from Phrygia in modern Turkey records a career in *legio I Italica*, *legio VIII Augusta* and *[legio I] Iovia Scythica* at the end of the 3rd century, reaching the rank of *optio* (a senior non-commissioned officer position). Although his epitaph is damaged, it mentions his service in an astonishingly broad range of places ranging across Europe, North Africa and the Near East: Asia (Minor), Caria, Lydia, Lycaonia, Cilicia, Phoenicia, Syria, Arabia, Palestine, Egypt, Alexandria, India (perhaps Yemen or Abyssinia), Mesopotamia, Cappadocia, Galatia, Bithynia, Thrace, Moesia, the Carpians' territory, Sarmatia four times, Viminacium, the Goths' territory twice, Germany, Dardania, Dalmatia, Pannonia, Gaul, Spain, Mauretania, and 10 other areas now lost from the stone. For Rome's enemies, most wars were similar, with Franks fighting near Trier, Moors near Carthage, or Saracens near Edessa. Aurelius Gaius, on the other hand, had probably forgotten more than most Picts or Sarmatians had ever learnt about warfare.

We tend to be better informed about individuals, but units also had such experiences. In the mid-4th century, we can trace the brigade of the *Celtae* and *Petulantes*, two regiments of elite field army troops in Gaul, 2,400 men at full strength. Here, after campaigns against the Franks and Alamanni in the late 350s, they were manipulated by Julian into declaring him full emperor. They fought a brief action against the Alamanni in 360 near the city of Sanctio, in which they were outnumbered and their commander, Libino, was killed. The Romans were aggressive in this action, because they could see their enemy. They then marched east with Julian to Persia in 363, where they gorged themselves on sacrificial meat in Antioch. Julian himself was wounded and killed in the same year, but the brigade participated in the march down the Euphrates to Ctesiphon and the subsequent retreat. The units then returned to the west in 364 with Valentinian I, campaigned in Gaul, and are next found fighting against the Alamanni again in Raetia in 378. Some of the men who fought the Alamanni in the 350s probably fought them again in 378. Some of their enemies may have been present at both actions too, but the intervening period would have been very different.

ENEMIES

As the Persians and Romans fought in Mesopotamia in 363, Julian's army had a clear view of the enemy. Ammianus Marcellinus, himself a participant in the Persian expedition, described the enemy: 'the Persians opposed to us ordered regiments of cataphracts so concentrated that the gleam of moving bodies covered with closely fitting plates of iron dazzled the eyes of those who looked upon them, while the whole throng of horses was protected by coverings of leather. The cavalry was backed up by companies of infantry who, protected by oblong curved shields covered with wickerwork and raw hides, advanced in very close order. Behind these were elephants, looking like walking hills and, by the movements of their enormous bodies, threatened destruction to all who came near them.'

In contrast, fighting Franks and Alamanni in the forests of Germany was a war of shadows and ambushes. Fallen trees often blocked pathways and clearing these tracks

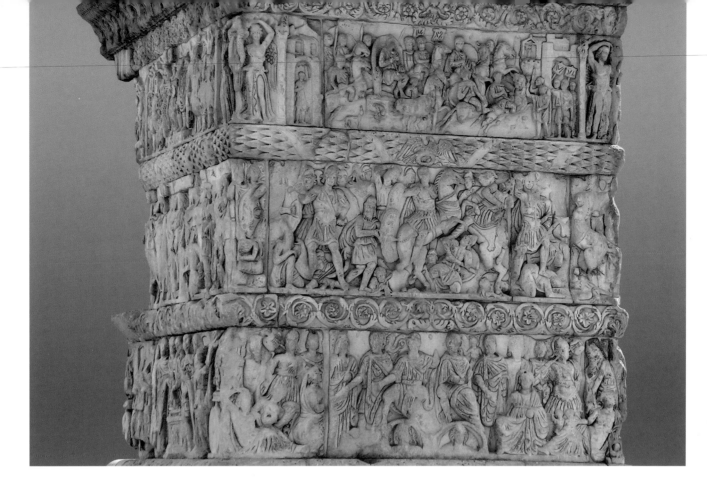

This frieze from the Arch of Galerius in Thessaloniki, Greece, commemorates eventual Roman victory in the Persian War (296–298) fought by the emperor Galerius. The arch was dedicated in AD 303. These panels show Roman cavalry in action against Persian infantry.

would have been a nerve-wracking activity. In the Rhineland, a Roman force pursued some Franks in 388 but 'ran up against an endless barricade solidly constructed from huge tree-trunks and then they tried to break out over the marshy fields which bordered the forests. Here and there enemy troops showed themselves, standing on the boles of trees or climbing about the barricades as if on the parapets of turrets.... Then the Roman army, now surrounded by the main force of the enemy, rushed desperately into the open meadows, which the Franks had left unoccupied. There the cavalry was bogged down in marshland and the bodies of men and animals, all mixed up together, were borne to the ground in one common catastrophe.' The problems in coming to grips with the enemy help to explain the aggressiveness of Libino and his brigade at Sanctio.

Although infantry were the core of late Roman armies, cavalry was always of great importance. One of the many advantages the Romans had over their enemies was that of strong cavalry. This started with an infrastructure to provide remounts, a supply system that fed horses in summer and winter, and a training mechanism that organized individual, unit, and army level exercises. The results could be impressive, as in 354 when a Roman line was wavering in an action against the Alamanni. At a moment when the Roman commander, Arbetio, appeared to be losing his nerve, three commanders of cavalry regiments struck. The Alamanni were rapidly scattered and the battle won. It is important to recognize that these tribunes' actions could be described either as initiative or as indiscipline. Similar action opened the battle of Adrianople prematurely in 378, and that was a battle that was lost (see box on pp. 206–7).

Beyond land combat and long-distance marching, other activities could include marine assaults and sieges. Julian ordered a commando raid across the Rhine in 359,

Fortified Farms in North Africa

A 3rd-century mosaic from Bardo, Tunisia, showing a typical country house in North Africa with an elaborate facade, gateway and corner towers. Despite its superficially military nature, the surrounding figures suggest that such sites were more concerned with agriculture than warfare.

In North Africa, the frontier area was studded with estates owned by Roman aristocrats. A good example is the farm of Marcus Cincius Hilarianus at Nador in Mauretania Caesariensis, built in the second quarter of the 4th century. Perhaps because of its location on the main road between Tipasa and Caesarea, it was decorated with a large facade and a dedicatory inscription. However, the simple interior, with no signs of luxury accommodation or mosaic decoration, suggest that Hilarianus himself lived elsewhere, probably in Caesarea. The facade gave the impression of a small fortress, with corner towers and a recessed gateway. But there was no surrounding ditch, the rear of the building lacked towers, and the rear entrance was undefended, so this suggests only a low-level threat. An inscription from a similar farm at Petra mentions the threat of 'the neighbouring peoples'.

An incident reported by Synesius, bishop of Cyrene in the early 5th century, suggests the sort of threat that Nador was probably intended to counter: 'we saw some wretched creatures on horseback, men who, to judge from the look of them, had been pushed into battle mostly by hunger…. However, the enemy did not seem in a hurry to open the attack any more than we were, for they drew up their line of battle and waited for us…. On both sides the troops stood watching each other. Finally, they drew off to the left and then we to the right, but at walking pace and without haste, so that the retreat might not have the appearance of flight.'

Although these farms might keep out such threats, they were not real forts. When the Roman general Theodosius attacked such an estate used by Moorish rebels at Gaio during a rebellion in 373, he used battering rams. The defences at Gaio were probably similar to those at Nador, and against soldiers would not have lasted long.

An early 4th-century panel from the Arch of Constantine in Rome, commemorating the defeat of his civil war rival Maxentius, showing Constantine's troops approaching the walls of Verona in AD 312. A second defeat at the battle of the Milvian Bridge at Rome itself sealed Maxentius' fate.

after receiving intelligence about a meeting of Alamannic kings. Some 300 men were loaded into 40 boats and crossed the Rhine at night, then marched inland and surprised the Alamanni at their feast. During Procopius' usurpation, he tried to seize Cyzicus in Turkey in the civil war of 365; the town's garrison had blocked the harbour with an iron chain. The commander of one of the attacking regiments, a certain Aliso, lashed three boats together, organized a shield wall, and then placed a block under the chain before breaking it with an axe. All of this while being shot at by the enemy. Procopius lost the civil war, but Aliso, because of this courageous performance, was allowed to keep his position.

The Roman army throughout the period was thus capable of effective performance and had a sophisticated infrastructure that supplied these forces with manpower, equipment and food. So what happened – why did the late Roman empire fall? Such a question, of course, is too simple. In the east, it continued as the Byzantine empire for a thousand years, and the military systems changed little in the immediate aftermath of the collapse of the western empire. This would suggest contemporaries felt that there was little wrong with the structure of the army itself. Nor, when we look at the army's performance, is there much to be seen as inadequate. Older explanations, particularly that the army was weakened by 'barbarization', are now generally rejected by historians. So too are issues of manpower shortages – though there were problems in gaining recruits, these were not confined to the late Roman empire. Far more critical was a lack of money. This is where we can see a difference between the eastern and western parts of the empire – most of the territorial losses, and thus losses of taxes, came in the west. The loss of Africa to the Vandals was particularly important here. On their first entry into Africa in 429, an immediate counterattack was launched in 431, involving both eastern and western forces. This failed. Carthage itself fell in 439, and was again followed by a counteroffensive in 441 that also failed. Now that the financial basis of the army was diminished, failures in leadership became far more critical. Western emperors found it impossible to assemble the resources to invade Africa (though Majorian was murdered in 461 in the midst of such preparations), and the great invasion of 468 was launched from the eastern empire. This also failed, and within a decade, Romulus Augustulus, the last western emperor, was deposed in 476 and the western empire faded away.

13 Central Asia from the Scythians to the Huns

Three warriors in combat are depicted on this 4th-century BC Scythian gold comb from Solocha, Ukraine. Two wear body armour and the horseman also wears an imported Greek 'Corinthian' helmet. Their weapons include a javelin, short swords and bowcase-quivers (*gorytoi*), and all three carry shields.

Eurasia, the landmass which stretches from Europe across to China, has a very varied geomorphology, but right across it there are connected regions of grassland steppe. The human cultures which the steppe favoured before the 20th century were based on animal herding and horse riding, a harsh way of life which encouraged stock-raiding, tribal warfare and occasional mass-movements out of the steppe into neighbouring regions of agricultural settlement and urban development. Horsemen wielding recurved, composite bows made up steppe forces, from small raiding bands to whole peoples moving as 'hordes'. Throughout history steppe cavalry had a profound influence upon Europe, Mesopotamia, Persia, India and China through both long-term coexistence and periodic horde invasions. From c. 700 BC to AD 550 the Greco-Roman world experienced and identified three distinct steppe peoples with whom peaceful trading and painful conflict might alternate. The Scythians generally affected the Black Sea region, and the Sarmatians extended down into what is now Hungary, but neither people ever mobilized in such numbers as to seriously threaten settled states. On the other hand, the Huns swept up a mass of peoples, including other steppe nomads, during their movement west into Europe and, for a short period under their horde leader, Attila, they dominated and terrorized the weakened and divided Late Roman empire.

STEPPE NOMAD CULTURES AT WAR

Asiatic steppe nomads relied heavily on herd animals which were grazed seasonally between uplands and lowlands, or moved from one grassland area to another with the seasons. Trade with sedentary neighbours was also important, providing, for example, grain, textiles and metalwork (especially armour and bladed weapons); such items could also be taken by force in war.

Steppe nomads excelled in horse breeding and horse riding, developing an equestrian culture of decorated saddlery and harness, herding tools and clothing fashions. They also combined certain forms of weaponry with horse riding so successfully that those weapons became synonymous with steppe identity. Foremost of these was the composite bow (known from about 1500 BC onwards; see box overleaf). Thus the steppe was dominated by groupings of consummately skilled horse-archers.

Horse-archers could shoot their bows around a full 360-degree arc from a fast-moving platform. This meant that mounted-archer warfare was mobile and fluid, individuals operating in a cloud of riders, concentrating on specific targets and then wheeling away out of reach when threatened. Shooting was rapid and at close range to defeat armour. All horse-archers could shoot backwards as they withdrew in the so-called 'Parthian shot' (made famous by Plutarch and Shakespeare), then turn in an instant on a pursuing foe. Such 'feigned flights' were specifically intended to lure out and isolate over-confident opponents to be destroyed piecemeal. En masse, nomad armies could harry slow-moving enemy infantry and avoid non-nomadic cavalry until they were exhausted. The further the enemy advanced the more vulnerable he was to being enveloped and surrounded. Until 19th-century improvements in firearms, conventional armies marched onto the steppe like rivers flowing into the desert. The skills of horsemanship and archery were seldom matched, and each successive wave of nomads brought new and often improved designs of archery equipment and horse-harness. The appearance of nomad hordes was often bewilderingly sudden and unexpected. The mobility of horse-archer groups meant that they could range widely in a short time and their numbers were difficult to estimate accurately. Nomads could also campaign much more effectively than sedentarists in winter, when steppe horses could forage in deep snow, and summer obstacles such as rivers and marshes were frozen over.

Study of steppe nomad peoples is sometimes reduced to moving ethnic labels around on a map with the ever-present difficulty that histories written by their sedentary neighbours employed ethnic names simplistically. A single label was often applied to an agglomeration of peoples based on the ruling group. Thus 'the Huns' invaded the eastern and western Roman empires in the 5th century AD having overrun numerous other peoples, tribes and cultures. Their horde represented a mass of Germanic, Iranian and Turkic groups dominated by a 'Hunnic' steppe nomad elite of disputed origin. Worse, the literary sources were often very conservative, and Greek writers, from the Classical period right through the Middle Ages, used the term 'Scythian' to denote any steppe nomad.

The main sites mentioned in this chapter – giving an impression of the vast area over which the Scythians, Sarmatians and Huns ranged.

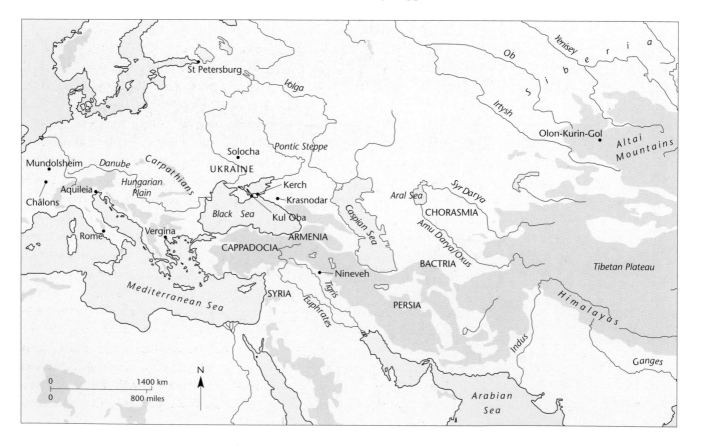

Steppe Composite Bows

The composite bow was the quintessential weapon of the steppe nomad. Its 'composite' construction required very little of the wood which was difficult to come by on the Eurasian steppe. Strips of horn were glued on the surface facing the archer, and sinew on the surface facing away. Late Sarmatian and Hunnic forms of the weapon also had antler or bone plates stuck to the grip, to stop it bending, and to the stave ends (ears) so that they could act as stiff levers to pull back the flexible limbs. The bow's constituents were applied in such a way that the stave formed a 'C' shape which had to be reversed to be strung. This allowed greater energy to be stored in a comparatively short weapon. The lower limb was always shorter than the upper, thus handy for use on horseback. Scythian and Early Sarmatian bows were short at 90 cm (3 ft), the handle set back and the limbs curving with slightly curled ends lacking laths. Middle to Late Sarmatian and Hunnic weapons were longer at 1.5 m (5 ft), and Late Sarmatian and Hunnic bows also bore three laths on the grip and two on each ear. Thus the handle was also set back but the ears were straight and angled forward from the limbs, especially when unstrung.

This 4th-century BC electrum vessel from Kul Oba, Ukraine, depicts a Scythian stringing his short composite bow.

THE SCYTHIANS

Iranian Scythians moved into the Pontic steppe north of the Black Sea in the 8th century BC, and several dynasties of Scythian kings ruled the region during the period 700–285 BC. Rather later, 4th-century Chinese sources mention horse-borne tribes which may have been culturally related to the Scythians: artifacts bearing 'Scythian animal style' decoration are distributed from North China, through the Altai Mountains and westward. The earliest recorded steppe nomad horde invasions were those of the Cimmerians and the Scythians who conquered Urartu (northern Iraq) in the 7th century BC. The Scythians went on to assault the Assyrian empire and to join the Medes in capturing Nineveh in 612 BC. Thereafter they were driven back north of the Caucasus. They dominated the hinterland of the Greek Black Sea colonies, and the regions north of the Caspian Sea, beyond the Syr Darya river, and into the Altai. In c. 514–512 BC the Achaemenid king Darius I led an expedition against the Scythians north of the Black Sea but was lured further and further away from his Danube bridgehead, his scouts and foraging parties being attacked, and his main body avoided. Unable to bring the elusive Scythians to battle, he was fortunate to bring back his army. In 329 BC Alexander the Great launched a campaign against the Scythian Sakai beyond the Syr Darya. His combination of long-range artillery, light troops and offensive use of cavalry enabled him to bring the nomads to battle and drive them off with considerable loss. Thereafter, pressure exerted by eastern nomads may have forced Saka groups to move south into Iran, where the Parni gradually

Opposite A mid-4th-century BC Scythian gold pectoral from Tolstaja Mogila in Ukraine, decorated with scenes of nomad life, animals and mythical creatures. The detail below, of the upper central figures, shows that each man has a bowcase-quiver (*gorytos*) close by.

Right Reconstruction of an armoured 5th-century BC Scythian warrior with shield, short sword, spear and *gorytos*, based on finds from a burial at Gladkovscina in Ukraine and figures on the Solocha comb.

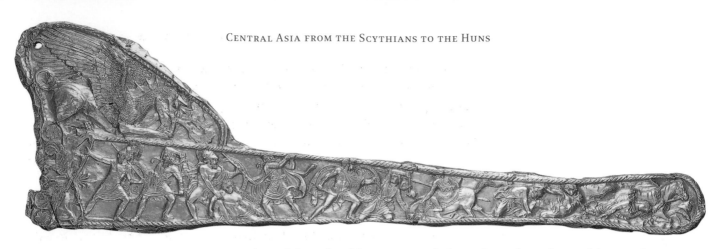

A gold scabbard of Greek manufacture, designed to hold a short Scythian sword. It was found at Chertomlyk in Ukraine, and dates to the 4th century BC.

supplanted the Seleucid successors of Alexander to form the Parthian empire (see Chapter 10). In the west Scythian tribes continued to raid and trade down to the Danube until Sarmatian peoples came to dominate the region.

Scythians are described in Greek literary sources, and are frequently depicted in Classical and Hellenistic Greek art wearing baggy trousers, a long wrap-around tunic, kaftans and felt boots. Concentrations of extremely rich Scythian burials in the Crimea and to the east (Ukraine and southern Russian Federation), and in the Altai Mountains (Mongolia), have provided a great deal of information about military equipment and horse-harness. The Altai finds, superbly preserved by permafrost, contained surviving horse-cadavers, tattooed human skin, wooden artifacts, clothing, textiles and felt horse trappings. The western graves revealed sets of copper alloy and iron scales for cuirasses, long sleeves, leggings and helmets. Imported Greek, Thracian and Macedonian helmets are preserved by burial in some numbers, as are metal greaves. Swords (*akinakes*) tend to be of a short type which also spread through the Parthian empire. Characteristic also of the Black Sea hinterland and the lands down to northern Greece are finds of gold sheet covers for bowcase and quiver combinations (*gorytoi*). These demonstrate that the bow was carried strung, on the

A recently excavated 3rd- to 2nd-century BC Scythian wooden burial chamber at Olon-Kurin-Gol in the Altai Mountains, Mongolia. The fragile contents have been beautifully preserved by permafrost.

horse-archer's left side. Some *gorytos* covers are decorated in Scythian animal style, but many bear bands of figural decoration in the so-called 'Greco-Scythian style', depicting Scythian warriors or Greek mythological scenes, which suggest manufacture for the Scythian market in Black Sea cities. One cover decorated with scenes from Homer was found in the tomb of the Macedonian king Philip II at Vergina in Greece, perhaps representing a trophy piece taken in conflict with Transdanubian Scythian tribes.

The Scythians directly influenced the military practices of neighbouring sedentary cultures, especially in the areas of long-term interaction, such as Chorasmia (north of the River Amu Darya) and the Black Sea-Danube region. In the former area the Massagetae were credited as the first to develop heavy bronze armour for man and horse. The Persian satrapy of Bactria supplied the king-of-kings with his best cavalry and Saka horse-archer mercenaries. The successor kingdom of Bactria seems to have relied upon archer-lancer armoured cavalry as part of its Macedonian-style army. In the Persian empire the archery technology was a blend of native Iranian and steppe nomad, but the arrowheads commonly found wherever Persian forces operated (e.g. Cyprus, western Asia Minor, Greece) conformed with the barbed, socketed bronze forms prevalent in Scythian use. The Parni in Parthia brought in new forms of bow and saddlery, and the characteristic dress of the Partho-Sasanian periods was essentially steppe nomad horseman's attire. In the west Macedonia developed its cavalry forces under steppe nomad influences.

THE SARMATIANS

From the 5th century BC Sarmatian groups were impinging upon the Pontic steppe, north of the Black Sea. Two groups of these Iranian nomads spread westwards into the Danube steppe lands; diplomatic contacts and confrontations with Roman forces commenced in the early 1st century AD. The Rhoxolani came to dominate the area between the Carpathians and the Black Sea, and the Iazyges came to rest on the Hungarian Plain. From these areas they were able to raid across the Danube into the Roman empire, which they did with some frequency through the 1st to 3rd centuries AD. Sometimes they were allied with other barbarian groups such as the Dacians or the Marcomanni, and these raids could be unexpected and costly. The Alans were another, more eastern Sarmatian grouping which raided down into the Parthian empire in the later 1st century AD and threatened Roman Cappadocia (in modern Turkey), only being warned off the latter by the military fame of the Roman governor, Arrian. The text of the latter's *Order of Battle Against the Alans* actually survives. The term 'Alans' continued to be applied to Sarmatian groups within and without the Roman empire into the 6th century AD.

Gold plaque depicting a man and a woman with a dying(?) man with two saddled horses beneath a tree on which hangs a *gorytos*. This is an undated piece from the Siberian Collection of Peter the Great at the Hermitage Museum, St Petersburg.

Above An iron Sarmatian sword with gold and silver inlay from near Krasnodar in Russia, 1st century BC to 1st century AD.

Right Detail of the early 2nd-century AD helical frieze on Trajan's Column, depicting three scale-armoured Sarmatian cavalry. The tight fit of the armour and its extension to the horses' legs are stylized features which cannot be taken seriously. However, the existence of heavily armoured Sarmatians is supported by ancient Crimean iconography and artifactual discoveries, and by Roman literature.

Opposite This marble plaque, found at Kerch in Ukraine, dates to the 1st or 2nd centuries AD. The rider is depicted in Sarmatian dress, a conical helmet and a scale cuirass, wielding a two-handed lance (*kontos*). Along with other iconography, this indicates the Sarmatian influence on the hunting and warfare cultures of the elites of the Crimean Greek cities.

Rich Sarmatian elite burials are accompanied by deposited weapons including long-swords, lance-heads and archery equipment. Some swords have Chinese jade fittings. In the Roman literary sources the Sarmatians were like other nomads in that they lived in wagons and tents, but unique amongst northern barbarians in being characterized as heavily armoured. This is corroborated by the tomb frescoes, sculptures and graffiti from the Crimea where the elites of the kingdom of Bosphorus became completely Sarmaticized in their burial customs, hunting, warfare and military equipment.

Sarmatian cavalry were brought into Roman service, but mainly in groups so as to maintain their specialized skills. Regiments of Roman cavalry were also armed in the Sarmatian style with the lance and employed both against Danubian nomads and on other fronts of the empire. An Asiatic form of military standard consisting of a metal wolf-head and a flowing textile body atop a shaft was almost immediately adopted by Roman cavalry after late 1st-century AD Danubian wars. Given a snake-head, this *draco* standard spread throughout the Roman army and even became the personal standard of emperors.

THE HUNS

Steppe nomad groups generically referred to as 'Huns' may be traced back at least to the 2nd century AD, successively occupying Sarmatian regions and pressing groups such as the Alans westwards. The ethnic definition of these Huns is disputed (Turkic, Mongolic, or mixed?). A horde crossed the Caucasus in c. AD 395, raiding into Armenia, Cappadocia and Syria. The Hephthalite Huns were raiding into Persia from the 4th century AD; in the 5th century they inflicted major defeats on Sasanian kings; in the 6th century they were defeated by the Sasanians using Turkish allies, but they also overran parts of western India. The historian Jordanes described the western Huns in terms which would have suited many other steppe nomad peoples, before and since: 'They are short in stature, quick in body movement, alert horsemen, broad shouldered, ready in the use of bow and arrow, and have firm-set necks which are ever erect in pride.'

For a short period of time (c. AD 440–55) the Huns created the first steppe 'empire' to seriously impinge on Europe. Their appearance in Roman consciousness was quite sudden in the later 4th century AD and was heralded by Goths, Alans and other peoples moving ahead of them and breaking into the Roman empire. Huns themselves raided Roman provinces in the 420s and parts of Roman Pannonia (modern Hungary) were ceded to them. Thereafter, the Hungarian Plain and adjacent areas became the centre of Hunnic power. The eastern Roman empire suffered a string of defeats and punishing raids which resulted in the siege and destruction of many major Danubian cities. In all the diplomatic negotiations the Huns demanded annual subsidies in gold, regular markets, the return of escaped Roman prisoners, and the expulsion of barbarians who sought refuge with the Romans. Further wars were sparked by perennial Roman refusal to fulfil these terms. The most famous and most successful Hunnic leader was Attila (see box overleaf). The Romans and his other enemies were reprieved in 453 when he died, and, led by the Gepids, his subject peoples revolted. Hunnic dominance was broken and this steppe empire dispersed.

Attila the Hun

Attila was the most prominent of all the steppe nomad leaders in the west, comparable with later great horde commanders such as Genghis Khan and Timurlane. He already had some experience of the west as a childhood hostage, and was clearly a calculating and charismatic leader who fully exploited the strengths of his diplomatic and military position. With his brother, Bleda, and then after *c.* AD 445 as sole leader, he dominated a host of steppe nomad and sedentary Germanic peoples, wielding them in raiding expeditions which swept through the Roman Danubian provinces, Gaul and Italy. The historian Jordanes called him 'the scourge of all lands'.

At the battle of Châlons in AD 451, with his composite horde of Huns, Gepids, Ostrogoths, Burgundians, Scirians, Thuringians and Franks in northern Gaul, Attila was met by a 'Roman' army under Flavius Aëtius, somewhere near Châlons in Champagne. Aëtius' army had few Roman troops and was likewise a conglomeration of barbarian groups: Visigoths, Sarmatians, Armoricans, Saxons, Burgundians and Franks. Thus the Gothic historian Jordanes referred to the battlefield as 'the threshing-floor of countless races'. The two armies fought for two days with great loss to both sides, Attila withdrawing to a fortified camp and reportedly preparing for death. Thereafter the protagonists drifted apart and the Huns withdrew from Gaul. Next year they ravaged Italy; nevertheless they had been stopped, having reached further west into Europe than any other nomad horde in history.

Attila's sudden death after a wedding feast in AD 453 ended the cohesion of the Hunnic 'empire' at a stroke, but there were already signs that the Huns were settling down and losing their military dominance. Steppe peoples which ended up on the Hungarian Plain just did not have the space to maintain their particular cultural traits: the Sarmatians earlier, and the Avars and Magyars later could not avoid culture-change and eventual dissolution.

Part of a mosaic floor from the great basilica at Aquileia in northeast Italy, all that is left after Attila raised the building to the ground in AD 452.

Hun leaders had ruled as an elite over a polyglot collection of Goths, Alans, Gepids and Burgundians, sometimes promoting individual barbarians or Romans as subordinate rulers. Wealth exacted from the Romans was shared by the elites of subject peoples. Finds of gold-sheathings from presentation bows in Hungary and Poland, and of gem-encrusted crowns, may represent diplomatic gifts or badges of status conveyed on subject leaders. The elites of Attila's empire are further identifiable in purely Hunnic burials (some 70 in Hungary) and in Germanic burials with Hunnic artifacts. Characteristic are Hunnic archery equipment, arched saddles and decorated horse-harness. Roman material is also prominent, including bullion items amongst which is at least one Roman helmet. Embassies from the eastern and western Roman courts were received at a centre which boasted wooden halls, colonnades, fortifications and even stone-built baths. The latter were a clear indication of the nomad readiness to employ the technicians of settled cultures, not least in constructing siege engines which successfully reduced such Roman cities as Naissus (Serbia) and Aquileia (Italy).

In the Hungarian Plain, the Huns, like the Iazyges, seem to have become sedentary, although the process was not far advanced before Attila's death. However, the impact of Hunnic culture on the sedentary neighbours was predictably profound in the area of military technology. Roman writers commented approvingly on the qualities of the 'Hunnic horse', and Roman armies were eventually transformed into forces in which the cavalry element was tactically dominant. Lance- and bow-armed horsemen combined steppe nomad weaponry, horse-harness, felt armour and attire with the metallic armours produced by urban craftsmen.

Gold plaques from Mundolsheim, France, dating to the 5th century AD, positioned on a reconstructed Hunnic saddle. The overlapping scale motif is characteristically Hunnic and spread into Roman, German and Persian decorative arts through steppe nomad contacts.

14 Warfare in Ancient South Asia

Detail of the stone-carved southern *torana* at Sanchi. These carvings are some of the first in South Asia that explicitly depict acts of warfare. Previously, monumental architecture had focused upon the Buddhist philosophies of forsaking violence, reverence of animals and rectification of evils.

Containing one fifth of the world's population, South Asia (modern India, Pakistan, Bangladesh, Sri Lanka, Nepal, Bhutan and the Maldives) is a melting pot of religions, languages, economies and traditions. Despite this diversity, frequent attempts have been made to integrate its disparate communities with resultant conflict and schism. This chapter explores the archaeology of South Asia's distinctive character of warfare and traces its development from the Indus cities of the Bronze Age to the fortified capitals of the Buddha's time. Whilst much of this period is prehistoric in nature, later Buddhist and Greek chronicles provide detailed records but suffer from propaganda and multiple-authorship. These sources are accompanied, however, by less subjective material evidence in the form of military architecture, sculptures and art depicting war and warriors, and excavated weaponry and armour.

Although the first known victim of conflict in South Asia is represented by a male with microlithic blade embedded in his rib at the Mesolithic site of Sarai Nahar Rai, our chapter will discuss the region's two great urbanized traditions, the Indus and Early Historic, and within each we will examine the relevant textual, architectural and archaeological evidence. Throughout, two themes unique to South Asian warfare will become apparent. First, the emergence of a tradition of non-violence and, secondly, the martial training of elephants – both of which were later to have an impact on European nations. Our chapter ends in AD 530 with the invasion of the Hephthalite Huns and the destruction of the great Buddhist monasteries and cities of northern India.

THE INDUS CIVILIZATION

The appearance of Bronze Age cities and states in Mesopotamia and the eastern Mediterranean was closely associated with the rise of warfare and the cult of the warrior. In contrast, the rulers of the largest polity of the Old World Bronze Age, the Indus, appear to have gone to extremes to ensure that warfare and conflict remained invisible.

With cultural origins in the Neolithic communities of the Baluchistan hills, farmers and herders colonized the fertile alluvium of the Indus river in modern Pakistan and by the 4th millennium BC developed small walled settlements. Cultural and economic convergence resulted in a single integrated system covering 1 million sq. km (385,000 sq. miles) in the 3rd millennium BC. Unified by the use of common town plans, drainage systems, writing, weights and measures, and even mudbrick dimensions, raw materials were channelled into the centres and finished products distributed to domestic and Mesopotamian markets.

Whilst suspecting the use of force and coercion in the fusing of this civilization, archaeologists have failed to identify any direct evidence more concrete than thin

Right The main sites and regions mentioned in this chapter.

Below Aerial view of the citadel of Mohenjo-daro, the largest city within the Indus valley. The huge fortified citadel housed a 'great bath', 'granary' and a pillared structure denoted as a 'college of priests' by the archaeologist Sir John Marshall. The large structure visible on the left-hand side of the mound is a 1st- to 2nd-century AD Buddhist stupa.

A 'massacre' at Mohenjo-daro? These human remains found below a street in Mohenjo-daro were for many years used to exemplify the invasion of the Indus valley by Indo-Aryan speakers in c. 1900 BC. Recently, they have been re-interpreted by archaeologists as deliberate burials complete with grave goods cut into an earlier layer.

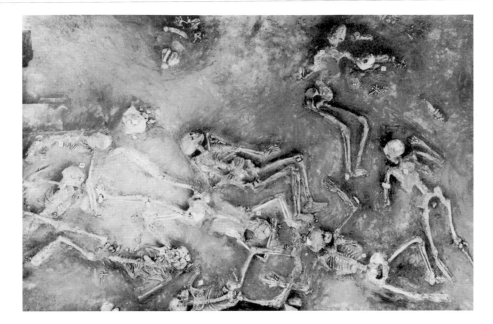

layers of burning at the regional centre of Kot Diji. More surprisingly, archaeologists have also failed to identify royal palaces and burials or even pictorial representations of elites. This has led scholars from the 1920s onwards to suggest that the Indus civilization was inherently peaceful and egalitarian, but others have argued that the invisibility of warfare and warriors is not necessarily indicative of their absence from Indus society.

The most visible (but indirect) evidence for warfare in the Indus civilization is in the form of defensive architecture: the great mudbrick platforms of its cities. A massive investment of labour, Mohenjo-daro's citadel stands 10 m (33 ft) above the Indus plain and enclosed over 80,000 sq. m (850,000 sq. ft) of structures. Towering above the inhabitants of the lower town, it was faced with baked mudbrick, although scholars are still unsure as to whether it was designed primarily to defend the citadel's residents against armies or floods. Walled centres are also found at Harappa where scholars have recently identified the presence of a further three walled mounds in addition to its original 'citadel'. More impressive than the others, the latter has clear bastions projecting from its walls and two gateways, one to the north and one to the west. This use of formal boundaries to control access and define space is also found in smaller centres such as Kalibangan and Surkotada. The latter, with buttresses and bastions built in stone, is thought to have offered a safe haven for merchants following the primary trade route to the rich carnelian sources of western India. The use of locally available stone for fortifications, also found at the great city of Dholavira, demonstrates the versatility of the Indus defensive architects.

Armies and rulers are frequently defined by the weaponry they bear, but within the Indus civilization, it has been extremely difficult to distinguish between weapons, hunting implements and agricultural tools. Similarly, it has proved impossible to identify evidence of a professional army; confusion surrounds the mechanisms through which the Indus defended itself from jealous neighbours, or subdued uncooperative elements within its boundaries. In the absence of an apparatus of physical coercion and enforcement, recent scholars have suggested

Excavations at Harappa. It was originally thought that only the citadel mound at Harappa was fortified, but recent excavations have demonstrated that at least four of the mounds at the site were circumvallated. None of the mounds at Harappa contain the monumentality witnessed at Mohenjo-daro.

A reconstruction of the gateway on Mound E at Harappa. The narrow gateway would have limited and controlled access in and out of the town. Even within the city itself, houses open onto small side streets rather than the main thoroughfares, suggesting an innate sense of privacy and control over one's own space.

that the Indus elite suppressed all outward manifestations of rank or competition between individuals and even cities. In such models, renounceants are thought to have wielded most authority thus removing the necessity of conflict and violence. However, other scholars have suggested that either stories of battles and wars were passed on through oral traditions or were recorded on perishable materials such as textiles. Until the Indus script is deciphered, this confusion is unlikely to change.

When it came at the beginning of the 2nd millennium BC, so sudden was the end of the Indus civilization that early archaeologists attributed its demise to invasions of Indo-Aryan speakers from western and Central Asia. Indeed, the archaeologist Sir Mortimer Wheeler supported such an explanation with reference to the clusters of human remains found in the highest levels of Mohenjo-daro: these were interpreted as a sign of Aryans' 'consistent hatred of the people of Mohenjo-daro' and for whom 'total extermination appears to have been their endeavour'. Equally conclusive for

Wheeler were references in the early Sanskrit text, the *Rigveda*, to the destruction of an urban people known as the Dasas by chariot-riding Arya, the burning of a number of sites in Baluchistan, such as Rana Ghundai, and the introduction of bronze artifacts with stylistic affinities in western and Central Asia. More recent studies have found the suddenness of this collapse to have been matched by its completeness as citadels and towns across the region were abandoned, and cultural and economic uniformity disintegrated.

This reliance on a human vector for the end of the Indus civilization has been weakened by subsequent re-analysis of the 37 'victims' at Mohenjo-daro, which suggests that they were conventionally buried and did not have injuries consistent with a 'massacre'. Additionally, the construction of an unfortified 'palatial' building at Mundigak in Afghanistan and the remodelling of the gateway at Surkotada in western India suggest that many aspects of Indus life continued unaltered. Indeed, scholars are becoming increasingly convinced that the Indus tradition was ended by a combination of increasing aridity, shifts in river channels and interruptions in trade with Mesopotamia rather than by warfare and that there was continuity rather than contrast between the Indus and Early Historic traditions.

THE EARLY HISTORIC PERIOD

The Early Historic period is generally associated with the advent of Buddhism, professing a creed of equality and striving for the amelioration of conflict, greed and suffering. In direct contrast, this period also witnessed the emergence and destruction of cities and states by professional armies and warrior elites. Unlike our knowledge of warfare and conflict in the Indus civilization, there is rich architectural, sculptural and textual evidence for its role and development in the Early Historic world.

Following the collapse of the Indus civilization a series of regional Chalcolithic (Copper Age) and early Iron Age communities established themselves across the subcontinent. Associated in northern India with the Pandava and Kaurava conflict, as described in the epic *Mahabharata*, little is known of the nature of warfare. What is clear, however, is the emergence during this period of what was to become the foundations of South Asian social organization: the caste system. Most importantly for this chapter, is the designation of the Kshatriya varna, the hereditary warriors of India.

Our knowledge of this period is also supplemented through explosive meeting of east and west in the northwest of the subcontinent as over a period of several hundred years, the region witnessed several invasions and retreats by expansionist Persian and Greek civilizations (see box on pp. 236-237). This began in the 5th century BC with the campaigns of Darius I, whose Achaemenid empire annexed the satrapies of Gandhara and Bactria. Introducing standardized silver currency and the Aramaic script to the region, recruits for the Persian army were raised and deployed across the empire.

To the east, 16 of the emergent Iron Age chiefdoms of the Ganges began to consolidate authority, centred on increasingly urbanized settlements. Subsequent competition between these centres opened one of the most brutal chapters of conflict in South Asia as powerful states consumed weaker neighbours in the period characterized as the *matsya-nyaya* or the 'maxim of the fish' – the analogy of fish eating smaller fish, and in turn being eaten by larger fish. This aggression was not only aimed at the destruction of rivals, but was also intended to extend access to adjacent agricultural lands and raw resources. One victim of this internecine warfare was the Buddha's own kingdom during his lifetime.

The failure of successive generations of archaeologists to identify physical evidence of Alexander the Great's Indian campaigns (see Chapter 7) throws into doubt the success of Macedonian military tactics. More apparent is the construction of massive strongholds as conflict between the surviving *mahajanapadas*, or great states, continued into the 4th century BC, until four remained. By 321 BC, Magadha had established its supremacy over the remaining territories and its first Mauryan emperor, Chandragupta (who reigned from 325 to 297 BC) ruled a centralized state from Afghanistan in the west to Bangladesh in the east and from Nepal in the north to the Deccan.

The post-Mauryan period witnessed a series of dynastic surges and dissipations as regional political authority was contested. It was not until the hegemony of the Kushans in the 2nd century AD that integration was again achieved across an area that stretched from Central Asia to the Indian Ocean. Depicted on their coinage in martial pose, these horse-riding warriors were to have a significant impact upon urban planning and religious patronage. Their control of the central element of the Silk Route brought them into contact with the superpowers of the ancient world, the Han Chinese, Romans and Parthians – effecting cultural, religious and military change. Finally, mention should be made of Sri Lanka which although frequently seen as a peripheral component of South Asia, provides valuable evidence as to the success of the policy of non-violence of the Mauryan ruler Asoka and the expansion of hegemony through the medium of *Dharma* (see box opposite).

Under Kanishka (AD 120–150), represented here in a 2nd-century AD statue from Mathura, the Kushan empire conquered a large portion of Central Asia and northern India. This imperial expansion allowed the Kushans to control both land and sea routes between Rome and China, and facilitated the transmission of Buddhism to East Asia.

EARLY HISTORIC DEFENSIVE ARCHITECTURE

Associated with the growth of urbanized settlements was the development of elaborate defensive architecture to protect them. Military and political competition between the emergent *janapadas*, or states, led to the construction of five fortified cities in northern India at Sravasti, Rajagriha, Champa, Kausambi and Varanasi by 550 BC. Massive ramparts, 9 m (30 ft) high and 20 m (66 ft) wide and using over 1 million cu. m (35 million cu. ft) of clay were constructed at Kausambi, encircling an area of 50 ha (125 acres); it has been estimated that it would have taken over 2,500 individuals two years to complete.

Equally impressive are the stone walls of Rajagriha in the Indian state of Bihar. Utilizing the topography of a small valley to full effect, the city was surrounded by a 3.5-m (11½-ft) high outer fortification wall stretching for 40 km (25 miles) along the ridge of the hills enclosing the valley. The most vulnerable points, the northern and southern openings of the valley, were secured through the construction of bastions 18 m (59 ft) long and 12 m (39 ft) high.

Whether all these great constructions were purely military in design has been actively debated. For example, when the earliest rampart and ditch at Anuradhapura

The Tradition of Non-Violence

As well as having a tradition of military campaigns, South Asia has an equally important tradition of non-violence as exemplified by this edict from Asoka (who reigned from 272 to 235 BC): 'this inscription... has been engraved so that any sons or great grandsons that I may have should not think of gaining new conquests... they should only consider conquest by *Dharma*.' In contrast, when Asoka bloodily acceded to the Mauryan throne in 272 BC he planned the annexation of the last independent state of northern India. Asoka was well trained for this task having governed the disparate Greek- and Aramaic-speaking populations of Taxila, followed by his appointment as viceroy of Ujjain in central India. In 261 BC, his army advanced on the kingdom of Kalinga, whilst his fleet secured its coastline. Asoka's campaign was extremely destructive, resulting in the death of 100,000 people and the deportation of over 150,000 others. The campaign complete, it is likely that the stronghold of Sisupalgarh was built by Asoka to dominate the ravaged kingdom.

Appalled at this suffering, Asoka revoked warfare and pursued the philosophy of *Dharma*, forsaking violence, revering animal life, building public works, supporting Buddhism, and rectifying bureaucratic and other administrative evils. Asoka had this philosophy inscribed throughout his empire in the various languages and scripts of its constituent members. The first attempt to create a pluralistic polity in South Asia, he extended his authority by

sending envoys and Buddhist missionaries to neighbouring kingdoms. The success of Asoka's campaigns of *Dharma* is illustrated by his bloodless expansion of hegemony over Sri Lanka, where missionaries converted the court to Buddhism and crowned its king with regalia sent by Asoka himself. This tradition of non-violence was never extinguished and was later used to great effect by Gandhi against the British empire.

An Asokan pillar at Lumbini, birthplace of Gautama Buddha. Asoka's edicts are found throughout the Mauryan empire, and are transcribed into several languages – an attempt to incorporate diverse populations into a unified whole.

in Sri Lanka were established in the 4th century BC they enclosed an area of 100 ha (250 acres) but only one third of this area was actually settled. Mirrored at other Early Historic sites, it has been suggested that such early defences may also have protected fields and gardens from flooding and the depredations of large mammals such as wild pig, elephant and deer. The impressive monumentality of the defensive architecture suggests that there was also a less functional motive for circumvallating South Asian cities and that their defences acted as part of a wider microcosm transforming the city into a plastic representation of the universe. Within such symbolism, the rampart and moat represent the boundaries of the world, the city symbolizes the universe itself, and by extension the ruler identifies with the king of the universe.

The Battle of the Hydaspes River

	MACEDONIAN, GREEK, PERSIAN AND INDIAN ALLIES	HYDASPES (PUNJABI INDIAN KINGDOM)
COMMANDERS	Alexander the Great	Porus
STRENGTH	28,000 infantry 8,500 cavalry	20,000 infantry 2,000 cavalry 60 chariots 200 war elephants
CASUALTIES	4,000 men killed 280 cavalry killed	12,000 men killed 400 cavalry killed 9,000 men captured 80 elephants captured

of the king of Taxila against his neighbour, Porus, they encountered no fewer than 200 of these pachyderms opposing them.

The army of Porus, king of Hydaspes, numbered 20,000 infantry supported by 2,000 cavalry and the 200 elephants. Cautious of Macedonian successes, the Hydaspes were drawn up on the bank of the river obstructing Alexander. To outflank Porus, Alexander crossed the river with a force of Macedonians at night and when Craterus led the frontal assault in the morning, Porus' right flank disintegrated as the new force joined. The Hydaspes held their ground and their elephants began to shatter Alexander's phalanx. In desperation, coalition archers picked off mahouts and blinded many elephants so that the creatures fled, trampling their own troops. Weakened, Porus fought

Weighing 5 tons and standing 3.5 m (11½ ft) high, a war elephant charging at 30 km (19 miles) per hour causes terror and confusion. With its thick hide covered with leather or metal armour, it is almost impervious to injury. These attributes made the elephant the choice vehicle of warrior elites in South Asia from the time of the Buddha to the Mughals. When the Macedonian, Greek and Persian armies of Alexander crossed the Hydaspes river in 326 BC in support

Left The strategic importance of war elephants was recognized by Alexander, who issued this silver decadrachm immortalizing his encounter with them.

Nandana Pass

Alexander's march

Hydaspes River

1 Marching through the Nandana Pass, Alexander approaches a fording point on the Hydaspes river only to find his path blocked by Porus' forces on the opposite bank

2 After moving along the riverbank, with Porus' forces shadowing his every move, Alexander decides to cross behind Admana island during the night

Admana Island

3 Once across the cavalry advances on Porus' forces with a screen of mounted archers. Porus sends his son with a force of chariots to meet the advance, but they are repelled and Porus' son killed

4 The two armies then manoeuvre their men ready for battle, Alexander's infantry being screened by cavalry, Porus' screened by elephants

Hydaspes

Hydaspes

until he was overwhelmed but was rewarded for his bravery by keeping his kingdom.

Although defeated at the Hydaspes, the elephant remained a key element of South Asian armies: Chandragupta Maurya amassed 9,000 of them. Their strategic importance was also quickly recognized by Alexander, who issued a silver coin immortalizing his encounter. Dying at Babylon, it was his successors in the east, the Seleucids, who exchanged part of their kingdom with Chandragupta Maurya for 500 elephants to use against their Macedonian rivals. Thus introduced to the Mediterranean littoral, they were to reach their full potential when Hannibal crossed the Alps and threatened Rome (see p. 147).

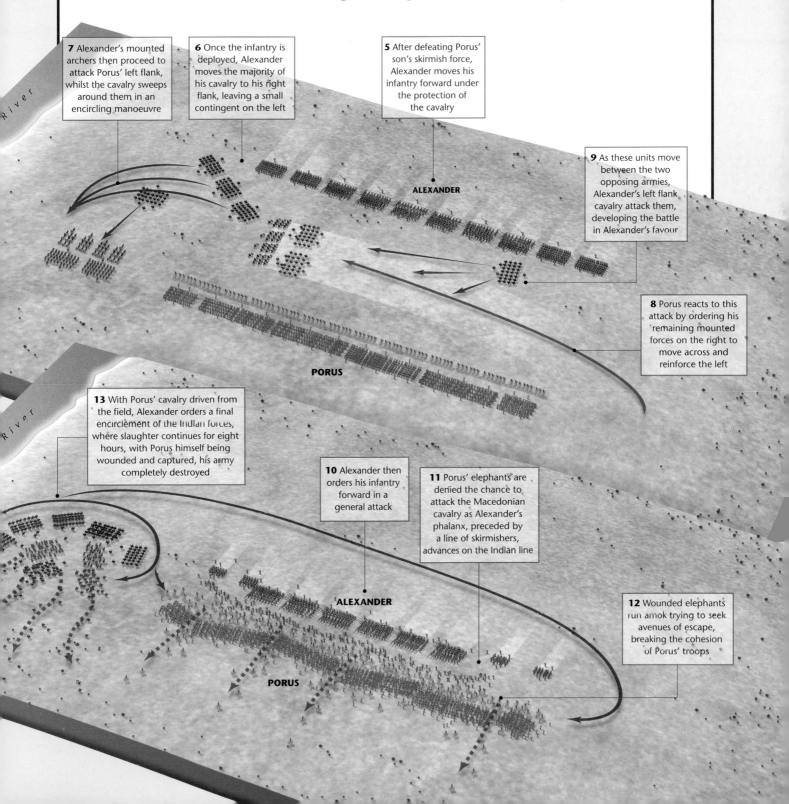

7 Alexander's mounted archers then proceed to attack Porus' left flank, whilst the cavalry sweeps around them in an encircling manoeuvre

6 Once the infantry is deployed, Alexander moves the majority of his cavalry to his right flank, leaving a small contingent on the left

5 After defeating Porus' son's skirmish force, Alexander moves his infantry forward under the protection of the cavalry

ALEXANDER

9 As these units move between the two opposing armies, Alexander's left flank cavalry attack them, developing the battle in Alexander's favour

8 Porus reacts to this attack by ordering his remaining mounted forces on the right to move across and reinforce the left

PORUS

13 With Porus' cavalry driven from the field, Alexander orders a final encirclement of the Indian forces, where slaughter continues for eight hours, with Porus himself being wounded and captured, his army completely destroyed

10 Alexander then orders his infantry forward in a general attack

11 Porus' elephants are denied the chance to attack the Macedonian cavalry as Alexander's phalanx, preceded by a line of skirmishers, advances on the Indian line

12 Wounded elephants run amok trying to seek avenues of escape, breaking the cohesion of Porus' troops

ALEXANDER

PORUS

Heaven on Earth? The Early Historic city of Sigiriya in Sri Lanka was deliberately planned as a microcosm of the Early Historic universe. The king's palace was situated on top of the high granite outcrop, commanding an almost impregnable defensive position. The city was designed to represent Alakamanda, projecting the king's divine authority over the landscape.

This cosmo-magical planning reached its zenith at the Sri Lankan city of Sigiriya. Occupied by the usurper Kassapa I (who reigned from AD 473 to 491), he transferred the capital of the island from Anuradhapura to a 182-m (600-ft) high outcrop. In an attempt to recreate Alakamanda, the home of Kubera (god of wealth), the city consisted of three main elements each representing a constituent of Kubera's celestial home. The lake and moat symbolize the ocean surrounding the universe; the inner zone of white-washed boulders the Himalayas; the outcrop Mount Meru, the home of the gods; whilst the palace structure on top of the rock is equated with the palace of Kubera. Thus, through the morphology of the city Kassapa identified himself as Kubera, outwardly projecting his divine authority over his subjects.

Less symbolically charged are the series of heavily fortified capitals securing the valley of Taxila in Pakistan and with it, the South Asian portion of the Silk Route. Reflecting its Hellenistic and Philhellene origins, the 2nd century BC city of Sirkap was surrounded by 4.8 km (3 miles) of stone wall strengthened by regularly spaced rectangular bastions. Additional security was provided by a walled acropolis on the Hathial ridge to the south of the rectangular city and the placing of the main gateway slightly to the east of the main street. Largely abandoned during Kushan domination of South Asia's northern territories, it was superseded by a new generation of military architecture developed in Central Asia.

Drawing inspiration from Central Asian cities such as Dalverzin-tepe in Uzbekistan, the fortified city of Sirsukh, also in the Taxila valley was roughly square in plan, measuring 1,375 by 1,000 m (4,500 by 3,250 ft). Its masonry-faced rubble walls were 5.5 m (18 ft) thick and were strengthened by a berm, or low buttress, to prevent undermining, whilst stirrup bastions punctuated the wall and numerous arrow-slits provided a wide field of fire for the defenders. The absence of densely occupied deposits within has suggested to some scholars that a largely mobile force occupied this site.

This investment in heavily fortified strong points reflects the Kushans' domination of a hostile landscape through the use of cavalry. This use of speed and mobility in combination with walled centres allowed them to control key access points and regulate trade networks across the Silk Route. The success of this strategy is illustrated by the caravan city of Begram where a double ditch and 12-m (39-ft) thick walls were strengthened by towers containing heavy ballista and catapults. Archaeologists excavating a sealed storeroom in the city's palace were amazed to find hundreds of ivory artifacts from South Asia beside Greco-Roman glass and Chinese lacquer work, reflecting the Kushans' unique position at the crossroads of Asia.

WEAPONS AND WARFARE

Greek and Roman accounts of Alexander the Great's expedition have provided us with clear insights into the general military techniques and weapons of South Asian warfare. However, these are augmented and expanded by the *Arthasastra* – the contemporary writings of Kautilya, chief minister of Chandragupta Maurya. Providing a unique record of the economic and political governance of a South Asian state and its professional instruments and strategies for war, the *Arthasastra* represents a record paralleling the thesis of Machiavelli.

According to the *Arthasastra*, the ideal army was composed of four main divisions: infantry, cavalry, chariots and elephants. The infantry comprised foot soldiers equipped with swords and spears supported by archers with bamboo longbows and slingers. Primarily utilized for hand-to-hand combat, they were augmented by cavalry units who made swift surprise attacks, scouted and raided enemy supply and communication lines. The chariot division consisted of vehicles drawn by two horses and was used for defensive and offensive deployments, such as protecting infantry ranks and

Although early examples have been found at Daimabad (dating to the 2nd millennium BC), the use of chariots, such as this one depicted on the main stupa at Sanchi, was at its peak during the Early Historic period. One of the four main divisions of the ideal Early Historic army, chariots were utilized both defensively and offensively. Their speed was vital for battlefield communication, and, according to Kautilya, chariots were the choice vehicles for kings.

239

breaking through enemy lines. The final and most decisive division of the army, the war elephants, were utilized crushing infantry deployments and destroying fortifications. Another contemporary source estimates that the Mauryan army consisted of 600,000 infantry, 30,000 cavalry and 9,000 elephants.

Equally important are Kautilya's treatises on political science. Writing at the formative stage of the Mauryan empire as it was still expanding its hegemony, Kautilya suggested that all neighbouring kingdoms were enemies of the state but that the neighbours of their neighbours were potential allies. Further categorizing neighbouring states, Kautilya considered strong kingdoms to be 'foes', weak kingdoms fit only to be 'exterminated' and kingdoms facing internal problems to be 'vulnerable'. From the Mauryan perspective, it was the duty of prosperous kingdoms like themselves to extend their control over weaker kingdoms. Rather more revealingly, Kautilya advocated expansion through the use of the triple strategy of open, concealed and silent warfare.

Whilst open warfare employed the professional army, Kautilya advised that it should be supported by concealed warfare, that is the use of guerrilla tactics. These more regular strategies were to be supported by a uniquely Mauryan tactic that involved the use of secret agents, female spies and assassins, and propaganda. Kautilya's concept of silent warfare was intended to create confusion, dissension and conflict within enemy kingdoms, weakening them both militarily and socially. Such an approach was a direct contradiction of earlier epics, such as the *Mahabharata*, in which tacit codes of war were outlined promoting honour during warfare.

THE ART OF WAR

The earliest depictions of South Asian troops come from outside the subcontinent at the spectacular spring capital of the Achaemenid empire, Persepolis. Confirming reports of Gandharan and Indian conscripts in the Persian armies opposing Alexander the Great, bas-reliefs on the staircase at the Apadana Palace at Persepolis illustrate Gandharan troops from an area equating to northwestern Pakistan and southern Afghanistan armed with lances and large round shields of dried skins. In a similar fashion, troops from a region corresponding with Punjab and Kashmir are depicted, although they are equipped with double-headed axes.

Despite the substantial corpus of textual evidence for the character of South Asian warfare during the Mauryan period through the writings of Kautilya, no representations of warriors or conflict are known. Perhaps associated with Asoka's later pursuit of non-violence, this remained the case for a number of centuries, until dramatically changed in the archaeological record by the great stone gateways or *toranas* at the Buddhist centre of Sanchi, in Madhya Pradesh.

Built by the great Sunga warrior-king Agnimitra in the 1st century BC, the southern *torana* of Sanchi's main stupa depicts scenes from the 'War of the Relics', in which neighbouring kingdoms fought over possession of the corporeal remains of Gautama Buddha. Agnimitra, the son of the commander-in-chief of the last Mauryan emperor, commissioned this carving of the siege of a fortified city by an army corresponding with Kautilya's blueprint with the four divisions of infantry, cavalry, chariots and elephants clearly visible.

Detail from the Apadana Palace at Persepolis. The bas-reliefs on the palace staircase depict soldiers from across the Persian empire, including Gandharan troops carrying lances and soldiers from Punjab and Kashmir wielding double-headed axes. These images demonstrate the control and taxation the Persians instituted across their vast empire, which incorporated northwestern South Asia.

Depicting a siege from the 'War of the Relics', this carving from the southern *torana* of the main stupa at Sanchi portrays the four main wings of an Early Historic army – infantry, cavalry, chariots and elephants (see also p. 228).

The city is centrally placed with high walls of mudbrick or stone, above which timber galleries or parapets may be seen. Mainly occupied by archers, raining arrows down on the advancing infantry, other troops can be seen hurling stone blocks over the walls. The siege army advances in full battle order with archers providing cover for foot soldiers armed with spears, lances, clubs and shields. In the immediate foreground, the vanguard can be seen scaling the outer walls of the city, only to be repulsed by spear and club-wielding guards. Charioteers and elephants mass menacingly in reserve, waiting to demolish the weakened fortifications and smash the demoralized troops within. Unsuitable for high humidity and temperatures, neither metal helmets nor body armour are worn by either side, who favour instead loincloths, sarongs, turbans and the protection afforded by three-quarter-length shields.

This chapter ends with the destruction of the Early Historic world through repeated incursions by the Hephthalites, or White Huns, in the 5th century AD. In the words of Sir John Marshall, Director-General of Archaeology in India from 1902 to 1928, they 'swept over Gandhara and Punjab... carrying ruin and desolation wherever they went'. Graphic evidence of this scorched earth policy is found in the valley of Taxila where human remains lie next to charred grain stores in the ruins of monasteries.

Despite the two hiatuses present within our coverage of South Asia, the continuum of Asoka's philosophy of non-violence or *Dharma* may be traced through the centuries culminating in the passive resistance of Mahatma Gandhi. Hugely successful, this simple approach baffled British military and political strategists and was to play a crucial role in ending imperial rule in South Asia. Unfortunately, such a policy appears absent in modern South Asia, with ongoing conflict present at local, regional, national and international levels practising strategies close to Kautilya's threefold division of open, concealed and silent warfare throughout the region.

15 Warfare in Ancient China

Infantryman of the famous terracotta army found in the tomb of the First Emperor, dating to the 3rd century BC. His armour is composed of leather platelets riveted onto knee-length leather jerkins. By the 4th century such armour was mass produced and became standard equipment for the infantry-based armies of the day.

The immense span of time treated in this chapter, c. 1600 BC – AD 589, is best approached through a division into four broad periods. All four saw distinct and significant developments in Chinese society and culture, including in the art of war. Long a cultural consciousness and identity, China only emerged as a single country recognizable to us today in the third of our periods. Politically, indeed, it enjoyed genuine unity only during that period, though from our terminus, AD 589, unity was the rule rather than the exception.

The geography of China is most obviously characterized by its two great rivers, the Yellow and the Yangzi, which served as the respective arenas for earlier and later development. The rim of highlands and mountains that encompass and demarcated most of traditional China (later largely absorbed) make up a further notable feature. Two related circumstances stand out as key determinants in the country's political and military history. First, as a land with ample arable land and other resources, China developed a productive agrarian economy which supported a large population, a network of towns and cities, an active trade and thus the capacity for large-scale war-making. Second, along the northern and northwestern borders a sharp division emerged in the societies, economies and cultures on either side: the pastoral, nomadic peoples to the north, the sedentary, agricultural Chinese to the south. This circumstance led to the most persistent and intractable external problem the Chinese were to face.

Warfare in China certainly dates from late Neolithic times, or by the middle of the 3rd millennium BC. The success of cereal agriculture had led to the emergence of numerous settled communities which, after a certain point, began surrounding themselves with defensive walls. There was conflict, probably in the form of raiding, defensive measures and counterattacks, but the archaeological record has not yet revealed how such fighting was actually conducted.

ARCHAIC CHINA

History, as defined by the appearance of writing, begins with the Shang dynasty, c. 1600–1045 BC, an era likewise characterized by bronze production. The Shang kingdom occupied the middle reaches of the Yellow River in north China, but its influence extended far beyond its political domain. In turn it profited from contacts with other cultures in the region. True warfare in China begins with the Shang. A formal organization of royal forces, apparently several thousand in number, permitted systematic attacks (and counterattacks) against enemies on all sides. Along with more conventional motivations, one goal of these wars was to obtain captives for sacrifice in Shang religious rites. Organization and the availability of ample resources go a long way towards explaining Shang's war-making capability, but technological advances must have played a role too: bronze weapons were unquestionably superior

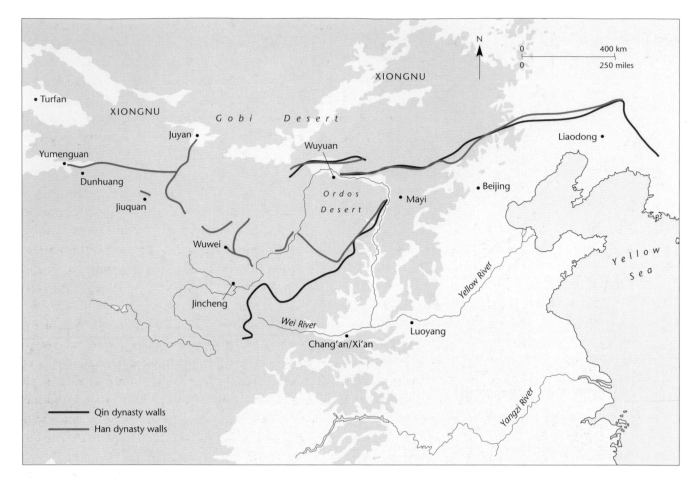

to those made of wood and stone. These included lengthy dagger-axes (*ge*), spears, various battle-axes and knives, and the composite reflex bow. A specialized unit of archers is indeed attested in the sources. The war chariot too makes its appearance, evidently an import from distant western Asia. It served largely as a status symbol, however, and played little if any role in combat.

The Shang kingdom was extinguished 1045 BC by a neighbour and one-time vassal to the west, the Zhou. Long established in the fertile Wei River valley, the Zhou house provided the leadership and core army for what may well have been an alliance of Shang enemies. Related to the Shang linguistically and culturally, the Zhou extended their conquests far beyond the former's borders to encompass most of north China. Politically, this resulted in a rather loosely jointed kingdom with large areas parcelled out to kinsmen and loyal generals, in effect an extended tribal system. Without doubt, however, this framework served to spread a common culture, eventually identified as Han.

Left Late Shang bronze helmet, probably worn only by aristocratic warriors. Bronze was the predominant metal throughout this early period.

Above The main sites mentioned in this chapter, and the courses of the Qin and Han dynasty walls.

The long-lived Zhou dynasty (c. 1045–256 BC) provides the chronological framework for the most momentous political and military developments in Chinese history. This was the period when literary, historical and philosophical works, later recognized as classics, appeared and when some of the most influential figures such as Confucius lived. Nevertheless, politically it was characterized by disunity. After a long initial period of rule, the Zhou house was expelled from its western base in 771 BC and forced to establish a new capital in the east at Luoyang. There, as its power steadily declined, it saw its role reduced to merely ritual head of an increasingly fragmented realm.

THE EVOLUTION OF A MULTISTATE SOCIETY

The political landscape of Zhou China after 770 BC reveals well over a hundred independent or autonomous territories, varying greatly in size and resources. The dominant tendency over the next three centuries (the so-called Spring and Autumn period) was for these nascent states to become fewer and larger, above all through armed conflict. Wars were frequent, typically short, small-scale and fought with limited aims. They carried sufficient cost, however, to inspire repeated efforts to control such conflicts. In the 7th century BC the institution of the hegemon was created: that is, recognition of a particular state as first among equals and charged to keep the peace. It had only limited effect as diplomacy and the forging of alliances invariably followed the course of strict self-interest. By the mid-5th century BC barely two dozen states survived, and the process continued. It is notable that leadership in each state was provided by an aristocracy who fostered the martial virtues and espoused a chivalrous code intended to keep war within limits, at least for those of their station.

This is also the age of the war chariot in China. The chariot now appears in the hundreds, in rare cases in the thousands, in battles of this period. A three-man crew included an archer (often a noble), a spearman and a driver, the horses two or four in number. Units of foot soldiers, commonly ten but often more, were attached to each chariot. Defensively, such units screened the chariot until it was ready to move into the attack. However, it is not at all clear what chariot tactics were. The chariots' great advantage, speed, would normally lead them beyond their foot escorts, and given the cost of the horses and vehicle and the presence of a nobleman, they would hardly be risked in literal shock fashion. Probably, certain conventions governed their use, observed by both sides, and in great numbers they must have been effective.

Some development of an independent infantry occurred as well. Southern armies (from the Yangzi basin), for example, were almost wholly infantry from the beginning because of the terrain. When towards the end of this period sieges began to be undertaken, only foot soldiers could manage this task. Archaeology reveals the presence of good infantry weapons, mostly continuing earlier designs. The *ge* dagger-axe had by now received an elongated blade at the end, permitting a thrusting movement and thus becoming a true halberd.

Two beautifully decorated bronze swords, inlaid with turquoise, both dating to around 500 BC. An inscription on the left-hand sword records that it was owned by Fu Chai, Prince of Wu. The right-hand sword has a very well-preserved incised design; both are still extremely sharp.

Three-bladed halberd or dagger-axe of the Warring States period. This weapon, long a standard infantry issue, reached lengths of 2.5 m (8 ft) and longer.

From the mid-5th century BC change accelerated in all sectors in all states. Though reforms, for example, in law and administration, had been underway since the 7th century, much more ambitious programmes were now initiated. Adopting the perspective of that time, we could describe these as efforts at modernization. Both external and internal pressures were at work. Externally, as China moved into the Warring States period (officially 403–221 BC), conflicts among the states became larger in scale, more deadly and of longer duration. Internally, measures intended to place increasing power into the hands of the ruling prince were accompanied by threats to him posed by prominent families. Tradition and precedent still weighed heavily, but the ability to mobilize resources and to use force effectively became even more decisive in determining the fortunes of a state's leadership.

Military growth and development were linked to a series of profound and widespread changes. Rulers adopted a variety of means to concentrate power in their own hands. The imposition of law codes, levelling the social playing field, eroded the privileges of the old aristocracy. To provide direct access to the populace for services and taxes, a system of household registration was implemented. Similarly, a cadre of officials was created, shifting over time from nobles to commoners, to staff the central government and assume direct control over local areas. The new state also fostered and benefited from economic growth which is itself demonstrated in the expansion of trade, appearance of money, spread of towns and demographic changes. There is an intellectual counterpart to these developments as well, since the period *c.* 500–200 BC was the liveliest and most creative in the history of Chinese thought.

In this environment a strong military was essential, not only to preserve the state but also to pursue the expansion necessary to keep it abreast of competing states. What, in short, happened was the transformation of an army based on the old aristocratic order and led by nobles to a mass army in the service of an autocratic ruler and led by officials appointed by him. Central to this change was registration of the population which permitted the direct conscription of peasants. The large, increasingly effective infantry forces thus created spelled the end of chariot warfare with its emphasis on individual heroism and chivalric behaviour. Up to a point at least, numbers were most important: we begin hearing in the Warring States period about field armies of 100,000 and more (in fact, much larger, surely fanciful, figures are given too).

The new infantry was also better equipped. Though bronze weapons remained dominant, iron appears and comes in for greater and greater use. Shock troops were primarily armed with halberds and spears and to a lesser extent swords. They were protected by coats of body armour made up of numerous plates of leather or metal sewn together, as seen in the famous terracotta army of the First Emperor (see box on pp. 254–255). Archers were joined by the bearers of a new weapon, the crossbow. Certainly present by 400 BC, the accurate and powerful crossbow became a crucial and lasting part of Chinese weaponry. The key component was the complex bronze trigger mechanism that by the end of this period even went into mass production. Unfortunately, we have no idea in what proportions these various shock and missile troops made up a standard unit.

In the 4th century BC rulers in the northern states began introducing cavalry into their armies. The Chinese had probably first encountered mounted nomads on the northern border a century earlier. Despite its obvious advantages, several factors must have inhibited the adoption and growth of cavalry – a poor supply of horses, the lack of experienced riders and conservatism. Until the imperial era, the cavalry's role remained limited.

Widespread improvements in fortification, dating from the 5th century BC, also called forth more systematic efforts at siegecraft. Town and city walls were renewed, heightened and generally strengthened. Walls intended to serve rather different purposes began appearing as well, constructed as defensive barriers along the borders of the various states. Though the northern states built walls too to safeguard newly acquired areas to the north, the internal walls were of much greater significance in this period. It is ironic that well before the Great Wall (better translated as 'Long Walls') was built to shield the Chinese from nomadic invaders, the Chinese were constructing walls to protect themselves from each other.

Many of the techniques of siegecraft call to mind those used in other parts of the world – the battering ram, the ramp, scaling ladders (here actually counter-weighted 'cloud ladders'), mining and so forth. Defenders placed geophones to detect mining activities and might also use a bellows-and-tubes arrangement to blow noxious fumes towards the miners. A variety of screens could be set up to intercept missiles, while an inflammable screen could be hung from the walls and ignited to dispatch would-be attackers on scaling ladders. There are questions about the kinds of artillery at the disposal of either attackers or defenders. It is certain that larger, heavier crossbows were developed, equivalent to the Greek and Roman ballistae. Rather than employing the principle of torsion like the latter, the Chinese models used an exceptionally strong bowstave or multiple bowstaves mounted on a stationary framework or even on a kind of cart. These were very effective weapons with ranges, depending on sizes of machine and bolt, up to 250 m (820 ft) and more. Information is surprisingly scarce,

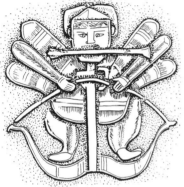

The heavy crossbow of the Warring States period was an arduous weapon to use: in this depiction, the soldier holds the bolt in his teeth before loading it; the bronze trigger mechanism and bolt heads of a slightly later Han crossbow are shown below. The crossbow was unquestionably the most important innovation in weaponry in this period.

however, regarding the other common type of artillery of the ancient world, the catapult, and accounts of its use in actual sieges are sadly lacking.

As wars thus became larger, more complex and farther-reaching in their consequences, a demand was inevitably created for professionalism and expertise. In the ranks, professionalism was fostered among officers whose leadership on all levels was critical in shaping, controlling and directing the new mass armies. It also appeared in the emergence of elite units within these armies, at times the bodyguard units of the rulers, at others commando or special assault units. Of most interest to us, however, are the experts who became advisers, commanders and sometimes authors. The best known of these, of course, is Sunzi, the author of *The Art of War*, the world's earliest military treatise (see box opposite). Yet, Sunzi was but one of many specialists on the art of war, albeit among the first and certainly the most influential. Moreover, the search for rational and pragmatic solutions to the challenges of war was typical of the many intellectual endeavours in this age of 'a hundred schools'. It was typical, as well, of the firm belief in the power of ideas and in the possibility of their successful application.

Military experts were among a new group on the scene, itinerant advisers – mostly on the political arts – who might move from court to court, seeking an audience and high office (Confucius was one of the earliest of these, though a firm proponent of persuasion rather than of force). In due course, the military experts developed distinct schools and approaches. One emphasized strategy, another technology, and a third metaphysical-cosmological calculations. Most are not well represented among the surviving sources, but they did share certain characteristics. They were pragmatic in their approaches and at least implicitly anti-traditionalist. They showed small concern for moral issues, or in the case of Sunzi none at all. They stressed the need for clear organization, strict discipline and unquestioning obedience. The army was to respond perfectly to the decision of the commander whose role was elevated to an extraordinary degree. By virtue of his thorough preparation of the army, his grasp of the potential uses of the terrain, and his acquisition of sound intelligence on the enemy's condition, leadership and intentions, the commander could in effect win the battle with minimal fighting. Nor did his superior conduct issue merely from the conventional qualities of a good general. More significantly, he must possess an almost mystical perspicacity that revealed the underlying, determinative pattern of events as they were to unfold. Most astonishingly, according to the theoreticians, he should enjoy complete independence on the battlefield and suffer no interference from the ruling prince.

The period of the Warring States was brought to an end by the best organized, most autocratic, most militaristic and, in the eyes of contemporaries, most ruthless state, Qin. Long regarded as rough and uncultured, Qin, its capital near modern Xi'an, underwent a series of reforms in the 4th century BC that allowed it to catch up with and, in some respects, surpass the other states. A good idea of the contemporary 3rd-century view of Qin can be obtained from the famous Confucian philosopher Xunzi:

'The rulers of Qin... employ [their people] harshly, terrorize them with authority, embitter them with hardship, coax them with rewards and cow them with punishments. They see to it that if the humbler people hope to gain any benefits from their superiors, they can do so only by achieving distinction in battle.... Rewards

Sunzi's *Art of War*

Sunzi identifies both the author ('Master Sun') of *The Art of War*, the world's oldest surviving military treatise, and the book itself. Though the work is attributed to a general and military adviser of the late 6th century BC, as a text it dates from the second half of the 5th century (thus, of different authorship or a later compilation of Master Sun's dicta). Until the early 1970s in fact, when a number of texts were discovered in a 2nd-century tomb, there was confusion over the real name and identity of the author. This find made it clear that there were two 'Master Suns', the earlier Sun Wu and a likely descendant who lived in the 4th century, Sun Bin, both authors of *Art of War* treatises. The latter incorporates nearly the whole of the former's work into his own while expanding into some new directions. The following characterization, however, focuses entirely on the earlier work.

Sunzi is not literally a military manual; it is, rather, a set of guidelines, even a psychological treatise, addressed to the commander. In this age, the Warring States, of growing military conflict and professionalization, Sunzi preached (and no doubt helped determine) many of the tenets advocated by other military experts, as indicated elsewhere in this chapter. Most striking in Sunzi is his emphasis on the use of deception and surprise, to further which he advocates employment of a full panoply of spies. He also stresses the absolute need for the commander to recognize the critical moment and place at which to strike in decisive fashion. In this as in other ways he reflects, explicitly or implicitly, a grasp of all the modern 'principles' of warfare. Notably too for someone in the business of war, he is keenly aware of its costs and even finds it feasible on occasion to win without actually resorting to battle.

Above These wooden 'pages', with the script running from top to bottom, are part of a much larger find of nearly 5,000 complete and incomplete pieces dating to the late centuries BC and buried in a Han tomb. Some 300 of these preserve most of the text of Sunzi's *The Art of War*.

increase to keep pace with achievements; thus a man who returns from battle with five enemy heads is made the master of five families in his neighbourhood.'

Having consolidated its external position in the west by 300 BC, Qin achieved effective dominance over the six large states remaining by c. 260 BC. The end, when Qin was duly prepared, came quickly: within the decade 230–221 BC Qin successively destroyed its rivals and unified the country under its rule. A new era was born.

THE FIRST EMPIRE: THE QIN AND HAN DYNASTIES

The first step in the Qin construction of empire was the extension of its own laws and institutions throughout the land. In some respects this did not entail such radical change in that all the states had been developing along similar lines anyhow. To be sure, and events bear this out, local resentment at the imposition of rule from the outside must have remained strong. It is not clear how the regime refashioned its military or even if it tried to. Presumably, it absorbed a substantial proportion of soldiers from the defeated armies and demobilized the rest. In view of the need to consolidate its control over the country and of the extensive military operations subsequently undertaken, the government must have kept a large number of men under arms, perhaps in the order of 250,000. The survival of the terracotta army in the tomb of the First Emperor, Shi Huangdi, has provided us with a better visual record than of any pre-modern Chinese soldiers (see box on pp. 254–255).

Qin launched an ambitious set of programmes, many of which had profound and lasting effects. For the most part they were also what one would expect of a national government. The whole country was carved up into 36 (later 42) administrative districts (with subdivisions), and the Qin law code was extended throughout. An effort was launched to make the Chinese script, till now featuring numerous variants, uniform. Similarly, standardization of currency, weights and measures, and road gauges was implemented. Enormous public works projects were undertaken, conscripting the labour of hundreds of thousands of peasants. Roads were constructed on a massive scale, totalling over 6,500 km (4,000 miles) by most estimates and suggesting an obvious parallel with the Roman empire. Several large-scale canal projects aimed at improving water transport as well. The tomb of the First Emperor itself was years and thousands of man-hours in the making, while construction of the Great Wall is probably Qin's most famous building effort.

Not surprisingly, expansion was also on the Qin agenda. Already in 219 BC forces were sent to the deep south, in the next few years extending north Chinese rule to the southern and southeastern coasts for the first time. Colonists were periodically sent both south and north to help stabilize these frontier regions with settlements. From 215 BC the accomplished Qin general Meng Tian launched a series of attacks against the nomadic Xiongnu which successfully added new territory to the empire. It was to enclose this and secure the whole northern frontier that the first Great Wall was built. These, literally, 'Long Walls' actually connected and extended three walls previously built by northern Chinese states, their trajectory lying north of the present Ming-Qing wall. In design, construction and strategic function they were very similar to the Han walls which we shall examine more closely below.

In all probability the Qin empire-building reached too far and moved too quickly, alienating many people who were otherwise politically neutral. No doubt too, the privileged classes of the formerly independent states remained unreconciled to the new regime. Above all, a leadership crisis followed the death of the First Emperor in 210 BC and continued unresolved until the dynasty met its end in 207 BC. In a state as absolutist as Qin, the lack of a firm hand at the centre was almost certain to prove fatal.

The years of civil war until pacification in 202 BC were costly to the country in both internal and external security but did not shake the unity already achieved. Indeed, the succeeding Han emperors by and large maintained Qin laws and institutions, albeit lending them a different, ultimately Confucian, ideological cast. The fact that the founder Liu Bang (who reigned from 206 to 195 BC, posthumously known as Gaozu) was a commoner who had fought his way to the top makes this all the more comprehensible. This long-lived dynasty suffered a rupture from AD 9 to 23, when a usurper attempted unsuccessfully to replace it. As a result, the period

Remnants of the Qin 'Great Wall' in Western China, the ambitious defence line and border intended to keep nomadic warriors at bay.

251

206 BC – AD 9 is known as Former (or Western) Han, the capital located at Chang'an, and the period AD 23–220 as Later (or Eastern) Han, with the capital at Luoyang.

The Han was an era of numerous accomplishments which made it the prototype of the successful dynasty to which all succeeding dynasties looked back. This was true in the military sphere as well, though in a period of such length fortunes inevitably rose and fell. Four aspects of the Han military record require our attention as the most significant: for the first time China had a government in place that over a period of decades could frame a national military and defence policy; this was the first dynasty confronted by a contemporary nomadic confederation of strength comparable to China's; in response to the nomadic threat Han developed the first large-scale and independent cavalry arm in Chinese history; and, again, in response to the external threat and to safeguard territorial and strategic gains, Han constructed the first comprehensive frontier defence system for China. The importance of all these points will emerge as we proceed.

Han was hardly less expansionist than Qin. It was only late in the 2nd century BC that internal conditions and stabilization of the northern frontier permitted initiatives to be pursued in other directions. Then came a series of aggressive moves: reassertion of the Chinese position in the south, even as far as Vietnam; invasion of north Korea; attacks on native rulers and seizures of their lands in the southwest; and to the west, advances far out into Central Asia. The basic rationale was that, as the quintessence of civilization, China should enjoy the subordination of surrounding peoples who themselves would benefit from the relationship. Thus, though there were frequent changes in local conditions and challenges to Han authority, the territorial empire was born.

Overwhelmingly, the major problem was posed by the Xiongnu in the north. Clan-based, migratory and herders by trade (of horses and sheep primarily), nomads were typically divided and resistant to non-tribal authority. The advances made by Qin may, however, have so threatened the income and security of the Xiongnu tribes as to unite them behind a new, able and aggressive leader, Modun (r. 209–174 BC). The consequences for China were not long in coming. When Liu Bang himself sought to regain lands along the northern frontier in 201 BC, he was defeated, trapped and forced to accede to an unfavourable treaty with Modun. In purely military terms, this result was not surprising. Having made the transition to horse nomadism some centuries earlier, these eastern nomads had developed a cavalry army whose speed, range and mobility gave it enormous advantages, especially in open terrain, over an infantry-based army such as the Han's. Individually, too, the skills of the nomadic warriors were honed by the routine activities of their daily life, riding and hunting, and they became expert shots with their composite reflex bows. Eagerness to fight was further encouraged by a martial ethos.

In consequence of this military imbalance, the first six decades of the dynasty saw a Han government committed to peace at almost any cost. To preserve it, the Han effectively sought to buy off the Xiongnu, providing under treaty terms an annual subsidy, a marriage alliance and trading rights. It was also pertinent that the reestablishment of true central control throughout the empire was not achieved until after the middle of the 2nd century BC. The problem with the treaty arrangement was

A bronze tomb figurine of a Han horseman, armed with a halberd. The lack of stirrups apparent here limited the effectiveness of such early cavalry.

that it did not work. The Chinese thought they were purchasing peace; however, all too often the Xiongnu launched raids for loot and even, in 166 and 158 BC, major incursions.

Obviously part of any solution to this aggression lay in the creation of a cavalry force that could counter nomadic strength. Precise dating of the inception of this effort is impossible, but cavalry units begin showing up in Han armies in about 170 BC. They were largely recruited from friendly peoples living along the border. A number of mounts were imported, but there was a serious effort at large-scale horse production too, so that by c. 140 BC numerous breeding farms had been established in the border lands. The majority of cavalrymen were horse-archers, armed additionally with a sword or other such weapons for closing. Surviving tomb figurines show some horsemen with polearms, so that there was certainly a shock component too (although since the stirrup had not yet been invented, shock tactics must still have been severely limited). The figurines indicate that horsemen wore long leather tunics rather than armour.

The infantry remained the backbone of the Han army, its strength in numbers reflecting China's vastly greater human resources. Han historians repeatedly emphasize the effectiveness of the crossbow, and there seem to be no good reasons to doubt their claims. The remarkable performance in 99 BC of Li Ling's 5,000-man force is ample testimony to this. Isolated on the steppe and constantly under attack and harassment by far superior Xiongnu numbers, this force almost made it back to the Chinese lines, succumbing only when it ran out of bolts and arrows. The great disadvantage of the crossbow was its slow rate of fire – hardly more than once a minute – due to the clumsiness of loading. This also explains why it was unsuitable as a cavalry weapon. Though explicit evidence is lacking for several centuries yet, we can speculate that the Han must already have worked out a system of staggered firing.

For the offensive operations that were to come, the Han should have enjoyed more than adequate manpower. A system of conscription was in place which required two years service of men in the age range 23–56. Given the estimated population figure of 58 million provided for the year AD 2, ample conscripts for any given year would have been available. Volunteers and convicts also served. The real task lay in training the men and then keeping experienced units intact. Probably compulsory extensions of the service period were common. There was, to be sure, a core group of professionals who made up the guard units at the capital and the cadres both for the field armies and the frontier defence system.

It was following the accession of the emperor Wudi (r. 141–87 BC) that a radical new political and military policy was set. The ground for this change was prepared by obtaining intelligence on the borderlands and beyond, scrapping the treaty with the Xiongnu, harbouring a full treasury, and reshaping the army for major offensive operations. For three decades, from 129 to 90 BC, Wudi launched a series of offensives against the Xiongnu, essentially on a search and destroy basis. Han forces were to engage and destroy the enemy and/or his herds and property. Given the hyperbole of the Chinese sources on the sizes of the armies involved, it is impossible to determine exact numbers. But using contemporary figures on supply and

The Terracotta Army

Discovered only in the 1970s, this assemblage of more than 7,000 life-size figures of soldiers was created to protect the First Emperor of Qin (and of China) in the afterlife. Despite the monumental scale of this find, it represents only one part of the gigantic necropolis whose construction lasted throughout his reign. The central part, visible as a huge tumulus, has not yet been excavated. A variety of soldiers are represented – infantry (including archers), cavalry and charioteers – and placed as if in battle array. The seven kinds of dress and variety of hairstyles shown testify to differences in rank and function. The faces exhibit a remarkable degree of individuality, whereas the body parts were mass-produced according to type and pose. Fine bronze weapons also turned up, but as this sector of the necropolis was looted in the post-Qin period, they are relatively limited in number.

The ranks of soldiers (and horses) of the terracotta army guarding the First Emperor's tomb. To date some 7,000 figures have been uncovered.

Late Han or post-Han warriors in full armour, holding spears that are now missing. These are probably officers and possibly non-Chinese.

consumption and bearing in mind that in such an environment living off the land was not an option, we can speculate that Chinese expeditionary armies ran a maximum of about 75,000 with cavalry contingents perhaps up to 25,000. Han was also fortunate in that the capable Modun line ceased ruling after 126 BC, so that the Xiongnu only intermittently enjoyed real unity and good leadership thereafter.

Wudi's great offensives were on the whole successful. The Xiongnu were fragmented; their capacity for major incursions was sharply reduced; and they were pushed back well beyond the borderlands. These new conditions enabled the Han to extend and consolidate their northern defence barriers (i.e. the Great Wall, see below). They also used the opportunity to strike out to the west into Central Asia where they extended a rather tenuous dominion across modern Xinjiang. Though this advance had the consequence of opening up the Silk Route (which through a succession of links reached the Roman empire), the main objective was strategic, not commercial. The Han sought to deny to the Xiongnu access to the wealth and material of the prosperous oasis cities such as Turfan.

These gains, naturally, did not come without cost. Because of the savagery of the fighting and the harsh conditions, casualties were high. So too was the expense. The bulging treasury of Wudi's accession was left empty at the time of his death, despite the imposition of numerous (and unpopular) new taxes. In view of the criticism of subsequent Chinese historians, there seems in Han expansionism to be more than a whiff of what in the modern era is labelled imperialism. Moreover, the nomadic threat could never be eliminated completely, for surviving tribes could always withdraw to safety and regroup, at some point, to fight again.

As a result of historical accident and the dry climate of Central Asia, the Han external defence perimeter has emerged from the shadows and assumed quite clear and substantial shape. Thousands of documents, or rather fragments thereof, have survived in the form of wooden strips which served as 'pages' in communications or records. The unique value of these materials lies in the everyday, concrete detail they provide which was never incorporated into our standard sources, edited and compiled as they were in the distant capital. These 'documents' range from reports on patrols to results of shooting proficiency, from inspections of facilities to specifications of brick size. They do not, of course, show the big picture, but they reveal the countless minutiae that made up reality along the frontier.

The border was, in fact, marked by walls, constructed of tamped earth to a height of 1.8–3 m (6–10 ft). They made effective use of natural features and were punctuated every mile or more by watchtowers, built of brick and plastered over and rising to a height of 6–9 m (20–30 ft). Since signalling was one of the critical functions of these towers and their five-man squads, visibility was a primary factor in their placement. At selected points behind this highly guarded perimeter, forts were placed with garrisons of perhaps a hundred men. Garrisons were also placed in towns and at military colonies, founded to support the frontier forces. Clearly, the walls were not intended as a serious barrier to any but a handful of marauders. Rather, they (and their attendant personnel) were intended to serve as an early warning system: sighting of the enemy in any number would bring an immediate alert and an appropriate response. A major enemy force would, to be sure, simply overrun the position. The system that the Han, as well as later Chinese dynasties, employed

Above Remains at Jiaohe of what was originally a mud-brick Han border fort. The site was eventually destroyed in the 13th century by the armies of Genghis Khan.

Right Remnants of the Han 'Great Wall' near Hengshan in Shaanxi province. Such remains are typically found in barren, unproductive areas – in more populated regions they are lost.

could be characterized as an elastic defence, at least in those areas of thin population. There was no expectation of preventing penetration by significant forces but only of halting them somewhere inside the border with units distributed for this purpose.

The lengthy subsequent history of Han saw a chequered pattern of gains and losses on the frontiers. The Xiongnu never regained the position of strength they had enjoyed early in the 2nd century BC, but they remained a threat nevertheless. A phenomenon of greater importance in Later than in Former Han was warfare in the interior, that is, between contending Chinese forces. This was characteristic especially of the interregnum of AD 9–23 and, then increasingly, of the period after AD 180. This meant wars of position and frequent resort to sieges in contrast to the wars of movement on the periphery. Two fundamental developments in Later Han help explain the fragmentation of China in the succeeding period. One was the imperial government's steady loss of revenue and local control to the landowners who built up large estates throughout the countryside. The other was its loss of military control to the powerful generals appointed to deal with rebellions, foreign incursion and general problems of security. These figures in due course became true satraps who divided the country among them. The Han dynasty was finished well before its official end in AD 220.

THE AGE OF DIVISION

This was a period of conflict, instability and rapid change. The break-up of the empire exposed China to attack from the outside and guaranteed violent competition among the surviving pieces. The disruption of civil life was severe, with the economy suffering reduced production and contraction in all sectors. A militarization of society occurred, not only on the level of large armies battling each other for supremacy but also on the local level where well-off families gathered private retinues around them and built walled villas for their protection. The conflict and insecurity also put large numbers of people in motion, often to any place that seemed to offer refuge but most of all south-ward as the Yangzi valley experienced its first great wave of migration. And in the north from the early 4th century foreign conquerors burst upon the scene. Mostly nomads but of differing ethnic identities, they did not so much destroy the old order as find it shattered and possessing little power to resist. For the next three centuries all the founders of dynasties in north China were non-Chinese, or in the cases of the reunifying dynasties of Sui and Tang, of mixed blood.

Replica for a tomb of a fort or fortified villa from the unstable years of late or post-Han when means of self-protection had to be found. Inside are figures of warriors, a master at the table, and kneeling servants.

The foreign conquerors of this time faced many of the same problems as the more famous Mongols and Manchus centuries later: how does a small conquering army and nation rule a vastly larger sedentary population different in culture and ethnicity? Where to draw the line between effective exploitation and self-defeating oppression? The more effective of these regimes learned on the one hand to draw Chinese into the ranks of leadership, and on the other to nurture agricultural production among the peasantry. Amid the competitive conditions of the time, moreover, they had to maintain a high level of military proficiency and preparedness. They made use of Chinese numbers to field an infantry and to serve as work battalions. But truly effective use of natives as soldiers only dates from the mid-6th century. Circumstances differed considerably in the south which remained wholly Chinese and benefited from large influxes of refugees. It enjoyed the protection afforded by its low-lying, watery terrain from the Northern cavalry armies. Yet, as an under-developed region, it was not in this period a major player on the political and military stage.

Unquestionably, the most significant technological-military invention of the age was the stirrup which made possible the first true heavy cavalry. As in the West, the written sources are silent on the subject, but material remains certainly reveal the presence of the stirrup in China by the early 4th century. Its origin is unknown. China might be proposed because of its long tradition of sophisticated crafts, though the horse-riding peoples of the steppe cannot be discounted as a possibility. In any event tomb figurines demonstrate the presence, henceforth, of armoured cavalry – wearing the typical eastern laminated armour – bestride mounts equipped with stirrups. Often the horses are armoured too. Heavy cavalry units became conventional parts of any army, as military texts shortly postdating our period indicate. The shock value gained by the cavalry, no longer mere horse-archers, must have been very significant, though the precise tactics employed remain obscure. Some changes in weaponry seem related to the development of cavalry too. A new kind of sword, single-edged and closer to the Western sabre, and lances became common. The Western knight, with his plate armour, heavy helmet and powerful lance, has, however, no equivalent in East Asia.

Despite the high incidence of warfare and general instability, the Age of Division was by no means a purely destructive and degenerate period in Chinese history. The level of intellectual life remained high, and numerous outstanding literary works were produced. The adoption of Buddhism on all social levels, including the alien conquerors, called forth enormous creative energies and deeply enriched Chinese life. The south, then understood as principally the Yangzi valley, underwent its first significant phase of development. In the north the foundations for reunification

Tomb figurines of armoured horsemen and mounts from the 4th or 5th centuries, when the advent of the stirrup made heavy cavalry (for shock purposes) possible.

Chinese horse-archers, a type of warrior widely used throughout Asia, depicted in a wall-painting of around AD 570 in the Tomb of Lou Rui.

were being laid, though that would hardly have been recognized at the time. As we enter the 6th century, we find – at the risk of oversimplification – that the most successful regimes were the most sinified ones. This does not mean that their leaders were necessarily wide-eyed admirers of Chinese culture but rather that they perceived the need to develop policies and institutions that made optimal use of Chinese resources. Though the Han ideal of a great, unified empire had been kept alive, it was ultimately the institutions developed in the Age of Division that underlay the success of the late 6th-century unifiers.

One of these institutions was the regional militia (*fubing*). Militias of various sorts had been employed periodically for centuries, usually formed on a local basis for temporary duty. The militia which evolved now from about AD 550 was created by the central government of Western Wei (AD 535–556), based in the northwest, out of a need for more manpower. Using the principle of regular annual training or service, it drew upon a kind of yeomanry among the peasants to whom certain privileges were accorded. Unlike the more traditional militias which served only locally, these units were liable for service, normally as infantry, anywhere in the interior or on the frontier. Once trained and battle-tested, they combined with the professional troops, mostly cavalry, to form the most potent army in China at the time and tip the balance in favour of Western Wei.

It is possible to trace a certain lineage of regimes, or dynasties, that employed such institutions as the regional militia with apparent success. Their leadership was not, however, insulated against usurpation. Northern Zhou (AD 557–580), unseating Western Wei, achieved unification of the north before being displaced by Sui (AD 581–617). The reunified empire which Sui brought about with its conquest of the south in AD 589 was inherited by Tang (AD 618–906), heralding one of the greatest ages in Chinese history.

16 Warfare in Early Korea and Japan

A 1.3-m (4½-ft) high fired clay haniwa (funerary sculpture) of a 6th-century AD warrior in eastern Japan, wearing the Koguryo-type lamellar armour favoured by horseriders. Such figures were designed to stand on the surface of large mounded tombs, representing the ruler and his retinue. From Iizuka-cho, Ota-shi, Gunma prefecture.

The Korean Peninsula and Japanese Islands form a regional cultural unit apart from China. The languages spoken ostensibly belong to Tungusic within the Altaic language family, and much of the prehistoric material culture is similarly derived from northeast Asia. The region's peoples maintained an existence based on hunting, gathering, fishing and horticulture long after China's agricultural regimes and complex societies were developed. But crops were eventually adopted: millet from perhaps 2000 BC and wet rice from 1500–1000 BC. Tungusic warriors are suspected to have brought bronzes to Korea in the early 1st millennium BC, mixing with the early agriculturalists. Migrations of the resulting Bronze Age peoples into the western Japanese Islands late in that millennium led to the creation of the Yayoi culture. Bronze Age Korea and Yayoi Japan witness the first incidents of warfare evident in the archaeological record of the region.

Bronze weapons were joined by iron weapons from China during the Han dynasty occupation of northern Korea and the Manchurian massif where four military commanderies were established. Lelang was the longest lived, from 108 BC to AD 313, but during the 3rd century AD, a newly established fifth commandery called Daifang was more active. The presence of Chinese military forces and the dynastic tributary network, which brought most Korean and Japanese peoples into its sphere of influence, served to distribute new types of iron weapons and tools as well as Chinese-style bronze mirrors from this technologically advanced society.

Following the demise of the Han dynasty, the Chinese chronicles record a long period of purported warfare among the Yayoi, referred to in Chinese as the Wa. The Wa Disturbances between AD 147 and 189 may have stemmed from disruption in the supply of Chinese goods, but relations were re-established with the Wei (220–265) and Western Jin (265–316). With the onset of political fragmentation across north China in the 4th century, secondary states began to rise in the political vacuum. In northern Korea, the Koguryo peoples formed a strong state (in the Yalu River valley), and the Paekche emerged in the southwest (around modern Seoul). The southeastern peninsula housed the Kaya chiefdoms (near the modern city of Pusan), and Silla emerged in the late 4th century (centred on Kyongju). The Koguryo and Paekche may have shared common roots but became vicious enemies; similarly, Kaya and Silla were from common stock but were politically opposed. Silla became the most powerful southern state, eventually swallowing Kaya in the 6th century and defeating Koguryo and Paekche in the 7th century to unite the lower peninsula in 668. During the same time period, the Yayoi polities in the islands, which had communicated separately with the Chinese court, were united culturally in the 4th century by the spread of the Mounded Tomb Culture emanating from the Kinai (subsuming the tri-city area of Kyoto, Osaka and Nara), where Miwa came to exercise political hegemony in the first stage of Yamato state formation.

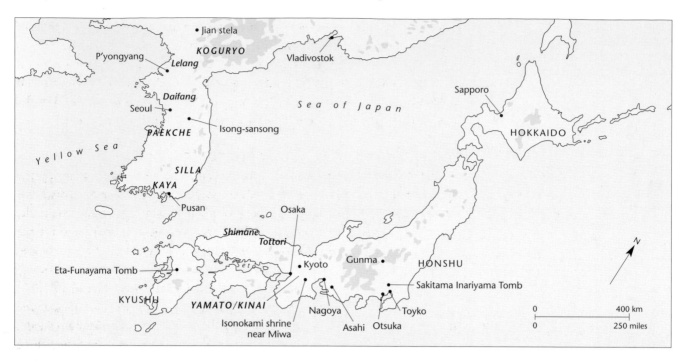

The main sites and regions mentioned in this chapter.

In the 4th century, local forms of iron weapons and body armour were developed in both Kaya and the Kinai. Ultimately inspired by armour styles from the steppes, these new types indicate the militarization of chiefly society in these two areas, though it is not thought they were in direct conflict. On the contrary, Kaya was the source of virtually all iron available to the Japanese Islands, and insular chieftains negotiated to protect their supply. In the late 4th century, the growing militancy of Koguryo in the north challenged Paekche, which called on the incipient Yamato state in the Kinai for assistance. Investment in the military brought Yamato a new source of power, and influx of Paekche allies and refugees in the 5th century transformed the economic and administrative framework of the new Yamato state.

Throughout the 6th century, Paekche and Yamato prepared against incursions by Koguryo and Silla. But when Silla formed an alliance with the new Tang dynasty in China in the 7th century in order to conquer Koguryo, Yamato courtiers decided the best way to protect themselves was to adopt the superior technology of Tang. Reforms beginning in 645 led to the voluntary transformation of Yamato into a sinicized administrative system, the Ritsuryo state, which included the provision of a standing army. Paekche, though having built many stone-walled fortresses along its border with Silla, was unable to keep its independence and succumbed to Silla in 660.

The major periods of warfare in early Korea and Japan ended with the establishment of strong, centralized states, one on the peninsula (United Silla 668–934) and one in the islands (Ritsuryo 945–1185). The Ritsuryo state managed militarily to extend its borders into northern Honshu and to the southwest into Kyushu during its period of power. In United Silla, specialized militarists called the Hwarang protected the state, but Koguryo's withdrawal to the north and establishment of the Bohai state in the Manchurian Basin left United Silla in relative peace. Both Bohai and United Silla also adopted Tang administrative technology and became, like Ritsuryo, large bureaucracies governing vast territories.

In the sections below, we will examine some of the more specific incidents of warfare in this historical trajectory from both archaeological and historical points of view. One focus will be on the weapons and armour used at different periods, reflecting on the scale, organization and interactions of the societies that made and employed them. Another will be the way warfare has been represented in the historical documents, from both international and internal perspectives.

BRONZE AGE WEAPONRY AND WARFARE

The tanged double-edged bronze thrusting sword, often termed a 'dagger', was the first and most enduring weapon of the Pen/Insular region. Derived from daggers of the steppe Bronze Age, this type of bronze sword had a unique pear-shaped profile, giving rise to one appellation: the *pipa* (lute)-shaped dagger. Quite exaggerated in its early versions but slimmed down later, it never lost the telltale flanges located three-quarters of the way down the blade. They have recently been renamed Liaoning-type daggers, referring to their main locus of distribution rather than shape.

Five stages of bronze weapon production and usage have been identified on the Korean Peninsula, beginning in the early 1st millennium BC. The Liaoning dagger was first accompanied by polished stone double-edged swords and polished stone arrowheads. Later in the millennium, its narrowed down version was joined by other bronze products: multi-knobbed mirrors, axes, chisels, small bells and cast sword hilts. These bronze objects probably belonged to Tungusic-speaking chiefs, giving them status and recognition as warriors. The third stage shows the influence of Chinese weaponry as the northern peninsula became drawn into the conflicts and confusion resulting from the Warring States period (403–221 BC). Bronze socketed spearheads and halberds joined the dagger to form the trinity of weapons imported into Kyushu in the middle of this stage, around the early 2nd century BC. Iron implements also began flowing into the peninsula and into the western islands, initiating the Iron Age in Korea and providing Yayoi with both metals simultaneously. Ceremonialization also began at this time, with socketed spearheads increasing in

Korean and Japanese bronze weapons included, from left to right, northeast Asian double-edged thrusting swords with either 'lute-shaped' or narrow blades, usually with detachable hilts; Chinese-style socketed spearheads; and Chinese-style tanged halberds, with holes to fasten the blade perpendicularly to a pole.

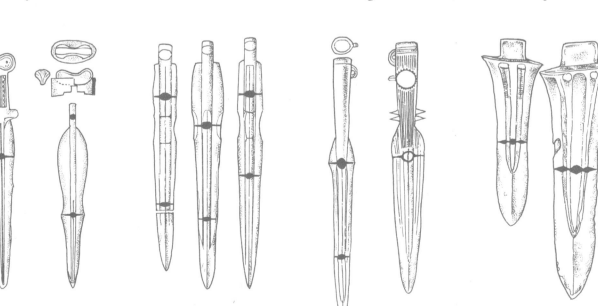

Otsuka site, Shizuoka prefecture, Japan: a Late Yayoi upland site surrounded by a moat. The removal of sites from the lowland plains to higher elevations is interpreted as evidence of unrest in this period.

breadth and length, up to 60 cm (24 in) in the fourth stage. These oversized weapons functioned in community ceremonies and ritual shows of power between chiefs into stage five. By this time, the Chinese commandery of Lelang had been established where modern P'yongyang stands today, and overt warfare on the peninsula was suppressed by the presence of the Chinese military and trading agents.

Bronzes and casting technology were introduced into Kyushu at the end of Early Middle Yayoi (c. early 2nd century BC), before the establishment of Lelang. The repertoire included all three major weapons, fine-lined mirrors and small bells. For decades it was thought that the weapons were used only as ceremonial goods in shows of prestige by emergent Yayoi chieftains, and indeed two types of bronze arrowheads, cast in Late Yayoi, have been identified: run-of-the-mill narrow ones and rarer wider, larger, flat arrowheads thought to be for show. Some of the weapons also grew broader and wider, with unsharpened blades and sand still embedded in the cast sockets, while decorative patterns were cast onto the objects themselves, hilts were adorned with sculpturesque elements and gemstones, and glass beads were attached to scabbards. In the 1980s, however, it was convincingly demonstrated that the narrower implements did serve as functional weapons.

Many Yayoi burial jars and wooden coffins have yielded the broken tips of not only narrow bronze swords and socketed spearheads but also polished stone swords. It has been argued that the tips had broken off upon impact and were embedded in the flesh and bone of the deceased. Using modern forensic techniques to examine

A Chinese-style 5th-century single-edged straight iron sword with a ring-pommel hilt containing a phoenix-head. The ring-pommel and anchoring cylinder are of silver plate. From the 4th–5th-century Kaya chiefdom in Korea.

wounds in surviving bones, correlations have been made with the unique size and diamond-shaped cross-section of the sword. Similar sword points have been recovered from peninsular burials, and even more telling, both stone and bronze swords with reworked edges are numerous, suggesting that broken tips were common.

The peak of warfare in North Kyushu – calculated by the number of wounded or mutilated deceased – occurred in the middle of Middle Yayoi (2nd to 1st centuries BC) and was accompanied by the fortification of lowland villages by providing them with deep enclosing moats and perhaps palisades as seen at the Asahi site in Aichi prefecture, which was surrounded by three rows of hurdles and stakes on level ground, then a moat and rampart topped with a fence. The late 1st century BC through the 1st century AD also saw the construction of many upland sites in coastal regions as warfare apparently spread out from North Kyushu into the Seto region and beyond.

It has been postulated that stone arrowheads in the Inland Sea area underwent a radical change from hunting tools to weapons in Middle Yayoi. Arrowheads used by Jomon hunter-gatherers (10,000–500 BC) and early Yayoi agriculturalists were small and light, mostly less than 2 grams in weight. But suddenly, the average increased to 4 grams and the weight range grew to parallel those of functional bronze arrowheads. These larger arrowheads are interpreted as weapons to kill people wearing protective clothing or armour made of organic materials.

Warfare in Middle Yayoi is understood to have been carried out between communities, led by emergent chiefs, to protect and/or expand their agricultural lands and water supplies. Rice agriculture in both Korea and Japan was several centuries old by this time, so that circumscription of resources was beginning to be felt. However, another source of competition may have been efforts to obtain Chinese prestige goods being offered through the Han tributary network regulated through the Lelang commandery. We know from the Chinese court histories that one Yayoi chief was given a gold seal and ribbons by the emperor Gwangwu in AD 57. The seal is inscribed with Chinese characters that can be translated as the King of Na of Wa, affiliated with Han. The Chinese record that the western Japanese Islands at this time were divided into more than 100 communities, termed *guo* by the Chinese; this word can be interpreted as 'polity' or 'state' and indicates the existence of many, possibly competing, local chiefdoms in the western archipelago.

IRON WEAPONRY: IMPORTS, COPIES AND NEW CREATIONS

Iron weapons are known from Middle Yayoi but occur almost entirely in North Kyushu. The iron weapon repertoire was different from bronze: iron halberds and socketed spearheads copied bronze ones, but spearhead sockets were often wrap-around rather than completely enclosed. These two weapon types are found in North Kyushu but rarely further inland, mostly disappearing by the 3rd century. Iron double-edged swords may also be copies of bronze daggers, but they did not have the characteristic flanges. Two new types of iron weapons were single-edged slashing swords and tanged spearpoints, the latter not occurring on the peninsula.

Single-edged swords have a straight or slightly curved tanged blade and generally measure 60–80 cm (24–31 in) long; however, many end in a simple ring pommel and are much longer – up to 120 cm (47 in). Ring-pommelled swords, especially the oversized ones, are thought to be political gifts from China through the tributary system. A considerable number occur in North Kyushu, dating to Middle and Late Yayoi, while those from beyond Kyushu, dating from Late Yayoi to Early Kofun, are fewer. One interesting development effected by blacksmiths along the Japan Sea coast was the removal of the ring to form a tanged blade; and Shimane prefecture is still renowned for its Japanese sword production. The burial of an inscribed Chinese sword in a 4th-century Nara tomb (see box on p. 272) suggests the Kinai was developing its own contacts with the continent, perhaps through the Japan Sea communities in opposition to North Kyushu.

THE WA DISTURBANCES

The Chinese dynastic records speak of great turmoil in the western Japanese Islands between AD 147 and 189. These have come to be known as the Wa Disturbances. Nothing else is recorded about them in the documents, so only archaeology can illuminate what was happening in Late Yayoi. Unexpectedly, moated villages were abandoned by this time throughout the Seto region, while a second tranche of upland sites were built. In general, violent deaths similar to the earlier period of warfare in North Kyushu are not found, but new discoveries may change this situation: in July 2000, skeletal remains of 53 individuals, 10 wounded, were recovered from a 2nd-century ditch in Tottori prefecture facing the Japan Sea. Some archaeologists emphasize that the 'disturbances' recorded by the Chinese may not have been caused by warfare but represent the disruption of the settlement pattern and general population movement within the region. Others interpret the Wa Disturbances in terms of competition between Eastern and Western Seto for Chinese bronze mirrors and Korean iron, with Eastern Seto as winner.

The aftermath of these disturbances throughout the western archipelago saw the emergence of regional chiefs who were buried with their iron swords in large burial mounds. From Terminal Yayoi into the Early Kofun period, double-edged iron swords far outnumbered Chinese-style single-edged swords, but often one of each was interred with a chief. Ongoing competition among regional chieftains is suggested by the development of unique burial-mound shapes to distinguish their regional cultures from others. Square mounds with corner projections along the Japan Sea coast stand in contrast to keyhole-shaped mounds in the Nara Basin in the Kinai region.

Nara is thought to be the location of one of the *guo* polities mentioned in the Chinese chronicles, Yamatai, and is understood to have developed into Yamato, the first state in Japan. Yamatai was said by the Chinese to have been ruled by a Queen named Himiko, who was promoted as a hegemon after the Wa Disturbances. The chronicles record that her direst enemy was the polity called Kunu; war between Yamatai and Kunu is mentioned for the early 3rd century, but since the location of Kunu is not known (though suspected to have been in the area around modern Nagoya city), it is difficult to pin down archaeologically.

KAYA IRON ARMOUR

In the mid-3rd century, the area around Pusan that hosted the Kaya chiefdoms was noted by the Chinese as an industrial area producing iron to supply all the

Iron horse armour is found in small quantities in Kaya and the Japanese Islands. Similar face guards are depicted in Koguryo tomb paintings, and such armour was probably introduced with Koguryo lamellar armour at the beginning of the 5th century.

surrounding peoples. This remained a literary observation until the 1980s, when Korean archaeologists suddenly began discovering iron armour and weaponry in Kaya tombs. Helmets and cuirasses were the major armour types, both constructed of vertical slats rather than the small squarish lamellae of Chinese Han armour. Since slatted armour is known from Northern (Toba) Wei art in China and the helmets are Mongolian forms, a northern steppe influence is presumed. Kaya cuirasses are all constructed slightly differently from each other, often with unique decorative attachments which may have served to identify the wearer. Such stylistic individualism suggests each Kaya chief had his own blacksmiths who produced armour to order.

The question is, who were the Kaya protecting themselves against? There is evidence of communications with the Wa in Yamato, as 4th-century prestige goods have been recovered from Kaya tombs. Since all iron in Japan was imported from the continent as either ingots or finished goods, open supply lines from Kaya were a necessity, though the traditional interpretation by Japanese historians of Kaya territory as part of a Japanese commandery called Mimana is most certainly unfounded. Paekche also must have been one of the 'surrounding peoples' to obtain iron products from Kaya, and it is possible that Paekche and Yamato elites became known to each other through the iron trade. But they were not enemies: on the contrary, they fought together against Koguryo.

WAR WITH KOGURYO

As the northernmost state, Koguryo was well positioned to draw on the influence and resources of steppe cultures. During the Han dynasty, the Koguryo became well known as a mounted mountain peoples who often swept down to raid the commanderies on the plains. These raids led to reprisals by the Wei dynasty in 244–45, when the Koguryo capital was sacked and its tributary peoples conquered by the Chinese. By 313, Koguryo regained enough strength to devastate the nearly abandoned Lelang commandery area. After the death of the last Chinese governor of Lelang in 357, it pushed southwards towards Paekche in the Han River basin. The Paekche looked to their back and developed communications with Yamato in Japan, sealing a new alliance with the gift of an inscribed 7-branched sword in 369 (see box on p. 272). In 372, Paekche further allied itself with the Chinese Eastern Jin Court to its west. In the late 4th century, it is thought Yamato supplied troops to help Paekche ward off Koguryo aggression, but we know of the wars only from the Koguryo point of view.

In 414, the son of King Kwanggaet'o erected a 7-m (23-ft) high granite stela, referred to as the Kwanggaet'o or the Kotaio stela, containing a long inscription detailing the exploits of his father from 391 until his death. The meaning of the inscription is highly contested, but the gist of the message is that Koguryo interpreted Wa military assistance to Paekche in 391 as an 'invasion', to which Koguryo responded. In 400, Koguryo swept down the peninsula and laid waste to the southern coast, destroying the coastal Kaya chiefdoms. The stela recounts dated interactions among the major players at the time, with a long list of battles and trading of 'hostages'.

Koguryo possessed the most feared and successful military machinery around. As shown in 6th-century tomb paintings, they had perfected the 'Parthian shot' of shooting bow and arrow backwards over a horse's flanks – a manoeuvre used both in hunting and warfare. It is not clear whether such skill was cultivated by Koguryo's enemies once they, too, adopted horse-riding, but by the medieval period in Japan, archery from horseback had become a samurai art. Instead, the horse-trappings and armour known from 5th- and 6th-century Paekche and Yamato suggest that Koguryo inspired a ceremonial preoccupation with horses among the elite.

After the devastation of the southern peninsular coast, Kaya regrouped inland in the Nakdong River valley, and craftworkers began to produce gilt bronze, riveted horse trappings; Paekche craftspeople learned how to make leather saddles. All these specialities as well as horses themselves were transferred to Yamato. Horse

Opposite above The King Kwanggaet'o stela (known in Japanese as the Kotaio monument), erected in Koguryo in AD 414 and standing nearly 7 m (23 ft) in height, bears an inscription of almost 1,800 characters coarsely carved into the granite. Now located in Ji'an, Jilin province, China.

Opposite below A 6th-century Koguryo tomb painting displaying elite archery skills. The contents of Koguryo pyramidal tombs have mostly been looted over the centuries, leaving only the informative murals (which themselves occur in just 3 per cent of tombs) to shed light on Koguryo life.

Below A riveted iron cuirass and visored helmet from 5th-century Yamato. The cuirass consists of horizontal bands in a surrounding frame – a distinctively Japanese construction. The helmet, however, comprises vertical slats as found in the so-called 'Mongolian' helmet used in northeast Asia.

A Silla stoneware vessel of the 5th–6th century, shaped as horse and rider, with spigot from chest and jar neck on flanks. The aristocrat rider is highly decked out, suggesting a ceremonial rather than military use of the horse.

'brasses' (actually bronze or gilt-bronze objects), filigree metalwork attached to saddles, and plume holders are common grave good deposits in Yamato tombs from the late 5th century. Suits of Koguryo lamellar armour, flexibly designed for horse-riding, became coveted possessions, relegating the fixed cuirass to the foot soldier. This continental influx has inspired the interpretation, known as the 'Horserider Theory' of Japanese state formation, that Yamato was conquered by Paekche at this time. But close analysis of the historical events suggests that Paekche was far too weakened by fighting against Koguryo and counted very much on Yamato's support; a far more plausible cause of the influx is the intimate relations between Paekche and Yamato from the late 4th century.

Further support for Yamato independence is borne out by the iron armour industry. The 5th century witnessed mass production of iron cuirasses and helmets in centralized Kinai workshops. Constructed completely differently from Kaya slatted armour or Koguryo lamellar suits, the cuirasses consisted of an outer stabilizing frame into which smaller rectangular or triangular plates were riveted in horizontal bands, and keeled helmets were also constructed of horizontal bands. Riveting itself was adopted from Kaya horse-trapping manufacture, whereas in Kaya it had previously been adopted for slatted armour production. Thus, technology transfer is recognized but not the imposition of foreign styles of manufacture.

In 427 Koguryo moved its own capital from the upper Yalu River valley to the coastal plains of former Lelang. In its continued push southwards, it sacked the Paekche capital on the Han River in 475, forcing the Paekche

271

Inscribed Swords from Japan

Iron swords with inscriptions on the blade, inlaid in silver or gold, were used as political gifts to consolidate alliances in Han-dynasty China. One such sword, with an inscribed reign date of AD 184–89, is thought to have been transmitted to Japan in the late 2nd century and buried in the mid-4th-century Todaijiyama Tomb in Nara prefecture. It has an unusual separately cast bronze ring pommel, highly decorated with an inner trefoil design and outer florid projections. Another inscribed sword has been preserved nearby at the Isonokami Shrine: the 7-branched sword bearing an inscribed date equal to AD 369 and presumably presented by Paekche to Yamato in negotiating their alliance against Koguryo. In the late 5th to early 6th century, Yamato adopted this continental practice while consolidating its frontiers against Silla aggression. Inscribed swords are known in Kyushu, from the Eta-Funayama Tomb in Kumamoto prefecture, and Kanto, from the Sakitama Inariyama Tomb in Saitama prefecture. Both inscriptions include the name 'Waka Takeru Okimi', who is thought to be the late 5th-century sovereign, Yuryaku.

Below and right A horse motif inlaid in silver on a 5th–6th-century iron sword blade from the Eta-Funayama Tumulus, Kikusui-machi, Kumamoto prefecture. The sword is 91 cm (36 in) long.

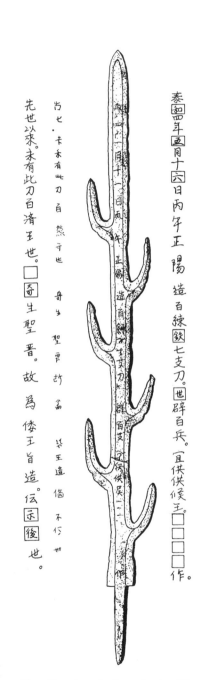

Above The 7-branched sword ostensibly gifted to Yamato from Paekche, inscribed with a cyclical date equalling AD 369. Preserved at Isonokami Shrine, Nara.

to remove themselves to the more southern Kum River basin. Yamato responded by petitioning the Chinese court five times during the 5th century for recognition as the suzerain of the entire Korean and Japanese region. During this intense 5th-century interaction between Koguryo, Paekche, Kaya and Yamato, the new state of Silla was undergoing consolidation in the southeast, eventually to become the dominant peninsular polity.

SILLA'S WARS OF UNIFICATION

Silla, formed from a coalition of six former chiefdoms, is known as the golden state: its major elite symbols – crowns, pendant belts, earrings and ear pendants – were all made of solid gold, and they have been preserved in mounded tombs which have a protective covering of cobbles and earth unlike any other in Korea. Thus, much is known of Silla material culture, but surprisingly little armour and weaponry have been recovered from these intact tombs, belying the strong military Silla developed in her quest for dominance.

References to warfare in the Silla chronicles of the medieval text, the *Samguk Sagi*, identify Silla's antagonists as Tang China, Paekche, Koguryo and Wa, as well as many smaller named polities (*guk*), such as Usan-guk, Somon-guk and Siljik-guk, and ethnic groups, such as the Malgal and Kitan. Interestingly, many of the incidents referred to were defensive operations by Silla. Offensive operations increased over time between the 4th and 7th centuries.

Historically, Silla began its predation by conquering and incorporating the Kaya chiefdoms first: coastal Kaya in 532, then inland Kaya in 562. Thereafter Silla turned its attention to Paekche, stimulating the construction of numerous stone fortresses along the border region. Most of these are stone walls that encircle mountain tops, being topographically defined in shape rather than geometrically laid out. Despite Paekche's desperate defensive operations, it succumbed in 660.

The most impressive Silla mountain-top fortress is Isong-sansong, positioned in former Paekche territory on the south side of the Han River, looking north into Koguryo. Koguryo was a formidable enemy, and to conquer it, Silla was inspired to complete a treaty with Tang China and mount a tweezer offensive simultaneously from the northwest and southeast. Isong-sansong, with its octagonal pagoda, also suggests that Buddhism was invoked to protect and promote Silla's interests. These strategies worked, as the Silla-Tang alliance defeated Koguryo in 668, whereupon Silla declared itself ruler of the united peninsula.

The loss of its peninsular allies in the wars of unification spurred Yamato in Japan first to consolidate its hinterlands in the 6th century, reconfirming alliances with peripheral chieftains through the time-honoured means of distributing inscribed swords (see box opposite). With Silla's victories in the 7th century and fears of attacks across the straits, many peninsular-style stone-walled fortresses were built in Japan on mountain tops overlooking sea passages in the western archipelago. Yamato's final defence against Silla was the adoption of Tang administration, perceived as the most advanced technology by which Yamato could rebuff continental incursions.

17 Mesoamerica from the Olmecs to the Aztecs

An elaborately garbed Maya warrior grasps a breechcloth-clad captive by the forelock in this detail from the wall-paintings at Bonampak. An eclectic assortment of arms is represented in these murals.

Armed conflicts in Mesoamerica are ancient, increasing with the rise of settled agrarian communities after 2500 BC, conflicts between adjacent settlements becoming widespread with urbanization. Chronicling each instance of warfare is neither useful nor feasible here, and we will concentrate instead on technological developments and warfare affecting societies beyond a polity's immediate locale. In short, the focus is not on the incessant conflicts between neighbours, but on the broad course of warfare influencing Mesoamerican culture and history from c. 2500 BC to AD 1520.

THE OLMECS

The earliest evidence of complex warfare emerged in Mesoamerica with the Olmecs (1150–400 BC) on the Mexican Gulf coast. They were the first to deal with a series of fundamental constraints that shaped warfare in Mesoamerica for 2500 years before the Spanish conquest. Primary among these was the monopolization of military force.

Like all complex societies, the Olmec polity organized, trained and concentrated force. Tools such as spears and atlatls (spearthrowers) and darts were superseded by specialized weapons of war. They developed maces, clubs and stone-tipped spears designed for slashing and thrusting, rather than throwing. Such shock weapons required soldiers to close with the enemy and were far more effective than projectiles in battles. The Olmec soldiers did not use armour or shields, but provide the earliest evidence of professionalism since the skills needed were not adapted from practical pursuits, but demanded specialized training, probably by military societies and likely only among the elite.

Olmec warriors are well represented in stone carvings and kings are depicted holding bound captives, evidence they had achieved the basic military capacity needed to create and sustain a kingdom. Moreover, they projected force well beyond their own frontiers into central and southern Mexico, later extending their presence as far as El Salvador.

Although their soldiers are depicted at many of these distant sites, Olmec centres each held only a few thousand people which could field only scores of elite soldiers, and the entire region perhaps 2,000 or less, and even fewer could be dispatched such long distances because of logistical constraints. The longer the distance travelled, the greater the logistical demands, and the smaller the party that could be sent, so a small army had less importance at this time. But cause or consequence, Olmec soldiers were associated with trade, not conquest, and their foreign influence changed over time.

From 1150 to 900 BC, the Olmecs traded with the more sophisticated cultures elsewhere in Mesoamerica: Oaxaca, highland and Pacific coastal Guatemala, and central Mexico. But from 900 to 400 BC, Olmec expansion bypassed more complex centres, notably Oaxaca and Kaminaljuyu in Guatemala, while creating a trade

A Teotihuacan figure holding rectangular fringed shields. The inside edges of the shields, around which the warrior would fight, are unencumbered – but no actual warrior would go into battle with both hands holding shields and no weapons.

THE EMPIRE OF TEOTIHUACAN

The first major empire, however, emerged at Teotihuacan in central Mexico. Driven by the twin need for far-flung resources upon which the increasingly complex economy depended, and a market for its output, which rapidly shifted from art to proto-industrial production, Teotihuacan began absorbing nearby towns as early as the 1st century BC, aided by significant military innovations.

Teotihuacan's material innovations were primarily defensive, but its most significant developments were organizational. Older weapons continued in use, notably thrusting spears, but Teotihuacan also began using the atlatl. Atlatls (spearthrowers) were ancient but heretofore unimportant in warfare, perhaps because of the logistical demands of a weapon that could quickly exhaust its ammunition. The requirement to use both hands made them difficult to use with shields, and they were less useful once an enemy closed. Among their virtues, however, was range, up to 70 m (230 ft), though they were most effective up to 45 m (148 ft), and had great penetrating power, their thrust being half again as great as hand-thrown spears. And it was these virtues that led the Teotihuacanos to adopt them in conjunction with their organizational and technological innovations.

The primary Teotihuacan technological innovation was armour, which developed gradually. Initially, they used protective helmets of quilted cotton, which allowed them to use smaller, more mobile shields. To these, they added hanging feather curtains on the left and bottoms to conceal their actual dimension and hide the tell-tale placement of their users' feet, while leaving the right side around which the soldiers fought unimpeded. Moreover, these smaller shields were used to parry blows, freeing the soldiers' arms for immediate counter-thrusts, and being lighter, they posed less of a logistical problem for long-range incursions. Held by a single top strap, these shields were probably tied to their belts until needed after the initial dart barrage. Spearmen, by contrast, used round shields carried on their left wrists, so they could be used in conjunction with thrusting spears.

But it was their organization that made Teotihuacan armies dominant. Their two types of soldiers were organized in complementary, cohesive formations, marking a major shift in Mesoamerican combat tactics. The role of projectiles was elevated, and massed atlatlists concentrated their fire to disrupt opposing forces. But being vulnerable to attack, atlatlists were functionally integrated with specialized spearmen when they closed with the enemy. Thus, Teotihuacan offers the first evidence in Mesoamerica of large armies and battle formations employing complementary weapons systems. But beyond their superior military organization, it was Teotihuacan's superior social-cum-military organization that was decisive.

Teotihuacan lacked the ethnic homogeneity of kingdoms; it was a multiethnic city with a social organization that incorporated outsiders by emphasizing residence over descent in citizenship. Kin links doubtless remained important, but the city's murals emphasize types and classes rather than individuals, suggesting some potential advancement by achievement which also characterized their army.

The extent of its incursions and depth of control demanded a larger army than could be fielded from the elites alone. Instead, it drew from all classes to create the large, well-trained army reflected in the uniform weaponry characteristic of state arsenals and central control. Complementary formations of spearmen and atlatlists also depend on drilled tactics that are difficult to achieve with fractious nobles, as they depend on a hierarchical command structure. In short, Teotihuacan fielded a true army, not just an aggregation of warriors.

By AD 100, at least 60,000 people lived at Teotihuacan, allowing it to muster a maximum army of about 13,000 men and it drew foodstuffs from co-opted areas within 200 km (124 miles) of the city. Farther afield, it expanded over much of Mexico and into Guatemala, targeting distant areas providing exotic goods, such as minerals, rare feathers and cacao.

Teotihuacan faced greater logistical constraints than the Olmecs, as its far larger armies moved more slowly and required more logistical support. But it minimized the latter by establishing relations with cities en route, or by creating its own centres to provide support, such as Matacapan on the southern Gulf coast. And in the Maya area, it colonized existing cities, notably Kaminaljuyu at modern-day Guatemala City. But travel remained costly and large-scale movements were probably limited to the post-harvest dry season from December through April.

Teotihuacan apparently relied as much on intimidation as force to rule, and the lack of direct control entailed a certain degree of political unreliability, limiting exploitation lest the provinces revolt. But its expansion within Mesoamerica was eased by basic cultural commonalities, in large part a legacy of the earlier Olmec expansion. Expansion into the north, beyond Mesoamerica, required the establishment of far costlier independent outposts that did not provide control over local peoples.

Within Mesoamerica, however, colonial occupation of distant centres was less expansive than control from the centre. Colonial enclaves facilitated the gradual

Uniformly attired warriors are depicted on this relief from the Maya city of Piedras Negras, suggesting arms and armour were furnished by the state like Teotihuacan, which contrasts with the more common Maya practice of each warrior arming himself.

build up of soldiers, merchants and political elites, and once in place, colonists exercised control over the surrounding area consistently and cheaply.

Some existing regional centres nevertheless persisted and new ones developed elsewhere. Monte Albán remained the capital of a small expansionist polity, employing the same weapons complex as previously, thrusting spears and clubs, with small shields worn on the forearm. But it never emulated Teotihuacan's military, as doing so would entail disrupting its existing social structure. It apparently continued with a nobles-only army, as there is no evidence of commoner soldiers, and little indication of military formations and an attendant command structure. This limited Monte Albán's expansion beyond its own ethnic group, and its boundaries were marked by a series of small fortifications. Yet Monte Albán's control over its region shrank as competing hilltop fortified sites arose in the first two centuries of the 1st millennium AD. And it regained its importance only after Teotihuacan entered the valley, and entered into a non-conquest relationship for the next 250 years.

Teotihuacan also encountered kingdoms in the ecologically homogeneous Maya lowlands, including the major centre of Tikal, where military victories were proclaimed on monuments, often showing nude, bound captives trodden underfoot. There is little evidence of centralized military structures, which suggests these clashes were not imperial, but aimed internally at legitimating and aggrandizing ruling lineages and externally at defining and clarifying tributary zones.

Most Maya cities lacked fortifications, and where they did exist, most were small, protecting only limited elite areas, and the more extensive examples, such as Tikal's earthwork walls, that were too extensive to be continuously manned and likely served as obstacles for withdrawing raiders. But Tikal differed from most lowland cities in having been unmistakably influenced by Teotihuacan at least as early as the 4th century AD, when it helped oust the ruling lineage and place an outsider on the throne.

Teotihuacan may have influenced Tikal to conquer and hold one or two smaller cities, but the limits of its forces and travel disruptions made year-round control from the centre difficult. Placing its nobles on foreign thrones was the more usual means of colonization, but did not guarantee stable imperial-like polities, as the descendants of grafted rulers typically broke away within a generation or two to became rulers of independent city-states. At best, the lowlands, or sections, were loosely linked by royal intermarriage.

Even though Teotihuacan's influence was felt in the Maya lowlands, sheer distance limited its influence as travel costs eroded its sustainable forces to the extent that larger cities achieved rough military parity. The friction of distance layered Teotihuacan's influence, from a tightly controlled inner hinterland to a reorganized and regionally controlled outer hinterland, to still more distant areas spotted with colonized sites whose peoples were more tenuously connected to the empire.

Teotihuacan's expansion slowed and stopped in the face of logistical limits and local competition. And with the growing sophistication of local groups, and the consequent rise in demand for the same goods Teotihuacan sought, the cost became unsustainable. Teotihuacan began withdrawing from its most distant outposts by AD 500, initiating a cascade effect of reduced markets for its manufacturers that had expanded to meet the demands of the earlier enormous market. Teotihuacan also began to take more from the remaining areas to compensate, and to increase repression of the inhabitants of its outlying regions, which further reduced the market for Teotihuacan wares.

Reflecting this growing resistance, or perhaps in response to the development of comparable armies elsewhere, militarism increased in Teotihuacan and the city made a major innovation by introducing the first heavy infantry in Mesoamerica. Teotihuacan invented, or adopted, quilted cotton armour up to 8 cm (3 in) thick in two basic types, suits that covered the body and limbs and tunics extended to the knees, and were effective against slingstones, most atlatl darts and spear thrusts. The cotton itself came from hotter, lowland regions, making the city dependent on the control of distant producing areas. Moreover, it was costly to import, spin, weave and fabricate the armoured garments, and while Teotihuacan held as many as 200,000 people in AD 500 and could thus field an enormous army, the cost of cotton armour caused a class-like division. Only a minority could be armoured, perhaps only front-line troops who bore the brunt of initial assaults. But at the same time, elite military orders emerged similar to the Aztecs' eagle and jaguar knights, though how they functioned in battle is uncertain.

These military innovations did not stem Teotihuacan's decline, however, and may well have accelerated its social fragmentation. After AD 500, the city's population declined until AD 650 when the ritual centre was burned in an apparent act of self-immolation, and Teotihuacan's day passed.

With the demise of the Teotihuacan empire, Mesoamerica again fragmented into semi-autonomous areas. No city adopted Teotihuacan's sophisticated military structure or armaments, which only broad-based armies required, and mobilizing that many people meant loosening class structures that could be fatal in kingdoms. Nor did costly armour persist. Thus, no empire filled the vacuum left by Teotihuacan's demise, only fragmentation and political disruption. A number of cities remained or became locally important, such as Chololland to the east and El Tajín on the Gulf coast, but others, including Monte Albán, declined into insignificance. And even distant Maya areas were affected.

MAYA WARFARE

Many Maya cities could have fielded sizeable armies had they mobilized their entire populations, and they likely did defensively, and perhaps even against adjacent cities where logistical constraints were minor. Though the period was one of proliferating conflicts and claims of victories, there is little evidence they projected force for any appreciable distance nor that they regulated arms in a manner indicative of large organized armies, which suggests the core of their armies remained elite and small. Arms used elsewhere, such as atlatls and slings, played no military role. Instead, the Maya used a wide and eclectic range of arms and armour typical of societies lacking military formations and attendant command structures. They did introduce flexible shields that could be rolled up in transit, and spears with inset blades extending down the sides, both elite arms.

Thus, most Maya warfare consisted of raids involving quick attacks and rapid withdrawals by relatively small groups of individually trained and eclectically equipped soldiers, rather than large-scale pitched battles between conventional

forces. These military limitations locked the Maya lowlands into a system of often mutually hostile city-states that fought wars with limited long-term effects.

Tikal was defeated in the late 6th century AD, and other centres became prominent, including Yaxchilan, Palenque, Calakmul and Caracol. The consequences of defeat do not appear to include occupation, but the stripping away of tributary areas unless and until a city regains the power to take them back can be seen by the lack of construction in Tikal after its defeat and the boom in other cities. Various cities became more or less important following battles, but stable regional powers failed to emerge.

Throughout Mesoamerica, the era was a period of political fragmentation dominated by regional powers largely employing earlier weapons and tactics. Among these in central Mexico was Cacaxtla.

Apparently built by a Maya group called the Olmeca-Xicalanca from the southern Gulf coast, Cacaxtla was a merchant entrepot for Maya seeking to reestablish trade ties with central Mexico. The same people also dominated Cholollan at this time. The Olmeca-Xicalanca focused on trade in such exotics as cacao, shells and feathers in exchange for Mexican goods, and their sites provided protection for their traders. But their military dominance was limited, and Cacaxtla owed its success to the lack of local competitors. Nevertheless, they brought new combinations of arms that influenced subsequent military practice.

Olmeca-Xicalanca soldiers merged Maya and Mexican arms, coupling atlatls and darts with fletched shafts for greater stability in flight, and barbed points that inflicted more damage and were difficult to extract. Thrusting spears with lanceolate points kept them from getting snagged in wounds, the Maya practice of insetting blades down the shaft was introduced, and unhafted stone knives became important for close-in work. These were accompanied by feather-fringed round shields carried by a strap on the forearm to free the left hand. But

Above In this rollout photo of the decoration on a vase, a procession of victorious, eclectically clad spear-carrying Maya warriors grasp two captives by their forelocks. The warriors hold no shields, and while they wear a type of shirt, they don't appear to be armoured.

Opposite A Maya warrior clad in Teotihuacan-style heavy armour of quilted cotton and carrying a feather-fringed shield. Heavy armour was very expensive, and was no longer used after the fall of Teotihuacan and a shift in emphasis towards more mobile combat.

body armour disappeared altogether, which reflects not only the cost, but likely the absence of serious enemies. Tactically, they emphasized individual combat rather than formations, with light, mobile forces well suited to quick strikes followed by withdrawals to fortified locations. And although the Olmeca-Xicalanca presence lasted almost 200 years, Cacaxtla was a minor military threat and prospered only in the period between empires.

Other regional centres built by Mexican groups that emerged in the chaos following Teotihuacan's demise, include Xochicalco and Teotenanco. These too were fortified hilltop cities and, like Cacaxtla, had extensive foreign trade ties.

Xochicalco, at least, became a regional power, as reflected in its many militaristic and sacrificial motifs. And here too, the army was composed of elites and dominated by military orders. Like Cacaxtla, Xochicalco's army was equipped with atlatls, secondarily with thrusting spears, and also knives, but retained the older Mexican rectangular shields which offered more protection in the absence of armour.

But unlike Cacaxtla, Xochicalco attempted to reestablish a tributary empire, which it controlled from its fortified hilltop location, through impressive displays of human sacrifice and the imposition of a new calendar.

Xochicalco established a new beginning date, a seemingly minor development that was key to synchronizing an empire, as it probably had been at earlier Teotihuacan and certainly was with the Aztecs. Disseminating a unified beginning date for the calendar enabled dependencies to function in unity with the centre for such purposes as the simultaneous payment of tribute. Xochicalco remained regionally dominant for two centuries.

Perhaps tied to the reemergence of strong city states, rising competition and the high cost of supplying a hilltop city, Xochicalco was overthrown and destroyed in the 10th century. The regionally important trader cities were likewise abandoned and another empire rose.

THE TOLTECS

The next major power emerged at the Toltec capital of Tollan (Tula), north of the Valley of Mexico. Immigrant Nahuatl- and Otomí-speaking groups from the north merged with local Mesoamerican groups to form Toltec society that the former soon dominated, along with much of central Mexico and beyond from approximately AD 950 to 1200.

The military again played a more obviously prominent role than in earlier groups, as reflected in Tollan's monuments. Part of their success was owed to the size of Toltec armies, which drew on virtually the entire populace, and was less a cultural innovation than a perpetuation of their past more egalitarian traditions. And part was owed to their innovations in arms and armour.

The Toltecs' ancestors brought their own weapons complex, which they merged with Mesoamerican arms, adopting some, replacing others and innovating in still others. They abandoned the thrusting spears that had dominated earlier Mesoamerican warfare, but adopted the Mesoamerican atlatl over their own, as North American varieties employed weights adapted to deer hunting that were both unnecessary and cumbersome in combat. Knives persisted but were now hafted onto wooden handles, providing the equivalent cutting surface with half the weight,

Toltec warriors at their capital of Tollan (more popularly known as Tula, the name of the present-day town), clad in headdresses, butterfly pectorals, v-shaped aprons, and carrying rabbit-fur-covered atlatls in their right hands. The left arms hold darts and short swords.

and which could be carried by tucking the handles into their armbands when not in use. But the most important innovation was the curved short sword as the primary shock weapon.

Perhaps adapted from curved wooden hunting clubs common in the north, the Toltecs used this as the platform into which they inserted obsidian blades as was already done with thrusting spears, to create a light, one-handed weapon with nearly half a meter of cutting surface. An excellent slasher, the short sword retained some of the impact benefits of clubs when used curved-end forward, as the Toltecs did.

The Toltecs adopted round shields carried on the forearm to free the hands, but re-introduced the use of armour, though a new type dominated. Full body armour was occasionally used, but the usual type armoured only the left arm which could then be used to parry even without a shield.

This complex allowed Toltec soldiers to merge atlatlist and swordsman into one combatant instead of requiring two separate forces. Toltec soldiers provided their own covering atlatl fire in battle, quickly consuming the four or five darts that were carried loose in their shield hands as they closed with the enemy, then shifted to short swords for hand to hand combat when they met. Combining arms in this manner doubled the effective size of Toltec armies, but demanded effective battlefield command and coordination, requiring drilling indicative of a large, highly organized and effective army. And while there were Toltec military orders, notably coyote and jaguar, the pictorial emphasis on classes of soldiers rather than individuals reinforced the broad-based egalitarian nature of the army. But even with a peak population of 60,000, which could be doubled by drawing on the dependent population in the city's immediate hinterland, Tollan could not field as large an army as Teotihuacan. By combining arms, however, it was probably as effective.

Whatever Tollan's role in the demise of the earlier fortified cities (and powers seldom tolerate fortified centres within their spheres of influence), the Toltecs seized control of the earlier trade network and significantly extended it, ultimately stretching as far south as Costa Rica and north into the desert, perhaps as far as the southwestern United States.

Like their predecessors, the Toltecs were less a military than a trading empire that operated through merchant enclaves and settlements instead of colonizing outlying areas. But military power protected their merchants, and dispatching large forces was eased by Mesoamerica's increased population and growing agricultural productivity.

Unlike Teotihuacan, there is no evidence that Tollan's mercantile empire contracted before it collapsed. Rather, it disintegrated from within as the capital was abandoned in AD 1179. The cause, in part, was the influx of barbarian groups (*Chichimecs*) who, though few, introduced long-range bows and arrows that frustrated conventional armies in raids and imperilled Tollan's trade links, raising the costs of maintaining its far-flung economic empire. But these incursions were only a symptom of a more widespread problem, the progressive desiccation of the north that had uprooted these people and sent them south. And as desertification reached Tollan, its agriculture became increasingly inadequate and the city was eventually abandoned, leaving Toltec enclaves scattered throughout Mesoamerica.

Yet during its florescence, Tollan also influenced political developments elsewhere in Mesoamerica. In Oaxaca, the 11th-century regional empire of Mixtec

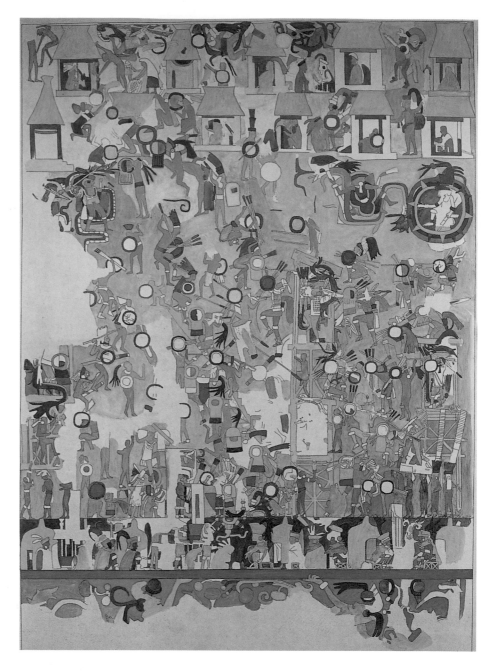

A watercolour of a mural showing an assault at Chichen Itzá (the original faded within days of being uncovered). The attackers employ a siege tower against a pyramid, improving covering fire for the attackers. When bows and arrows were introduced, their far greater ranges minimized the need for siege towers, and no later ones than this are known.

ruler, 8 Deer, had ties to Tollan and may have been inspired by it, though it was poorly institutionalized and failed to outlive its founder.

Yucatan too, felt a pronounced Toltec influence, though of a different type. After a 10th-century struggle in Tollan, the losing Toltec faction emigrated to Chichen Itzá on the Yucatan peninsula, where they are historically known as the Itzá. They conquered the local Putun rulers and established their own empire and introduced Mexican weapons and tactics to the lowland Maya. These included the standard Toltec armaments of atlatls, short swords, knives, shields and cotton arm armour, which made the Itzás superior to equal, or even larger, Maya forces in hand-to-hand combat. And since virtually all the Toltecs were soldiers, their per capita armies outnumbered those of far larger cities that drew only on elites.

This era also offers the first definitive evidence of naval warfare, siege devices and the use of fire as a weapon, though all probably had precursors earlier and elsewhere. Itzá canoes are shown in military contexts, and their atlatl attacks from sea-going rafts against Maya warriors are graphically depicted. Three- and four-storey-tall siege towers were used against pyramids, though not to storm it, as the pyramid's sloped construction meant the temple at the top is increasingly distant as the height of the vertical tower mounts. Rather, these elevated platforms allowed atlatlists to pour suppressing fire onto the temple's defenders while attackers scaled the sides. Fiery spears were also used against the roofs of thatched buildings, though this doubtless had long antecedents. But the use of fire in battle was not common, possibly because thatch is not easy to ignite without an accelerant, especially in rainy areas.

The Itzá empire was relatively small, occupying the northwestern Yucatan peninsula. This was the driest region in the Maya lowlands within which their armies could best march, aided by the logistical support of tortillas which the Itzá introduced. The extent of the Itzá domain is indicated by a series of small fortified sites.

In rainier regions beyond this area, and perhaps in reaction to the Itzá expansion, some greater Maya political integration was achieved, notably at Cobá in eastern Yucatan. As large as Chichen, inland Cobá controlled a series of settlements, including a satellite on the coast that allowed maritime trade without exposing the main city to surprise attack from raft- or canoe-borne troops. And they achieved this not through superior military organization, but by building roads. Though not extensive, Cobá created perhaps the most sophisticated road system in Mesoamerica, constructing at least 16 lime-plastered stone roads that ran in exceptionally straight lines, elevated above the undulating land to maintain a level surface and cambered to shed water. These roads permitted year-round travel, minimized the march time between centres, and sped Cobá's armies to its many dependencies, night or day, rain or shine. They also afforded Cobá unusual precision in timing and logistics, permitting far greater regional control than other polities in Mesoamerica. As a result, Cobá and its dependencies remained independent of Chichen Itzá for two centuries, collapsing only after the Itzá severed its trade routes.

Chichen Itzá itself was overthrown by a coup in the early 13th century. Aided by Mexicans who introduced the bow, the nearby centre of Mayapan engineered the coup but failed to sustain Chichen's regional political integration. By the 13th century, the partial political unity of Yucatan was gone, as was Tollan's in central Mexico.

Mesoamerica disintegrated into a plethora of kingdoms, city-states and minor multi-city polities, but no persistent empires. Another rough military parity existed, and while there were wars, either no city was strong enough to achieve long-lasting conquest and political integration, or none sought it. The next, and last, great empire that arose in Mesoamerica, was the Aztecs', and it did so in the midst of competing small empires and pretenders.

THE AZTECS

The Aztecs were the last immigrants from the north, settling in the Valley of Mexico in the 13th century where they established their capital in 1325. And in 1428, with allies, the Aztecs overthrew the dominant Tepanecs to begin their own empire. The motivation to expand came not from the people but the rulers; tributary lands provided

Above Life-size terracotta figure of an Aztec Eagle Warrior excavated at the Great Temple in Tenochtitlan, representing one of the two major knightly orders, whose meeting rooms were adjacent to the temple.

Opposite Goods given as tribute to Tenochtitlan from Cuauhnahuac (Cuernavaca) are shown in this page from the Codex Mendoza, including four types of Aztec warriors' uniforms and shields, all awarded for military exploits. Aztec arms, armour and raw materials for them were drawn from throughout Mesoamerica in both trade and tribute.

a new source of wealth that reduced the ruler's dependence on the bottom-up flow through which traditional neighbourhood (*calpolli*) leaders exercised power. And their military success was aided by martial innovations, both material and organizational.

The Aztecs merged bows and arrows with traditional Mesoamerican weapons such as atlatls, slings and perhaps short swords. They also replaced the thrusting spear's stone point with a long wooden ovoid head into which were set obsidian blades, producing a cutting surface on a third of its 2-m (6½-ft) length. But their primary invention or adoption was the broadsword. This wooden sword with inset obsidian blades along both sides was a logical extension of the earlier sword toward greater size that probably developed in the 15th century.

The Aztecs retained round shields but augmented it with a new type of armour. A jerkin-like tunic of quilted cotton covered the torso to or below the waist, leaving the limbs unencumbered in battle. The wearer remained vulnerable to slashing wounds, which were treatable by Aztec medicine, while protecting the body from deadlier puncture wounds. Cotton helmets were available, but could partially obscure vision and most soldiers fought without them.

Conventional battles typically began at dawn with the two sides confronting each other about 60 m (196 ft) apart. Drums or trumpets signalled the opening arrow and slingstone barrage under which the two sides closed. The military orders advanced first, followed by veteran soldiers leading organized units, and wearing tall battle standards to signal their movements despite the din of battle.

While the two sides closed, the soldiers cast darts to disrupt the opposing formation. But once they met, the barrage stopped and hand-to-hand battle began. Front-line fighters wielded broadswords and thrusting spears in an exhausting melee, and soldiers were rotated in and out of battle about every 15 minutes for rest and rearmament.

Each soldier's flanks and rear were protected by the formation's solid front. Accordingly, the goal was to disrupt the enemy's line, break the opposing front and pour through the gap to divide his forces. But since only the first few ranks could bring their weapons to bear, numerical superiority became important in wearing down opponents or by extending the front farther than the enemy could match, then turning their flanks and enveloping them.

But feints were also a significant part of Aztec military strategy. They would seemingly break and run in battle, drawing deceived opponents after them, past where other Aztec forces were hidden before turning and renewing their attack with assistance from behind.

Surrender was negotiable at any point, though the farther the war went, the greater the tribute demanded. Indeed, emissaries were often dispatched to a targeted city to ask for gifts before a war as a tacit acknowledgment of tributary status. If refused, the war was announced and troops were mustered, retrained and dispatched. But the defeat of the city's army usually meant its capitulation, which, if refused at this point, meant the city would be sacked and razed.

The wounded were tended after battle, and the dead were cremated, records being kept to notify and compensate their families. Captured soldiers were taken if the city capitulated after battle, but women and children were also taken in the sacking

Right King Nezahualcoyotl of Tetzcoco (who died in 1472) holding a feather-fringed shield, wielding a broadsword, and carrying a small drum on his back to signal the attack. His feather tunic probably covered an armoured one beneath. He also wears a cotton quilt more typical of the eastern side of the Valley of Mexico, and a helmet.

Below An ornate Aztec featherwork shield with a coyote figure and speech glyph, similar to the one held by Nezahualcoyotl. Typically, the ornate exteriors of shields were overlaid on cane and hide backings. Only a handful survive.

Right Indigenous drawing of the Great Temple in Tenochtitlan. The twin pyramid housed two temples, for Tlaloc (on the left) and the Aztec patron god Huitzilopochtli. The human sacrifices associated with war were carried out in the temple to Huitzilopochtli.

Below The Stone of Tizoc (Aztec king from 1481 to 1486) depicts a series of town conquests. The Aztec warriors (in Toltec attire) grasp the forelocks of captured (and armed) warriors, representing the towns indicated by their respective place glyphs.

if surrender was refused. These were bound and led back to Tenochtitlan for eventual sacrifice. While there were religious motives for human sacrifice, the political display of Aztec might was paramount. Most were sacrificed in a festival in April, which all the tributaries were required to attend.

Nobles had an incentive to fight in all Mesoamerican societies, but in Tenochtitlan, so too did the commoners. In addition to booty and tribute, a successful warrior could be elevated to noble status. And with a city population of 200,000 to draw on, and 1.2 to 2.65 million people living in the Valley of Mexico as a whole, the Aztecs could field far larger, and more motivated, armies than anyone else in Mesoamerica. Moreover, they not only drew on their entire male populace, the Aztecs established formal schools that produced soldiers of an elite calibre among all classes. But size and skill alone do not obviate the difficulties in projecting force at a distance.

The army was organized into 8,000-man units (*xiquipilli*), each of which was subdivided by towns or calpollis, these subunits varying with each mobilization according to how many men each contributed. Aztec armies began marching at dawn, limited to two columns by road width and march times, stretching out each xiquipilli at least 12 km (7.5 miles) on the march, so the last man would start three to four hours after the first. Thus, additional xiquipillis on the same route were sent on subsequent days. But the more days on the march, the greater the toll on their foodstuffs as they waited for everyone to assemble. So for large campaigns, the Aztecs sent multiple xiquipilli forces on separate routes to assemble at a prearranged site before the attack.

And to overcome the severe logistical constraints, the Aztecs harnessed their empire, requiring each tributary to cultivate foodstuffs for the army. It has been estimated that each 8,000 man unit consumed over 8 tons of maize per day. Two days before the army's departure, runners were sent to alert the towns along the

The Battle for Tenochtitlan

Though the Aztecs used traditional weapons and tactics, the battle of Tenochtitlan was largely fought not on their terms, but Spanish. The king who first welcomed Cortés to Tenochtitlan, Moteuczoma Xocoyotl (Montezuma), died in late June 1520 when the Spaniards were driven out. His brother and successor, Cuitlahua, died in early December of that year, almost a month before Cortés returned, so it was their young nephew, Cuauhtemoc, the Spaniards confronted during the battle for Tenochtitlan. Faced with considerable political turmoil, the Aztecs withdrew into Tenochtitlan, attacking the Spaniards and their allies by canoe assaults.

In the first four months, the Spaniards fought in and around the valley, cordoning Tenochtitlan off from its tributaries, then launched a combined naval/land assault. With 13 brigantines built in the valley, each manned by 25 soldiers and a falconet, the Spaniards and allies cut the city off from canoe supplies and destroyed its freshwater aqueduct. Then three armies attacked the main causeways connecting the island city to the lakeshore. Each army had about 200 Spaniards and an undercredited 25,000–30,000 Indian allies. With the brigantines fending off Aztec canoe assaults, the three armies battled for three months, pushing forward and being thrown back, across the causeways. Spanish projectiles disrupted enemy barricades and formations, allowing them to push forward, while Aztec counterattacks pushed their exposed forces back in a seesaw along the causeways that limited the numbers the Aztecs could bring to bear, but also hindered the mounted Spanish lancers. With each Spanish victory, Indian allies flocked to their standard, and left just as quickly with each Aztec triumph. But eventually, the defenders weakened, though they never gave up, until Spanish forces reached the city, razing it as they went, and the starving Aztecs submitted on 13 August 1521. The victory was a triumph of assertion over reality, as throughout the battle, Spaniards amounted to less than 1 per cent of the forces arrayed against the Aztecs.

A depiction by Diego Durán, a Dominican friar, of Cortés besieged in Tenochtitlan before the main events of the battle.

line of march to gather the supplies, and the army collected them en route, giving the Aztecs a far greater range than any other city in Mesoamerica.

Still, the costs of projecting force were daunting, and smaller forces were typically dispatched for lengthy campaigns, creating rough parities with large cities at great distances. And fortifications complicated this because sieges quickly consumed their food supplies and siege machines were no longer employed. But huddling behind fortifications was uncommon since if the walls were not breached or scaled, the surrounding fields and villages upon which the city depended lay open to destruction.

While battles against individual city-states were usually decisive, as they occurred near the city, and victory meant capture whereas defeat meant a later return, confederacies and empires were more difficult. Their armies could meet the Aztecs at their borders so defeat meant only the loss of that peripheral place. The enemy would withdraw into the interior where the Aztecs had no logistical support and could ill-afford to follow. So the conquest of multi-city polities was a slow, costly process of chipping away at the edges.

The prospect of prolonged wars with few immediate gains was, however, problematic for an empire where the loss of tribute threatened the king's rule. So rather than risk only slow victory, if not defeat, the Aztecs often engaged powerful opponents in flower wars (*xochiyaoyotl*). These seemingly ritual wars began as demonstrations of prowess between strictly limited equal forces. If the Aztecs successfully demonstrated their superiority, their opponents would capitulate and acknowledge subordination. But if they did not, the war gradually escalated into a larger, more vicious, conflict until it became a war of attrition. This system kept the enemy engaged without hindering their other conquests, and the Aztecs gradually conquered the surrounding cities, until the enemy was completely encircled, then chipping away, draining them of strength and allies, before crushing them outright.

Aztec expansion continued until the Spanish arrival, incorporating most of central Mexico, and reaching well into Guatemala with little sign of abatement. Only the encircled Tlaxcaltec confederacy to the east and the partially encircled Tarascan empire to the west posed significant obstacles.

The Spaniards, however, brought new military technologies that decisively altered the prevailing military balance. But the conquest of Mexico was far less theirs than their Indian allies'. Cortés claim of defeating the Aztecs, who controlled millions, with a few hundred Spaniards mirrors his claims to royal favour and reward, but does not truly reflect reality.

When Cortés marched inland and fought Tlaxcallan, his certain defeat was only days away when the Tlaxcaltecs decided to ally with him. Locked in a flower war with the Aztecs, and likely less than 15 years from final defeat, the Tlaxcaltecs recognized that by allying with the Spaniards, they could defeat their enemies (see box on the battle for Tenochtitlan, the Aztec capital, opposite). Though there were few Spaniards, the Tlaxcaltecs recognized that their weapons, notably crossbows, harquebuses, falconets and mounted lancers, could do the one thing their own forces could not, penetrate and disrupt the enemy front. The credit-claiming Spaniards never amounted to more than 1 per cent of the forces arrayed against the Aztecs, even when Spanish forces reached a thousand. It was the 100,000 Indians who exploited the Spanish wedge to defeat the Aztecs.

18 Ancient Warfare in the Andes

Scenes of combat and prisoner
capture adorn this Moche bowl. At the
top, a warrior leads a captive by a rope
around the neck, accompanied by blasts
on strombus-shell trumpets. The captive
has been stripped of his gear, which hangs
from his captor's mace. Unlike most
depictions, here Moche warriors fight
and defeat clearly non-Moche enemies.

A long sequence of civilizations arose in the Andes of western South America, and
with them a long history of wars, conquests and fortifications. In contrast to the
history of warfare in the Old World, this sequence was not primarily driven by
revolutions in military technology such as iron weapons or advances in siegecraft,
but by changes in social organization, as more populous and hierarchical societies
developed larger armies, better logistics and new ways to tax and govern conquered
subjects. Evolving in parallel was a deeply rooted system of beliefs about combat,
sacrifice and warlike supernatural beings. Andean elites extended their power
through both military victories and violent, post-victory displays that referenced
these beliefs. These developments eventually led to the remarkable military
achievements of the last of the Andean cultures, the Incas. Because our knowledge
of Inca warfare is so much more complete than for previous cultures, we devote the
majority of this essay to it.

THE ORIGINS OF ANDEAN WARFARE

The beginnings of warfare in the Andes can be glimpsed only dimly, but almost as
soon as sedentary, pre-agricultural peoples settled on the western coast of the
continent, supported by rich marine life, there is evidence of war. Lines of slingstone
piles defend the Ostra site, a small village and work camp on the north-central coast
of Peru, dated to at least 3000 BC. Far to the south, a large sample of human remains
from the Chinchorro culture, *c.* 2000 BC, reveal surprisingly high levels of cranial
fractures from impacts with stones – probably evidence of warfare, since males had
more injuries.

From about 2000 to 500 BC, a series of more complex societies arose first on
the coast and later in the highlands, anchored at monumental temple and court
complexes and participating in shared stylistic traditions. Although warfare was
not so intense or destructive that these centres were fortified, we can detect its
presence as well as its initial uses in ritual and iconography. Slings, lances and
spearthrowers were the weapons used, and rock art suggests that by this time,
the bow and arrow were employed in warfare as well as hunting. Disembodied
male heads and headless male bodies at the site of Asia on Peru's central coast
signal the beginning of a long Andean tradition: the taking and curating of heads
as trophies, most likely from slain enemies. Gruesomely detailed carvings of
dismembered limbs, severed heads and armed warriors cover the massive granite
slabs of Cerro Sechín's temple (*c.* 1500 BC), making a powerful statement of military
domination. Imagery of supernatural decapitators conceptually linked power to
sacrifice, setting the stage for elites to buttress their legitimacy with violent
displays and images.

From about 300 BC until *c.* AD 300, hilltop forts with massive walls became common in the northern coastal valleys, suggesting warfare on a larger scale and with more severe consequences. Maces – doughnut shaped stones set on a wooden haft – appeared, the first specialized weapon that was not also a hunting tool. Starting as defences for clusters of communities pitted against each other, forts eventually made up integrated systems of defence against incursions from other valleys or from the highlands, and defensive needs may have been one of the factors knitting together and sustaining larger, valley-wide polities. These fortified sites were rarely inhabited, serving instead for residents of lower-altitude settlements to take refuge in. In some cases, as in the Moche valley, they were also placed to block access to valuable irrigated lands, suggesting that warfare involved the destruction of crops or canal systems. But people and lands were not the only targets. At the centre of the famous fort of Chankillo, shielded by triple concentric walls, baffled gates and parapets, and warriors armed with slingstones and maces, was an important temple aligned for astronomical observations: a giveaway that sacred locales and structures were targeted in war. Despite its defences, this temple was sacked, probably by victorious invaders.

WAR AMONG THE MOCHE AND NASCA

The celebration of warfare in art reached its height with the Moche culture (*c.* AD 1–700) on Peru's northern coast. Emerging from a period of warfare and fortification, the Moche successfully repelled highland invaders, unified nearby coastal valleys and achieved a remarkable florescence. Famed for their exquisite ceramics and metalwork, Moche artisans repeatedly portrayed warriors, battles and the sacrifice of war captives, revealing the centrality of warrior ideology to the culture. In these detailed images, a typical warrior's kit includes a mace with a sharp point at the staff end; barbed spears and spearthrowers; a small round or square shield; a helmet; and adornments such as crests, backflaps and earspools. The standardization of these portrayals may indicate a specialized warrior class.

Once defeated, a captive was stripped of his regalia and led bound, naked and bleeding to his eventual fate: sacrifice by high-ranking priests or officials, his blood drunk from a cup. Archaeologists have found the victims of such sacrifices where they were killed atop the Huaca de la Luna, a magnificent adobe-brick temple; they have also found the fabulously rich tombs of the elites who presided at such rites, wearing the same regalia depicted on the pots. Archaeologists debate whether the battles which yielded captives for sacrifice were staged, ritualized combats between members of the Moche elite, or more destructive political wars against outsiders, in which captives were not the only outcome. In either case, the numerous images of combat and sacrifice, the monuments on which captives were sacrificed, and the richness of the elites who conducted and oversaw these sacrifices, show the intimate link between elite power and violence in Moche culture.

Like the Moche, the Nasca culture of southern coastal Peru combined militaristic iconography with material evidence for violence, in this case, trophy heads. Their frequent portrayal in art indicates their great symbolic importance. Trophy heads that have been recovered archaeologically were carefully prepared, displayed, curated and eventually cached or buried. Though most frequently taken from men, heads of women and children have also been found. Were these heads trophies from defeated foes, or revered ancestor relics? The case for war is strengthened by the fact that Nasca skeletal remains often have cranial fractures indicative of combat. If trophy heads were taken in war, the fact that women and children were also targeted suggests that they were taken not

Above This Moche vessel portrays the moment of victory as a warrior takes his opponent captive. Striking him with a mace, his other hand seizes his foe's hair, a Moche artistic convention for captive-taking.

Opposite above The fort of Chankillo in the Casma valley (320–200 BC). Here, a temple aligned with the December solstice was surrounded by three massive walls up to 8 m (25 ft) high and 6.5 m (20 ft) thick and augmented with parapets. Thousands of slingstones litter the slopes nearby, relics of Chankillo's final battle.

Opposite At the temple of Cerro Sechin in Peru's Casma valley, monolithic carved granite panels dating to *c.* 1500 BC depict warriors (bottom) and their dismembered victims (top). Sites in Casma at this time are not defensive or fortified. These images may have commemorated a rare, singularly important conflict, or even a mythic battle.

Left Two sacrifice victims among approximately 70 excavated at the Huaca de la Luna, an elaborately decorated temple at the Moche capital. The victims were probably captured warriors: young, strong men, many with healed fractures from previous battles, and some with fresh injuries from their recent defeat. They were killed with knife or club blows, partially dismembered, and left to decompose on the temple platform, perhaps to propitiate the gods.

Right Nasca trophy heads were elaborately prepared: the base of the skull was opened to remove the brain, a hole was drilled in the forehead to pass a carrying cord through, the eye sockets were sometimes stuffed with cotton, and the lips held together with cactus spines. It is estimated that some 5 per cent of Nasca people ended up as trophy heads.

Below Later Nasca pots such as this one often show elite men dressed in fine garments and carrying trophy heads – perhaps a visual shorthand for their power or military prowess.

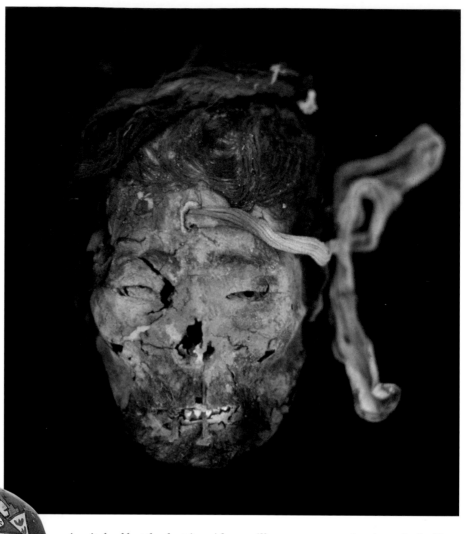

in pitched battles but in raids on villages, a pattern that is typical of less centralized societies. The Nasca now appear to have been organized as a series of local polities based at different drainages; they may have warred over the limited water and arable land of their region.

HIGHLAND WARFARE OF WARI AND TIWANAKU

The era of the Moche and Nasca waned around AD 600 with the rise of the highland states of Wari and Tiwanaku. Both were based at urban capitals replete with monumental architecture and art, and in this art and in remains from ceremonial spaces we can see the continuity of traditions of warrior valorization and violent displays. Warriors and armed deities are frequently depicted. Trophy heads are emphasized in the art of both societies; actual heads have been found in a temple at the Wari site of Conchopata. There is evidence of the public sacrifice and dismemberment of victims, possibly war captives, at Tiwanaku's monumental Akapana pyramid. But now we see a new type of warfare: the permanent conquest of subject peoples far from the centre. Wari, in particular, established administrative centres across a 1,300-km (800-mile) long expanse of the Andean highlands, resulting in an archipelago of controlled nodes rather than a territorially unified empire; Tiwanaku's similarly patchy realm was somewhat smaller, and may have been characterized by more Tiwanaku influence than outright control.

These feats were probably accomplished with much larger and more organized military forces than the Andes had seen previously. The warriors depicted on Wari ceramics brandish bows and arrows or axes, and bear variations of face paint, dress and shield motifs, perhaps suggesting several levels of military rank. Excellent logistical support would have been necessary for Wari long-distance campaigns and for the initial establishment of colonies, and it is likely that the use of storehouses for staple foods at provincial centres that would prove instrumental to Inca military success was pioneered by the Wari; blocks of repeated small rooms at highland Wari centres such as Jargampata and Azángaro are most convincingly interpreted as storage rooms. The initial conquests may have been bloody – human remains both from Wari's heartland at Conchopata and from a distant area that came under its sway show unusually high levels of cranial injury – but once established, control may have been largely uncontested, for most Wari and Tiwanaku provincial centres are not particularly defensible.

Both Wari and Tiwanaku collapsed around AD 1000, leaving in their wake a fragmented political landscape of small regional polities. The exception was the Chimu state on the north coast, which retained symbolic traditions surrounding militarism, and quickly expanded from its dense urban capital of Chan Chan in the Moche valley to conquer an empire spanning the northern coastal valleys. But outside the orbit of the Chimu, by AD 1200 or 1300 much of the Andean highlands and western upper valleys were engulfed in internecine warfare. Because the polities involved tended to be small, this warfare would have involved brief, fierce assaults aimed at raiding, harassment and extermination, rather than large, organized armies on campaigns of conquest, and it did not include prolonged sieges, judging by the lack of water sources at most highland forts. It was nonetheless the most pervasive and

A hilltop fort (c. 1400) north of Lake Titicaca. Three high walls protect a village of about 300 houses inside. Some two or three centuries after the collapse of Wari and Tiwanaku, many walled hilltop settlements like this one dotted the Andean highlands as warfare swept through the land with unparalleled ferocity.

destructive warfare of the Andean sequence, causing a dramatic settlement shift to ridges and hilltops, often defended by massive stone-built fortifications and slingstone caches. Scarce resources may have caused or exacerbated conflicts, since the period was one of reduced rainfall. These conflicts left their mark in the high rates of cranial fractures from slingshot wounds found at sites such as San Pedro de Atacama. Documents from the period of European contact refer to this time as a chaotic age in which communities led by petty warlords vied for control of lands, camelid flocks and crop stores. In these accounts, the power of local political leaders is closely tied to their military prowess. However, the warlike iconographic themes of preceding periods largely disappeared at this time; perhaps as war became a part of everyday life, it lost its romance. It was from this context of fragmentation and competition that the Incas emerged to conquer their empire.

THE RISE OF THE INCAS

At its height, on the eve of European contact, the Inca empire stretched some 4,000 km (2,500 miles) along western South America, incorporating a population of at least six million and much of modern-day Ecuador, Peru, Bolivia, northern Chile and northwest Argentina. The perimeter of this vast empire was defined by a series of outposts and fortifications. Within the empire, the Incas built a complex system of roads, storehouses and large administrative centres to serve the needs of the state. With these facilities and a well-developed system of labour-taxation, the ruling Inca could call forth armies at a moment's notice to fight invaders or quell rebellious ethnic groups.

The main sites mentioned in this chapter, with, inset, the Inca road system.

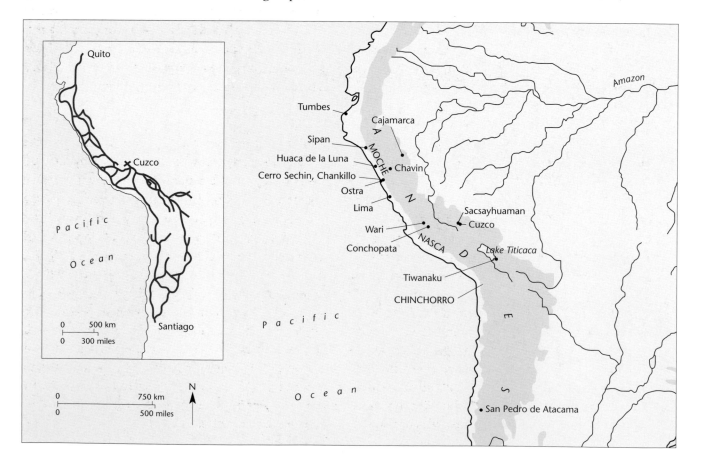

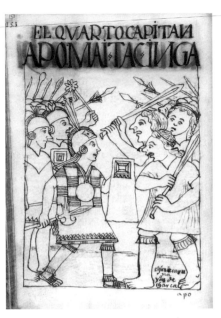

EL QVARTO CAPITAN
APOMAITAC̃INGA

The indigenous author Felipe Guaman Poma de Ayala wrote a long protest letter to the king of Spain in 1516 which included over a hundred drawings. Here he illustrates a battle between Inca troops (left) and those of another ethnic group (right). Both sides use a variety of weapons.

Historical sources and archaeological data suggest that the Inca incorporation and domination of the Andes began sometime in the late 14th or early 15th centuries. However, this rapid expansion did not develop in a vacuum, but has been traced to a series of important alliance-building policies which began several centuries earlier in the Cuzco region, the traditional highland heartland of the Inca ethnic group. Nevertheless, once expansion began, largely implemented through military force, this relatively small polity came to dominate hundreds of disparate ethnic groups within just a few generations.

The city of Cuzco was the political and religious centre of the Inca empire and the seat of the dynastic order that ruled the realm. Traditionally, the Incas are thought to have aggressively expanded the geographical limits of their state beyond the Cuzco region during the reign of Pachacuti Inca Yupanqui (1438–71). A warrior-king of legendary proportions, Pachacuti is frequently credited with reorganizing much of Cuzco as well as its social and political institutions. It is also said that Pachacuti made the first imperial conquests well outside the Cuzco region. These conquests continued for the next three generations of kings. At the time of Spanish contact, the empire was at its maximum extent, and Huayna Capac, the great-grandson of Pachacuti, was attempting to expand the area of Inca rule into northern Ecuador and southern Colombia. Huayna Capac's sudden death around 1528, the subsequent dynastic wars between his sons Atahualpa and Huascar for control of the empire, and the arrival of Francisco Pizarro's forces on the shores of the Inca empire marked the beginning of the end of indigenous rule in the Andes.

Our best descriptions of Inca warfare, ironically, come from those very forces that came to culturally transform them. The Spaniards described many features of Inca warfare in large part because they themselves had a long history of militarism in both the Old and New Worlds. Additional information is preserved in rare illustrations, especially those provided by Guaman Poma de Ayala, an indigenous writer who composed a 1,000-page letter to the king of Spain in 1615.

THE INCAS AT WAR

The bulk of the Inca armies were drawn from the general population. Military service in the empire was part of a much larger system of labour tax imposed by the state on their subjects. Each year, the numerous ethnic groups of the empire were required to send hundreds, and in some cases thousands, of individuals to work for the state in various positions including herders, coca farmers, craft specialists and of course soldiers. Under this system of labour tax, called *mita* (turn), the individuals served the state for a fixed period of time. After their service obligations had been fulfilled, they were replaced by others also sent by their own ethnic lords. However, at times of war, additional calls were sent out to local leaders and they were expected to provide additional men to serve in the army. If the conflict lasted for an extended period, the men might be replaced on a rotational basis. While away from their villages, it was expected that local leaders and the community would provide for the soldiers' families. Nevertheless, many conflicts appear to have been limited to the dry season (June–September), for as the rains approached in October, not only did moving armies across the landscape become more difficult, but the peasant ranks felt greater pressure to return to their fields.

By all accounts, the late prehistoric battles of the Andes were chaotic and bloody events which took the form of either great clashes across open terrain or frontal attacks upon hilltop fortifications. Before battle, the Incas offered sacrifices to local shrines, idols and oracles, asking for their advice. Spies were used to gather information on the upcoming battle. Commonly dressed as members of the opposing side, spies would infiltrate the enemy's encampments, providing estimates of troop strength and potential battle plans. Using this knowledge, the Incas often organized armies much larger than necessary. This strategy was meant to overwhelm their opponents through sheer numbers. At times, Inca military commanders merely concentrated their forces on an enemy's border, hoping that this display of military might would be sufficient to bring the opposite side to negotiations.

If negotiations or intimidation failed, the two sides approached each other. Soldiers on both sides taunted their opponents while their ethnic lords, clearly differentiated by coloured plumes and precious metal adornments, called to each other. These displays could last for hours and, if neither side backed down, the two sides would eventually be drawn into combat. The conquistador Pedro Cieza de León described such a scene in the civil war between Atahualpa and Huascar: 'They began to yell loudly and howl at each other... and they played many kettledrums and shell trumpets and other of their instruments. They insulted each other... those of Huascar asked [those of Atahualpa] why they were following a usurper, a son of a low woman; they responded to the tune that Atahualpa was the true king and Huascar not worthy to be one because he enjoyed such delights in Cuzco surrounded by women and concubines.'

Once armed conflict began, there was little control of strategic movement, with each army hoping to win through a combination of numerical strength and individual skills. Though some writers describe more organized attacks, and the use of reserve troops in late-flanking manoeuvres, most suggest that the squadrons quickly dissolved in the heat of battle, with troops fighting individually. This could dissolve the advantage in numbers that the Incas tended to have, and made Inca armies difficult to command.

Initial battle formation followed distinct ethnic lines. Trusted leaders of incorporated groups, who understood how to organize their people and more importantly who spoke the same language, led their own ethnic divisions into battle. Each group also specialized in their own type of weaponry. For example, the Incas preferred stone or bronze star maceheads mounted on wooden handles or double-edged palmwood clubs. Incorporation of Amazonian groups brought the bow and arrow to the battlefield. However, it appears that throughout the empire, clubs, spears and slings were the most common weaponry.

Although many battles took place on open plains, the Inca armies also made frontal assaults on fortifications. Perhaps the most famous assault was conducted by Huayna Capac during the Inca-Canari war in Ecuador. Several historical accounts suggest that the Canari retreated into a hilltop fort surrounded by a series of defensive walls. We are told that after several unsuccessful attempts at taking the fort, Huayna Capac hid many of his forces and feigned withdrawal as if routed. When the Canari came out to exploit their perceived advantage, the Incas cut them off and drove them into a nearby lake which was later renamed Yahuar cocha (Lake of Blood) due to the slaughter that ensued there.

Following a successful campaign the Inca armies would return to Cuzco. Various writers note that the leaders of opposing armies were killed and made into drums or stuffed and placed on display. The high-ranking leaders who were not killed in battle or immediately afterwards were paraded in the city and then executed. Several authors also describe how the spoils of war were placed at the feet of the ruling Inca so that he might walk over them and thus claim the victory as his own. A 16th-century Spanish explorer, Pedro Sarmiento, describes such an event: 'The warriors marched in order of their squadrons, dressed in their best regalia, with many dances and songs. And the imprisoned captives, their eyes on the ground, were dressed in long robes with many tassels. They paraded through the streets of the town, which

The fort of Sacsayhuaman stands high above the city of Cuzco. Its massive gateways, zigzagging walls, and enormous stones make this fort one of the greatest feats of construction in the ancient Americas. The Spanish and the Inca fought for control of the fort during the early years of the conquest.

were very well prepared for this. They went on, reenacting the victories and battles they had won. On arriving at the House of the Sun, they would cast the spoils and prisoners on the ground, and the Inca would walk on them, treading on them and saying: "I tread on my enemies."' After large celebrations, which are said to have lasted weeks, the army was disbanded and the soldiers were allowed to return to their villages, families and fields.

SUPPLYING AND SUSTAINING INCA ARMIES

Since logistics are key to the long-term success of any military campaign, especially when battles are fought far from the heartland, any discussion of Inca militarism inevitably revolves around their impressive ability to conduct and maintain war. Here we will examine two inter-related aspects of the empire's infrastructure – their road system and their regional storage facilities – both of which played critical roles in supporting their great armies.

Provisioning soldiers with food and supplies is one of the greatest concerns for expansionistic states. Enormous amounts of military gear, from sandals to shields, are consumed by troops. In addition, feeding large forces becomes increasingly difficult as extended campaigns take place further and further from the homeland. To meet these challenges, the Incas developed a storage system that spanned the length of their empire. Large amounts of agricultural surplus were produced each year for the state through the *mita* labour tax system. Being both heavy and bulky, this food was generally placed in storage units within the province where it had been grown. Thousands of storage houses were built on the hills surrounding the major Inca provincial centres to hold maize, quinoa and potatoes. Hundreds of other storage units were built around secondary and tertiary centres of Inca administration. These vast food resources could be called upon by the armies in times of need.

Large numbers of storehouses were built in areas surrounding major Inca administrative centres. This set is located above the Inca town of Ollantaytambo in the Inca heartland and most likely held agricultural surplus from the large terrace systems located in the nearby valleys.

Inca Roads and Bridges

The two largest Inca roads ran the length of the empire from Ecuador to Chile (see map on p. 300). One of these traversed the coastal desert while the other ran along the spine of the Andes. Various secondary roads ran between the coast and the highlands; others descended from the highlands into the upper reaches of the Amazon forests. Numerous way stations, or *tambos*, were constructed along the Inca roads. These way stations frequently included small clusters of buildings as well as storage houses, and provided lodgings for travellers. Runners, called *chaski*, traversed the roads to bring news from army commanders and regional administrators to the ruling Inca in Cuzco.

To cross the numerous rivers of the Andes, the Incas constructed bridges along their road system. Where the rivers were too large to be spanned by wooden beams, they built suspension bridges of grass and other fibres. These bridges, the largest suspension bridges of the pre-industrial age, represent one of the Incas' most impressive engineering achievements. The largest were built across narrow gorges in deeply incised river valleys.

Various early colonial writers tell us that the largest and most important bridges of the Inca empire had full-time overseers. In one of his many drawings, Guaman Poma de Ayala depicts such a guard in front of a suspension bridge. The guard's large earspools indicate that he is a man of considerable importance in the empire. Behind the guard, a traveller with a large load can be seen crossing the bridge. The bridge is made of woven materials and mounted on stone platforms.

The Inca guards for the bridges lived nearby and always kept weaving materials and ready-made cords to mend the bridge. They were especially important during periods of war when the bridges, critical control points in the countryside, were frequently attacked and burnt. One early colonial writer describes how an Inca overseer was able to rebuild a suspension bridge within days after it was destroyed by enemy forces, which allowed the Inca army to continue unabated.

Above and left The Pampas River Bridge is one of the best-documented bridges of the Inca road system. The American diplomat and explorer E. George Squier crossed the bridge in 1865 and took two photographs of it. One shows the thick matting that covered the bridge floor.

Below An Inca bridge from Felipe Guaman Poma de Ayala's protest letter.

Non-food items of use to the military were also stockpiled by the Incas. Francisco Xerez, a member of Francisco Pizarro's Spanish force that conquered the Incas, provides a first-hand account of Inca storehouses in the town of Cajamarca: 'In this town ... they found certain houses filled with clothes packed in bales that reached to the ceiling of the houses. They say that it was a deposit to supply the army. The Christians [i.e. Pizarro's men] took what they wanted, and still the houses remained so full that what was taken seemed not to be missed.'

To move their army and supplies across the rugged terrain of the Andes, the Incas built a vast network of roads and bridges (see box on p. 305). Spanish forces reserved their highest praise for these monumental constructions. Cieza de León, a young Spanish foot soldier, recorded his thoughts on these engineering achievements, writing: 'In the memory of people I doubt there is record of another highway comparable to this, running through deep valleys and over high mountains, through piles of snow, quagmires, living rock, along turbulent rivers; in some places it ran smooth and paved, carefully laid out; in others over mountains, cut through the snow; everywhere it was clean-swept and kept free of rubbish, with lodgings, storehouses, temples to the Sun.'

THE SPANISH CONQUEST OF THE INCAS

When Pizarro and his forces arrived on the shores of Peru in 1531, the Incas had forged the largest empire in the Americas. How then did this small band of soldiers defeat the Inca empire with its large army? Many researchers have stressed the advantages of European weapons and their horses, both of which did play important roles in winning numerous skirmishes. Yet the Spaniards could not have achieved such a stunning defeat without a series of other important factors which tipped the balance of war heavily in their favour. These included the introduction of European diseases before contact, Spain's prior experiences in the Americas, and Pizarro's skilful use of indigenous allies.

When Pizarro entered the Inca empire it was already reeling from a series of calamities. European presence on the American mainland, first established in 1510, had sent waves of deadly European diseases into the Andean region even before Spain had established direct contact with the Incas. In fact, the dynastic struggle between the two brothers Atahualpa and Huascar was sparked by the premature death of their father Huayna Capac in a smallpox epidemic around 1528. On Pizarro's arrival at the port of Tumbes, he saw the carnage of the civil war. The Inca empire was weakened by disease – millions had already died – and its leaders were distracted by internal strife. The timing for Spain could not have been more fortuitous.

The Spaniards soon left the coast and advanced towards the highland city of Cajamarca where Atahualpa, who would soon emerge victorious in the civil war, was camped. The Inca could have sent his army to engage the Europeans, but in the grander scheme of the civil war, this group of newcomers was seen as more of a nuisance than a threat. Atahualpa also knew that these same strangers had arrived on the coast approximately three years earlier and then departed, so he did not see the return of the Spaniards as a long-term threat to the empire. Furthermore, Atahualpa was curious to see these strangers for himself and assumed that he could effectively deal with them once they arrived near his army. In contrast, Pizarro was

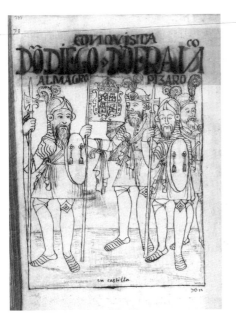

Francisco Pizarro arrived on the shores of Peru in 1531 and soon captured the ruling Inca Atahualpa in the Andean city of Cajamarca. The Spaniards had better weapons, but the fall of the Incas was accelerated by the introduction of European diseases, knowledge of Cortés's dealings with the Aztecs, and Pizarro's skilful use of indigenous allies.

a well-seasoned leader of expeditionary forces in the Americas and was aware of the successful tactics which Cortés had used during his conquest of the Aztecs in 1519 (see box on p. 292). Among Cortés's most important manoeuvres was the capture and prolonged ransoming of Moteuczoma which gained the conquistadors time to solidify their foothold in the empire. A similar situation would unfold in Cajamarca and Pizarro took full advantage of it.

The war between the Spaniards and the Incas began with a checkmate. Atahualpa, blind to the true intentions of the Spaniards, entered the plaza of Cajamarca poorly prepared. His royal guard and many of the most important officials of the empire who travelled with him were killed, and Atahualpa fell victim to Pizarro's boldness. With the Inca as his prisoner, Pizarro gained valuable time to sack the empire, wait for additional forces to arrive from the coast, and to establish contacts with rivals to the throne.

The ransom for the Inca, set at one room of gold and two of silver, took many months to raise. During this time, Pizarro sent expeditions to Cuzco and to Pachacamac, an oracle centre on the central coast, which gave the Spaniards a better understanding of the empire. The delay also gave time for the news of Atahualpa's capture to spread throughout the empire. When Pizarro resumed his march towards Cuzco, eight months later, not only had Atahualpa been executed but his greatest general Calcuchima had willingly entered imprisonment in order to speak with his lord.

Much of the Spaniard's advance towards Cuzco was unimpeded and while en route they used the vast storage systems created by the Incas to supply their own army. Atahualpa's death also provided numerous indigenous groups the opportunity to ally themselves with the Spaniards, so their forces grew larger as they moved across the countryside. The aid provided by the Canari and Chacapoya, both ethnic groups recently defeated by the Incas, was so important that the Spanish crown granted their descendants a tax-exempt status.

By the time the Spaniards entered Cuzco, they were seen as liberators of the city, which had been occupied by Atahualpa's forces. To solidify their position in the capital the Spaniards immediately selected Manco Inca, one of the few sons of Huayna Capac to survive the civil wars, to serve as ruler of the realm. Manco Inca's coronation not only raised the Spaniards higher in the eyes of the Cuzco elite but also ensured further allegiance with the remaining remnants of the empire.

The coalition between Manco Inca and Pizarro collapsed three years later, in 1536, but by then thousands of Spaniards had arrived in Peru and a new capital city (Lima) had been established on the coast. Although the descendants of Manco Inca continued armed resistance against the Spaniards until 1572, they were ultimately unsuccessful. Without direct access to the former imperial armies and the complex state infrastructure, and weakened by decades of depopulation and rival alliances with the Spaniards, forces loyal to the former rulers were unable to alter the tide of historic change.

Further Reading

INTRODUCTION AND GENERAL SOURCES

Bradford, A.S. *With Arrow, Sword and Spear: a history of warfare in the ancient world* (Westport, CT, 2001)

Carman, J. and A. Harding, *Ancient Warfare: Archaeological Perspectives* (Stroud, 1999)

Connolly, P. *Greece and Rome at War* (London, 1981)

Dawson, D. *The Origins of Western Warfare: militarism and morality in the ancient world* (Oxford, 1996)

Ferrill, A. *The Origins of War from the Stone Age to Alexander the Great* (London and New York, 1985)

Garlan, Y. *War in the Ancient World: a social history* (London, 1976)

Lloyd, A.B. (ed.). *Battle in Antiquity* (London, 1996)

Raaflaub, K. & N. Rosenstein (eds.). *War and Society in the Ancient and Medieval Worlds* (Cambridge, MA, 1999)

Sabin, P., H. van Wees and M. Whitby (eds.). *The Cambridge History of Greek and Roman Warfare* (2 vols, Cambridge, 2007)

Sidebottom, H. *Ancient Warfare: a very short introduction* (Oxford, 2004)

Yadin, Y., *The Art of Warfare in Biblical Lands*, (London, 1963)

WAR BEFORE HISTORY

Arkush, E.N. and M.W. Allen (eds.). *The Archaeology of Warfare: prehistories of raiding and conquest* (Gainesville, FL, 2006)

Guilaine, J. and J. Zammit. *Origins of War: Violence in Prehistory* (Oxford, 2005)

Keeley, L.H. *War Before Civilization* (Oxford, 1996)

Kelly, R. *Warless Societies and the Origins of War* (Ann Arbor, MI, 2000)

Kristian Kristiansen and Thomas B. Larrson, *The Rise of Bronze Age Society: travels, transmissions and transformations* (Cambridge, 2005)

LeBlanc, S.A. and K.E. Register. *Constant Battles: the myth of the peaceful, noble savage.* (New York, 2003)

Otterbein, K. *How War Began* (College Station, TX, 2004)

Martin, D.L. and D.W. Frayer (eds.). *Troubled Times: violence and warfare in the past* (Langhorne, PA, 1997)

Parker Pearson, M. and I.J.N. Thorpe (eds.). *Warfare, Violence and Slavery in Prehistory: proceedings of a Prehistoric Society conference at Sheffield University* (BAR International Series 1374, 2005)

Tacon, P. and C. Chippindale. "Australia's Ancient Warriors: changing depictions of fighting in the rock art of Arnhem Land, N.T.," *Cambridge Archaeological Journal* 4:2 (1994), 211–248

Wendorf, F. "Site 117: a Nubian Final Paleolithic graveyard near Jebel Sahaba, Sudan," in *The Prehistory of Nubia*, vol. II, 954–995 (Dallas, 1968)

ANCIENT EGYPTIAN WARFARE

Davies, W. V. *Catalogue of Egyptian Antiquities in the British Museum, VII: tools and weapons, 1. axes* (London, 1987)

Emery, W.B., H.S. Smith and A. Millard. *The Fortress of Buhen: the archaeological report* (London, 1979)

Goedicke, H. (ed.). *Perspectives on the Battle of Kadesh* (Baltimore, MA, 1985)

Landström, B. *Ships of the Pharaohs* (London, 1970)

Littauer, M.A. and J.H. Crouwel. *Chariots and Related Equipment from the Tomb of Tut`ankhamun* (Oxford, 1985)

McLeod, W.E. *Composite Bows from the Tomb of Tut`ankhamun* (Oxford, 1970)

Morris, E. *The Architecture of Imperialism: military bases and the evolution of foreign policy in Egypt's New Kingdom* (Leiden, 2005)

Murnane, W.J. *The Road to Kadesh: a historical interpretation of the battle reliefs of King Sety I at Karnak* (Chicago, 1985)

Schulman, A.R. *Military Rank, Title and Organization in the Egyptian New Kingdom* (Berlin, 1964)

Shaw, I. *Egyptian Warfare and Weapons* (Princes Risborough, 1991)

Spalinger, A.J. *Aspects of the Military Documents of the Ancient Egyptians* (Yale, 1982)

Spalinger, A.J. *War in Ancient Egypt* (Oxford, 2004)

ANCIENT NEAR EASTERN WARFARE

Beal, R.H. *The Organisation of the Hittite Military.* (Heidelberg, 1992)

Dalley, S.M. *Mari and Karana: two Old Babylonian cities* (London, 1984)

———"Foreign Chariotry and Cavalry in the Armies of Tiglath-Pileser III and Sargon II," in *Iraq* 47 (1985), 31–48

Heimpel, W. *Letters to the King of Mari: a new translation, with historical introduction, notes, and commentary* (Winona Lake, IN, 2003)

Littauer, M.A., & J.H. Crouwel. *Wheeled Vehicles and Ridden Animals in the Ancient Near East.* (Leiden, 1979)

Malbran-Labat, F. *L'armée et l'organisation militaire de l'Assyrie: d'après les lettres des Sargonides trouvées à Ninive* (Genève, 1982)

Nissen, H.J. *The Early History of the Ancient Near East 9000–2000 BC* (London, 1988)

Postgate, J.N. *Early Mesopotamia: society and economy at the dawn of history* (London, 1992)

———"The Assyrian army at Zamua", in *Iraq* 62 (2000), 89–108

Roux, G. *Ancient Iraq* (3rd ed, Harmondsworth, 1992)

Stillman, N.R. and N. Tallis. *Armies of the Ancient Near East 3000 BC – 539 BC* (Devizes, 1984)

Ussishkin, D. *The Conquest of Lachish by Sennacherib* (Tel Aviv, 1983)

Van de Mieroop, M. *A History of the Ancient Near East, c. 3000–323 BC* (Malden, 2003)

THE MIGHT OF THE PERSIAN EMPIRE

Bittner, S. *Tracht und Bewaffnung des persischen Heeres zur Zeit der Achaimeniden* (München, 1985)

Briant, P. *From Cyrus to Alexander: A History of the Persian Empire* (translated by P.T. Daniels, Winona Lake, IA, 2002)

Cook, J.M. *The Persian Empire* (London, 1983)

Curtis, V. Sarkhosh and S. Stewart (eds.). *Birth of the Persian Empire, vol. 1* (London & New York, 2005)

Head, D. *The Achaemenid Persian Army* (Stockport 1992)

Olmstead, A.T. *A History of the Persian Empire* (Chicago, 1948)

Rahe, P. "The Military Situation in Western Asia on the eve of Cunaxa," *American Journal of Philology* 101 (1980), 79–96

Sekunda, N.V. "Achaemenid Military terminology," *Archäologisches Mitteilungen aus Iran* 21 (1988), 69–77

———"The Persians" in General Sir J. Hackett (ed.) *Warfare in the Ancient World* (London, 1989), 82–103

———and S. Chew. *The Persian Army 560–330 BC* (London, 1992)

Tuplin, C. "Xenophon and the Garrisons of the Achaemenid Empire," *Archäologisches Mitteilungen aus Iran* 20 (1987), 167–245

MINOAN AND MYCENAEAN WARFARE

Crouwel, J. "Fighting on Land and Sea in Late Mycenaean times," in Laffineur R. and J. Driessen (1999), 455–464

Dickinson, O. *The Aegean Bronze Age* (Cambridge, 1994)

Driessen, J. "The Archaeology of Aegean Warfare," in Laffineur R. and J. Driessen (1999), 11–20

Fitton, J.L. *Minoans* (London, 2002)

Laffineur R. and J. Driessen (eds.). *POLEMOS, Le contexte guerrier en égée à l'âge du bronze, Aegaeum 19* (Liège, 1999)

Molloy, B. (ed.). *The Cutting Edge: archaeological studies in combat and weaponry* (Stroud, 2007)

Niemeier W-D. "Mycenaeans and Hittites in War in Western Asia Minor," in Laffineur R. and J. Driessen (1999), 141–156

Peatfield, A. "The Paradox of Violence: weaponry and martial art in Minoan Crete," in R. Laffineur & J. Driessen (1999), 67–74

WAR IN ARCHAIC AND CLASSICAL GREECE

Anderson, J.K. *Military Theory and Practice in the Age of Xenophon* (Berkeley, 1970)

Gabrielsen, V. *Financing the Athenian Fleet* (Baltimore, 1994)

Garlan, Y. *War in the Ancient World: a social history* (London, 1975)

Greenhalgh, P. *Early Greek Warfare* (Cambridge, 1973)

Hanson, V.D. *The Western Way of War* (London, 1989)

———(ed.). *Hoplites: the classical Greek battle experience* (London, 1991)

———*Warfare and Agriculture* (2nd edition, Berkeley, 1998)

Hunt, P. *Slavery, Warfare and Ideology in the Greek Historians* (Cambridge, 1998)

Lendon, J.E. *Soldiers and Ghosts: a history of battle in classical antiquity* (New Haven and London, 2005)

Morrison, J., J. Coates and B. Rankov. *The Athenian Trireme* (2nd edition, Cambridge, 2000)

Rawlings, L. *The Ancient Greeks at War* (Manchester, 2007)

Rich, J. and G. Shipley (eds.). *War and Society in the Greek World* (London, 1993)

Sabin, P., H. van Wees and M. Whitby (eds.). *The Cambridge History of Greek and Roman Warfare* (Cambridge, 2007)

Snodgrass, A.M. *Arms and Armour of the Greeks* (2nd edition, Baltimore, 1999)

Spence, I. *The Cavalry of Classical Greece: a social and military history* (Oxford, 1991)

Trundle, M. *Greek Mercenaries: from the late archaic period to Alexander* (London, 2004)

van Wees, H., *Greek Warfare: myths and realities* (London, 2004)

———(ed.). *War and Violence in Ancient Greece* (London and Swansea, 2000)

ALEXANDER THE GREAT AND HELLENISTIC WARFARE

Bar Kochva, B. *The Seleucid army* (Cambridge, 1976)

———*Judas Maccabaeus: the Jewish struggle against the Seleucids* (Cambridge, 1989)

Bosworth, A.B. *Conquest and Empire: the reign of Alexander the Great* (Cambridge, 1988)

Cartledge, P. *Alexander the Great: the hunt for a new past* (London, 2004)

Chaniotis, A. *War in the Hellenistic World* (Oxford, 2005)

Hammond, N.G.L. and G.T. Griffith. *A History of Macedonia 2* (Oxford, 1979)

Holt, F. *Into the Land of Bones: Alexander the Great in Afghanistan* (Berkeley, 2005)

Lane Fox, R.J. *Alexander the Great* (London, 1977)

Marsden, E.W. *Greek and Roman Artillery: historical development* (Oxford, 1969)

McNicoll, A.W. *Hellenistic Fortifications from the Aegean to the Euphrates* (Oxford, 1997)

Morrison, J.S. *Greek and Roman Oared Warships 399–30 BC* (Oxford, 1996)

Walbank, F.W. *A Historical Commentary on Polybius* 3 vols (Oxford, 1957–79)

———, A.E. Astin, M.W. Frederiksen and R.M. Ogilvie (eds.). *The Cambridge Ancient History vol. 7.1* (Cambridge, 1984)

ARMIES OF THE ROMAN REPUBLIC

Cornell, T. *The Beginnings Of Rome: Italy and Rome From the Bronze Age to the Punic Wars*, c. 1000–263 BC (London, 1995)

Eckstein, A.M. *Senate and General: individual decision making and Roman foreign relations, 264–194 BC* (Berkeley and Los Angeles, 1987)

——— "Conceptualizing Roman Imperial Expansion under the Republic: An Introduction," in N. Rosenstein and R. Morstein-Marx, (eds.) *A Companion to the Roman Republic*, 567–89 (Malden, MA, 2006)

Erdkamp, P. *Hunger and the Sword: warfare and food supply in Roman Republican warfare (264–30 BC)* (Amsterdam, 1998)

Goldsworthy, A. *The Roman Army at War, 100 BC – AD 200* (Oxford and New York, 1996)

Harris, W.V. *War and Imperialism in Republican Rome, 327–70 BC* (Oxford and New York, 1979)

Holmes, T. Rice. *The Roman Republic and the Founder of the Empire* (Oxford, 1923)

Keppie, L. *The Making of the Roman Army: from Republic To Empire* (London, 1984)

Lazenby, J.F. *Hannibal's War: a military history of the Second Punic War* (Warminster, 1978)

——— *The First Punic War: a military history* (Stanford, 1996)

McCall, J. *Cavalry of the Roman Republic: cavalry combat and elite reputations in the Middle and Late Republic* (London and New York, 2002)

Rosenstein, N. *Rome at War: farms, families, and death in the Middle Republic* (Chapel Hill, 2004)

CELTIC AND IBERIAN WARRIOR CULTURES

Arnold, B. "Power Drinking in Iron Age Europe," *British Archaeology* 57 (2001), 12–19

Berresford Ellis, P. *Celt and Greek* (London, 1997)

Chadwick, N. *The Celts* (Harmonsworth, 1991)

Champion, T.C. and J.V.S. Megaw (eds.). *Settlement and Society: aspects of west European prehistory in the first millennium BC* (Leicester, 1985)

Collis, J. *Oppida: earliest towns north of the Alps* (Sheffield, 1984)

Cunliffe, B. *The Ancient Celts* (Oxford, 1997)

Green, M. (ed.) *The Celtic World* (London, 1996)

James, S. *Exploring the World of the Celts* (London and New York, 1993)

Moret, P. & F. Quesada Sanz (eds.). *La guerra en el mundo ibérico y celtibérico (ss. VI-II a. de C.)* (Madrid, 2002)

Rankin, H.D. *Celts in the Classical World* (London, 1987)

Rawlings, L. "Celts, Spaniards and Samnites: Warriors in a Soldier's War," in Cornell, T., B. Rankov and P. Sabin (eds.) *The Second Punic War – A Reappraisal* (London, 1996), 81–117

——— "Caesar's portrayal of Gauls as Warriors," in Welch, K. and A. Powell (eds.) *Julius Caesar as Artful Reporter: the war commentaries as political instruments*, (London and Swansea, 1998), 171–192

Ritchie, W.F. and J.N.G. Ritchie. *Celtic warriors* (Princes Risborough, 1985)

Roymans, N. *Tribal Societies in Northern Gaul: an anthropological perspective* (Cingula 12, 1990)

The Celts, Catalogue of the Exhibition in Palazzo Grassi, Venice (Milan, 1991)

PARTHIAN AND SASANIAN WARFARE

Brosius, M. *The Persians: an introduction* (London, 2006)

Curtis, J. *Ancient Persia* (London, 1989)

Curtis, V. Sarkhosh and S. Stewart (eds.). *The Age of the Parthians. The Idea of Iran, vol. 2* (London, 2007)

Dodgeon, M.H. and S.N.C. Lieu. *The Roman Eastern Frontier and the Persian Wars (AD 226–363): a documentary history* (London, 1991)

Greatrex, G., and S.N.C. Lieu. *The Roman Eastern Frontier and the Persian Wars: Part II, AD 363–628* (London, 2002)

James, S. *Excavations at Dura Europos 1928–1937: final report VII, the arms and armour and other military equipment* (London, 2003)

Wiesehöfer, J. *Ancient Persia: from 550 BC to AD 650* (London, 1996)

Wheeler, E.L. "Why the Romans can't defeat the Parthians: Julius Africanus and the strategy of magic," in Greonmann van Waateringe, W., B.L. van Beek, W.J.H. Willems and S.L. Synia (eds.) *Roman Frontier Studies 1995. Proceedings of the XVIth Congress of Roman Frontier Studies* (Oxford, 1997), 575–9

IMPERIAL ROMAN WARFARE

Bishop, M.C. and J.C.N. Coulston. *Roman Military Equipment from the Punic Wars to the Fall of Rome* (Oxford, 2006)

Brewer, R.J. (ed.). *Roman Fortresses and their Legions* (London, 2000)

Campbell, B. *The Emperor and the Roman Army, 31 BC–AD 235* (Oxford, 1984)

——— *The Roman Army 31 BC–AD 337: a sourcebook* (London, 1994)

——— *Warfare and Society in Imperial Rome, c. 31 BC–AD 230* (London, 2002)

Coulston, J.C.N. "The archaeology of Roman conflict," in Freeman, P.W.M. and A. Pollard (eds.) *Fields of Conflict: progress and prospect in battlefield archaeology* (Oxford, 2001), 23–49

Farnum, J.H. *The Positioning of the Roman Imperial Legions* (Oxford, 2005)

Gilliver, C.M. *The Roman Art of War* (London, 1999)

Goldsworthy, A.K. *The Roman Army at War, 100 BC–AD 200* (Oxford, 1996)

——— *The Complete Roman Army* (London and New York, 2003)

Keppie, L. *The Making of the Roman Army from Republic to Empire* (London, 1998)

Maxfield, V. *The Military Decorations of the Roman Army* (London, 1981)

Saddington, D. *The Development of the Roman Auxiliary Forces from Caesar to Vespasian (49 BC–AD 79)* (Harare, 1982)

Spaul, J. *Ala 2: the auxiliary cavalry units of the Pre-Diocletianic Imperial Roman Army* (Andover, 1994)

——— *Cohors 2: the evidence for and a short history of the auxiliary infantry units of the Imperial Roman Army* (Oxford, 2000)

Watson, G.R. *The Roman Soldier* (London, 1969)

Webster, G. *The Roman Imperial Army of the First and Second Centuries AD* (London, 1986)

ROME AND THE BARBARIANS

Blockley, R.C. "Warfare and Diplomacy," in *The Cambridge Ancient History vol. 13* (Cambridge, 1998), 411–436

Elton, H. *Warfare in Roman Europe: AD 350–425* (Oxford, 1996)

Hoffmann, D. *Das spätrömische Bewegungsheer und die Notitia Dignitatum* (Düsseldorf, 1969)

Jones, A.H.M. *The Later Roman Empire* (Oxford, 1964)

Lee, A.D. "The Army," in *The Cambridge Ancient History vol. 13* (Cambridge, 1998), 211–237

Nicasie, M. *Twilight of Empire* (Amsterdam, 1998)

Shaw, B.D. "War and Violence," in Bowersock, G. et al., *Interpreting Late Antiquity* (Cambridge, MA, 2001), 130–169

Whitby, M. "The Army c. 420–602," *The Cambridge Ancient History vol. 14* (Cambridge, 2000), 286–314

CENTRAL ASIA FROM THE SCYTHIANS TO THE HUNS

Barfield, T.J. *The Perilous Frontier: nomadic empires and China, 221 BC to AD 1757* (Oxford, 1989)

Braund, D. (ed.). *Scythians and Greeks: cultural interactions in Scythia, Athens and the early Roman Empire (sixth century BC – first century AD)* (Exeter, 2005)

Coulston, J.C.N. "Tacitus, *Historiae* I.79 and the impact of Sarmatian warfare on the Roman empire," in von Carnap-Bornheim, C. (ed.) *Kontakt – Kooperation – Konflikt: Germanen und Sarmaten zwischen dem 1. und dem 4. Jahrhundert nach Christus* (Neumünster, 2003) 415–33

Grousset, R. *The Empire of the Steppes: a history of Central Asia* (New Brunswick and London, 2000)

Hartog, F. *The Mirror of Herodotus: the representation of the other in the writing of history* (Berkeley, 1998)

Hildinger, E. *Warriors of the Steppe: a military history of Central Asia, 500 BC to AD 1700* (Staplehurst, 1997)

Khazanov, A.M. *Nomads and the Outside World* (Madison, 1994)

Maenchen-Helfen, O.J. *The World of the Huns: studies in their history and culture* (Berkeley, 1973)

Phillips, E.D. *The Royal Hordes: nomad peoples of the Steppes* (London, 1965)

Rolle, R. *The World of the Scythians* (London, 1980)

———, M. Muller-Wille and K. Schietzel. *Gold der Steppe: archäologie der Ukraine* (Schleswig, 1991)

Sinor, D. (ed.). *The Cambridge History of Early Inner Asia* (Cambridge, 1990)

Sulimirski, T. *The Sarmatians* (London, 1970)

Thompson, E.A. *The Huns* (Oxford, 1996)

Torday, L. *Mounted Archers: the beginnings of Central Asian history* (Durham, 1997)

Trippett, F. *The First Horsemen* (Amsterdam, 1974)

Wright, D.C. *Peoples of the Steppe: historical sources on the pastoral nomads of Eurasia* (Needham Heights, 1998)

WARFARE IN ANCIENT SOUTH ASIA

Allchin, F.R. (ed.). *The Archaeology of Early Historic South Asia* (Cambridge, 1995)

Coningham, R.A.E. *Anuradhapura, Volume 1: The Site*. Society for South Asian Studies (British Academy) Monograph no. 3. (Oxford, 1999)

——"Contestatory urban texts or were cities in South Asia built as images," *Cambridge Archaeological Journal* 10 (2000), 348–357

——"South Asia: from early villages to Buddhism," in Scarre, C.J. (ed.) *The Human Past* (London and New York, 2005), 518–558

——*Anuradhapura, Volume 2: The Artefacts*. Society for South Asian Studies (British Academy) Monograph no. 4. (Oxford, 2006)

——"The antiquity of caste and the timeless nature of south Asia's subordination," in Reid, A. and P. Lane (eds.) *Studies in Subordinate Archaeologies* (Leicester, 2006), 50–74

Dani, A.H. & V.M. Masson (eds.). *History of Civilizations of Central Asia, vol. 1* (Paris, 1992)

Hsuan-tsang, Si-Yu-Ki. *Buddhist Records of the Western World*. Translated by S. Beal (London, 1906)

Huntingdon, S. and J. Huntingdon. *The Art of Ancient India* (New York, 1985)

Kenoyer, J.M. *Ancient cities of the Indus* (Oxford, 1999)

Kulke, H. and D. Rothermund. *A History of India* (London, 1990)

Marshall, J.H. *Mohenjo-daro and the Indus Civilization* (London, 1931)

——*A Guide to Sanchi* (Delhi, 1936)

——*Taxila: an illustrated account of archaeological excavations* (Cambridge, 1951)

Thapar, R. *Asoka and the Decline of the Mauryans* (Oxford, 1961)

Trautmann, T.R. *Kautilya and the Arthasastra* (Leiden, 1971)

Wheeler, R.E.M. *Early India and Pakistan* (London, 1959)

——*The Indus Civilization* (Cambridge, 1968)

WARFARE IN ANCIENT CHINA

Di Cosmo, N. *Ancient China and Its Enemies: the rise of nomadic power in East Asian history* (Cambridge, 2002)

Graff, D.A. *Medieval Chinese Warfare, 300–900* (London, 2002)

Hsu Cho-yun, *Ancient China in Transition: An Analysis of Social Mobility, 722–222 BC*, (Stanford, 1965)

Kierman, F.A. Jr. (ed.). *Chinese Ways in Warfare* (Cambridge, MA, 1974)

Kolb, R.T. *Die Infanterie im Alten China: Ein Beitrag zur Militärgeschichte der Vor-Zhan-Guo Zeit* (Mainz, 1991)

Lau, D.C. and R.T. Ames. *Sun Bin: The Art of Warfare* (New York, 2003)

Lewis, M.E. *Sanctioned Violence in Early China* (New York, 1990)

Loewe, M. and E.L. Shaughnessy (eds.). *The Cambridge History of Ancient China* (Cambridge, 1999)

Loewe, M. and D. Twitchett (eds.). *The Cambridge History of China, vol. 1: the Ch'in and Han Empires* (Cambridge, 1986)

Loewe, M. *Records of Han Administration*, 2 vols (Cambridge, 1967)

Minford, J. *Sunzi, The Art of War* (Penguin, 2002)

Needham, J. *et al. Science and Civilisation in China, vol. 5, part 6. Military Technology: Missiles and Sieges* (Cambridge, 1994)

WARFARE IN EARLY KOREA AND JAPAN

Anazawa, W. and J. Manome. "Two inscribed swords from Japanese tumuli: discoveries and research on finds from the Sakitama-Inariyama and Eta-Funayama tumuli," in R. Pearson *et al.* (eds.) *Windows on the Japanese Past: studies in archaeology* (Ann Arbor, 1986), 375–96

Barnes, G.L. *The Rise of Civilization in East Asia: the archaeology of China, Korea and Japan* (London and New York, 1999)

——*Clashes of iron: armour, weaponry, and warfare in early East Asian states*. Thematic issue of the *Journal of East Asian Archaeology*, vol. 2:3–4 (2000)

——*State Formation in Korea: historical and archaeological perspectives* (London, 2001)

——*State Formation in Japan: the rise of a 4th-century ruling elite* (London, 2007)

Brown, D.M. (ed.). *Cambridge History of Japan, vol. 1: Ancient Japan* (Cambridge, 1993)

Hudson, M.J. *Ruins of identity: ethnogenesis in the Japanese Islands* (Honolulu, 1999)

Imamura, K. *Prehistoric Japan: new perspectives on insular East Asia* (London, 1996)

Jamieson, J.C. "Collapse of the T'ang Silla alliance: Chinese and Korean accounts compared," in Wakeman F. Jr. (ed.) *Nothing Concealed: essays in honor of Liu Yu-yun* (Taipei, 1970)

Kang, H. "The historiography of the King Kwanggaet'o stele," in Pak Y. and J. Yeon, *History, Language and Culture in Korea* (London, 2001), 28–42

Kim, J.Y. "The Kwanggaet'o stele inscription," in Nish, I. (ed.) *Contemporary European writing on Japan: scholarly views from Eastern and Western Europe* (Tenterden, 1988)

Kitamura, B. "Five kings of Wa," in *Kodansha Encyclopedia of Japan, vol 2* (Tokyo, 1983), 287–8

Nelson, S.M. *The Archaeology of Korea* (Cambridge, 1993)

MESOAMERICA FROM THE OLMECS TO THE AZTECS

Coe, M.D. *The Maya* (7th edition, London and New York, 2005)

Cowgill, G.L. "Teotihuacan, Internal Militaristic Competition, and the Fall of the Classic Maya," in Hammond, N. and G.R. Willey (eds.) *Maya Archaeology and Ethnohistory* (Austin, 1974)

De Fuentes, P. *The Conquistadors: first-person accounts of the conquest of Mexico* (Norman, 1993)

Diehl, R.A. and J.C. Berlo (eds.). *Mesoamerica After the Decline of Teotihuacan AD 700–900* (Washington, 1989)

Durán, D. *The History of the Indies of New Spain*. Translated by Doris Heyden (Norman, 1994)

Evans, S.T. *Ancient Mexico and Central America* (2nd edition, London and New York, 2008)

Hassig, R. *Aztec Warfare: imperial expansion and political control* (Norman, 1988)

——*War and Society in Ancient Mesoamerica* (Los Angeles, 1992)

——*Mexico and the Spanish Conquest* (London, 1994)

——"The Collision of Two Worlds," in Meyer, M.C. and W.H. Beezley (eds.) *The Oxford History of Mexico* (Oxford, 2000)

——"The Siege of Tenochtitlan," in Black, J. (ed.) *The Seventy Great Battles of All Time* (London and New York, 2005)

Martin, S. and N. Grube. *Chronicle of the Maya Kings and Queens* (2nd edition, London and New York, 2008)

Leon-Portilla, M. *The Broken Spears: the Aztec account of the conquest of Mexico* (Boston, 1966)

Pohl, J. *Aztec, Mixtec and Zapotec Armies* (London, 1991)

Sahagún, B. de. *Florentine Codex: general history of the things of New Spain. Book 12 – The Conquest of Mexico*. Translated by Arthur J. Anderson and Charles E. Dibble (Salt Lake City, 1975)

Tsouras, P.G. *Warlords of the Ancient Americans: Central America* (London, 1996)

Webster, D. "Warfare and the Evolution of Maya Civilization," in Adams, R.E.W. (ed.) *The Origins of Maya Civilization* (Albuquerque, 1977)

ANCIENT WARFARE IN THE ANDES

Arkush, E.N. "Collapse, Conflict, Conquest: the transformation of warfare in the late prehispanic Andean highlands," in Arkush, E.N. and M.W. Allen (eds.) *The Archaeology of Warfare: prehistories of raiding and conquest* (Gainesville, FL, 2006), 286–335

Bauer, B.S. *Ancient Cuzco: Heartland of the Inca* (Austin, TX, 2004)

——"Suspension Bridges of the Inca Empire," in Silverman, H. and Isbell, W.H. (eds.) *Andean Archaeology Vol. 3* (New York, 2006), 468–493

Bourget, S. and N.E. Newman. "A Toast to the Ancestors: ritual warfare and sacrificial blood in Moche culture," *Baessler Archives N. F* (1998), 85–106

Bram, J. *An Analysis of Inca Militarism* (New York, 1941)

D'Altroy, T.N. *The Incas* (Oxford, 2003)

Donnan, C. *Moche Art and Iconography* (Los Angeles, 1976)

Ghezzi, I. 2006. "Religious warfare at Chankillo," in Silverman, H. and Isbell, W.H. (eds.) *Andean Archaeology Vol. 3* (New York, 2006)

Haas, J., S. Pozorski and T. Pozorski. *The Origins and Development of the Andean State* (Cambridge, 1987)

Hemming, J. *The Conquest of the Incas* (New York, 1970)

LeVine, T. (ed.). *Inka storage systems* (Norman, 1992)

Moseley, M.E. *The Incas and their Ancestors* (2nd edition, London and New York, 2001)

Pillsbury, J. (ed.). *Moche Art and Archaeology in Ancient Peru* (New Haven, 2002)

Rostworowski de Diez Canseco, M. *History of the Inca Realm*. Translated by Harry B. Iceland (Cambridge, 1999)

Rowe, J.H. "Inca Culture at the Time of the Spanish Conquest," in Steward, J. (ed.) *Handbook of South American Indians, vol. 2, The Andean civilizations* (Washington, D.C., 1946), 183–330

Silverman, H. and D.A. Proulx. *The Nasca* (Malden, MA, 2002)

Standen, V.G. and B.T. Arriaza. "Trauma in the Preceramic Coastal Populations of Northern Chile: violence or occupational hazards?" *American Journal of Physical Anthropology* (2000) 112, 239–249

Verano, J.W. "Where Do They Rest? The treatment of human offerings and trophies in ancient Peru," in Dillehay, T.D. (ed.) *Tombs for the Living: Andean Mortuary Practices* (Washington, D.C., 1995), 189–227

List of Contributors

Philip de Souza is Lecturer in Classics at University College Dublin, specializing in Greek and Roman history. He was born in Usk, South Wales and studied History and Classics at London University. He is a Fellow of the Royal Historical Society and a leading authority on ancient warfare and maritime history. His books include *Piracy in the Graeco-Roman World* (1999), *Seafaring and Civilization: Maritime Perspectives on World History* (2001), *The Peloponnesian War* (2002) and *The Greek and Persian Wars* (2003). He has also edited (with John France) a volume of essays on *War and Peace in Ancient and Medieval History* (2008).

Elizabeth Arkush received her doctorate from UCLA, where she researched late pre-Columbian forts of the southern Andes. She recently co-edited *The Archaeology of Warfare: prehistories of raiding and conquest* (2006) and has written about the difficulties of interpreting Andean warfare. She is an Assistant Professor at the University of Virginia.

Gina Barnes, Professor Emeritus of Durham University, is currently Professorial Research Associate at the School of Oriental and African Studies, University of London. Her publications include: *Protohistoric Yamato* (1988); *The Rise of Civilization in East Asia* (1999); *State Formation in Korea* (2001); and *State Formation in Japan* (2007).

Brian S. Bauer is Professor of Anthropology at the University of Illinois at Chicago. His scholarly interests are focused on the development of complex societies in the Americas and the European–American contact period. He has published nearly a dozen books and monographs on Andean prehistory and is particularly well known for his work on the Incas.

Daniel Boatright is currently studying for his doctorate at the School of Archaeology, Classics and Egyptology, University of Liverpool. His principal area of research is the cultural transmission of weapons technology in Egypt and the East Mediterranean during the Late Bronze Age.

Robin Coningham is Professor of Archaeology at Durham University and has conducted fieldwork throughout South Asia, directing excavations at the Citadel of Anuradhapura in Sri Lanka, the Bala Hisar of Charsadda in Pakistan and Tepe Pardis in Iran. Currently, he is co-directing a five-year survey of the extra-mural hinterland of Anuradhapura and a programme of survey and excavation in the Tehran Plain of Iran.

Jon Coulston is a Lecturer in Archaeology and Ancient History at the University of St Andrews, Scotland. His PhD thesis concerned the sculpting and relief content of Trajan's Column in Rome. He has published widely on the Roman army, ancient warfare, military equipment, Roman art, and on the city of Rome.

Hugh Elton has published monographs on Late Roman warfare and Roman imperial frontiers, and has edited essay collections on 5th-century AD Gaul and Regionalism in Hellenistic and Roman Asia Minor. His current research focuses on the areas of Cilicia and Isauria in southern Anatolia. After teaching at several US universities, he was Director of the British Institute at Ankara from 2001, and from 2006 has been working at Trent University in the Department of Ancient History and Classics.

R. Brian Ferguson is an anthropologist at Rutgers University, Newark, specializing in the study of organized violence. He has written on many aspects of war, including the biology of war, tribal warfare, war in ancient civilizations, and contemporary ethnic violence (see www.newark.rutgers.edu/socant/brian.htm). He is currently researching lethal violence among chimpanzees, and gang violence leading to organized crime in historic New York City.

Ross Hassig is an anthropologist specializing in the Aztecs. His publications include *Trade, Tribute, and Transportation: The sixteenth-century political economy of the Valley of Mexico* (1985), *Aztec Warfare: imperial expansion and political control* (1988), *War and Society in Ancient Mesoamerica* (1992), *Time, History, and Belief in Aztec and Colonial Mexico* (2001), and *Mexico and the Spanish Conquest* (2006).

Mark Manuel is a PhD student at Durham University working on the Indus civilization. He has conducted a survey in Gujarat in India, has excavated at Pompeii in Italy, and is currently working on projects at Anuradhapura in Sri Lanka and the Tehran Plain in Iran.

Alan Peatfield has taught Greek Archaeology at University College Dublin since 1991. From 1986 to 1990 he was Knossos Curator for the British School at Athens. He is director of the Atsipadhes Peak Sanctuary excavation project on Crete, and he has published extensively on Minoan religion, martial arts, and ancient combat.

Charles A. Peterson taught premodern Chinese history at Cornell University where in 2006 he was named Professor Emeritus. His research interests have encompassed politics, administration, military affairs and foreign relations, mostly in China's middle period. His publications include much specialist literature as well contributions to the *Cambridge History of China*.

David Potter, Arthur F. Thurnau Professor of Greek and Latin at the University of Michigan, is the author/editor of seven books about Roman history, including *The Roman Empire at Bay* (2004). He is currently writing a book on ancient warfare, and a general book on Roman History for Thames & Hudson.

Louis Rawlings is a Lecturer in Ancient History at Cardiff University. He has written numerous articles on Gallic, Iberian and Carthaginian warfare, and is author of *The Ancient Greeks at War* (2007).

Nathan Rosenstein is Professor of History at the Ohio State University. He is the author of *Imperatores Victi: Military Defeat and Aristocratic Competition in the Middle and Late Republic* (1992) and *Rome At War: farms, families, and death in the Middle Republic* (2004), and the editor (with Kurt Raaflaub) of *War and Society in the Ancient and Medieval Worlds: Asia, the Mediterranean, Europe, and Mesoamerica* (2001), and (with Robert Morstein-Marx) of *A Companion to the Roman Republic* (2006).

Nicholas Sekunda studied Ancient History and Archaeology at Manchester University, obtaining a doctorate in 1981. Following research positions in Australia and Oxford, he taught at Manchester before leaving for Poland in 1994. He is currently a Professor of Gdansk University in the Department of Archaeology, and has previously taught at the Military Academy for Teaching Foreign Languages in Lodz, and at Torun University.

Ian Shaw is Senior Lecturer in Egyptian Archaeology at the School of Archaeology, Classics and Egyptology, University of Liverpool. His publications include *Egyptian Warfare and Weapons* (1991), *The Oxford History of Ancient Egypt* (2000) and *Ancient Egypt: a very short introduction* (2004).

Joseph Szymczak holds a BA in Anthropology from the University of Pittsburgh and a MA in Anthropology from the University of Illinois at Chicago. His interests are focused on the prehistory of the Andes and evidence of warfare in the archaeological record.

Nigel Tallis is a curator in the Department of the Middle East at the British Museum, where most recently he was co-curator of the exhibition *Forgotten Empire: the world of Ancient Persia*. He is a specialist in the history and archaeology of ancient and medieval Near Eastern warfare and land and sea transport – especially the development of wheeled vehicles and the use of the horse.

Hans van Wees is Professor of Ancient History at University College London. He is the author of *Greek Warfare: myths and realities* (2004) and *Status Warriors* (1992), and editor of several volumes, including *War and Violence in Ancient Greece* (2000) and the *Cambridge History of Greek and Roman Warfare* (2007).

Sources of Illustrations

1 akg-images/Nimatallah; **2** akg-images/Erich Lessing; **4–5** akg-images/Erich Lessing; **6** Egyptian Museum, Cairo; **9** Vatican Museums; **10** National Museum of Afghanistan, Kabul; **11** akg-images/Laurent Lecod; **13** National Museum of Anthropology, Mexico City; **14** © Pierre Colombe/Corbis; **15** National Museum, Copenhagen; **16a** Pacheco, *Estudios de arte Prehistorico*, Revista de la Real Academia de Ciencias 16, 1918; **16b** © LRMH, 1998; **18a** Landesdenkmalamt Baden-Württemberg; **18b** Schmidt; **19a** Déri Múzeum, Debrezen; **19b** Antikvarisk Topografiska Arkivet, Stockholm; **20** © Richard A. Cooke/Corbis; **22a** © Paul C. Pet/zefa/Corbis; **22b** after Seler, 1923; **23** Whites Aviation; **25a** Southern Methodist University, Dallas; **25b** Robert Layton; **26a** National Maritime Museum, Greenwich; **26b** Museum of Anthropology & Ethnology, Cambridge; **28** Jürgen Liepe; **30** Egyptian Museum, Cairo; **31a** Egypt Exploration Society, London; **31b** Newberry, *Beni Hasan*, London, 1900; **32** © Paul Almasy/Corbis; **33** Sammlung des Ägyptologischen Instituts der Universität Heidelberg; **35** akg-images/Hervé Champollion; **37** Jürgen Liepe; **38a** © Roger Wood/Corbis; **38b** © Griffith Institute, Oxford, 2005; **39a** British Museum, London; **39b** Egyptian Museum, Cairo; **40** © Griffith Institute, Oxford, 2005; **41a** Peter Bull Art Studio © Thames & Hudson Ltd, London; **41b** Metropolitan Museum of Art, New York; **42–43** Jürgen Liepe; **42bl** Metropolitan Museum of Art, New York; **44** After Champollion, *Monuments de l'Egypte...*, 1835; **45** akg-images/Erich Lessing; **46** © Gianni Dagli Orti/Corbis; **48** Iraq Museum, Baghdad; **49** Photo RMN, Hervé Lewandowski; **50a** Musée du Louvre, Paris; **50b** Peter Bull Art Studio © Thames & Hudson Ltd, London; **51a&b** British Museum, London; **52** © Gianni Dagli Orti/Corbis; **53** Musée du Louvre, Paris; **54a** Iraq Museum, Baghdad; **54b&c** British Museum, London; **55** Peter Bull Art Studio © Thames & Hudson Ltd, London; **56** akg-images/Erich Lessing; **57** British Museum, London; **58** British Museum, London; **60–61** British Museum, London; **60** British Museum, London; **62** British Museum, London; **63** British Museum, London; **64** Photo RMN, Les frères Chuzeville; **66** Nicholas Sekunda; **67** Peter Bull Art Studio © Thames & Hudson Ltd, London (after M.B. Garrison, M.C. Root, *Persepolis Seal Studies*, Leiden, 1996); **68** American Journal of Archaeology; **69al** Ashmolean Museum, Oxford; **69ar&b** Bibliothèque Nationale de France, Paris; **70** University of Mississippi Museum; **71a** Staatliche Antikensammlungen und Glyptothek, Munich; **71c** Nicholas Sekunda; **71b** bpk/Ethnologisches Museum, Staatliche Museen zu Berlin; **72al** after Franz Georg Maier, *Alt-Paphos auf Cypern*, 1984, pl.II, 3; **72ar** Universität Zürich; **73a** Ashmolean Museum, Oxford; **73bl** State Hermitage Museum, St Petersburg; **73br** Dura Europos Collection, Yale University Art Gallery, New Haven; **74al** University of Tubingen, Institute of Archaeology; **74ar** akg-images/John Hios; **74b** Oriental Institute, University of Chicago; **75a** British Museum, London; **75b** © Gianni Dagli Orti/Corbis; **76** Ashmolean Museum, Oxford; **78** Nicholas Sekunda; **79a** British Museum, London; **79b** akg-images/Erich Lessing; **80l** Antikensammlungen, Staatliche Museen zu Berlin; **80r** Private Collection, Basel; **81a** Peter Bull Art Studio © Thames & Hudson Ltd, London; **81b** Courtesy Professor Machteld Mellink; **82** British Museum, London; **83a** after C. Texier, *Description de l'Asie Mineure*, Paris, 1849; **83b** Courtesy Hector Catling; **84** akg-images/Peter Connolly; **85a** State Hermitage Museum, St. Petersburg; **85b** Dr Marius Mielczarek; **86** National Museum, Athens; **87** Metropolitan Museum of Art, New York; **88** National Museum, Athens; **89l&c** National Museum, Athens; **89b** Heraklion Museum; **90a** Alan Peatfield; **90bl** Heraklion Museum; **90bc&br** National Museum, Athens; **91a&b** National Museum, Athens; **92** Mycenae Archive: Piet de Jong; **93a** National Museum, Athens; **93b** Alan Peatfield; **94a&b** National Museum, Athens; **96** National Museum, Athens; **97a** akg-images/Peter Connolly; **97b** DAI, Athens; **98** National Museum, Athens; **99al** National Museum of Denmark, Copenhagen; **99ar** Archaeological Museum, Volos; **100** akg-images/Erich Lessing; **103** akg-images/Peter Connolly; **104** Antikensammlungen, Staatliche Museen zu Berlin; **105al** Museum für Kunst und Gewerbe, Hamburg; **105ac** akg-images/Nimatallah; **105cl** akg-images/Erich Lessing; **105cr** Nobert Schimmel Collection, New York; **105b** akg-images/Peter Connolly; **107** Staatliche Antikensammlungen und Glyptothek, Munich; **108** British Museum, London; **109** Photo RMN © Hervé Lewandowski; **110** Antikensammlungen, Staatliche Museen zu Berlin; **111** Staatliche Antikensammlungen und Glyptothek, Munich; **112a&b** The J. Paul Getty Museum, Malibu, California; **113** Photo RMN © Les frères Chuzeville; **116** British Museum, London; **117** Mike Andrews/Ancient, Art & Architecture Collection; **118** akg-images/Erich Lessing; **120** Archaeological Museum, Istanbul; **121** British Museum, London; **123** Museo Archeologico Nazionale, Naples; **124a,b&c** Royal Tombs at Vergina, Imathia, Greece; **125** akg-images/Peter Connolly; **126** Archaeological Museum, Istanbul; **128a&b** akg-images/Peter Connolly; **129** British Museum, London; **130** akg-images/Erich Lessing; **131a** Musée du Louvre, Paris; **131c** State Hermitage Museum, St. Petersburg; **131b** Museo Nazionale di Villa Giulia, Rome; **132a** Peter Bull Art Studio © Thames & Hudson Ltd, London; **132b** State Hermitage Museum, St Petersburg; **135** Antikensammlungen, Staatliche Museen zu Berlin; **136** akg-images/Peter Connolly; **138** Museo Nazionale di Villa Giulia, Rome; **141** Peter Inker; **142** Museo Archeologico Nazionale, Naples; **143l** Mike Craig © Salamandar Books Ltd; **143b** Museo Capitolino, Rome; **144** Peter Inker; **146a** National Museet, Stockholm; **146b** akg-images/Peter Connolly; **147** Musée du Louvre, Paris; **149** akg-images; **151a** Peter Inker; **151b** British Museum, London; **152** The Art Archive/Museo della Civilta Romana, Rome/Dagli Orti; **153a&b** British Museum, London; **154** Roger Wilson; **155a** Ny Carlsberg Glyptothek, Copenhagen; **155b** Vatican Museums; **156** Musée Departmental de l'Oise, Beauvais; **158** akg-images/Nimatallah; **159** akg-images/Nimatallah; **162a** Museo Numantino, Soria; **162b** National Archaeological Museum, Madrid; **163** Simon James; **164** Musée Calvet, Avignon; **165a** British Museum, London; **165b** akg-images/Peter Connolly; **166** Fitzwilliam Museum, Cambridge; **167c** Centre Camille Julian, CNRS, Aix-en-Provence; **167bl** Musée Borély, Marseilles; **167br** Simon James; **168** Naturhistorisches Museum, Vienna; **169a** Museul National de Istorie, Bucharest; **169b** National Museum of Denmark, Copenhagen; **170** akg-images/Erich Lessing; **171** Museo Nazionale delle Terme, Rome; **172** British Museum, London; **174** British Museum, London; **175** akg-images/Gérard Degeorge; **176** © Paul Almasy/Corbis; **177a** Erik Smekens, reproduced with the kind permission of the late Louis Vanden Berghe and Ernie Haerink; **177c&b** Dura Europos Collection, Yale University Art Gallery, New Haven; **178** Dura Europos Collection, Yale University Art Gallery, New Haven; **179** © Roger Wood/Corbis; **180a** after Duruy, *Histoire des Romains...*, Paris, 1843; **180b** akg-images/Tristan Lafranchis; **181** akg-images/Erich Lessing; **182** akg-images; **185** Rheinisches Landesmuseum, Bonn; **186** Musée du Louvre, Paris; **187** © Skyscan/Corbis; **188** Colchester Museum, England; **189al** © Richard T. Nowitz/Corbis; **189ar** Gary Braasch/Corbis; **189b** © Ted Spiegel/Corbis; **190a** Sally Nicholls; **190b** Landschaftsverband Rheinland/Archäologischer Park/Regional Museum Xanten; **191a** akg-images/Hedda Eid; **191b** Peter Inker; **192** Römisch-Germanisches Zentralmuseum, Mainz; **193a** British Museum, London; **193b** Roger Wilson; **194** British Museum, London; **195** © Vittoriano Rastelli/Corbis; **197** © Vittoriano Rastelli/Corbis; **201** Centre Belge de Recherches Archéologiques à Apamée, Apamea; **202** akg-images/Andrea Jemolo; **204** akg-images/Erich Lessing; **205** Hirmer Verlag; **208** Giraudon; **209a** Sonia Halliday; **209b** Narodni muzej, Belgrade; **210** Museo Regionale Villa dei Casale; **211** Bodleian Library, University of Oxford; **212** Rijksmuseum van Oudheden, Leiden; **213** Snowdog; **214** Bardo Museum, Tunis; **215** © Araldo da Luca/Corbis; **216** State Hermitage Museum, St. Petersburg; **219** State Hermitage Museum, St. Petersburg; **220** © Charles O'Rear/Corbis; **221** National Museum of the History of the Ukraine, Kiev; **222a** State Hermitage Museum, St. Petersburg; **222b** © Deutsches Archäologisches Institut/epa/Corbis; **223** State Hermitage Museum, St. Petersburg; **224l&ar** State Hermitage Museum, St. Petersburg; **224b** akg-images; **226** Jonathan Coulston; **227** Musée Archéologique de Strasbourg, photo Musées de Strasbourg, A. Plisson; **228** akg-images/Jean-Louis Nou; **230b** Georg Helms; **231** Georg Helms; **232a** © Harappa Archaeological Research Project, Courtesy Dept. of Archaeology and Museums, Govt. of Pakistan; **232b** © Chris Sloan, Courtesy J.M. Kenoyer; **234** Archaeological Museum, Mathura; **235** Robin Conigham; **236** British Museum, London; **238** © Christophe Boisvieux/Corbis; **239** © Adam Woolfitt/Corbis; **240** © Corbis; **241** akg-images/Jean-Louis Nou; **242** Qin Terracotta Museum, Lintong, Shaanxi Province; **244** Jiangxi Provincial Museum, Nanchang; **245** Morning Glory Publishing, Beijing; **246** Leigudun Provincial Museum, Wuhan; **247c** after Loewe; **247b** akg-images; **249l&r** Morning Glory Publishing, Beijing; **251** Morning Glory Publishing, Beijing; **253** akg-images/Erich Lessing; **254–255** Gavin Hellier/Robert Harding; **255** State Bureau of Cultural Relics, Beijing; **257** akg-images/François Guénet; **258a** akg-images/Suzanne Held; **258b** © Liang Zhouming/Corbis; **259** Morning Glory Publishing, Beijing;

260 Morning Glory Publishing, Beijing **261** State Bureau of Cultural Relics, Beijing; **262** DNP Archives; **265** Peter Bull Art Studio © Thames & Hudson Ltd, London; **266** Yokohama City Miazanbunkazai Center; **267** DNP Archives; **269** National Museum of Korea, Seoul; **270a** Gina Barnes; **270b** © Korea News Service/Reuters/Corbis; **271a** National Museum of Korea, Seoul; **271b** DNP Archives; **272** DNP Archives; **274** © Charles & Josette Lenars/Corbis; **277** © Richard A. Cooke/Corbis; **278** National Museum of Anthropology, Mexico City; **279** Peabody Museum of Anthropology and Ethnology, Harvard University, Cambridge MA; **282a** © Justin Kerr; **282b** National Museum of Anthropology, Mexico City; **285** © Angelo Hornak/Corbis; **286** City of Bristol Museum and Art Gallery; **288** Photo Salvador Guilliem, The Great Temple Project; **289** Bodleian Library, University of Oxford; **290a** Bibliothèque Nationale de France, Paris;

290b Museum für Völkerkunde, Vienna; **291a** Biblioteca Nacional, Madrid; **291b** National Museum of Anthropology, Mexico City; **292** Hunterian Library, University of Glasgow; **294** Mireille Vautier; **296a,b&c** Elizabeth Arkush; **297a** National Museum of Anthropology and Archaeology, Lima; **297b** Dr Steven Bourget; **298a** Helaine Silverman; **298b** Amano Museum, Lima; **299** Elizabeth Arkush; **301** Det Kongelige Bibliotek, Copenhagen; **302** © Fridmar Damm/zefa/Corbis; **304** © Galen Rowell/CORBIS; **305a&bl** Courtesy of The Latin American Library, Squier Collection, Tulane University, New Orleans; **305br** Det Kongelige Bibliotek, Copenhagen; **307** Det Kongelige Bibliotek, Copenhagen

All 3-d battle plans: Red Lion Prints © Thames & Hudson Ltd, London
All maps: ML Design © Thames & Hudson Ltd, London

Sources of Quotations

30 After R. Parkinson, *Voices from Ancient Egypt* (London, 1991); **35** K. Kitchen, *Pharaoh Triumphant: the Life and Times of Ramesses II* (Warminster, 1982); **36** E. Wente, *Letters from Ancient Egypt* (Atlanta, 1990); **36–7** J. Breasted, *Ancient Records of Egypt II: The Eighteenth Dynasty* (Chicago, 1906); **44** W.F. Edgerton and J.A. Wilson, *Historical Records of Ramesses III: The Texts of Medinet Habu I* (Chicago, 1936); **45** J.B. Pritchard, *Ancient Near Eastern Texts Relating to the Old Testament* (Princeton, 1955); **50** After J.S. Cooper, *Reconstructing History from Ancient Inscriptions: The Lagash-Umma Border Conflict. Sources from the Ancient Near East 2/1* (Malibu, 1983); **57** B.R. Foster, *Before the Muses* (Bethesda, 2005); **61** After R. Borger, *Die Inschriften Asarhaddons, Königs von Assyrien. Archiv für Orientforschung, Beiheft 9* (Graz, 1956); **65** After S. Parpola, *The Correspondence of Sargon II, Part 1: Letters from Assyria and the West. State Archives of Assyria I* (Helsinki 1987), no.240; **68** Hdt. 1.155–7; **74** Strabo XV.3.17; **74** DB iv 54–6, R.G. Kent, *Old Persian: Grammar, Texts, Lexicon* (Newhaven, 1953); **76** Hdt. 7.83; **77** Hdt. 5.52; **78** Hdt. 8.98; **83** Diodorus 14.98.3; **111** Dem. 9.48; **125** Dem. 2.17; **144** Polybius, 15.15.7–8; 18.30.6–8, 32.10–12, trans. Shuckburgh (London & New York, 1889); **165** Diodorus 5.29; **168** Strabo 4.4.4; **173** Cassius Dio, *Roman History* 40.14.4ff; **173** Tacitus, *Annals* 6.31.3; **176** Justin, *Epitome of the Philippic History of Pompeius Trogus* 41.2;

178 Libanius *Or.* XVIII.264; **178** Ammianus Marcellinus, *History* XXIII.6.83; **178** See discussion of the sources in J. Howard-Johnson, "The Two Great Powers in Late Antiquity: A Comparison" and Z. Rubin, "The Reforms of Khusro Anushirwan" in A. Cameron (ed.), *States, Resources and Armies, The Byzantine and Early Islamic Near East III* (Princeton, 1995); **178** After C.E. Bosworth, *The Sasanids, the Byzantines, the Lakmids, and Yemen. The History of al-Tabari V* (New York, 1999); **181** After J.M. Unvala, *King Husrav and His Boy* (Paris, n.d.); **205** Synesius, *Ep.* 78; **210** Theodoret, *Historia Religiosa* 13.5; **212–3** AM 24.6.8; **214** ILS 9351; **214** Synesius, *Ep.* 104 (trans. A. Fitzgerald, *The Letters of Synesius* (Oxford, 1926); **225** Jordanes, *The Origin and Deeds of the Goths* XXIV.128; **226** Jordanes, *The Origin and Deeds of the Goths* XXXV.182; XXXVI.191; **235** R. Thapar, *Asoka and the Decline of the Mauryans* (Oxford, 1961); **241** J.H. Marshall, *A Guide to Taxila* (Cambridge, 1960); **248–9** Xunzi, *Basic Writings*, trans. B. Watson (New York, 2003); **303** Cieza de León, Pedro de, *The discovery and conquest of Peru*, trans. and ed. by A.P. Cook and N.D. Cook (Durham, N.C., 1998); **303–4** Sarmiento de Gamboa, Pedro, *The History of the Incas*, trans. and ed. B.S. Bauer and V. Smith (University of Texas Press, 2006); **306** Xerez, Francisco de, *Verdadera relación de la conquista del Perú* (1534), (Madrid: Historia 16, 1985); **306** Cieza de León, Pedro de, *The Incas of Pedro Cieza de León* (Part 1, 1553, and Part 2, 1554), trans. H. de Onís, ed. V.W. von Hagen (University of Oklahoma Press, 1976)

Index

Page numbers in *italic* refer to illustrations.